FLOSS

+ Art

= = = = = = = = = = =

Published 2008 by GOTO10
in association with OpenMute

GOTO10
12 rue Charles Gide
86000 Poitiers
France
contact@goto10.org
www.goto10.org

ISBN 978-1-906496-18-0

= = = = = = = = = = =


Compiled and edited by: Aymeric Mansoux and Marloes de Valk

= = = = = = = = = = =



= = = = = = = = = = =

= = = = = = = = = =

TABLE OF CONTENTS

# Preface

Aymeric Mansoux
Marloes de Valk

The relationship between artist, tool, content and audience has never been of greater importance than in digital culture. Data has become both instrument, material and medium, all of which are reproducible without cost and distributable instantaneously. The software industry is well aware of this, and consequently has adopted the model of selling licenses instead of software. Similarly, the entertainment industry does not release movies and music to an audience, but instead sells end-user license agreements that provide a limited right to the playback of digital content. In both cases the study, modification and redistribution of this digital information is forbidden. At the same time, content creators are inclined to use software specifically tuned and developed for such a distribution system. As a consequence creativity becomes a passive input for a content distribution machine the output of which feeds a passive audience. The lack of freedom and the absence of connection between the two opposed components of this production chain give the system all rights to control both culture and its usage. But is there any alternative?

Actually, yes. What about a model, in which artists and their audience simply refuse the passive role of user and instead persevere as creators and collectors of great ideas? In this model, artists could own their own 'tools', would be free to use them whenever and however they want, and could dissect, hack, embellish and share them, without breaking any laws. The creative process of an artist is no longer restricted by what software companies dictate, only by his or her own skill. Software, being more than a means by which ideas are expressed technically, functions as medium. Software *is* the artwork and its code is an integral part of it. In this model, artists would give free access to this layer of the artwork. Free distribution of the work would break the artist out of isolation and put him/her in contact with an audience, a community. Such a model is not utopian, it is already practised by those artists who choose Free Software and copyleft.

Free/Libre/Open Source Software (FLOSS) can be used, copied, shared, modified, and redistributed with little or no restriction, always allowing free access to its source code. The term FLOSS refers to both Free Software as well as Open Source Software, without bias towards one single approach. Free Software, as defined by Richard Stallman and promoted by the Free Software Foundation, puts the emphasis on the freedom that Free Software gives to its users. The four freedoms of Free Software are: the freedom to use the software for any purpose, freedom to study and modify its source code, freedom to share and redistribute the software, and the freedom to improve the software and release your version of it to the public. Open Source Software on the other hand, tries to avoid the philosophical and political implications of the interpretation of free as in freedom, and emphasises the strengths of the peer to peer development model of Open Source Software, thus trying to appeal more to the corporate world.

The Free Software definition has its roots in the GNU project. In 1983, Richard Stallman announced the plan for the GNU operating system, composed of 100 percent free software. The GNU project was initiated to give computer users back their lost freedom. In the fifties, sixties and seventies, software was mostly produced by its users, and in many ways software was free. In the late seventies and eighties, companies started to put increasingly tight restrictions on software through copyright, making the earlier freedoms illegal. Suddenly, volunteer programmers that were sharing and improving code were considered thieves. Software became an extremely profitable business.

Most components of the GNU operating system were developed between 1983 and 1991, but the kernel kept on being delayed. When in 1991 Linus Torvalds released the Linux kernel, and changed the license to the GNU General Public License in 1992, the lack of a kernel was resolved and the first free operating system was a reality.

The GNU General Public License was written by Stallman in 1989 for the GNU project. The GPL is a strong copyleft license, it ensures the 4 freedoms of Free Software, access to the source code of a work and requires all derivative works to preserve the same freedoms. A work licensed under the GPL is copyrighted, thus making sure that licensees are bound by the terms of the license, and therefore can be sued by the original author if they break the conditions of the license. Next to that, the copyleft principle is a workaround to copyright, meant to protect the freedom of licensees instead of the exclusive rights of the author, with the sole restriction that all derived and redistributed works must be GPL licensed as well. The GPL is one of the most popular licenses used for FLOSS.

The development and use of GNU/Linux has exploded during the last few years. This explosion has resulted from the positive feedback of an increased number of users, increased needs from users, triggering more development of software to fulfil those needs, which eventually resulted in even more users. Much of this increase is due to the massive developments made at the level of the desktop. Friendlier user interfaces and the more familiar environment of the desktop have brought a lot of fresh attention to GNU/Linux. The Ubuntu campaigns have played a big role in this, focusing on usability, accessibility and 'user friendliness'. The results of these recent developments are more GNU/Linux powered desktops and more high quality open source desktop applications. On top of this, the sheer amount of GNU/Linux distributions has grown exponentially. In May 2008 Distrowatch lists an increase from three main distributions in 1995, to a total of 354 active distributions in the database today, many of which are branches of a few main distributions.

While this increase is undeniable, thoughts along the line of 'GNU/Linux is nice but if you want to do some real work you have to use proprietary operating systems' are still quite common. This is true as long as you consider 'real work' to consist of working the way proprietary software companies want you to work. In real life, you are more often confronted with the need for tailored solutions that can not be delivered by ready made problem solvers. For example, in the early days of computer animation it was not unusual to work on proprietary UNIX based systems. With the democratisation of PC hardware and GNU/Linux in the mid '90's, it started to be possible to provide cheaper, and most of all more flexible, production environments than the single-vendor solutions and high-priced specialised hardware ones could offer. It only took a few years for the special effects industry to move its 'pipeline' to GNU/Linux and more generic hardware. At the same time, software companies, although most of them still following closed source models, ported a great number of animation, modelling, rendering and post production software to the free platform. The side effect of this wave in the VFX industry was that GNU/Linux started to gain popularity outside of the computer science arena. GNU/Linux became visible to computer artists through the marketing campaigns of the VFX industry. This triggered a lot of curiosity, and more and more computer artists gave GNU/Linux a try and discovered there was much more to it than rendering farms and fancy post production tools.

The user base was steadily growing, and small communities quickly grew into bigger groups, focused on particular aspects of open source artistic software and technology, and started to organise large scale events and conventions, such as the Linux Audio Convention and the Libre Graphics Meeting. The main difference between users grouped as customers, and users who are part of a FLOSS community, is that the latter have the ability to be pro-active in the process of software development by way of writing documentation, providing support, reporting issues, and in some cases participating in the writing of the software. The latest iteration of this change in the position of the user has made the redistribution and customisation of artistic software possible to the point where groups of practitioners have been able to provide free operating systems tailored to the needs of artists, performers and musicians. This development resulted in art and multimedia centred additions to the growing list of GNU/Linux distributions, with systems such as 64 Studio, APODIO, dyne:bolic, Musix, pure:dyne, and Ubuntu Studio.

Using FLOSS within digital and software art practice brings lots of added value to artists. The most immediate benefit is that the software comes with, instead of just a shrink wrapped box with glossy print, an active and lively community of users and developers. As a user you are not isolated, but part of this community. The software doesn't come with a help desk phone number, but something much better, other users that help each other via mailing lists, forums and IRC channels. Once you've made it through the first part of the learning curve, moving from newbie to more advanced user, you discover you have gained great freedoms. No longer are implementations of artistic concepts bound by the limits of the software applications that exist. You are free to create your own tools by combining or modifying existing ones, using the modularity and flexibility of the GNU/Linux operating system and the accessibility of the source code of all applications. Small scripts function like a glue between different low level software. Suddenly you are materialising your concepts as you would create objects using LEGO blocks. The learning has paid off, this lower level access to the operating system, software and network greatly enhances the freedom to technically implement artistic ideas.

In a similar way, the resulting work itself can use a free license and there are quite a few good reasons for an artist to do so. With respect to generating an audience for ones work, the choice of an open license will greatly increase the number of viewers or listeners, especially when published on an online platform such as archive.org. From a curatorial point of view, the choice for open systems and licenses can simplify the preservation and maintenance of an artwork, independent of fickle proprietary standards and limited edition habits inherited from previous non-digital media. Last but not least, this new distribution framework seems well suited for today's prosumer approach, as demonstrated by the increasing number of independent artist-led organisations, productions, festivals and distribution platforms such as net-labels.

The openness of an artwork does not only impact its release and relation to its audience, it also greatly influences the process underlying the artwork. That's why it's important to understand that software is not just a technical component of digital art, it *is* the artwork and its code provides another reading of it. This often forgotten layer of interpretation should be open for others, to study and understand the work, to learn from, get inspired by and comment on. It is unfortunate that many artists, including those working with FLOSS, still resist to this call for openness. They are unwilling to show the inner workings of their art, for fear of giving away their identity and ruining their chances of generating income, not realising the latter in fact relies solely on the performance, exhibition, commissioning and teaching of their art, not on the software that enables its manifestation.

Beyond the use of artistic and multimedia software, software art using an open license can have an afterlife the artist releasing it never could have foreseen. At the moment, this is still quite rare, but this might change and provide a rich environment for works that could branch and fork into many directions, passing through many hands, gracefully escaping the fate of a final resting place in a dusty corner of a forgotten hard disk.

Using FLOSS automatically gives an artists work an extra dimension, a political statement that is embedded in the choice to use FLOSS instead of proprietary software. This political statement may seem unrelated to the artistic concept of a work, but it is far from trivial. It implies an awareness of the fact that software is the base material of a work of art, like the clay of a sculpture, and that this choice of material greatly influences the eventual work and its context. This awareness often leads to the choice of open licenses for the artistic work itself, feeding developed ideas and technical implementations of ideas back into the community, enabling the reuse of code and facilitating the sharing of knowledge. The demystification of software and code is an important result of this.

This is why it is rare to come across isolated artists using FLOSS. Most of them quickly find their way to online communities that provide help and support. The FLOSS scene is also booming with communities and distributed collectives focused around politics, art and Free Software. Here, artists frequently show each other bits of code, inspire each other, and most of all, teach each other. This form of circularity generates an engagement with digital art that is close to a form of continuous open artistic research, and marks a strong opposition with the classic top-down design approach of an end-product form of media art.

Of course, getting started with FLOSS and GNU/Linux within an art practice can be quite a rocky ride. Even though some Linux distributions would have you believe otherwise, it is not that easy to learn a completely new system. GNU/Linux, compared to most proprietary operating systems, takes a very different approach to its users. Its design is based on the assumption that users are capable of learning to master the system, instead of the assumption that users are helpless. At the beginning, you have to unlearn a lot of habits and constructs you've build up using proprietary systems, and no matter how nice the user interface and desktop of some distributions look, you cannot avoid the system that lies behind the Graphical User Interface (GUI). Things have improved a lot in the past few years, and continue to improve, making Linux much more accessible for new users, but it still remains a challenge for many.

One of the first things that takes getting used to is how and where to find documentation. A lot of applications lack the famous 'help' button which brings you to a searchable database of topics, or a step by step 'how to'. The writing of documentation is very often at the bottom of the priority list of any FLOSS development team. This is changing rapidly, and more and more efforts to write good documentation are undertaken, but until this change has properly kicked in, users need to use different tactics to find their way around. The best strategy is learning to do accurate online searches. This will open up a world of information – sometimes scattered, often incomplete, but most of the time extremely helpful – written by other users encountering the same problem as you and describing how to deal with it, on mailinglists, forums, blogs and wikis.

Switching from a proprietary system to GNU/Linux, or from proprietary software to FLOSS takes time. As with all new tools, you need to learn a whole new set of skills before you feel like you can fluently express yourself with them. For many artists, the time it takes to reach this point means a loss of productivity. Before you have mastered the new software or system, you find yourself struggling with tasks you would normally have no problems with. Besides the frustration this brings, artists need to generate income and this loss of productivity needs to have a big pay off in the end to be worth this investment of time. The benefits of using FLOSS can be obscure at first, but due to more and more artists making the switch and developers aiming to improve the accessibility of FLOSS, these benefits are becoming increasingly apparent.

The greatest obstacle blocking people from easy access to FLOSS is the fact that students are very rarely introduced to it at art schools and universities. The best time to get familiar with computers and software is at school, especially considering that most people stick with what they've learned after graduating. But most schools and universities are only offering courses using proprietary software running on proprietary systems. Art students will most likely only be introduced to the biggest and most dominant producers of closed commercial tools for artistic production, such as Adobe. Students rarely are given a choice. The choice of schools and universities to only offer this type of product has its reasons. Learning to use the most dominant proprietary software and operating system will make a student much more employable, since those products are also the ones used in the industry. This of course only goes for studies aiming at industry, it has no meaning in an art context. And even when considering employability, skills like concept development, creativity in the use of tools and thinking outside the box, are much more valuable to a future employer than knowing how to use a certain product. Those skills will be outdated as soon as this product gets updated, and learning technical skills takes less time and expertise than developing a strong artistic and creative practice.

The wider use of FLOSS is not only blocked by external factors, it is also due to its community shooting itself in the foot with internal conflicts. The most famous one being the conflict between the Free Software Foundation and the Open Source Initiative. Flame wars around notions of freedom haven't contributed much to enhance FLOSS' friendly face. Neither have the many flame wars and various witch hunts between users of FLOSS and proprietary software. For those new to the community, it is hard to understand the almost religious fanaticism and intolerance with which some people express their opinion regarding these topics. In fact, it seems very much at odds with the philosophy of openness and sharing that is associated with this community.

This sometimes brutal online behaviour, unorthodox social organisation, and chaotic spreading of information might come as a shock to those arriving from the scripted, polished and secure world of customer support. These are not bugs though, they are features. Indeed, while the basic ideas behind FLOSS are rather simple and trivial to understand, their practical interpretation, use and influence remain free from the diktat of a control structure. So, to understand the nature of it, you have to picture FLOSS as part of an emerging transdisciplinary field that deals with different forms of openness. The resulting complexity stems from the confrontation of the many different disciplines and groups involved, and the many people forming them.

FLOSS+Art, or the interaction between the FLOSS philosophy and digital art, should not be seen as yet another category of art, but as an added layer. It acts as another dimension on top of existing fields of digital art and enriches the way artists and collectives can work by adding another degree of freedom in the creative process. We think this openness will create more transparency and bring to light otherwise hidden properties of digital art practice in the world of connected artist communities and collectives. And although it is too early to speculate on the long-term influence FLOSS will have on digital art, we believe it will bring a better understanding of software as an artistic medium beyond the simplicity of neoclassical code aesthetics.

# Artists and Free Software - an Introduction

Pedro Soler

(The first version of this text was written at the request of LABoral in July 2007 and then updated for publication in November 2007. Thanks to Erich Berger, H.C. Steiner and Aymeric Mansoux for comments)

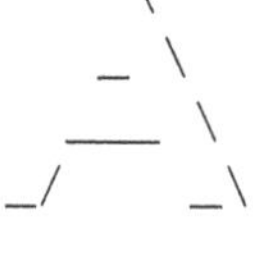

n artist is an investigator. Always pushing the frontiers of the possible. The artist works to change our perception of the world. She digs into the medium and techniques she has chosen, experimenting and developing new ways and visions. Whether this is paint, stone or code, the process is the same.

Nobody creates alone, as Virginia Woolf pointed out,

> *Masterpieces are not single and solitary births; they are the outcome of many years of thinking in common, of thinking by the body of the people, so that the experience of the mass is behind the single voice.*

But for the artist to create, this thinking in common must be available and shareable. She must be able to discuss and talk about it, use it, abuse it and expand it. Thus the artist's work will often enter into conflict with current copyright laws and, in the case of the digital artist, can be completely blocked by code that is protected or beyond reach. It is here that free software is so important for an artist. The capacity to intervene in the code, redistribute the interventions, to build with the blocks that other people have made available is absolutely essential to drive forward the creative process. Software moves from read only to read/write.

A good example is the development of Pure Data, a program for manipulating data and media. As needs emerge developers write the code necessary to resolve those needs, thus many authors have contributed to the ever growing library of code.[1] A recent example are curves for animation – these are mathematical formula that have now been implemented in objects for Pure Data by Hans Christoph Steiner in collaboration with Golan Levin.[2] These curves are needed for an animation to 'breath', for its elegance and beauty. If Pure Data had been closed code it would have been impossible to implement these curves and the artistic work is stopped or greatly delayed as one attempts to negotiate with a company to include your creative needs. Once implemented by the company it becomes another selling point. On the contrary, once implemented in free software these tools become available to the community, permitting everybody's work to reach a new level.

[1] http://puredata.org/

[2] http://artengine.ca/~catalogue-pd/39-Steiner-Henry.pdf the mapping library is included in pd-extended package : http://puredata.info/downloads

[3] http://www.blender.org

[4] http://arduino.cc

Art is continual change and the only way to advance is together. No single developer can create everything from scratch.

When you work with any software you are unavoidably involved in the process of testing that software. Simply to use it and comment on it, look for solutions to the problems, is to contribute to the development of that software. With a commercial software you are essentially working for the company, helping their profits and development that will only benefit users in the way that the software company decides. With free software your efforts contribute to the efforts of the community as a whole – nobody is profiting from your investigation, all are benefiting.

Many artistic investigations suffer from a lack of funding. It is only in academia that the concept of investigation is considered valid and financed. This is a serious problem for any independent artist developing her work. The art world still only considers creation in terms of the finished product, the logic being that you sell the work and cover your development costs. But investigation, as the academic world itself shows, does not work so logically and discoveries can come in the most unexpected moments. Free software is making artistic investigation more accesible in the sense that, while not resolving rent and food for the artist, it at least avoids license fees. As an example, a license for the 3D modelling program 3D studio Max costs US$3,495 while Blender, a comparable program, is free and, in addition, connectable to other programs, reusable and distributable.[3] Another example, this time in the field of hardware, is the Arduino project – suddenly, building physical interfaces has become much more accessible due to the open source nature of the electronics.[4]

This in no way means that the artist has to accept lower quality or unreliable work: a recent installation by Fernando Sanchez-Castillo (a sculpture that responds to the sending of SMS) was developed by Alex Posada in Hangar and used Arduino and its accompanying free software.[5] It worked without a flaw for the three months of the exhibition in the Centre d'Art Santa Monica in Barcelona. Another example, currently used by Björk in her concerts, is the ReACTable – an electronic instrument completely programmed with free software by a team from the Universitat de Pompeu Fabra.[6]

[5]
http://cultura.gencat.net/casm/butlleti/hemeroteca/n28/sp/article_01.htm
http://www.hangar.org

[6]
http://mtg.upf.edu/reactable/

[7]
http://www.ubuntu.com/

[8]
http://piksel.no
http://makeart.goto10.org/
http://www.laboralcentrodearte.org/

[9]
http://www.craslab.org/
http://www.hangar.org/wikis/lab/doku.php

Apart from the technical and economic considerations there is the question of ethics. The relationship between ethics and aesthetics is an increasingly important area of philosophical investigation for very good reasons. Our aesthetics – what we find beautiful or good – are indissociably linked to the world that we create. Divorced from ethics we plunge headlong to disaster. How do we think about the creation of beauty in the midst of an ecological disaster? When the difference between the rich and the poor is ever more abysmal? Can we find something beautiful that accentuates this difference, that contributes to the disaster? Is a work made with free software more beautiful than one made with proprietary software? The decision to work with free software is also an ethical decision, the expression of a desire to live in a world organised in a different way, where the artificial barriers that benefit only a few are eliminated.

The barriers that do remain in the use of free software are of a purely intellectual nature – the capacity to understand and work with code, for there is no doubt that more is demanded of the user. This, however, is changing greatly as free software reaches a new maturity, the Ubuntu distribution of Linux especially has made free software accessible to the non-technical 'standard' user.[7] For this reason it is so important that events, workshops and gatherings such as the Piksel festival in Bergen, make art in Poitiers, or the workshops organised by Hangar in Barcelona and at LABoral in Gijón, are organised in a way that permits the circulation of knowledge and learning.[8]

These gatherings are just one of the aspects of the community based nature of free software. Many coders never actually meet face to face but develop intense collaborations through mailing lists, IRC chat, CVS, Sourceforge.net and other internet tools. Labs like Hangar in Barcelona or CRAS in Paris are also important meeting points and places where work gets done and collaborations are extended.[9] Many people point out that

Google is the programmer's best friend but this would be useless without the conscious effort that developers and users put into documentation – both in the code and in the form of HOWTOs. Documentation is an absolutely essential part of working with free software and is fundamental to maintaining and extending the community. Which is, after all, what it's all about.

# Generous Practices: A Fictional Conversation, Based on Emails, Physical Encounters, IRC and a Skype session

Femke Snelting

FS: Femke Snelting
LR: Laurence Rassel
MK: Maja Kuzmanovic
TL: Thomas Laureyssens
GB: Guy van Belle
NG: Nik Gaffney

## A Cultural Ecosystem

FS: Reuse, free distribution and the free flow of ideas are concepts I often encounter on your websites and in your publications. Do you use these terms because you consider culture as an eco-system?

LR: I'm not sure I would use the term 'ecology' literally, but we like to work with open source software for example, because it exposes a network of relations between communities, tools and audiences. Of course, these relations go much further than art, literature, theatre or dance. Culture is embedded in social, economical and technological structures.

MK: Culture is much more than a series of static objects and statements; it is an ongoing process. So naturally you start to think about the interdependency between different elements.

LR: ... and this type of culture has a longer storage life than the modernistic idea that every artist is autonomous and avant-garde, has to do away with history, and destroy and discard everything in order to start again.

[1]
groWorld initiative: minimize borders and maximize edges, http://fo.am/groworld/

[2]
'The Viridian Design Manifesto', http://viridiandesign.org/manifesto.html

MK: What's important is how you interact with your environment; how, as a maker, you are an essential element in a larger system and vice versa, how small differences can determine who and what you are. In our groWorld project we try to reflect on the way you 'cultivate' your cultural milieu. For instance, how do you maintain the conditions by which culture can exist?[1]

GB: The interesting thing about a cultural ecosystem is the fact that it's not only about a literal exchange of information and products, but that the system also allows you to share behaviours, approaches, and working methods. The participation of the public also plays an important role.

TL: My association is perhaps even more direct, but the fact that digital media literally have a smaller ecological impact, really interests me. As a student, I read Bruce Sterling's 'Viridian Design Manifesto', and it still has a great influence on the way I approach digital media.[2] 'Replacing natural resources with information', as he calls it, is an important challenge for designers, artists and other creative people. I believe that if we can find a clever way to use these media, we can reduce the use of energy.

FS: Is the use of virtual space actually 'greener'?

TL: Obviously the production of computers does have an effect on the environment... and there's the catch.

NG: I agree with Thomas. Digital media provide a range of options; some of which might be very useful. First of all, they have a wider reach and a lower environmental impact than print for example. Software systems can also help to visualise ecological processes or to regulate those processes, such as with the distribution of electricity.

MK: There is so much in digital culture that could be used to change the unsustainable aspects of our social economy! The culture of open re-sources, for example, is very important. And as we are living in a technological society, the solution to environmental problems should be formulated from a technological point of view. There is no going back to an imaginary agrarian utopia.

## Copyright Alternatives

FS: In his article 'Aan auteursrecht heb je niets', Joost Smiers writes that 'exclusivity' is not an adequate criterion in terms of determining the value of culture. 'Copyright nowadays revolves almost exclusively around so-called intellectual property. This is a problem, since the traditional notion of property is largely irreconcilable with intangible concepts such as knowledge and creativity; a tune, an idea or an invention will not lose any of its value or usefulness when it is shared among any number of people.'[3]

[3] Joost Smiers in: Aan Auteursrecht heb je niets, De Volkskrant, 2005

[4] Creative Commons, http://creativecommons.org/ Licence Art Libre, http://artlibre.org/

[5] GPL, http://www.gnu.org/licenses/licenses.html#GPL

MK: Creative work consists of so many different media, disciplines, activities and products that if even the smallest part remains closed and is unable to benefit from the free flow of processes, ideas and products, it is precisely here where cancerous growths start to develop.

GB: Media artists do not gain recognition as individuals as such, but more often as a group. The value is not determined by an object or a specific result, but rather by a special moment where artists and public meet. And those moments are more important than individual glory.

FS: Do you use copyleft licences such as Creative Commons or Licence Art Libre?[4]

NG: Our projects are published under Creative Commons and the General Public Licence for example, in order to make sure that we share copyright with the people we collaborate with. And since it once got us into trouble, we also categorically refuse to sign non-disclosure agreements.[5]

GB: I use alternative licences especially when I develop projects with other artists and cultural organisations. They are very useful for making agreements about the correct use of each other's material.

LR: Constant often uses these licences as a 'performative' act! When you release a work under a copyleft licence, you immediately address intellectual property issues.

FS: But in fact you add an extra legal document...

LR: You mean that each creative act is preceded by ten or sometimes hundreds of contracts? I know, that frightens me too. It seems as if in the future 'fair use' will only occur very rarely... and that's exactly the opposite of what we want.

FS: Copyleft licences are an interesting alternative to the traditional copyright system, but the individual author still remains the starting point.

GB: For me and many people around me, the copyright system has never really been a solution. If you look at its history, it's a very commercial mechanism and I think for experimental artists who are not market driven, the system has no value at all. I myself refuse to be a part of any copyright system at all.

LR: An author never has a neutral position; he or she is an active thinker and player. It's always interesting when creators use their position as an author to give others the opportunity to use their work, instead of protecting everything, but that's just one way of questioning the concept of 'originality', authority and the power an author can exercise.

TL: It's very important to be part of a network where you can profile and represent yourself so that you get invited to give performances and to work on new projects for example.

FS: Is this way of operating inspired by the fact that you work with digital media?

TL: I guess so. I think that new economic structures such as micro payments and a decentralised distribution system based on downloads can be very helpful for media artists. The rules and structures of a long tail economy are more appropriate for small alternative organisations than for large conglomerates.

GB: Today's society is dictated by a whole bunch of contradictory economic principles, and media artists are in a vulnerable position anyway. This kind of experimental art is continually threatened by politicians who exploit culture, so we should be careful.

FS: As an artist, why is it important to think about intellectual property?

[6] CopyCult - the original Si(G)n, http://copycult.constantvzw.org/

LR: We were often asked the same question when we organised CopyCult in 2000.[6] At that time, you could really start to feel the impact of digital media, for example, in new distribution systems such as Napster and the issues it raised, but also in the work of artists such as Harun Farocki, Jean-Luc Godard or Chris Marker who were busy recycling existing images in an intelligent way. At what price can you re-use an image? That was and still is a very relevant question for artists.

FS: Shouldn't that discussion be left to lawyers?

LR: The law is the law, but there is also the actual practice and that became very clear to us when we started to work with lawyers specialised in intellectual property. We showed them how we felt restrained by restrictions that were seemingly intended to protect us. After that, we started to work out a different way of dealing with copyright. We learned a lot from them, but they also learned a lot from us.

**On Collaboration**

FS: You are all involved in collective practices. Why do you think these collaborations are so important in media art?

GB: A lot of media artists I work with were already experimenting with music in the early eighties, and via computer music and video they gradually moved over to media art. In music, you have this almost utopian optimistic attitude of 'hey, let's play music together!'. Someone has an idea and that's how it starts. And the person who has the original idea doesn't feel misused or anything, on the contrary, he or she is charmed by the fact that others want to collaborate.

TL: The habit of collaborating is something I learned gradually, as I moved more from an assignment based design practice towards becoming an autonomous artist. In fact, media art is always multidisciplinary and the complexity of the technologies used makes collaboration practically a must. It just broadens your range, technological as well as content-wise.

GB: You also work on things longer; together you can be much more critical. When you collaborate, somebody can suddenly come up and say: was this me or was it you? And at that point you realise that it's going in the right direction; when you are no longer able do distinguish who is doing what. In my terms, that's a successful collaboration.

MK: It's a way to start off a process that you can't predict, and we happen to like unpredictable projects. Unfortunately, there are a lot of artists whose rhetoric is steeped in 'collaboration' and 'collaborative', but when it comes down to working in a group, a lot of them still want to have their name as the author. On the other hand, we see a lot of scientists and technologists who, surprisingly enough, don't want to take credit for their role as a cultural 'author' in the projects that we develop with them... which I think is an interesting phenomenon.

FS: The subtitle of the sutChwon project is: 'connecting everything to everything else: flexible system for remote collaboration'.[7]

NG: We were planning to pull together all the half formed systems we were using, to get them to talk to each other. There was a lot of overlap because we kept on developing new software, hardware and equipment for specific purposes, so we needed a kind of connection kit. SutChwon is not really a tool as such, but it does have an effect on the way we design software and connect things together.

FS: So you're developing a kind of technological Esperanto?

NG: It's more a protocol than a language. Something like a plumber's van full of gaffer tape. And the instructions are written in a dialect of Esperanto that looks suspiciously like the Perl programming language![8]

## Free Tools

FS: The free software movement is in favour of computer programmers releasing the source code of their programs; giving each user the right to study, copy, change and distribute it.[9] Is the use of free software relevant for media artists?

[7] sutChwon uses computers to technically and socially facilitate collaboration. Http://www.fo.am/sutchwon/sutchwon_text.html

[8] Perl (Practical Extraction and Report Language) is a popular programming language.

[9] 'Free software is a matter of liberty, not price. To understand the concept, you should think of 'free' as in "free speech", not as in "free beer".' http://www.gnu.org/philosophy/free-sw.html

GB: When I first came in contact with software, internet didn't even exist (laughs). There was an enormous amount of code circulating. Artists and developers were sending each other disks. If someone would ask me to show them how I did this or that, I would. The idea that it was 'free software' came only later. At that time, we had no idea that code had a market value. Now it's a whole different story.

TL: It really surprises me that subsidised institutions continue to invest in new systems for themselves without sharing them with the community. So everyone keeps on putting in the same data, while you could be using your time for more creative and content related work! That's why I think that all governmental institutions should only use Open Source Software and open standards. This way, smaller organisations can benefit from the investments made by the bigger ones.

FS: Media artists work very intensively with their digital tools. The esthetical and material quality of their work is very much defined by it. What role does software play in your practice?

GB: I like to compare it to playing an instrument. Musicians, no matter how much they practice, they can only reach a certain level. They are physically limited by their instrument. I started programming when I realised that I could suddenly expand my range of expressive operations that way.

FS: You mean that you started to create your own digital instruments?

GB: Exactly. The idea is that you can behave a bit like a clumsy inventor. With software you can really experiment. I'm not a programmer, but in order to go beyond the limits of standard software, you need to be able to perform a few basic interventions. I like to go as far as I can in changing all possible parameters in order to create my own sound. And to come back to your question about collaboration, the limit of your own technical abilities is no longer an issue, because there is always the possibility of collaborating with other people.

LR: For me, software is more an instrument in the metaphorical sense. By asking 'who uses what, what for and with who?' it becomes a tool to help you think. I am interested in the fact that each program also programs in a figurative sense: it prescribes specific forms, sounds and images.

TL: It's amazing how easily you accept the default settings of a program.

FS: How would you describe the software that you develop?

TL: For some time now I've been working on a narrative game system.[10] I think it differs from conventional systems because it allows me to develop my own narrative structures without conforming to existing patterns and the users of the game can also contribute. And of course because it all goes very slowly!

NG: All the software we have developed so far has been an adjustment to existing systems for a specific purpose, or the 'glue' to keep several elements together. For us, software can sometimes be a medium, but usually it's a tool for making connections flexible.

MK: We like to build on existing systems, or actually we prefer to collaborate with people who want to further develop and/or use the software. But it doesn't mean that we are afraid to get our hands dirty, if something doesn't exist yet.

**Sharing Knowledge**

FS: Since 2004 Foam and OKNO have been working on X-med-K, a series of workshops on the experimental use of new media.[11] Constant is involved with Femmes et logiciels libres, a project in which the participants themselves are responsible for the organisation of the learning process.[12] Can you tell me something more about your interest in sharing knowledge and why it is important as artists to organise these workshops?

GB: For OKNO it's a way to get together with a few people and to investigate a technology or an idea. At this moment, for example, we are working on a workshop around wireless modems. Reseau Citoyen has put up a few of them.[13] Through sensors, they can communicate with each other. We have invited Maxigas and Ákos Maróy join us in making an interactive work with this equipment in a week's time.

FS: You use the term 'workshop'?

[10] Lakshmi, http://www.toyfoo.com/lakshmi/index.html

[11] http://xmedk.be/

[12] Femmes et Logiciels Libres, http://samedi.collectifs.net/

[13] http://www.reseaucitoyen.be

GB: I would like to find a different word for it though... it's about doing things together, about discovering how to be practical and creative with technology. It's not about institutional learning, but we do invite experts to work on projects together with participants.

FS: Can learning and collaborating go hand in hand?

MK: That brings us back to the beginning of this conversation. It's important to feed the ecology that keeps you going. We don't consider our work to be the mere production of unique art works, but as the production of *knowledge.* If not shared through an educational process, be it a traditional workshop, a discussion or any form of exchange, this knowledge is reduced to superficial 'information'.

FS: How do you deal with the hierarchical relationship between yourself and the one you are sharing knowledge with?

MK: In the beginning we used to work with workshop instructors who taught something to the group, but eventually we moved towards participatory models where instructors can become participants and vice versa and we find this method to be much more productive.

TL: It's really great when you get this flow where others start to run wild with something you have instigated.

FS: If you want to share knowledge, experience, tools and/or a platform, the 'opening' of sources is just the beginning.

MK: Of course it doesn't stop at the opening of source files. Hopefully, we can change our consumers' society into a responsible participatory culture. One of the people we work with, pointed out that perhaps instead of cultural '*open source*', we should refer to it as '*ajar* (half open) *source*', because it's not about leaving the door wide open.

LR: It's wrong to assume that all free software is automatically open. Because who really has the opportunity to participate? Who has time for it, who does it lend authority to and who gets into trouble by it?

MK: So much 'open source' media works and artistic software are being dumped online, which supposedly makes them 'open' but they are incomprehensible and undocumented, so they remain closed for most people. Participation is the key, and that means that not only the end result is shared, but the whole process.

Notes

This text was originally published in:
Mediakunst in Vlaanderen, BAM, 2007.
Translation from Dutch by Sophie Burm.

Contributors

Guy van Belle (GB) is a developer of creative tools for networked performances and installations. In projects such as mXHz and Society of Algorithm, he researches modes of collaboration around audiovisual artefacts. Since 2005 he also works in Bratislava under the name Gívan Belá.

Nik Gaffney (NK) is a systems and media researcher and a co-founder of FoAM. Gaffney focuses on biological and physical computer models, generative systems and responsive media environments.

Maja Kuzmanovic (MK) is a generalist and interested in the small miracles of everyday life. As a co-founder of FoAM, she is involved in many different projects, be it commissioned by European research institutes or as an independent artist.

Thomas Laureyssens (TL) develops integrated systems for interactive storytelling. His practice consists of experimental interface design, video work and public installations.

Laurence Rassel (LR) is a cyberfeminist and a member of Constant (Organisation for art and media). She works together with organisations such as Interface3, Arteleku and Fundació Antoni Tàpies, on projects around archive policy, the position of the author and technology.

Femke Snelting (FS) is involved in various projects at the intersection of free software, feminism and design. She is an active member of Constant, De Geuzen (a foundation for multi-visual research) and the Open Source Publishing design team.

# The 'Free' and New Creative Practices: Open Source Modular Art-efacts

Julien Ottavi

## The Intuitively Free and the Free as Practice

The free software movement came into existence with the GNU philosophy, originally developed by Richard Stallman, through the GPL licence and the GNU operating system, and later, through GNU/Linux. It was called 'Free' from the beginning, already an attitude, a choice for a certain kind of society and human behaviour, even before involving software and encoding; which should be considered in terms of continuous development, an in-progress operation, a sharing process. Gathered under this name the enduring questions of what constitutes sensible, intuitive and practical approaches to reality frequently arise. The 'free' movement cannot only be thought of as a practice limited to the realm of computing and art, since its origin was the result of a relation to production and to social exchange. The concept of 'free' was not born out of the '70 and '80s, but had previously travelled through various periods, various processes, feeding off all sorts of cultures.

Tales, myths, the learning of techniques – all new knowledge enriched through the exchange and circulation of content and of practices in communities which shared the same interests and the same desire to understand their times. However, with the onset of capitalism the notion of property – the ownership of knowledge and of technology, dominates the processes by which knowledge is handled and obtained, especially with relation to the invention of copyrights. Yet, contrary to this 'free' movement is an intuitive and deeply engrained attitude that has traversed the centuries. Rather than being detached from an extinct tradition, the 'free' movement continues to enlarge those ideas of its ancestors – which, only recently replaced by a new language and new ideas, is now confronting a society where everything is bound by the concepts of property, the licensing of individual rights and commodity exchange – objectifying every germ of an idea or a product.

The GPL aims to overturn such limitations by upsetting that infamous right not to copy and instigating a new process of creation, of sharing and of the diffusion of source code. But how do we move from the intuition of the 'free' to implementing its practice? By opening up the faults that undermine a system, those cracks created beneath capitalist structures, through practices contrary to those structures which seek to reach a new kind of stability in a society whose systems are crumbling, the 'free' movement is beginning to get a foothold. Practising the 'free' signifies exiting the spheres of trade and fetishistic capitalism; questioning the system (even its reality), organising its mutation, allowing others to develop their own ideas, projects and practices beyond the schemes imposed by the corporate machine. The practice of the 'free' can be found at all levels of human activity, be it immaterial (ideas, digital data, knowledge) or industrial, agricultural, manual (craft) or artistic. It becomes ever more obvious that praxis and production can exist under different guises, outside the notion of property. The 'free' unlocks the doors of fear or ignorance, of dead end economics.

## Free Software and Creation: Beyond Models, Synergy and Mutation

How do free software and open source influence each other and encourage creative processes and artistic practices? For a few years now, free software has been deployed, through creation-oriented tools, in artistic practices which are, as a consequence, set free from the domination of large proprietary data processing corporations. But we now discover a whole field of concepts through free software: the logic of source code, of sharing and open distribution, the freedom to modify sources, new modes of sharing, new ways to learn or to transform other people's work, working in a net or a collective, questioning copyrights and other property rights... . The first effects of the 'free' upon creation were felt against the notion of copyright in addition to the invention of new modes of distribution and sharing content or knowledge – especially digital content (audio, text, video, image). Questions concerning authorship had already been raised by previous avant-garde artistic groups, such as Dada, Lettrists, Situationists, as well as through unclaimed works and imaginary names, and so on. Yet the concept of authorship eventually returned with a vengeance; the individual's wish for recognition prevailed, programmed into us by the system and its formatting devices (family, school, prison, army, media...). The 'free' movement does not negate the existence of an author. On the contrary, the author introduces him/herself and allows us to develop his/her work beyond any denial to share and transform. What we call 'author-owner', as opposed to plain 'author', is controlled by jurisdiction, his/her ideas or products (books, CDs, films, sculptures, clothes, designs...) would remain restricted or regulated. In many countries, all works of art or of the imagination, are 'copyrighted' by default, i.e. Their use is regulated and they are legally protected from copying freely or unauthorised transformation. The red tape of the bureaucrats has already decided what is best for us, we are entwined from the start; new concepts must necessarily belong to somebody; hence, they must be protected and licensed. At this stage, the notion of 'free' comes onto the scene, and licences such as the GPL become essential, allowing again the creative process to be developed outside of the rigid proprietary rules that binds it. The product is now set free from the world of traded commodities, ready to be shared, distributed or transformed. The author can now let his/her work proliferate and generate new processes. In a world of (almost) costless reproduction, the outmoded notion of the 'unique' has no reason to subsist; objects, concepts are no longer irreplaceable. We now live in a time of proliferation, of (digital or industrial) diffusion, when production can be multiplied, in different modes, from different points of view – not just from perspective of the originator, the 'owner'. The doors of fear and ignorance, of one-way economics, may be set ajar. Things can now be copied at will and immediately, as soon as they have been created or expressed. Reality now confronts the great propagating machine which can swallow anything and regurgitate so many of its replicas. More and more ants stream out of a digital planetary ant-hill.

The author has now been 'liberated' through the opening of source codes and by the possibility of their modification. This trend can be observed in the artistic arena, thanks to many kinds of licences that have been chosen specifically for creation (Creative Commons, Art Libre, gnu-art etc.), and including works open to transformation, modification or reappropriation. Where this opening had previously been intuitive, now it has become the conscious choice of the original author; there is no more talk of 'influence', 'quotes' or other ways to modify works (previously considered as 'assets', liable to be 'controlled'). When governed by these new licences, works become part of an ongoing process, they are 'in progress', part of a multi-layered product. In this context, any member of the art community may consciously develop, disrupt, aestheticise, redefine, divert a piece of work, a process, an idea, originated by others. Questions can now be openly raised, the author/genius can be upstaged and the author/owner becomes rather run-of-the-mill. Everybody can now believe that the part of the gap that separated them from creativity has been bridged and that art can penetrate our most trivial actions. More and more projects are using the concepts of open codes as a basis to push and encourage future transformations by individuals and groups. This means we may now imagine sharing what we are and what we mean without fear, fear of the other, of whoever might contradict us, question us or our project. We can now proliferate, become multi-cellular, imagine a manifold entity in each work, each process. History is no longer made of Great People only, but of multi-generational nuclei. We contemplate the renaissance of the collective author.

## New Practices Influenced by the Free Movement

For a few years, free software has been engaged in network practice. Through these first networks, source code has been able to circulate, it has been shared, modified, copied. GNU/Linux first met recognition when it engaged in network technology. Free software could only be developed out of collaborative work, multi-authored projects, programming, corrections, beta-tests etc. From the outset the 'free' project participated in the internet project and the practice of networking. Without free software and the options of out-of-copyright licences, the notion of digital networks would have found itself limited to paying sites, or sites controlled by specialised companies. Whilst these companies are visibly present in the current system, they have to compete with more open techniques in addition to a mass of products stemming from the free movement, such as; software, texts, ideas, documentation, distribution, community, mutual aid, forums, modes of sharing etc. Many forms of creation implicating contemporary notions of networks, sharing and collaboration have been developed in and outside of the internet. They intuitively borrowed concepts from the net and the digital, and from the resulting multiplication of forms and layers, the deregulation of time (stretched), the new ubiquity of our way of life. When the author is multiplied tenfold, thousandfold, when the machine (prosthesis of the human) becomes creator, autonomous and almost unbound, we can see a new society being born where new visions mingle and get bruised, pile up and explode, new hopes arise leading to mutations. Machinic mutations lead to chaos, the unknown, and unexpected behaviour. We are now running into darkness with fear as our only light, maybe toward our termination, like Icarus aiming for the sun, trying to disappear into the sun. However, what has this got to do with artistic practices? Maybe these practices only mirror our the scope of our desires, phantasms? Maybe desire is necessary for our transformation, and we need to create, with machines, through networks. To participate collectively in an incommensurable and endless work of art, with networks acting as multipliers in a myriad of permutations. The continual production of a work, forever ongoing in its actualisation, can now be considered, with so many layers or versions, temporary endings and pauses, as a new process that explodes the myth of the completed work of art, of achievement. Work that is perpetually in progress is no longer the dream that was previously imagined – rhetorically invoked it can actually be realised. Relayed by many craftsmen, artists, technicians, who modify the very concept of a work of art, are no longer caught up in a 'movement', nor prisoners of the framework of Art History (as in Conceptual art), but free to shift within an ongoing practice, across diverse milieus and activities. New creative forms can connect, through networks, feeding and exchanging data from afar, ubiquitous. New forms of creation everywhere, reproducing like organic cells. Creators can now exchange in real time, content and/or processes, as well as receive some form of instant feedback. They can imagine catching or transforming things differently, and hope that their own contribution will participate in a gigantic constellation. Any experiment has the potential to continue beyond any pre-defined framework, following directions never conceived previously. The notion of a categorised, quantified product could sometimes disappear, being replaced by undefined forms destined to evolve unexpectedly. The machine becomes poetical, almost human. Or, we are becoming our own prosthesis, the cosmic phantasm that we exhale, integrating the here and there, the now and after. Free software and the practice of the 'free' in general liberates the desires that we have not yet expressed. Here they appear, suddenly realised, developed, diverted, recuperated and they communicate, but they dissolve as soon as they are born, and multiply to an infinity of forms, shared and open; their mere existence is questioned as much as their future and their definition. The pirate does not depend on the fake, the *faux* (remaining a prisoner of corporations or institutions), he explores the unknown, beyond definitions, beyond routine.

By developing from free content, by sharing with multiple authors, we can reconsider the various co-actors or co-producers of a collective work, who are no longer prisoners of a specific role: the concept engineer, the author, the technician, the producer, the distributor, the artist, the spectator, the participant... we can now become all or anyone of these. And we know our (and *their*) work can now be distributed without any legal or technical constraints.

With gratitude, we are lost. We have derailed the beaten path of easy categorisations and obvious histories, new modes are open; real-time, permanent diffusion, network distribution, countless copies, ubiquity on the net and the division of product source. Even this text has not been written where you/they think: it's here and it's there, everywhere, you read it in one form but, maybe, it has already been copied and modified in ways you can't imagine. It is becoming something else, it has become already, it does not wait for us before it dissipates or proliferates into the universe.

Notes

Original text written in French :
http://www.crealab.info/ecriture/doku.php?id=version_en_ligne
translation by Hervé Gosselin.

version 0.1 (source : Julien Ottavi)

# Information Nomads and Community Surfing

oRx-qX

## Information Pursuit

In the early phases of the development of internet connectivity, the information banks were the FTP archives of mostly academic institutions and the key to their resources was anonymous FTP and a command line of a terminal. Computer guys played with BSD, the first free software. Also on commercial Unix, one could finger people, SMTP servers were open. Communication culture was based on the ideas of the '70s post-hippie movement transformed into the electronic sphere. The address of the FTP server could sometimes be found in printed magazines or a randomly obtained electronic text, and in order to connect, knowledge of control commands were necessary. An abundance of texts existed about drugs, underground zines, postmodern texts, one could find the Anarchist cookbook, Phrack. And yes, there was ASCII art and there were text games... However, only a relatively limited group of people had access to this information.

After a short episode with the hypertext system Gopher, a WWW boom followed in 1995-96. The number of private or theme sites began to grow, although they could only be placed at the predominantly academic or the emerging freehosting servers. And you could hear the phreaks saying: 'Look, we can have Microsoft server and Novell both here, on the machine under the table, for free, connect to our network!' And it was Linux, a breakout from the institutional bindings. One could easily envisage that on the academic website CV-type information was expected – photographs, information about professional interests, projects. The administrators didn't cherish other types of info. According to the graphical nature of the WWW, all was suddenly uncovered, the login and password and dark command line disappeared, information so far hidden in the net was at once made outright public. Information on the World Wide Web had to abide by certain rules of the server or institution where it was located.

Freehosting providers censored the web for two main reasons – bandwidth and complaints about indecent content from companies and individuals hardened by threats of legal prosecution. Areas of unsuitable information rapidly proliferated – porn, drugs, warez, hacking, cracks, guides on how to produce chemicals, spreading racism, fascism but also 'different opinions'. The scenario was simple. The author created his website, uploaded it onto the server, and let everyone know about it. On other websites links to this site would emerge, thus more and more people would find out about it. Because everything was public, sooner or later someone who found some information unacceptable would come across a site containing it. Someone whose perception of the world was scattered or the administrator himself detected an increased data transfer from the statistics, and a problem would arise. After hackers, information liberators of the late '80s, the information nomads emerged, authors of websites incessantly driven from server to server because they couldn't stay long anywhere.

Thing.net is a network where The Yes Men, a group of political artists and activists hosted a parody site, dow-chemical.com. In 2002, the creators of the site sent out a false press release, in which Dow admitted responsibility for the Bhopal catastrophe in India, where the leak of chemicals killed 5,000 people and 150,000 have died in the following years as a consequence of the contamination of the environment. The press release stated that Dow would like to compensate the victims and face the environmental damage, however, the interests of the shareholders do not allow that and it would be a dangerous precedent for other corporations in the field, such as Exxon, Amoco, BP or Shell. The company Dow consequently filed a DMCA complaint against Verio, the Internet provider of the whole network thing.net, achieving a momentary disconnection for 15 hours. Thing.net had its 7-year contract terminated and got 60 days to relocate to a different provider. The domain dow-chemical.com was redirected to Dow company's own site. Free speech? Dow called it defamation, trademark infringement, and cybersquatting.

**Cyberdissent**

Liu Di, a 22-year-old student of psychology from Beijing wrote contributions in discussion groups under her nickname 'stainless steel mouse'. When police closed her favourite chatroom, she set up her own. She published various articles on the online bulletin board and criticized the government restrictions of the internet. Furthermore, she expressed sympathy for the webmaster, who had been imprisoned for publishing articles dealing with forbidden topics, such as the demonstration at the

Tian'anmen Square in 1989. The police arrested her for threatening state security, searched her house, seized her computer, notes and floppy disks. Her parents don't know where she is.

Amnesty International publicly accused top US producers and distributors of computer technologies. Microsoft, Sun microsystems, Cisco systems and others were among those who supplied China with technology enabling restriction of freedom of speech on the internet. They are in league with Yahoo and Google providing the Chinese government with the Golden Shield, the largest political filtering system. Now, the side effect of various restrictions on internet access and information content filtering is that people are being arrested for transmission of subversive information. Some of them are already dead. The censorship of the internet is most severe in China and Burma, but in a number of other countries where state-controlled information infrastructure exists internet access is censored on a national level. The protocols on foreign connectivity lines are restricted and filtered. Internet is only accessible in state-controlled cafes, email communication is monitored. In 2000 the founder and editor of the online daily Ukrainian Truth, Georgij Gongadze, was murdered. He was monitored by the state police for a couple of months prior to his disappearance.

Censorship appears in most countries of the world. Even in countries generally considered as democratic, such as the USA or the UK, sites and servers are classified according to their suitability or danger. You can't browse through Helmut Newton's web which is classified as sex/nudity or read about fascism. Proxy servers and search engines contain lists of unacceptable words and filter unsuitable sites. 50 to 80 percent of email is filtered and disappears without any rules or notice. Hidden restrictions shape and cut information flows more and more and everything is closely monitored. The decision is made by the provider or employer, and is arbitrary and secret. Isn't the situation in Malaysia better in that things are censored only if they're breaking written laws? Reporters Without Borders have a record of tens of imprisoned cyber dissidents. The demonstrations (even in Paris!) for their release are mostly suppressed by the police.

Software and information are closely connected, maybe they are the two sides of the same coin. Software is just encoded thought, different for commercial monopolies, different for common people. Free software means free information and vice versa. Remember the case of Phil Zimmermann's Pretty Good Privacy. This encryption software was released with complete source code and led in 1993 to criminal investigation for export of forbidden technology. Now, everything is available, from operating systems to web and proxy servers for building communication infrastructure, independent of political and economic restrictions and for sure it is massively used. Open source ideas allowed the creation of personal, DIY, community and small business fields supporting and running the samizdat of the 21st century, a global network penetrating any firewall. Don't think you can download hacktivism as Tor or Freegate. In 2007, a Swedish hacker infiltrated the Tor network meaning to provide anonymous communication routing, and gained access to hundreds of governmental and corporate emails, which he published later on his security blog. Staying free is a way of thinking, understanding, a long term building of infrastructure and tools.

**Anonymity**

Publishing information, but also browsing and reading poses a risk. As a precaution against hackers or viruses, the ISPs in the USA were forced to bug their system logs by secret service and police, which are thus able to track down from which telephone number or place the user connected to a certain IP address. Through this they can trace the visitors of websites, the origin of emails, etc. Interestingly, an important producer of log data mining technologies is Microsoft, whose OS and Office software is a heaven for viruses. The security holes in its internet tools are often hard to grasp. It surely might be intentional, the Microsoft management calls the computer underground the Darknet and organizes seminars about cyberterrorism as PR for their products.

Eventually, weapons against prosecution of information have developed naturally. It is something that could be called a non-linear way of communication – stepping out of the mainstream, closed and multi-layered communication. Login boxes in discussion forums requiring a password initially started to appear for identification reasons – to make the contributions more coherent and identifiable. Nevertheless, at some places one had to fulfill certain criteria in order to register, at some places you have to be someone's friend to get in. Closed content started to increase. Nowadays, most of the quality information is behind doors which are difficult to pass through. Robots cannot scan this content; personal contacts are required for access. We can speak about community sites, which have their entry games and rituals (typically, a new member must write something about himself and has to be recommended by an existing member). In open systems, only forums with restricted access emerged. To allow free communication, there is a rule which forbids publishing contributions that appeared on a closed discussion system anywhere else without the author's consent. A similar etiquette of links and citations has been created by bloggers.

**Copyright and Corporate Culture**

Etoy.com, one of the first art projects on the internet, got into trouble with its domain name when it became an object of interest for an online toy store which succeeded in acquiring the domain through a tough court case. Interestingly, after the bursting of the dotcom bubble, the toy company went bankrupt and the domain came back into the hands of the activists.

Free sites are facing problems and dying. Police and corporations have learned to monitor the web and terminate uncomfortable sites by threats to the ISP and the hosting provider, usually without any legal backing. The weapons the corporations use against freedom of speech on the internet are WIPO and DMCA – the World Intellectual Property Organisation and the infamous US authorship law the Digital Millennium Copyright Act. And of course, the Terrorist Threat. These acts basically work for state and large corporations, because an individual cannot compete on trademarks and patents with corporations. Thanks to the DMCA hundreds of internet radio stations have been closed down. The copyright organisations together with distribution companies – or rather under their pressure – prosecute the spread of music and films, despite the fact that the change of their business model after the arrival of the internet is inevitable. The Napster trial was the beginning of the witch hunts. New systems for file sharing have developed, such as Gnutella, which surpassed the centralized and easily assailable model by distributed network. RIAA has placed spies in these systems, traced downloads, sends out accusatory mails which report downloaders to providers and litigates with under-age children the same as elders. The only thing achieved is a growth of new generations of file-sharing networks with new technologies for anonymising, distributing transfer, routing mechanisms where every node becomes the server. This could be BitTorrent, Muse or any other software. Companies spread hidden malware and adware to sniff on people's behavior and preferences, on the other hand, youngsters stick at nothing and abuse the servers to make them serve their movies and when the exploit is discovered, they move to another. Napster was an easily recognizable center, but you cannot hit a network which has no center.

Legislation in many countries is so screwed, that when you write your own music and want to play it, or sing a traditional song, you have to pay for it. This comes from the US, the world's biggest media market dominated by major studios, and reaches the UK and EU and the domino goes on. The same way it makes celebrity pop-stars on one side, it kills free creation of most of the individual artists and people on the other. Sharing and remixing as natural principles of artistic expression are there at least the whole 20th century, says Lawrence Lessig in his book *Free Culture.* And above the subtitle 'How Big Media Uses Technology and the Law to Lock Down Culture and Control Creativity' the Creative Commons logo emerges from the book cover. CC is the answer of the people who do not want to be pushed to or over the legal border. Before CC, free content was illegal, with it we can now clearly explain what we do when running public archives of music, video and literature.

In 2004, I downloaded A. Jodorowsky's movie *The Holy Mountain* from suprnova.org, before it was shut down. I didn't know what kind of film it was and nobody knew. I started using it in a VJ projection for Bruno Ferrari, obscure, but in its refined style a trendsetting band. People wondered. Later, small screenings of Jodorowsky's movies went through and after three years, *The Holy Mountain* was screened at a mainstream film festival and thus came into national distribution. So does downloading spoil film business?

The fight is reverted from online back to the ordinary world. There are restrictions imposed upon parties and public appearances, efforts exist to enforce built-in protection against unauthorized use of author creation directly in the technology (players, projectors, memory cards). The protection goes so far that on your expensive player it might not be possible to play legal DVDs or CDs. Linux with Xine or VLC plays anything, region, CSS or not, it brings new logic into home entertainment and revolution into consumer electronics. Free software does not breach the DVD or MPEG licenses, it just came with a new point of view. Linux is in cameras, portable technology, set-top boxes, mobile phones... licensing models simply change. And the glimpsy FLOSS is left out of it.

There is often a misunderstanding, that open source or open content redistribution rules deny copyright or intellectual property. No, not at all. They are *based* on copyright. BSD, GNU GPL, Creative commons... these all are licences, pretty strict licences. And there could be no licence without accepting the principle of authorship. But there is a difference, instead of binding people, they make people free.

## Technological Communities

Czfree.net is a large WiFi network without an official administration structure, composed of hundreds of access points and nodes with a possibility of a free broadband connection. Parts of its backbone are carried out by DIY 10mbit/s Ronja optical links, home-made at a fraction of the price of similar commercial products. A license dispute arose between Clock, the author of the original open source hardware design and a small company Alphawave belonging to one of the founders of czfree. Alphawave didn't provide all the documentation with the product, according to the licence. The author's accusations ended up in developing the proprietary model of the laser by the company.

It all begins with a server running free software, the true community heartbeat. Some personal computers and at least partially freely accessible space, a small company, graphic or recording studio. Larger communities create strong information portals, they dispose of their own hosting capacities or internet connection. Having control over the medium enables one to set one's own rules, create a space which differs from the rigid and aimless economic conditions that are blocking alternative projects, from license arrangements or terms of service. Everything has to be paid for in the commercial sphere – information, patents, technologies, the smallest piece of software, standards or for using certain formats. The high technological level of the communities provides them with some financial freedom. However, it can't be said, that the financial issue would be the growth factor of the communities. They do not grow on money, they grow with people.

We can think further. Own wireless connection, telephone connection, open source software, special operating systems, encrypted short message systems, cryptographic authorities, streaming radio and video, multi-user virtual worlds and games.

From impulsive demo groups to the metropolitan networks, we are not talking about the forefront of the development but the bazaar. Their equipment, a mixture of commercially sold parts and other self-produced independent technologies, while the role of the independent ones keeps increasing. Simply said – they cannot develop new algorithms, but they know how to implement and use them. The central principle intertwined with this process is hacking of high-tech high-price equipment or programs, developing similar lo-tech devices from cheap DIY components, replacing commercial programs and formats with open source alternatives, utilization of the technology in other ways than had been intended, removal of protection mechanisms, reverse engineering, ripping, cracking.

At the beginning, there were revolutionary ideas – technology for everyone. Local self-sufficiency against global conglomerates. From open software, the virus spread and infected the hardware. Maybe you know Arduino, open design physical computing device used for interactive artworks of all kinds and operated by the open languages Processing and Wiring, which made its way into the ranks of stylish gadgets without the need for a SONY logo. There is more and more open source firmware, open processor designs, MIDI controllers... as software grows into hardware and the generation of hackers gets older and gains decisive influence in companies, the barriers fall down and many drivers, interfaces, formats and protocols become open and the remaining are under strong pressure. Fights for patented technologies that can make some money still remain. But the advantage is so brief. The new development processes adopted from open software, which count on co-development or at least modding by the users have proved to hold a much greater potential.

**Infocommunities**

Indymedia.org – during demonstrations against the WTO in Seattle in 1999 CNN broadcasted news, which said that the police didn't use rubber projectiles against the demonstrators. The Independent Media Center (IMC) gave another story. While the CNN reporters interviewed the police spokesman and recorded their official version, IMC had over a hundred cameras in the streets. On its website, the IMC published proofs about rubber shots and provided a video, which documented the use of police guns. CNN was pushed to correct its news and inform about the violent conflict.

Do broadcasters tell us lies and disinformation? Why not read news from reporters who are real people living in the actual places of conflict? Yes, time to talk about different structures of organization, self-organization, decentralization.

Open source software developers do form a similar global network around the idea expressed by the GPL license, which, apart from the economic aspect, has also some social impact regarding the rules of distribution. Open source is supported by companies, corporations, totalitarian governments or military subjects, which realize that it brings them profit. It is absurdly symptomatic that the most wide-spread distribution of Linux is the Chinese Red flag. Structure of open source development is more relaxed than classical corporate hierarchical bindings with managed motivation, but on the whole it can hardly be called a community. Post-industrial, post-modern and post-cybernetic community has multi-layered relationships, more social aims – and a personal dimension.

Communities are always somehow closed. They have their mantras and sound informations that unite them. In communities based around graphic style it is a more complex network of ties, however, there is a greater independence, or sometimes abstract. The feature of information communities is the acquisition of new information, discussion, creation of opinion systems, spreading of alternative information, that is pushed out of the mainstream media or misinterpreted, information liberation, creation of information bases and sources with an open license. Naturally developing community sites often contain a public layer – articles at a level generally accepted by other media. Under the systems of access rights there is a strong discussion core, a system of private messaging, user journals or blogs, tools for expressing identity and relationships between users (karma, friends, icon, nickname, avatar, etc).

The type of communication according to Flusser has generally got a tree type structure, in contrast to the pyramidal schema of centralized media. The discussion ramifies at all levels, everyone can reply, create new threads and forums. Corporate discussion can have the same features, however, the result is different. Discussion acts as an illusion of openness, where those who possess power generally don't respect the results, to say the least. They misuse them for their own aims and interpretations, or follow the discussion only to identify the potential opponents. This sometimes soaks even into Wikipedia. Didn't I mention Wikipedia yet, and other open publishing systems?

Within the community, the process and results of a discussion are integral and the arguments approach consensus. The deeper, the more specific is the communication of the community. As Flusser notes, modern national languages are more or less artificially created from many local ones in the era of the letterpress for economical reasons – because they enable a higher impression. Thanks to the internet, where the costs of text publishing is zero, we are digitally returning to the pre-literary period of oral communication with many varied communication codes and slangs of a mythical-ritual origin. Furthermore, they develop rapidly and change, which is another element of the protection of communication except the fact that information is strongly contextual.

## Creative Communities

Except of the transfer speed and personalities the growth factors of communities are dreams as well. To have one's own living space, autonomous zone for different opinions and ideas, own club, own network. The internet isn't about a physical space, but about people's thinking. Communities arise around certain kind of music, soundsystem or visual style. It can be seen vice versa, too. The style arises as a characteristic feature of a community. Thanks to the control over the (mass) medium, they can spread information about events, or creative results such as music tracks and records, comics, videos and texts without financial costs. Thus, an autonomous group of authors as well as an audience comes into being. In every case, encounters, communication possibilities and removing barriers constitutes a strong acceleration. Sub-cultural potential of interconnected communities is immense.

Node9.org has arisen during 2003 and hosts cultural websites such as alternative music magazines and other musical projects, performance and theatre activities, it was at the birth of media study projects, websites of artists and independent producers or designer web-boutiques, all sorts, usual web citizens. The server carries on mailinglists, streaming and thousands of people use it on a daily basis. In the year 2005 with the freetekkno VJs, video recordings were published of brute attacks by policeman on the free festival Czechtek, which was taken up by major Czech television stations, some of them claimed exclusivity of the shots downloaded. Heavy load during this cause, abuse by pirates or attempt to cut out some unhandy websites to make a subsidy goldmine out of it – every now and then the server, run mostly by artists, stands in a different kind of attack and strengthens the communities' immunity system.

As Lev Manovich notes, traditional division of art into genres according to a medium (photography, film, video) is pointless in cyberspace. Through transmitting onto the internet, everything is sampled into a digital version, which accentuates some of it's attributes and other (traditional) lose significance. Hypertext, net-art and new forms of art, the process of cut, paste, rip and remix are natural information patterns of behaviour. Freedom of interconnection of anything crashes linear ways of expression and thinking. Interactivity wipes out and reverses the roles of author/audience. It is interesting to note, that even DJ and party culture was based on deposing the musician from the stage star into the crowd, where he was one of the present, peer to peer. Nowadays, anyone can choose what he or she wants to play on an internet radio. Anyone can stream his or her own music mixes. The ratio of those who broadcast to those who listen keeps increasing. As opposed to the classic media with one transmitter and masses of thoroughly passive recipients of social programming, we are talking about a post-media and post-net culture. On the net stands who isn't creative, doesn't exist.

In creative communities, hacktivism is an interconnection of artistic expression, open source programming, performance and cultural/social/political activism. They use and provide audio and video streaming using free tools, which they often develop. Jaromil, a rasta coder, started the live linux distro dyne:bolic in 2001, meant specifically for artists and loaded with ready to use programs for audio, video, streaming, VJing. Later, the GOTO10 collective customized the dyne core and built a distro around pure data and other realtime audiovisual processing software. Pure Data, a ray of light for the nomad gone astray in the dark digital chaos... PD creates a new space between technology and people. Miller Puckette once had made a mistake, developing MAX/MSP as proprietary software, so he started PD as a free clone. This kind of visual programming environment doesn't tell you how you have to use it. Instead, it lets you create a patch which works the way you think, and doesn't limit you, of course you can interconnect with others and send live data over the network. Yves Degoyon, PiDiP library coder, or Riereta.net, if you want some nodes of avant-garde post-underground.

We talked about information, more or less textual. This is the freedom of audiovisual expression.

**Imminent Future of the Semantic Universe**

Maybe you already know, when I say 'online existence', I'm really not talking about sheep on the counter in the MySpace supermarket.

I talked about communities and the philosophy of their communication and organisation. The net is a textual and visual semantic space, in which various opinion maps meet. These maps are relationship networks of notions. Each map shapes up around an idea – open semantic maps, forced (state system), maps with a concealed idea (commerce), community maps. Each of these basically originates from a certain spiritual system, often in a postmodern mix of Buddhism with traces of Christianity, enriched with political, cultural, social or professional influence – students, punks, sharps, nazis, slackers, programmers, artists, dealers... The struggle arises as a result of the expansion of semantic systems with an imperative structure (mostly with democratic propaganda), which are not able to coexist in an information organism in an ecological way. The frontier between thought territories is based on individual attacks, counterattacks and defence. It can be said, that it is a kind of blade, dividing a realized future from hopeless dreams. The words border or frontier usually mean a line. Here, it is perhaps the surface of a multidimensional structure, which keeps changing, growing and withdrawing. The struggle doesn't happen at one place, but at all network nodes simultaneously. The response in a global electronic organism is immediate, information is pursued by disinformation. I mentioned several actions and stories which are significant, but there are thousands and thousands of events which make the movement. Thought viruses the same way as the code are spreading avalanche like, everything is happening online. Some people call it infowar, others say cyberspace is burning.

Time implodes. We're facing an epoch, in which the development of technologies, media and transmission of information will be uninterruptible. Information technology will soon be ready to generate our reality realtime. Whoever will not be ready to react – be it through the technological level or structural complexity – will be sucked into the elaborate addiction pyramids of corporations. Many people decide to follow this way voluntarily. I feel better with those who try to reclaim the future...

# Software Cult

Ivan Monroy Lopez

## 1 Metamathematics

The use of the axiomatic method goes back to the time of greek math. Basically it's the idea of developing theories from a small number of axioms via logical deduction. The classical example of this is Euclid's geometry. Euclid starts his 'Elements' treatise by stating five postulates and five common notions.[1] From this seed, he develops his theory of geometry by logically accumulating result upon result.

[1] In the first two sections, italics are used when the phrase or word has a special meaning for the math in question.

In the 1920s, David Hilbert proposed a metamathematical plan of action that now goes by the name of 'Hilbert's program'. It is called metamathematical because it is not really concerned with say, the properties of triangles, but rather with the properties of the properties of triangles.

Were it possible to carry out, Hilbert's program would be like the natural conclusion to the use of the axiomatic method. At some level of naïve intuition, it even feels plausible and doable. One thinks: 'if the axiomatic method has so far proved very effective, why should it not be able to fulfill Hilbert's wishes?' In a nutshell, he proposed to (a) axiomatize all of math, and (b) derive the *soundness* of the axiomatization from the axiomatization itself.

In books like 'Principia Mathematica' people like Russell and Whitehead put years of work trying to advance the Hilbert program. Now we know – thanks to Gödel's *incompleteness* theorems – about the recursive shortcircuitry that kept all those efforts from making much progress.

One could roughly say that Gödel showed that no axiom system that contains arithmetic can (a) account for its (the system's) *soundness*, and (b) account for all arithmetic truth. This means that – in a way – all axiom

[2] http://plato.stanford.edu/entries/logic-ai/#jmc

[3] S. Levy, Hackers, New York, Delta, 1985. Chapter 1

systems that contain arithmetic are incomplete – hence the name. What's interesting about these theorems is that they reduce an involved math/philosophy issue to a simple yes/no question, and then they answer this question with a no.

## 2. Logic, Computer Science, Artificial Intelligence

Gödel's negative results brought new energy to the field of mathematical logic. It is out of this period of intense activity that Computer Science springs. In this respect, the classical example is that of the Turing machine – a theoretical construct for today's computers that was employed by Alan Turing when tackling the metamathematical *halting problem.* Another lesser known and more recent result in this direction is the so-called 'Curry-Howard' isomorphism.

This result expresses rigorously the intuition that a lot of computing is already implicit in abstract math. It asserts the equality of the apparently disparate concepts of computer programs and mathematical proofs. One informal way of stating it is: programs are proofs.

With regards to this theorem Berline cites an avenue of experimentation that looks interesting. If programs and proofs are equivalent, then we can ask ourselves: 'what programs correspond to the proofs that we already know?' In that there's a long history of mathematical proofs that precedes the invention of physical computers, this is a rather arbitrary way of coding – math becomes like a clunky mindless interface that churns out potentially useless software.

At least historically, there are also connections between mathematical logic and Artificial Intelligence. Alongside chess playing, theorem deduction is one of the classic types of reasoning that AI research tried to emulate. Apparently there's even a whole subfield called logical AI. According to some website, 'the most influential figure'[2] in logical AI is John McCarthy, the creator of LISP. He also makes an appearance in the retelling of early hacker history that occupies the first chapter of Steven Levy's *Hackers* – he's the professor that taught the first course on programming that the Signals and Power members of the Tech Model Railroad Club enrolled in:

> *That spring of 1959, a new course was offered at MIT. It was the first course in programming a computer that freshmen could take. The teacher was [...] John McCarthy.*[3]

Later in that story, McCarthy – who was also trained as a mathematician – gets the hackers to work in the computer chess problem.

[4] http://www.oreilly.com/catalog/opensources/book/stallman.html

[5] http://en.wikipedia.org/wiki/Abstract nonsense

So far, I've tried to give an overview of some of the ideas at the intersection of math and computing that I find interesting. I've done this in an effort to sketch one of the traditions that Richard Stallman belongs to. I think that he belongs to this tradition because he was a good mathematician who got into computers, and who ended up working at the MIT AI Lab.

In general, I think that hacking not only finds its roots in things like the Tech Model Railroad Club, but also in the sort of stuff that I've been talking about. There's – or there could be – both engineering and pure science in hacking. If anything, this heritage may help in understanding the more utopian strains of software development.

Take for example, Stallman's classic: 'With my community gone, not continuing as before was impossible.'[4] If we take into account Stallman's roots, his words could be interpreted as nostalgia for a time when the hacker community still fell under the official protection of the academic institutions of science; a time before it was discovered that software could be sold as a commodity (unlike other more abstract mathematical products.)

### 3. TV-Edit

I think that the story that I've been sketching is also about the materialization of abstract concepts. Computers are in the flesh realizations of metamathematical concepts. I think that this could be one way of enriching the discussions about computing. We could, for example, search for traces of platonic contemplation in 'staring into monitors' phenomena – all the way from monastic laptop music performance to computer addiction anxiety.

If anything, mathematical abstraction can be difficult. It's hard to get your head around objects whose only distinguishing features at times are like fleeting shadows. This is probably the reason why abstraction is also one of the things that some people strive for in their work style. In this respect one of many possible references is 'abstract nonsense' an idea that finds its origins in Category Theory. Though it may sound derogatory, it is actually used 'as an indication of mathematical sophistication or coolness.'[5]

A book that also talks about the intersections of computing and math, but from a slightly different angle is Douglas Hofstadter's *Gödel, Escher Bach.* One of its weaknesses is that it is the type of book with an authoritative tone. When reading it, one imagines big men tackling big questions: Hofstadter is at the cutting edge of science (in 1979), working in the novel field of AI. Not only is he a very intelligent human being, he's also investigating human intelligence – in an intelligent manner, one would gather.

There are also good things about *GEB.* It is a book that exudes energy. Its gross generalizations[6] make me think of Hofstadter as a high-speed idea-spewing machine that has little time to double-check every single fact. His book may even belong to a self-publishing tradition – he was afforded the luxury (at the time) of typesetting his own book. In terms of book design, it even has style:

> *Equally important to me, however, is Pentti's rare quality: his sense of style. If my book looks good, to Pentti Kanerva is due most of the credit.* [7]

In this quote from the 'Word of Thanks' Hofstadter is referring to TVEdit, one of the alternatives to Emacs that were available at the time. It was built by Kanerva, and it's the text-editor that Hofstadter used to write *GEB.* It's remarkable that he decided to thank someone who was involved in the making of his book at such a fundamental level. Nowadays, this extended credit sequence could painlessly be skipped.

I think that this quote gives us a glimpse into the world that hackers like Stallman inhabited. It would seem that the boundaries between hackers and users were blurry back then. At least the two social groups were on better terms than they are today. It's hard to generalize, but these days the profusion of abuse on the user's part is almost like genuine class exploitation. The sys-admin hell that this gives rise to is obliquely hinted at in things like the dice.com 'success stories.'[8]

## 4. Free as in O'Reilly

Let's talk about the O'Reilly book *Free as in Freedom.* In Chapter 11, it chronicles a meeting organized by Tim O'Reilly during which important work towards cementing the open source definition was done. This was a meeting that snubbed[9] Stallman, as he was not invited. After reading

[6] 'Every mathematician has the sense that there's a kind of metric between ideas in mathematics - that all of mathematics is a network of results between which there are enormously many connections.' D. Hofstadter, Gödel, Escher, Bach, New York, Vintage Books, 1980, p. 614

[7] D. Hofstadter, Gödel, Escher, Bach, New York, Vintage Books, 1980

[8] http://www.dice.com/stories/successstories.html

[9] I'm using Williams' exact wording. He leaves the question on whether Stallman was or was not snubbed unresolved.

this, I could not help but wonder about O'Reilly's intentions in publishing a book that deals with something that he was involved in undermining. Although the book ends with the requisite appendices containing an 'introduction' into hacker culture, and the GNU Free Documentation License (GFDL), its real end is a rosy epilogue. In this epilogue we're afforded a look into the red tape that went into writing the book:

> *The drama in front of the curtain often pales in comparison to the drama backstage [...] The story behind this story starts in an Oakland apartment [...] Ultimately, however, it is the tale of two cities [...] The story starts in April, 2000 [...]* [10]

Williams does go to great lengths to explain how Stallman was the intellectual best man of his wedding. But – aside from a good account of the implications of the GDFL for his own book – all we get in the pages where he talks about O'Reilly is praise.[11] No indications as to why O'Reilly chose to publish it are given.

Parts of the book read like welcome elaborations on parts of the Stallman essay from 'Open Sources.' Take for example, the chapter 'For Want of a Printer' – it's a retelling of the story about how someone refused to give Stallman the source code for the MIT AI Lab's printer. Also interesting, is the way in which Stallman's launch of GNU is portrayed, especially in relation to anger and angst as creative drives.

I'm not entirely at odds with the portrayal of hackers as angry or disaffected teenagers – some hackers may actually fulfill the cliché. The allusions to dice.com in the previous section are indications of how teenage alienation can turn into worker exploitation beyond the realm of the abstract. Stallman may have even fallen into this hacker category at some point. Maybe there were even elements of solitude[12] and anger[13] in Stallman's decision to start GNU development. However, to put so much weight on such sentimentality is to turn a blind eye to the politics of Stallman. *Free as in Freedom* didn't have to be a GNU propaganda pamphlet, but it didn't have to be an depoliticized book, either. Its psychological absolutions of radical postures are condescending, at best.

An actual discussion of GNU politics could have been more interesting. I for one sometimes feel that operating system development is too abstract a field for activism. In my view, there are more urgent issues to

[10] S. Williams, Free as in Freedom, Sebastopol,O'Reilly, 2002. p. 185-6

[11] 'Of all the publishing houses in the world, O'Reilly [...] seemed the most sensitive [...] As a reporter, I had relied heavily on the O'Reilly book 'Open Sources' [...] During the O'Reilly Open Source Conference in 1999, I [...] had been wowed.' S. Williams, Free as in Freedom, Sebastopol, O'Reilly, 2002 p. 194-6

[12] 'Richard built up an entire political movement to address an issue of profound personal concern [...] [c]rushing loneliness.' S. Williams, Free as in Freedom, Sebastopol, O'Reilly, 2002 p. 198

[13] 'righteous anger [...] has propelled Stallman's career as surely as any political ideology or political belief.' S. Williams, Free as in Freedom, Sebastopol, O'Reilly, 2002. p. 12

attend to. Still, I'm sympathetic to GNU and would like to be convinced otherwise.

The next section is devoted to painting a portrait of GNU as a cult. In the face of the Magic Pixie Dust that something like O'Reilly Media seems to embody, I've chosen to play with the idea of a cult as a way of showing support for a more radical current of software development.[14] In this I'm inspired as much by the Church of the SubGenius, as by the Church of Emacs. I should also mention that the focus on GNU is largely rhetorical. Beyond GNU, there are other mock cults in FLOSS.

[14] More recently, Tim O'Reilly coined another term, namely Web 2.0. Magic Pixie Dust . This comes from an early survey in which Register readers were asked to 'redefine the paradigm': http://www.theregister.co.uk/2005/11/11/web_two_point_naught_answers/

[15] 'OK, I can now carry on six phone conversations at once. But what difference has this made in my ordinary life? [...] Frankly, I already had plenty of data to enrich my perceptions', H. Bey, Temporary Autonomous Zone, New York, Autonomedia, 1985, 1991 , http://hermetic.com/bey/taz_cont.html

## 5. Software Cult:

### 5.1. Isolation

Cult membership sometimes entails changes that could lead members to isolate from their social circle. Extreme cults demand that their members entirely break any contact with even their closest relatives and friends if they have not been already converted. Likewise, the use of GNU could translate into an implosion of someone's social life. If you use Skype on a power pc, switching to GNU would mean closing an avenue of communication with your acquaintances. There are other communication technologies, but these may be populated by people who are already GNU users. Any emotional attachment to utilities like Powerpoint will have to be severed. For some people, this could be painful.

### 5.2. Conversion

In general, computing-related activities involve some degree of coercion. In the end, computing is a surplus. To paraphrase Hakim Bey, we got along fine without the ability to sustain six phone conversations at once.[15] In this context, usability could be seen as a business strategy aimed at maximizing consumption. It's strange that at its basest level, this approach leads to things like idiotic instant messaging emoticons.

At the other extreme lies terminal-based work. Hackers have had the privilege of going through a 'learning period' in one way or another. However, for many people who come later in life to free software, especially if they have had previous experience with GUIs, the experience can very easily lead to frustration. The paradigm-shift can be so daunting, that it can be likened to thought reform or brainwashing.

## 5.3. CSS Asceticism

The design of the gnu.org webpage changed a few months ago.[16] It now boasts an enormous grey/blue header. It has a navigating bar that makes heavy use of the a.hover pseudo-element. Its ubiquitous unordered lists have also been styled – bullets are now bluish squares.

It's strange that even with that re-hash, its designers did not decide to make much use of the link variety of pseudo-elements. Most unvisited links are still blue, and they turn magenta once they've been clicked. The a.hover pseudo-element is used, but only to turn links red – the default color they take on when active. Overall, the GNU webpage gives the impression of being on the verge of losing its styling.

[16] This section makes reference to the design of gnu.org at the end of 2006. There are some approximations at the internet archive: http://web.archive.org/web/20061219051658/http://www.gnu.org/

[17] http://web.archive.org/web/19990125085924/http://gnu.org/

[18] Examples of these may be found in http://www.gnu.org/graphics/graphics.html This tradition is fleeting, and almost non-existent.

Before its redesign, the homepage of GNU was for many years a practically unformatted page. Sometime in early 2004 it acquired those sans-serif fonts, and its present right column / horizontal bar layout. Its earliest recorded version at the internet archive[17] dates from 1998, when it was apparently updated by rms himself. The design is as sober as it gets – a few h2 tags, one h3 tag, and one image. The contact information is inside a pre tag.

## 5.4. Iconography

There's also asceticism in some of the GNU imagery. I'm thinking particularly of the many simple black and white anthropomorphic gnu illustrations.[18]

There's a connection between this imagery and a certain para-mathematical visual tradition – the type of images that are sometimes used as book adornments. Like the GNU drawings, these images tend to also be naïve, and a bit outer-worldly, even when they're not lacking in conceptual depth. Some of them veer closely to the mnemonic research map genre. The best of them have a sense of humor, and play on a sort of 'less is more' strategy – like Guy Steele Jr.'s 'Crunchly Saga'.

## 5.5. Guru

There are few interest groups which have such a clear and visible leader as Stallman. This is probably due to a strong personality that sometimes veers on the aggressive. In his St. IGNUcius persona, Stallman

[19] 'Free Software: Freedom and Cooperation' speech, http://www.gnu.org/philosophy/audio/audio.html#NYU2001

himself plays with the idea of being a religious leader. He's probably the principal free software evangelist, a term that already has cultish overtones.

All free software is open source software, and vice versa. It could be argued that the open source definition came into being just to get Stallman out of the picture. Conversely, he has a reputation for not budging an inch, thus alienating a lot of potential allies. This has the effect of increasing the isolation of his followers that was alluded to previously. In this, GNU is like a political cadre.

Even though Stallman is an atheist, he speaks about the beginnings of GNU in almost religious terms. In his own narrative, ethical choices were involved; a community was dispersed; and Stallman played a role akin to that of a messiah:

> *I had just the right skills to be able to do it [...] and nobody was there but me [...] I felt: 'I'm elected, I have to work on this. If not me, who?'* [19]

References

C. Berline, 'A Presentation of the Curry-Howard Correspondence', http://www.pps.jussieu.fr/~berline/Cur-How.ps

H. Bey Temporary Autonomous Zone, New York, Autonomedia, 1985, 1991, http://hermetic.com/bey/taz cont.html

C. Dibona, S. Ockam, M. Stone, eds, Open Sources, Sebastopol, O'Reilly, 1999.

D. Hofstadter, Gödel, Escher, Bach, New York, Vintage Books, 1980.

S. Levy, Hackers New York, Delta, 1985.

S. Williams, Free as in Freedom Sebastopol, O'Reilly, 2002.

# Free Time

Martin Howse

*Hello everybody out there using minix –*

*I'm doing a (free) operating system (just a hobby, won't be big and professional like gnu) for 386(486) AT clones. This has been brewing since april, and is starting to get ready. I'd like any feedback on things people like/dislike in minix, as my OS resembles it somewhat (same physical layout of the file-system (due to practical reasons) among other things). I've currently ported bash(1.08) and gcc(1.40), and things seem to work. This implies that I'll get something practical within a few months, and I'd like to know what features most people would want. Any suggestions are welcome, but I won't promise I'll implement them :-)*

*Linus (torva...@kruuna.helsinki.fi)*

In contrast to economies of drudgery, functionality and productivity ensnaring the unwitting desktop slave within closed and circumscribed time at all levels of so called functionality, there exists an idea of free time, under the obvious caveat that free time is only defined thanks to its enchained brother worker. Free time demands parallel introductions, an array of simultaneous entry points into the history of free software in relation to artistic computing and indeed the very nature of time within computation. Such a notion equally leads well into the terrain of homebrewing, of DIY solutions outside established economies and of a hobbyist scene which free software promotes and descends from in part. It's all about time: time of computation; time within an embedded simulation and stories of past times, of other times; a parallel connection machine of ideas, individuals and advanced concerns.

In a misreading of the modern coding scene, inveterate naysayers maintain that free software is irrelevant to artistic computation, readily citing the now worn and ill considered cliché that open source imitates rather than innovates. Under such argument, centring in the main on GUI design, free software coders are damned if they experiment, damned if they try and make things easy for users of other systems. Such ill-attributed, authorless trash, repeated across newsgroups and blogs, acts as a viral meme, obscuring the truth.

Just by way of contrast, without even entering into argument on the misplaced field of functionality, it's worth imagining a present time without open code; a harsh contemporary reality of proprietary compilers and IDEs shoehorning artistic work within the deterministic confines of industry. Within this total terrain of locked down trusted computing and without free distribution or unhindered content creation, free time computing becomes a luxury of consumption. For why implement standards within a world of competing locked-down products which are better served by obscuring such details? It's a world of macro media solely offered to consumers and such a vision gives a good idea of the absolute necessity of free software for creativity, indeed an historical necessity well realised under varying narratives.

It's worth remembering that proprietary code historically is the exception rather than the rule. The story of Emacs and GNU Emacs, lying at the root of the free software movement gives a good picture of the transition from shared code to locked down executable, the rise of the license as a central issue for software as coders are outnumbered by 'end users.' And the history of UNIX is very much about free software, rather with tacit agreements between coder and industry; a loose limbed creature in comparison with the strictures of the GPL which present a necessary enforcement in the light of an increasingly hard nosed scene. At the same time such histories show how proprietary code was always engaged in a battle with the network; and, after all, the inevitable rise of network by way of BBSes (Bulletin Board Systems) proved highly significant in the development of GNU/Linux.

These simple facts are often obscured within comparisons which focus too heavily on a binary edge of perceived functionality, for example in judging which OS possesses the best application for deterministic content creation such as digital audio sequencing. Terms such as 'application', 'user' and 'interface' are already too weighted. The model of contemporary computing appears set in stone as a proprietary software industry conditions us blindingly to the only thing it has to offer, bland naked functionality. Richard Stallman makes plain in 'The GNU Project' how the true landscape of computing was historically rewritten by proprietary interests:

> *The idea that the proprietary software social system – the system that says you are not allowed to share or change software – is antisocial, that it is unethical, that it is simply wrong, may come as a surprise to some readers. But what else could we say about a system based on dividing the public and keeping users helpless? Readers who find the idea surprising may have taken proprietary-software social system as given, or judged it on the terms suggested by proprietary software businesses. Software publishers have worked long and hard to convince people that there is only one way to look at the issue.*

Free software means thinking outside the black box of application, the iconic stone GUI. In contrast to begrudging desktop mimicry along a dull axis of functionality, and key applications such as GNU Emacs stress this flipside with extensibility and self investigation, self reflection by way of prevalent source, customisation and internal documentation are dominant new themes.

## LAC, DAC, DIPPY DAP, LIO, DIO, JUMP2

Anecdotal stories recounting the early days of the AI labs at MIT which truly forged hacker culture and the core tenets of free software, are well documented in Stephen Levy's *Hackers* and elsewhere, including Sam Williams' account of Richard Stallman's work, *Free as in Freedom*. By default these histories can little ignore an involvement with the military by way of ARPA funding from the DoD (Department of Defence) for MIT AI lab projects.

What's interesting to unpick from both UNIX and hacker culture accounts is how issues of security splinter, reflect and contrast across the two narratives. A culture which values leaving files open for all to enter, share and improve their code is recounted through *Hackers* and stands in stark relation to the hierarchical design of the UNIX operating system with ringfenced superuser valued and rewarded above a swarm of trusted common users.

Stephen Levy recounts not just the opening of code and terminal to all fellow hackers partaking of a shared ethic, but also an openness which extended to the physical world. Doors, filing cabinets and desks would be left open by the initiated. Locked doors were viewed as an insult, to be answered in true hacker spirit with ingenious circumvention, or rather, lock hacking. Openness was valued above all else in the light of a grander Gnostic project of total knowledge, a shared Game of Life; in Levy's terms, 'the hacker quest to find out and improve the way the world works.' Yet at the same time, such a spirited game, a crusade for shared and active knowledge was carried out within a closed environment with hackers wilfully ignorant of the radical outside world at the end of the '60s. Their Game of Life was very much terminal bound, as advanced locks and hardcore security matters became de rigeur in the light of increased protests against defence funding. A boundary was established, yet internally, property rights remained an absurd concept.

In contrast, the words of Ken Thompson, from his key text 'Reflections on Trusting Trust', goes as far as to argue that 'The act of breaking into a computer system has to have the same social stigma as breaking into a neighbour's house.' From here on such metaphors have stuck, bridging the digital and physical divide under the sign of intellectual property. From UNIX to trusted computing.

Compare this with the words of Richard Stallman, reprinted in the same anthology as Thompson's work, *Computers Under Attack*, '... I judge computer security as a disease rather than a cure, except for banks and such.' ('Are Computer Property Rights Absolute?'). And although it's a rank cliché that all history is political, tracing the uses and so called abuses of the word 'hacker' through varying narratives unpacks both this quality and the political use of the term itself. Differing uses of the word both reflect the then current culture and forcefully impact on interpretations of the past. In the context of free software the past is most definitely rewritten. Stallman himself does an excellent job of dissecting this shifting field of reference in an appendix to *Free as in Freedom*, with the term hacker transformed into a 'linguistic billiard ball', ripe for further language hacks or games.

As an aside it may well be worth noting the relation of the pranksterish spirit of hacking, which Stallman and others rightly identify as one of the roots of the term within MIT student jargon, with Neoism through the removal of a subsequent emphasis on craft and a new stress on playful poetics. And yet we should walk carefully. Any investigation of Neoism must surely enter a veritable lion's den given that in the words of Stewart Home, '... every narrative constructed around Neoism is inaccurate and manipulative.' Nevertheless it is an entertaining and rhetoric ridden lair with respect both to 20th century artistic endeavour such as Dadaism and in the light of an aesthetic which dare not speak its name under the viral signature of plagiarism. Neoism hacks aesthetics, plays with history and context.

It can readily be argued that some aspects of the UNIX model, though delightful in terms of modularity and sheer pluggability which adds up to a certain openness, do not seem so well suited to the freedom-obsessed vision of Stallman and fellow free software travellers. In Stallman's own words from the GNU Manifesto:

> *Unix is not my ideal system, but it is not too bad. The essential features of Unix seem to be good ones, and I think I can fill in what Unix lacks without spoiling them. And a system compatible with Unix would be convenient for many other people to adopt.*

A good many alternative systems have tackled such issues with varying degrees of success, and under a range of implemented philosophies which break down across the, to some degree artificial, divide between core privileged kernel functionality and free running, readily modifiable user space.

## KILL SYSTEM

Any history of such free and open OSes is forced to return to hacking's roots at MIT in the '60s, with reference to the wonderfully titled Incompatible Time-sharing System (ITS), which, whilst parodying the then frowned upon and overly secure Compatible Time-sharing system, also neatly dovetails with the concerns of free time. ITS, which spawned a good many significant subprojects still in use today such as GNU Emacs itself, discards the very notion of security with a completely open architecture unhindered by passwords and the like. ITS was designed to allow and encourage sharing of both user data and even live hacking attempts, with coders able to snoop and comment on the terminal sessions of co-hackers. In the words of Levy, 'ITS proved that the best security was no security at all,' citing the KILL SYSTEM command, which would crash the funky PDP-6 system, as itself a deterrent through rendering the fatal hacker action simply too trivial.

Aside from such an open architecture, already connected to the burgeoning ARPAnet, ITS proved revolutionary in a good many respects, laying the foundations for future operating systems with sophisticated process management and transparent networked filesystem access. Through both a rich donated feature set and the involvement of key figures such as Richard Stallman within both the MIT AI labs where ITS was spawned, and the future GNU (GNU's Not UNIX) project, ITS occupies a vital position within the history of free software. Yet, through historical contingency it could well be argued that the hefty and embedded philosophical impetus of ITS is far from inherited by the technologies of contemporary GNU/Linux.

The GNU project itself kicked off in the '80s, as Stallman witnessed the demise of the hacker ethic at MIT, with quite obvious and well expressed political concerns centring around freedom and flexibility. Under its own terms, the GNU project and embracing Free Software Foundation (FSF) '... helps to spread awareness of the ethical and political issues of freedom in the use of software.'

An OS which addressed such issues within the harsh contemporary landscape of proprietary systems was first up on the agenda, with a UNIX model highly acceptable for both practical and conceptual reasons. The modular and eminently pipeable UNIX way of doing things was attractive to those seeking flexibility and a more modular, compartmentalised core toolset meant that free software could be worked on in small pieces by diverse coders within a collaborative development environment.

UNIX does stress standards and portability, both underrated features within anyone's definition of OS freedom; the freedom to run anywhere, on anything. Work on a GNU OS continued throughout the '80s with supremely usable free software created across the board. Yet, as all good GNU/Linux scholars know, there was one rather large piece of the UNIX puzzle which hadn't been made a GNU, and that was the kernel. By the early '90s, a Mach-based microkernel approach seemed to be finding favour, and the coding for the Hurd on Mach commenced around the same time as Torvald's famous 'just a hobby, won't be big and professional like GNU' announcement. The Hurd was and still is the official GNU kernel, but just as key Hurd developer, Michael Bushnell was implementing the necessary kludges for the Hurd's filesystem and boot strap code, Torvald's creation loomed large on the Free Software Foundation's (FSF) radar, and the rest is history. It's worth remembering that, at least in the eyes of the FSF, Linux is viewed more as a rather wayward, adopted son rather than a true family member, and is often castigated in this respect with regular infights centring on the Linux moniker.

**Back to the Future**

And in contrast to what could well be regarded as an arbitrary historical detail, though one which in a story of free software is of intense importance, namely the coding of the so-called hobby UNIX-like OS as kicked off by Torvalds, other narratives could well be regarded as furnishing a certain inevitability for free software. It can readily be argued that both the political impetus of the free software movement and the GNU project, and the social scale and ambitions of the homebrewing scene, under both the wirewrapping, seriously DIY '70s and the more code-based small home computer scene of the '80s, provided the necessary and inevitable emphasis for free software. Without this movement there would be no alternative to a proprietary environment barely brightened by the presence of crippled and ugly freeware. And Torvald's 'just a hobby' hint, however self-effacing, rightly roots GNU/Linux, one of the most visible manifestations of free software and an open development model, within such fascinating, early scenes.

The story of homebrewing exposes the true roots of creative computing and it's surely to the credit of the free software movement that it has both successfully re-energised the artistic visions of this scene and provided a unique spotlight on an engaging history. Rewinding 20 or even 30 years, and examining the ideas and connections made by artistic figures such as Alan Kay or Ted Nelson within a grass roots terrain proves illuminating if not somewhat disheartening in the light of a contemporary scene more occupied with porting a stable OS to a series of random hardware platforms. Under the sign of retrofuturism, as coined by Howard Rheingold, and by way of Stallman perhaps acting as some kind of medium, a psychic channeller, imbuing the creative world of free software with the spirit of the past, it's more rewarding to hark back to the heady days of both MIT and home experimentation.

Homebrewing, based around the semi-affordable 8-bit systems of the mid '70s, such as the exposed KIM-1 board, was all about recovering computational autonomy from institution and corporation for those who could by no means afford mainframe access. Such a spirit of creative computing continued well into the '80s, with low cost microcomputers only proving functional when combined with an autodidact's expertise in programming and the provision of a suitable language interpreter; the operating system tended to be minimal, far from a fully blown OS sitting on top of an 8-bit processor. Sure, code could be loaded from tape, shared across the airwaves or distributed on vinyl, but such dull and lengthy processes paled in comparison to hacking out applications or, more commonly, games. Printed source code, shared across magazines and photocopies, to be inputted by hand was very much the norm. Binary distribution was subject to noise; textual distribution was far more efficient.

Yet, as such systems grew in complexity and the operating systems of otherwise liberated home computers (no more time sharing for the eager hacker) expanded in terms of size and functionality, so the OS provided an entry point for the stranglehold of proprietary systems within the otherwise autonomous environment of home computing. As the first so-called desktops appeared, offering now ubiquitous metaphoric access to content or media, contrary to the dreams of the '70s outlined in magazines such as *Creative Computing*, the personal computer acceded to the domain of the corporate. Productivity and the machinic merged under a self-identical interface and the battle for a truly artistic and divergent political reading of the OS began.

**Radio On**

> *A radical realisation of art, then, would be the deposition of the sovereign producer and a return of the shared wealth of creativity to its true owners: the multitude. For this reason, a reappropriation and transformation of the artistic means of production comes to the fore – an opening up of cultural source codes to an undetermined end.*
>
> *– 'Bare Code', Josephine Berry Slater, 2002*

It's possible to argue coherently that free software can itself be considered a work of art, when considered as open culture and as self-referencing writing or intertextuality. Visible code, free distribution and a healthy set of political concerns are the watchwords here which inspire creative computing. In 1999 the Linux kernel was itself awarded the Golden Nica in the Net category of Ars Electronica, the world's most prestigious digital arts festival. And in February 2002, the 4,141,432 lines of code which then made up the Linux kernel commenced broadcast online and on air as computerised spoken word by Free Radio Linux, an initiative set up by the online art collaboration r a d i o q u a l i a. Free Radio Linux obviously runs using free software such as Ogg Vorbis, and its creators argue with great wit that the project continues the tradition of the FM code stations in the '80s who distributed source via radio, allowing early hackers with home computers, such as Sinclair ZX81s or Commodore 64s, to demodulate the analogue signal through a modem and run the code.

Free Radio Linux obviously provides a similar service for contemporary hackers, equipped with pen and paper for code transcription. Berlin-based theorist, Micz Flor, argues that Free Radio Linux digs deep into questions of code and language, technology, art, and culture as well as opening up debates on freedom of speech and copyright protection. Free Radio Linux exposes the wider cultural context surrounding free software, and as Larry Wall, creator of Perl, argues, a language is not just a set of rules or semantics, it is rather the complete culture which surrounds the language. This context includes all the people involved in the language, how people learn the language and help each other with the language and interact with each other. And it's tough not to argue that such a rich cultural context can only exist under a free software development model. This is one message that Free Radio Linux clearly broadcasts. And the political dimensions, which boil down to questions of code and language, of Free Radio Linux are even plainer, with clear parallels to the publication of Pretty Good Privacy (PGP) source code by MIT in 1995 which unhinged legal prohibitions placed on its distribution.

And it's also worth mentioning the DeCSS debacle, with T-shirts bearing the utilities source code being examined in court. Such a distribution model was neatly plagiarised by the Bologna-based artists group 0100101110101101.ORG in their Biennale.py work, a Python-based fake computer virus, which was exhibited on a thousand T-shirts during the opening of the Venice Biennale in 2001. Given the readily acknowledged Neoist influence on 0100101110101101.ORG, and in the light of the similarly inspired MacMag virus, Biennale.py enacts an homage to the truly artistic nature of the computer virus, with code rendered as common and highly contemporary language; a question always of the means of distribution and thus attribution disturbed increasingly within mass media by the flat binary.

**Substance**

Free software is concerned with opening up the mysterious substance of code, that vertiginous obscuring of hardware, and indeed computation. GNU/Linux laid out in all its glory across a mountainous landscape of printed source shows up all the hierarchies of abstraction enacted. For example, within a free software environment it's possible to read the living narrative of the boot process, a transition from mute hardware to active interrogative and linguistic software; a story which starts in /usr/src/linux/arch/i386/boot.

Yet to ask questions of the very substance of software, this otherwise closed code, it's perhaps worth examining another text, embedding within its title the key concern: 'There Is No Software', by theorist Friedrich Kittler (1995). It's a rich work which is perhaps immune to summary, but the core argument that software obscures lower levels of hardware, the hardwired, can be cleanly extracted. Further:

> *Precisely because software does not exist as a machine-independent faculty, software as a commercial or American medium insists all the more.*

The shrink-wrapped license is the insistent fact in this instance; that which renders effervescent software real. It's worth quoting the conclusion in full with the caveat that Kittler's arguments could well be viewed in a good many respects as referring solely to proprietary code:

> *Silicon hardware obeys many of the requisites for such highly connected, non-programmable systems. Between its millions of transistor cells, some million to the power of two interactions take place already; there is electronic diffusion, there is quantum mechanical tunnelling all over the chip. Yet, technically, these interactions are still treated in terms of system limitations, physical side-effects, and so on. To minimise all the noise that it would be possible to eliminate is the prize paid for structurally programmable machines. The inverse strategy of maximising noise would not only find the way back from IBM to Shannon, it may well be the only way to enter that body of real numbers originally known as chaos.*

Substance is articulated through noise and the real; all that which, according to Kittler, software as an industry-led phantom must obscure; a one way cryptography of closed data. Yet such concerns, and Kittler's writing can be situated very much in the fallow years of DOS, with GNU/Linux only exposed to small groups of hackers, point well towards a new aesthetics and culture of computing liberated by the free software movement. Further essays, such as Kittler's wonderfully titled 'Protected Mode', from 1993, just two years after Linus Torvalds 'just a hobby' post, illuminate his own feelings as a 'subject' of Microsoft, subjugated to embedded and hidden machinations within DOS; proprietary code obscuring and denying access to underlying hobbyist hardware. Such subjugation is well embedded in talk of working 'under' an operating system. Yet under the sign of free time we can now easily work 'on' an OS, hacking and diverting functionalities exposed by a code body.

And perhaps, in an ideal world of solely free software, there is ONLY software. Hardware vanishes in a reverse transubstantiation enacted by Saint Ignacius, as RMS playfully references himself in performance, wielding the sacred GNU GCC compiler.

Resources

Offline:

Free as in Freedom, 2002, Sam Williams.

Computers Under Attack, 1990, Peter J. Denning.

Neoism, Plagiarism and Praxis, 1995, Stewart Home.

'Bare Code', 2005, Josephine Berry Slater.

Literature, Media, Information Systems, 1997, Friedrich A. Kittler.

Online:

'The GNU Project', http://www.gnu.org/gnu/thegnuproject.html

'Linux and the GNU project', http://www.gnu.org/gnu/linux-and-gnu.html

'The Evolution of the UNIX Time-sharing System', http://cm.belllabs.com/cm/cs/who/dmr/hist.html

UNIX history, http://www.columbia.edu/~rh120/ch106.x09

'Tools For Thought', http://www.rheingold.com/texts/tft

Alan Kay, http://gagne.homedns.org/~tgagne/contrib/EarlyHistoryST.html ala

r a d i o q u a l i a, http://www.radioqualia.net

Micz Flor, http://mi.cz

Biennale.py, http://0100101110101101.org/home/biennale_py

'There Is No Software', http://www.ctheory.net/text_file.asp?pick=74

# All Problems of Notation Will be Solved by the Masses: Free Open Form Performance, Free/Libre Open Source Software, and Distributive Practice

Simon Yuill

In recent years, the foregrounding of 'collaboration' in artistic practice has acquired an aura of inherent benevolence and emancipation, as though the very act of working with others in itself ensures some form of resistance, or alternative, to conventions of cultural production. The recent valorisation of collaboration within the arts, however, merely elides the basic condition of collaboration that all forms of production ultimately rely on in various degrees and arrangements. This can be seen as one part of the larger growth in service and communications industries whose 'labour' and 'produce' are primarily invested in the structuring and intensification of various collaborative exchanges, often minute and ephemeral, yet, when harvested on a vast scale, capable of generating seemingly endless amounts of profit.[1] Collaboration in this form of production extends beyond the contracted employees into the consumers themselves, who help define and create the products they themselves consume. This is exemplified in the proliferation of highly 'personalised' products and services, reality entertainment, and the social networks of Web 2.0, with the virtual world of SecondLife notably combining all three factors.[2] Those artforms which most consciously foreground collaboration, as described in Bourriaud's *Relational Aesthetics*, merely echo this situation.[3] The social relations constructed by the artist in gestures of collaboration with audiences and others become spectacularised and commodified in forms that often do not return to those who created them but rather

[1] The relation of profit to surplus value in regard to so-called 'immaterial labour' have been much contested in recent debate, particularly in light of the controversial rejection by Negri of the application of Marx's 'law of value' to modern economies. For a critical overview of these issues, and a response to Negri, see: George Caffentzis, 'Immeasurable Value? An Essay on Marx's Legacy', The Commoner, issue 10, Spring/Summer 2005, http://www.commoner.org.uk/10caffentzis.pdf

[2] SecondLife http://secondlife.com

[3] Nicolas Bourriaud, Relational Aesthetics, translated by Simon Pleasance and Fronza Woods, Paris: les Presses du Reel, 2002.

become tokens circulated within the art market.[4] In a funding system that prioritises social inclusion within the arts, like that of the UK, collaborative projects can tick the box that unlocks the piggy-bank of state patronage. In such contexts, collaboration quickly becomes little more than a revenue stream.[5] Similarly, the rise of relational aesthetics has accompanied the embrace of artistic practice by the commercial sector, often drawing upon the strategies of such art to enhance collaboration and 'creativity' within the workplace.[6]

For some, Free/Libre Open Source Software (FLOSS) appears to offer a model of practitioner-led collaborative practice that, through its legislative mechanisms such as copyleft licensing, could be applied to artistic practice in a way that might counteract such problems of recuperation.[7] An initial enthusiasm for this, however, has given way to disenchantment as the application of FLOSS to artistic practice appears to create more problems than it solves.[8] These problems have arisen through an emphasis upon issues of collaboration and legislation that often fails to recognise the proper relation of these to FLOSS's primary mode of production – the notational medium of code.[9] Enthusiasts for a FLOSS inflected approach to artistic practice have similarly failed to properly consider forms of cultural practice that have been emerging from within FLOSS and how these may relate to other forms of cultural production outside of that community. A consideration of these reveals that such practices are not so much collaborative but rather distributive. Rather than accumulating and cohering the labour of others they enable capacity for self-production elsewhere. Through a comparison of current FLOSS-related arts practices to related earlier artistic forms this article outlines the relation between notational production and distributive practice.

## Livecoding

Of all the artforms supported and enabled through FLOSS, 'livecoding' has emerged as the one which most directly embodies the key principles of FLOSS production in the creation and experience of the work itself. In livecoding the artwork is expressed in software code that is written and re-written live during its performance. Many livecoding artists write their own software tools to support this way of working.

[4] For one perspective on this see: Saul Albert, Who Will Be Transformed?, http://twenteenthcentury.com/saul/who_will_be_transformed.htm

[5] See: Eleonora Belfiore, 'Auditing Culture: the subsidized cultural sector in the New Public Management', International Journal of Cultural Policy, 10.2, 2004.

[6] This was a model promoted by think-tanks such as DEMOS in London in the late 1990s, the artist Carey Young both works within and exposes this area.

[7] One of the earliest such statements was Saul Albert, Open Source and Collective Art Practice, http://twenteenthcentury.com/saul/os.htm

[8] These issues were brought up in the discussions looking back on the NODE.London festival, see: http://www.mazine.ws/NodeL_NMC, Al Altendrof, 'Calling Time Out', http://altendorf.enemy.org/en/works/texts/calling-time-out.html, and the 'NODE.London Evaluation Report', http://eval.nodel.org

[9] An initial example of such an approach can be found in Felix Stalder, 'On the Differences between Open Source and Open Culture', Media Mutandis: a NODE.London Reader, edited by Marina Vishmidt, Mary Anne Francis, Jo Walsh and Lewis Sykes, London:

Alex McLean's 'feedback.pl' was one of the first such tools.[10] It is a simple Perl script that continuously reads and executes an extract of its own code displayed in a text editor. This code defines various algorithms from which music is generated. During performance this is re-written by the performer, changing the musical structure and effectively improvising from within the code. A projection of the performer's desktop makes this visible, thereby emphasising how the code and the changes made to it are integral to the work and to the audience experience of it. The material and formal relationships between code and music are therefore discernible, even though many audience members may be unfamiliar with programming languages themselves.[11] To some extent this is comparable to witnessing a performance on an acoustic instrument such as guitar or clarinet. Whilst we may not understand how to play such instruments ourselves, we can relate the gestures of the performer to the sounds that we hear and thus acquire a sense of the relation between the sound and its material production. This contrasts sharply with previous forms of electronic music performance, such as those of Jean Michel Jarre and Todd Machover, in which interface devices are presented on stage often simulating and referring to acoustic instruments. Livecoding dispenses with such 'fetishes' and is unashamed to expose the bare materiality of its production. The unfamiliarity of presenting code as a raw material, however, results in something very different from that of the guitar or clarinet performance, and more akin to revealing the stage machinery in a Brecht play. It creates a virtue by exposing something that is normally concealed.

Whilst livecoding has initially developed as a form of music, it is not restricted to this. David Griffith's 'fluxus' and Tom Schouten's 'PacketForth' are tools for creating visual works, the first based on a 3D graphics engine and the second a video processing system.[12] Some existing tools, such as SuperCollider, Chuck and Pure Data have also been used for livecoding work.[13] In fact, any programming language or tool that can execute code on the fly can potentially be used for livecoding. The concept has also been extended into other forms of work. 'Social Versioning System' (SVS) enables multiplayer simulation games to be created and coded live, with new code distributed amongst the players as a game evolves.[14] Ap's 'Life Coding' is a large scale performance combining software coding, circuit bending and conference-style spoken presentations.[15]

OpenMute and NODE.London, 2006.

[10] Alex McLean, 'Hacking Perl in Nightclubs', http://www.toplap.org/index.php/Hacking_perl_in_nightclubs, originally published in 2004 at http://www.perl.com/pub/a/2004/08/31/livecode.html

[11] For an overview of livecoding issues see the TOPLAP website: http://www.toplap.org, as well as discussions on the TOPLAP and OpenLab (London) mailing lists: http://www.pawfal.org/openlab

[12] fluxus: http://www.pawfal.org/fluxus, PacketForth: http://packets.goto10.org

[13] SuperCollider: http://www.audiosynth.com, Chuck: http://chuck.cs.princeton.edu, Pure Data: http://www.puredata.info

[14] http://www.spring-alpha.org/svs

[15] http://1010.co.uk/xxxxx_at_piksel2007.html

## Livecoding Aesthetics

There are two key aspects of livecoding that embody FLOSS principles. Firstly, the way it makes the continual re-writing of code a primary mode of artistic production and, secondly, in its presentation of the 'work' itself as an open-ended mutable piece of code rather than as a static discrete artefact. In distinction to most non-digital and new media art that is presented solely as a commodity to be consumed, livecoding makes its own materials and practices of production available to others.[16] Livecoding emphasises the FLOSS principle of code-based production as a form of production that is itself 'live' and living, that enables the possibility of production by others for their own purposes.

This 'enabling the possibility of production by others' is often continued outside of performance not only in the use of FLOSS-style distribution, but also in the conscious use of workshops as a means of presenting works and teaching the skills used in their creation. This pedagogic aspect extends to the importance given to technical meetings and development workshops in artist-run festivals such as Piksel and MAKEART, or groups such as Dorkbot and OpenLab, and into the creation of dissemination platforms and projects such as pure:dyne and FLOSS Manuals.[17] The often ad-hoc workshop nature of many livecoding performances and projects themselves is an extension of the livecoding ethic of sharing and making materials generally available. In the case of the ap events that are deliberately staged over long durations of 12 hours or more, this includes participants learning and adapting the tools of the performance as they take place. On a smaller scale, the London OpenLab group host 'drumming circle' performances in which anyone can join in with their own algorithms and code, constructing and developing a collective rhythmic work, as well as performances that start from one piece of code that is rewritten by successive performers. Rather than something marginal or extraneous to the 'art', the idea of the workshop has been absorbed as an integral aspect of livecoding aesthetics.

Livecoding is not the sole or even dominant form of practice pursued by all those involved in FLOSS-related arts. What all practitioners involved in these projects do share, however, is a commitment to the broader notion of 'live code' as a mode of production and a common

[16] Livecoding differs, for example, from Manovich's model of 'new media' defined primarily as the relation of an artist-created interface providing an aestheticised visualisation with limited forms of manipulation to a database of media such as video clips or statistical info. Whilst presenting an experience that is dynamic, such new media works nevertheless often remain closed unmutable artefacts rather than exposed working processes, see: Lev Manovich, The Language of New Media, Cambridge, MA: MIT Press, 2001.

[17] Piksel: http://www.bek.no, MAKEART: http://makeart.goto10.org, Dorkbot: http://www.dorkbot.org, OpenLab (London): http://www.pawfal.org/openlab, OpenLab (Glasgow): http://www.openlab-glasgow.org, pure:dyne: http://puredyne.goto10.org, FLOSS Manuals: http://wwwflossmanuals.net. The pure:dyne project is a version of the GNU/Linux operating system specifically geared towards artistic usage and supports many livecoding tools.

preference for a workshop aesthetic. It is also within these more 'pedagogic' practices that artistic production within FLOSS meets with other aspects of the FLOSS world, and specifically the political and socially engaged practices emerging from hacklabs and hackmeets.

## Hacklabs & Hackmeets

Hacklabs are voluntary-run spaces providing free public access to computers and internet. They generally make use of reclaimed and recycled machines running GNU/Linux, and alongside providing computer access, most hacklabs run workshops in a range of topics from basic computer use and installing GNU/Linux software, to programming, electronics, and independent (or pirate) radio broadcast. The first hacklabs developed in Europe, often coming out of the traditions of squatted social centres and community media labs. In Italy they have been connected with the autonomist social centres, and in Spain, Germany, and the Netherlands with anarchist squatting movements.[18] Hackmeets are temporary gatherings of hackers and activists in which skills, tools and knowledge are exchanged and projects developed. Amongst the first hackmeets were those in Italy in the 1990s.[19] There are direct connections between many of these and artists working with FLOSS. The dyne:bolic project (from which pure:dyne evolved) partly developed through the Italian hackmeets and Dutch hacklabs.[20] RampArts hacklab in London has provided a meeting point for the local OpenLab group, and in Barcelona, spaces such as Hackitectura and Riereta have supported several FLOSS-based art and political projects.[21] Not all artists working with FLOSS and livecoding necessarily share the politics of the hacklabs scene, nor do all hacklab participants necessarily look upon their own activities as art-related, and some are, sometimes rightly, sceptical of artistic involvement in what they do. Hacklabs, however, have been absolutely fundamental to the development of FLOSS in recent years, especially in Europe and South America, and have provided a clear political and ethical orientation in contrast to the somewhat confused and often contradictory political and social perspectives articulated in the other communities and contexts of the wider FLOSS world.[22]

If livecoding is one of the most emblematic artistic manifestations of FLOSS, hacklabs have become one of its most emblematic social forms. Whilst the two may not occupy identical trajectories, they nevertheless

[18] Important early hacklabs include LOA in Milan, http://www.autistici.org/loa, and ASCII in Amsterdam, http://scii.nl, see also: http://www.metamute.org/en/Real-Meet-the-Hackers-Hackers-this-is-the-Real

[19] The Transhack meetings, for example, began in Italy but have spread elsewhere, the Chaos Computer Club meetings in Germany provide a similar context.

[20] dyne:bolic project: http://dynebolic.org

[21] RampArts: http://rampart.co.nr, Hackitectura: http://www.hackitectura.net, Riereta: http://riereta.net

[22] For information on the Autolabs in Sao Paulo, Brazil, see: Ricardo Rosas, 'The Revenge of Lowtech: Autolabs, Telecentros and Tactical Media in Sao Paulo', Sarai Reader 04: Crisis/Media, edited by Shuddhabrata Sengupta, Monica Narula, et al. Delhi: Sarai Media Lab, 2004, available online: http://www.sarai.net/publications/readers/04-crisis-media

overlap and compliment one another in many significant ways. Central to this is their shared principle of 'enabling the possibility of production by others'. This is an issue of distribution, not simply distribution at the level of product, in the way a piece of software can be easily distributed for example, but at the level of practice. The practice itself is inherently distributive, for it integrates the distribution of the knowledge of how to produce into that which it produces.[23] Whilst this allows for possibilities of collaborative production, it should be seen as distinct from collaboration in itself. For whereas a practice that is collaborative coheres the production of many under a single goal, thereby directing the disposition of their labour, a practice that is distributive enables the disposition of labour by others under their own direction. This is facilitated in the output of production as notation, as code that not only creates a product, but enters into an active life beyond its initial implementation.

[23] It might be assumed the 'distributive practice' deliberately echoes or relates to notions of 'distributive justice' but the similarity in the names is purely coincidental. There are many different models of distributive justice, with the liberal model of John Rawls and right-Libertarian model of Robert Nozick being amongst the most widely discussed. Both of these are based around an allocation of material resources. Where the notion of distributive practice discussed here may relate to distributive justice is in those which are based on, or identify a form of distributive justice in Marx, where the emphasis is upon creating capacity for production amongst others.

## Notational Production

Notational production is not unique to software. The emergence of livecoding as an initially musical activity reflects the engagement with notational production that has characterised many different musical traditions. The application of computer code to the construction of sound is, in one sense, simply one more episode in this process. Livecoding works from within a particular relation between notation and contingency. The specificity of code is opened towards the indeterminism of improvisation. In this respect livecoding not only adds to the evolution of notational production within music but echoes a particular period where a similar relation between notation and contingency came to the fore. This was a period in which the 'free playing' of experimental jazz developed by the likes of John Coltrane, Ornette Coleman and Sun Ra, met with the 'open' compositional systems of the avant-garde that had been developed by John Cage, Karlheinz Stockhausen, and Earle Brown. Just as FLOSS brings together two related, yet differing, ethics of software production ('Free Software' and 'Open Source'), we might describe this music as Free Open Form Performance (abbreviated as FOFP). 'Free playing' was a term preferred by Coleman and other jazz musicians who rejected the use of the term 'improvisation' on the grounds it was often applied to black music by white audiences to emphasise some innate intuitive musicality that denied the heritage of skills and formal traditions that the black musician drew upon.[24] 'Open' comes from Umberto Eco's 'Poetics of the Open Work', an essay from 1959 which was amongst the first to survey and analyse the experiments with aleatoric, indeterminate and partially composed works that were emerging in the classical avant-garde.[25] By the late 1960s these two strands of development had crossed over, with jazz composers such as Coleman and Anthony Braxton consciously working with the instrumentation and structural forms of the classical avant-garde, and groups such as the Scratch Orchestra adopting the collective structure of ensembles such as the Art Ensemble of Chicago. Experiments with notation were significant to many of these groups and composers, but in the Scratch Orchestra, the exploration of notational production was a cornerstone of the project.

**Scratch History**

The Scratch Orchestra grew out of a series of public classes in experimental music that Cornelius Cardew and other composers had been running in London in the late 1960s. These began at the Anti-University on Rivington Street and then at Morley College, a workers education centre set up in the 19th Century.[26] It was here that the original members of the Scratch Orchestra first came together: Cornelius Cardew, Michael Parson, Howard Skempton and people attending their classes. The foundation of the Orchestra was officially announced in June 1969 through the publication in the Musical Times of 'A Scratch Orchestra: draft constitution' written by Cardew.[27] The constitution defines the Orchestra as

> *[...] a large number of enthusiasts pooling their resources (not primarily material resources) and assembling for action (music-making, performance, edification).*

Membership was open to anyone, regardless of musical ability. Many visual artists, such as Stefan Szczelkun, joined and brought with them an interest and experience of art happenings and urban intervention works.[28] Through these, and more conventional concerts, the Orchestra aimed to 'function in the public sphere' presenting works developed by the group. The constitution outlined various forms of activity

[24] Ornette Coleman, 'Something To Think About', Free Spirits: Annals of the Insurgent Imagination, volume 1, San Francisco: City Lights, 1982, p.117, for other aspects of the free jazz scene see: Bill Cole, 'Improvisation in Music - A Black's View', Free Spirits: Annals of the Insurgent Imagination, volume 1, San Francisco: City Lights, 1982; Frank Kofsky, Black Music, White Business: Illuminating the History and Political Economy of Jazz, New York: Pathfinder, 1998; Graham Lock, Forces in Motion: Anthony Braxton and the Meta-reality of Creative Music, London: Quartet Books, 1988; Benjamin Looker, Point From Which Creation Begins: the Black Artists' Group of St. Louis, St. Louis: Missouri Historical Society Press, 2004.

[25] English translations have been published in Umberto Eco, The Role of the Reader: Explorations in the Semiotics of Texts, Indiana: Indiana University Press, 1979, and in Audio Culture: Readings in Modern Music, edited by Christopher Cox and Daniel Warner, London: Continuum, 2004. The references in this article are taken from the latter.

[26] Information about the Scratch Orchestra is taken from the following sources: Cornelius Cardew (editor), Scratch Music, Cambridge, MA: MIT

Press, 1974; Cornelius Cardew and Rod Eley, Stockhausen Serves Imperialism, London: Latimer new Dimensions, 1974, available online: http://www.ubu.com/historical/cardew/cardew_stockhausen.pdf; Stefan Szczelkun, 'The Scratch Orchestra', http://www.stefan-szczelkun.org.uk/phd102.htm; Stefan Szczelkun, '25 years from Scratch', http://www.stefan-szczelkun.org.uk/PHD-SCRATCH2.htm; John Tilbury, 'Cornelius Cardew', in JEMS: An online Journal of Experimental Music Studies, originally published in Contact no, 26, Spring, 1983, pp.4-12, http://www.users.waitrose.com/~chobbs/tilburycardew.html; Michael Chant, 'A Turning Point in Music History', in Experimental Music Catalogue, http://www.users.waitrose.com/~chobbs/chant.html; Michael Chant, et al., Twenty Five Years From Scratch, catalogue for event at ICA London,: London: London Musicians Collective, 1994, available: http//metamute.org/files/25years_scratch.pdf

[27] The constitution is reprinted in Cornelius Cardew (editor), Scratch Music, Cambridge, MA: MIT Press, 1974, pp.10 - 11.

[28] Stefan Szczelkun was involved in a number of different forms of art collective from the late 1960s onwards, see: Stefan Szczelkun, Exploding Cinema 1992 - 1999, culture and democracy, PhD Thesis, Royal College

that the Orchestra would follow in creating these works. One of the most important activities was the writing of 'Scratch Music'. Each member of the Orchestra had a notebook, or 'Scratchbook', in which they would write small works that could be combined into larger ensemble pieces.[29] The constitution emphasises that these Scratch Music pieces should be an active process of experimentation with different notational forms: 'verbal, graphic, musical, collage, etc.'. By 1972 a clearly defined process for the development of Scratch Music had emerged. Each piece was originally performed by its author, the scores were then exchanged and performed by other Orchestra members, providing a kind of 'peer review' critique of the pieces. 'Scratchers' were asked to write no more than one new piece per day, but encouraged to keep a 'regular turnover', so that there was a tight feedback loop between writing and performing.[30]

From the very beginning the Scratch Orchestra took a conscious decision to make all their notations freely distributable, stating that the Scratch Music works were without copyright.[31] One of their first collections of scores, published in 1969 and called *Nature Study Notes: Improvisation Rites*, replaced the conventional copyright notice with the following:

> *No rights are reserved in this book of rites. They may be reproduced and performed freely. Anyone wishing to send contributions for a second set should address them to the editor: C.Cardew, 112 Elm Grove Road, London SW13.*[32]

Whilst rejections of copyright restriction were nothing new, both the Situationists and the folk singer Woody Guthrie had placed anti-copyright notices on their works, it is notable that the Scratch Orchestra also encouraged others to modify and add to their scores, stating that these may be incorporated into the next version.[33]

The works in *Nature Study Notes* are all textual instruction pieces. Few of them describe ways of making sound however, and instead focus around various social interactions that construct and play with power relations amongst the performers. Some are like party games:

> *Form a standing circle. Nominate a leader, who stands in the circle with eyes blindfolded. The remainder of group rotate slowly around him/her. ... When the leader is touched, he forfeits his role and so doing shouts 'Porridge'.*[34]

Others like generative automata:

> *Each person entering the performance space receives a number in order. Anyone can give an order (imperatively obeyed) to a higher number, and must obey orders given him by a lower number. No. 1 receives his orders from the current highest number (the most recently entered player); the highest number can give orders only to No. 1.*[35]

## Noise Interrupts

Many of the scores in *Nature Study Notes* set up small scale 'operating systems', simple organisational structures that enable other works to be produced within them. The notion of the performance as an operating system is one that ap have taken up in their *Life Coding* project. Adapting mechanisms from computer systems, the interaction of performers is dictated by interrupt signals connected to actions defined in look-up tables.[36] In conventional computers, the interrupt mechanism enables signals from peripheral devices such as mice, keyboards or network cards to enter into the operating system. When an interrupt signal is received, the computer selects a response action by matching an identifier code for each signal against a look-up table of programmed routines known as 'interrupt handlers'. In this way pressing keys on a keyboard or moving the mouse can change the course of events currently in action. The interrupt creates a vector between the internal operation of the central processing unit (CPU), the domain of notational operations, and the contingency of the outside world. As Edsger Dijkstra, one of the inventors of the interrupt system, noted:

> *It was a great invention, but also a Box of Pandora. Because the exact moments of the interrupts were unpredictable and outside our*

of Art, 2002, available online: http://www.stefan-szczelkun.org.uk

[29] Examples of these are reproduced in Scratch Music, 1974, and in Twenty Five Years From Scratch, 1994.

[30] This does not mean that Orchestra members wrote a new score everyday, however, as the rate of composition would vary between members and over time. The process described here is summarised from the various revisions of the Scratch Orchestra constitution and from information offered by Stefan Szczelkun in personal correspondence.

[31] As Michael Chant stated: 'no Scratch Music is copyright', Scratch Music, p.17, see also discussion of copyright in Cardew and Eley, Stockhausen Serves Imperialism, p.5.

[32] Scratch Orchestra, Nature Study Notes: Improvisation Rites 1969, edited by Cornelius Cardew, London: Scratch Orchestra, 1969.

[33] The Woody Guthrie and Situationist anti-copyright notices are discussed in Dmytri Kleiner, WOS4: The Creative Anti-Commons and the Poverty of Networks, http://info.interactivist.net/article.pl?sid=06/09/16/2053224

[34] Nature Study Notes, score PDIR3, p.3

*control, the interrupt mechanism turned the computer into a nondeterministic machine with a non-reproducible behaviour, and could we control such a beast?*[37]

The interrupt breaks the closed linear unfolding of the Turing Machine, enabling programs to be stopped, altered and restarted. This enabled the development of languages that could be executed as individual statements one step at a time, giving rise to shell commands (the basic text-based commands used in the UNIX terminal) and the read-evaluate-print-loop (sometimes 'read-eval-print-loop' or REPL for short) that forms the basis of interactive programming languages such as Lisp.[38] The interrupt and read-eval-print-loop lie at the heart of any livecoding program and all UNIX-derived operating systems. In his notes for the first release of Linux, Linus Torvalds wrote: 'interrupts aren't hidden' - a statement that is as much aesthetic as it is technical.[39] It is here where contingency and notation meet, but it is here also that the possibility of error enters. For some, however, rather than treading lightly for fear of a crash, the error carried on an interrupt signal is a positive, productive opportunity. This is not restricted to computer interrupts. During rehearsals, Sun Ra would deliberately interrupt and trick his performers. The 'errors' this produced, however, were not mistakes but rather forms of evolution:

> *There are no mistakes. If someone's playing off-key or it sounds bad, the rest of us will do the same. And then it will sound right.*[40]

The operating system of Ra's Arkestra incorporated such 'noise' and restructured itself in the process. This 'noise' is not simply that of unmusical sound, but also in the sense that Jacques Attali adapts from information and systems theory, any material that is not recognised by an existing system, and is therefore opposed to 'information' which is material that has value or significance in a given system.[41] Attali describes the evolution of musical styles as one in which an existing system of music becomes exposed to 'noise' that at first disrupts it, but then, through incorporation restructures it and gives rise to a new system. In the voyage of the Arkestra, systems would collapse and be reborn on a daily basis.

[35] Nature Study Notes, score FRMEVR4, p.3

[36] The performance is described in more detail at: http://1010.co.uk/xxxxx_at_piksel2007.html

[37] Edsger W. Dijkstra, 'My recollections of operating system design', handwritten memoir, 2000 - 2001, pp.13 - 14, available as an electronic document, EWD1303, from the Dijkstra archives: http://www.cs.utexas.edu/users/EWD/transcriptions/EWD13xx/EWD1303.html, and http://www.cs.utexas.edu/users/EWD/ewd13xx/EWD1303.PDF. See also: Simon Yuill, 'Interrupt', in Software Studies: A Lexicon, edited by Matthew Fuller, Cambridge MA: MIT Press, 2008.

[38] Louis Pouzin, 'The Origin of the Shell', http://www.multicians.org/shell.html, 2000, Paul Graham, 'The Roots of Lisp', http://www.paulgraham.com/rootsoflisp.html, 2002.

[39] Linus Torvalds, 'Notes for linux release 0.01', http://www.kernel.org/pub/linux/kernel/Historic/old-versions/RELNOTES-0.01, 1991.

[40] John F. Szwed, Space is the Place: The Lives and Times of Sun Ra, Edinburgh: Mojo Books, 2000, p.114.

[41] Jacques Attali, Noise: the Political Economy of Music, translated by Brian Massumi, Minneapolis: University of

## Schooltime Compositions

This power over systems was not limited to the Demiurge or intergalactic jazz master. During the same period in which the Scratch Orchestra were re-inventing music from the ground up, a group of children at Muzzey Junior High School in the US were experimenting with their own improvised notation systems. These children were not writing music however, but teaching themselves to program computers. They were part of the first LOGO Lab, a project initiated by Seymour Papert, a researcher from the MIT Artificial Intelligence Laboratory.[42] LOGO was a simple programming language that directed an entity called a 'turtle'. The turtle could either be an on-screen virtual character or a small robot that was instructed to move around their terrain (screen or floorspace) and that could draw a trail on its path. LOGO Lab students developed their own programs in which the turtles would act out drawings or spatial exercises. In so far as LOGO expresses a series of potential actions out of which a drawing emerges it has an analogy to the notations of the Scratch Orchestra, which often did not express sound directly but rather actions from which sound could arise. As Cardew wrote in his notes to *Treatise*: 'Notation is a way of making people move.'[43]

Like the Scratch Orchestra, the LOGO Labs grew out of a conscious pedagogical interest directed towards developing forms of collective, self-directed practical research. These were realised through semi-structured 'improvisational' activities and used self-developed notational systems as a means of constructing, communicating and reflecting upon these. As the constitution makes clear, the Scratch Orchestra was a conscious exploration of what notation could be and how that related to establishing another understanding of what the practice of music itself might be. This came out of the pedagogic context of the Morley College classes, and, in a perhaps self-mocking gesture, the Orchestra's *Nature Study Notes* and Cardew's earlier *Schooltime Compositions* scores deliberately took the form of school exercise books.[44] Papert believed that programming was a skill that should be available to everyone not as a 'technology' – a mechanism for manufacture abstracted from human labour – but as a means of conceptual exploration. There are political parallels between the two projects. Papert had come to computing from a prior involvement in radical left-wing politics, and in the 1950s had been involved in the group running *Socialist Review* in London.[45] The LOGO Lab concept combined

Minnesota Press, 1985.

[42] For information on origins and development of the LOGO Labs see: Seymour Papert, Mindstorms: Children, Computers, and Powerful Ideas, Brighton: The Harvester Press, 1980, and Cynthia Solomon, Logo, Papert and Constructionist Learning, http://logothings.wikispaces.com, c2007.

[43] Cornelius Cardew, 'Treatise: Working Notes', in Cornelius Cardew, Treatise Handbook, London: Editions Peters, 1970, p.iii.

[44] Cornelius Cardew, Schooltime Compositions, self-published, London, 1968.

[45] This is referred to in the Wikipedia entry on Papert: http://en.wikipedia.org/wiki/Papert

insights from Jean Piaget's and Lev Vygotsky's psychological studies of child development with the non-schooling principles of Ivan Illich.[46] It advocated an approach in which: 'the child programs the computer rather than the computer is being used to program the child.'[47] Papert also argued that the design of a programming language could reflect a particular political and ethical position. He criticised BASIC, another language originally designed for teaching programming, as demonstrating 'how a conservative social system appropriates and tries to neutralise a potentially revolutionary instrument.'[48] Although the Scratch Orchestra did not initiate from a defined political program, it nevertheless acted as a context for the development of a politicised arts practice informed by both Marxist and anarchist tendencies. It was through the Scratch Orchestra that Cardew was to acquire a profound political self-awareness, applying an explicit Maoist perspective to his own practice, and leading to his involvement in founding the Revolutionary Communist Party of Great Britain (Marxist-Leninist). Echoing Papert's criticisms of BASIC, Cardew similarly criticised the institutionalised conservativism of much music notation, demanding instead that 'all problems of notation will be solved by the masses.'[49] For both Papert and Cardew, pedagogy was a two way thing. The lab and the orchestra broke down distinctions between pupil and tutor, and placed learning in the context of self-directed production. In these ways they were forms of distributive practice.

[46] Ivan Illich, Deschooling Society, new edition, London: Marion Boyars, 1995.

[47] Papert, 1980, op. cit., p.34.

[48] Ibid., p.5.

[49] Cardew made this statement as part of his response to the International Symposium on the Problematic of Today's Musical Notation, held in Rome, 1972, see: Cornelius Cardew 'Self Criticism: Repudiation of Earlier Works', in Cardew and Eley, 1974, op. cit., p.88.

[50] The classic account of hacking and the MIT AI Lab is Steven Levy, Hackers: Heroes of the Computer Revolution, updated edition, London:Penguin, 2001. It is worth noting that Papert was not really one of the 'core' hackers, however the parallels between the practices of hacking and the LOGO Labs are clear.

## Training in Contingency

An element of the contingent was essential to this. In Papert's eyes, one of the strengths of programming as a tool for learning, was the attitude to error that it encouraged. Encountering error, in the form of bugs, was an inevitable and necessary part of programming, especially that particular practice of programming developed at the AI Labs known as 'hacking'.[50] Papert pointed out that in conventional education, errors had a purely negative connotation. When a student makes a mistake they are discredited for it, losing marks or being punished, thereby encouraging a fear of error, leading to an unwillingness to stray from conventional boundaries and take risks. For the hacker, conversely, what mattered is not whether or not a mistake is made but rather how creatively it can be responded to. As with the Arkestra, embracing error is a productive possibility. The embracing of error is reflected in documents such as HAKMEM.[51] Short for 'hack memo', this was a collection of code snippets and programming ideas distributed amongst the hackers within the AI Labs – contributors include Richard Stallman, James Gosling and Marvin Minsky. Many of the entries utilise possibilities discovered through bugs and inconsistencies within the PDP computers that the AI Lab worked on. Other entries suggest ways that a particular algorithm might be played with, encouraging people to mess around with it in what can only be described as a form of aesthetic code play.[52] HAKMEM can be seen as the AI Lab's equivalent of the Scratchbooks exchanged between Scratch Orchestra members. Within the LOGO Labs, code was written and exchanged between students in a similar manner. Rather than planning out programs in advance, pupils would 'improvise' with their code responding to the how the turtle performed and modifying their programs accordingly. LOGO learning thereby operated through a similar feedback loop of coding-performing that livecoders such as Alex McLean identify as the basis of their practice and which builds upon the principle of the read-eval-print-loop.

Computers and programming languages present highly constrained environments that limit the possible varieties of interpretation that a particular notation may be subject to. The interpretation of notation by a human may be far less constrained. For Cardew this was a major concern in the development of new notations, for it presented both a danger and an opportunity. The opportunity was that notations need not only encode existing patterns or defined systems of sound, but could also be proposals and provocations to create new ones. The danger lay in the fact that a trained musician, when confronted with an unfamiliar notation system, rather than responding to it directly, might fall back into their personal predispositions and ingrained habits. The performance may simply become the regurgitation of old cliches and formulas like that of the amateur jazz musician described by Adorno, unable to stray from the existing models to which he has adapted and subordinated himself.[53] The trained musician approached a performance with a predefined system of producing sound against which the new notation was interpreted. What was novel in the new notation may simply be responded to as 'error' or noise within that system and

[51] Michael Beeler, William R. Gosper, and Rich Schroeppel, 'HAKMEM', Memo 239, Artificial Intelligence Laboratory, Cambridge, Mass: Massachusetts Institute of Technology, 1972. HAKMEM was originally published as an internal memo within MIT AI Lab, a copy of the document is available online: http://www.inwap.com/pdp10/hbaker/hakmem/hakmem.html, and at: ftp://publications.ai.mit.edu/ai-publications/pdf/AIM-239.pdf. Many of the HAKMEM examples also engage with code in a way that conscious exposes the materiality of the machines on which they run, see: Simon Yuill, 'Code Art Brutalism', in READ_ME 0.4, edited by Olga Goriunova and Alexei Shulgin, Aarhus: Aarhus University, 2004.

[52] For example:

ITEM 146: MUNCHING SQUARES
Another simple display program. It is thought that this was discovered by Jackson Wright on the RLE PDP-1 circa 1962.

```
DATAI 2
ADDB 1,2
ROTC 2,-22
XOR 1,2
JRST .-4
```

2=X, 3=Y. Try things like 1001002 in data switches. This also does interesting things with operations other than XOR, and rotations other than -22. (Try IOR; AND; TSC; FADR; FDV(!); ROT -14, -9, -20, .)

therefore avoided. New notations required performers with a similar attitude to that of the hacker and LOGO Lab student, one who could respond creatively to the unknown and unexpected. The performer, therefore, could not rehearse such music but rather 'trained' for it like a martial art, developing ways of acting upon contingency.[54] This similarly developed through a feedback loop of coding-performance that formed the basis of Scratch Music practice.

Through such feedback loops notation incorporates the experience of the contingent into future practice. What was the unexpected 'error' of the past becomes preparation for unknown future possibilities. In absorbing this a notation records the historical development of a practice, capturing different versions of how things could be done, and enabling comparison, analysis and synthesis of these. In both the LOGO Labs and Scratch Orchestra, this process of versioning was consciously engaged in, with the evolving knowledge, purposes and standards of the practitioner community acting as a form of version control identifying those practices that are most current and those which are conflicting or branching off.[55]

## The Virtues of Practice

These examples emphasise practice over product. This is practice realised as more than just a set of techniques and skills however. It is practice that is consciously linked to, and helps define, particular practitioner communities: groups defined not by a common aesthetic, style, nor common collection of cultural references, therefore, but by commitments to shared practices. This socialised notion of practice parallels that outlined by Alasdair MacIntyre.[56] Whilst any practice may comprise of certain techniques, skills or activities, the practice itself is not determined solely through the performance of these. The activities of a given practice exist within a set of relations that are both social, in the relations between each practitioner and his or her contemporaries, and historical, in the relations of current activity in regard to an understanding of its past development, to how it has been practised in the past.[57] A practice may be judged in terms of its internal goods, those qualities and characteristics that enable it to flourish, and external goods,

[53] Theodor Adorno, 'On the fetish character in music and the regression of listening', in The Culture Industry: Selected Essays on Mass Cuture, edited by J.M. Bernstein, London: Routledge, 1991, p.48. For some, Adorno's teatment of jazz music has been seen as problematic due to the somewhat limited forms of jazz music available through the European music market at that time, if anything Adorno's criticisms exemplify the gulf between jazz as practicised within the black community and jazz as experienced by consumers of the commodified forms that Adorno had access to, for a discussion of this see: Frederic Jameson, Late Marxism: Adorno, or, The Persistence of the Dialectic, London: Verso, 1990, p. 141.

[54] Cornelius Cardew, 'Towards an Ethics of Improvisation' in Cardew, 1970, op. cit., p.xvii. Nick Collins has outlined a series of training exercises for livecoding: Nick Collins, 'Live Coding Practice', paper presented at New Interface for Musical Expression 2007, New York, available online at: http://www.cogs.susx.ac.uk/users/nc81/research/livecoding practice.pdf

[55] Conflicts and branches are two common features of version control systems, such as CVS, used for managing source code in programming projects.

that which a practice produces which may become a property or possession of others who themselves are not practitioners.[58] Within a practice such as medicine, for example, an internal good may be the development of a new technique or understanding that enables doctors to realise more effective treatments, an external good would be the improved health of those patients who receive such treatment.

MacIntyre's model of practice is central to his retrieval of Aristotelian 'virtue ethics', informed by Marxist social and economic analyses and developed as a critique and alternative to post-Enlightenment Liberalism and individualist ethics.[59] In MacIntyre's reading 'virtues' are those internal goods through which 'we define our relationships to those other people with whom we share the kind of purposes and standards which inform practices', and 'vices' those which inhibit or undermine that.[60] MacIntyre's notion of virtue is not a conservative one, virtues are not defined as a static table of tropes set down by institutions such as the church or state. In contrast to an ethics of duty based on obligation to a set of external standards to which the individual must aspire, virtue ethics arise from and are directed towards forms of practice. They are defined and realised through action rather than regulation or law and aim towards a general ethic of self-actualisation.[61] Different virtues may be open to change and development within the unfolding and evolution of a given practice. It is the practitioners who define that which is virtuous in regard to the aims of their practice. In applying MacIntyre's virtue ethics to contemporary anarchist practice, Benjamin Franks has emphasised this dialogic and immanent model of ethics that evolves through the interplay of practitioners and social situations: 'different virtues take priority in different contexts rather than conforming to a set of universal values'.[62]

The history of FLOSS, as given in the accounts of its formative practitioners, has very much been one of the evolution and discourse of practices. In 'The GNU Project', Richard Stallman writes about the MIT AI Lab as the first 'software-sharing community' in which building upon and adapting the code made available by others within the lab was the key basis through which ideas were developed and realised.[63] This is embodied in documents such as HAKMEM, and expressed in the form of a virtue ethic that echoes

A conflict occurs when two or more programmers attempt to submit changes to the same section of code at the same time. Branches are a means of enabling programmers to work on copies of the code that have been 'branched off' into a separate development line from that of the main codebase, it can be used for testing out ideas before they are merged back into this. many aspects of the development of a software project can be traced in the records of a version control repository, making it a kind of discursive archive of how the software has been produced. For a discussion of these issues see: Simon Yuill, 'CVS' in Software Studies: A Lexicon, edited by Matthew Fuller, Cambridge MA: MIT Press, 2008.

[56] Alasdair MacIntyre, After Virtue, third edition, University of Notre Dame Press: Notre Dame, Indiana, 2007.

[57] Ibid., p.194.

[58] Ibid., p.190-191.

[59] Aristotle was a major influence on early Marx informing both his development of economic theory and his ideas on how a communist society might operate, particularly in terms of the capacities and potentials it might offer its citizens. See, for example, articles in: George E. McCarthy (editor), Marx and

Aristotle: Nineteenth-century German Social Theory and Classical Antiquity, Rowan and Littlefield, Maryland: Savage, 1992.

[60] MacIntyre, 2007, op. cit., p.191.

[61] Self-actualisation, selbstbetatigung, was for Marx the opposite to alienated labour. It is an aspect of his thought that was informed by his readings of Aristotle.

[62] Benjamin Franks, 'Anarchism and the Virtues', 2007, originally presented as 'Virtues and Anarchism: A non-essentialist account' at Alasdair MacIntyre's Revolutionary Aristotelianism: Ethics, Resistance and Utopia conference London Metropolitan University, June 2007. Franks also presents an outline of how MacIntyre's notion of virtue can be separated from previous essentialising models. As examples Franks gives the development of non-hierarchic organisational structures and forms of self-governance that emerged in the road protest camps of the mid-nineties and have evolved through the urban protest actions and social projects of the early 21st Century, in which hacklabs and FLOSS-based autonomous media (such as Indymedia and free networks) have formed a significant part. These have been accompanied by a growing sense and application of historical narratives

Aristotle: 'The fundamental act of friendship among programmers is the sharing of programs.'[64] Demonstrating how such a virtue ethic contrasts with that of regulative duty ethics, Stallman continues:

> *...marketing arrangements now typically used essentially forbid programmers to treat others as friends. The purchaser of software must choose between friendship and obeying the law.*[65]

Within the practice of hacking, the sharing of code is an internal good. Stallman also relates the basic principles of hacking to an external good. In arguing against the ends orientated values of the 'proprietary-software social system' he proposes that the way in which software is made (its mode of production) is reflective of the 'kind of society we are allowed to have.'[66] Free Software hacking is therefore also a prefigurative practice in the sense outline by Franks, as it seeks to realise its ends within the means that achieve them.[67] When the 'proprietary-software social system' came into contact with the 'software-sharing community', the latter was brought into crisis due to the conflict of values that this provoked. This forced the need to explicitly define what were previously tacit values held by mutual consent, articulated by Stallman as the four freedoms of 'Free Software'. The four principles of Free Software can be seen as the articulation of a particular virtue ethic applicable to the production of software and the practice of programming. The fourth freedom specifically relates the internal good of hacking to an external good:

> *You have freedom to distribute modified versions of the program, so that the community can benefit from your improvements.*[68]

Eric Raymond's *The Cathedral and the Bazaar* develops its definition of 'Open Source' through a similar emphasis upon practice.[69] It appears that Raymond is also promoting a kind of virtue ethic that develops and articulates a particular practitioner community. The various references to Kropotkin's notions of 'mutual aid' and governance through 'the principle of common understanding' that are found in this and other of Raymond's writings would also suggests that he shares the kind of communitarian ethos of Stallman and one that might even relate to the 'practical anarchism' of Franks.[70] Raymond's approach, however, is fundamentally different. Whereas Stallman outlines a set of values appropriate to realising a form of socially-directed and self-actualised production, Raymond provides an analysis of how such production can be utilised for productive efficiency. In doing so he severs the relationship between the internal goods of hacking practice and the external goods of communitarian production that are the basis of Free Software. The virtues of Free Software are replaced by the rules of Open Source – Raymond literally defines 19 rules of Open Source production. In place of an ethics of production we are presented with a management model which, according to MacIntyre, is antithetical to virtue, aiming only towards 'the most efficient means of achieving whatever is proposed.'[71] Whilst both Free Software and Open Source offer models of production that are collaborative they differ fundamentally in how this is orientated. Free Software presents a model of collaboration that is distributive, it seeks to enable others to have disposition over their own production.[72] MacIntyre would argue that this demands an ongoing process of critical judgement and the 'exercise of the virtues' appropriate to such a practice which cannot be subject to a 'routinizable application of rules.'[73] Open Source, on the other hand, presents a model of collaboration that is acquisitive, it seeks to harness the labour of others so as to reduce production costs and increase profits (reducing liability is often identified as a key saving within commercial Open Source projects), or create profits in previously unrecognised areas. This can be seen in tracing the evolution of Open Source style licensing and production models away from a set of positive freedoms enabling self-disposition towards a set of negative freedoms acting upon a liberalised sharing economy. These are exemplified in the variations of the Creative Commons licenses and the regulative, aspirational (rather than virtuous) sharing of Web 2.0.[74]

As with Free Software, the history of the Scratch Orchestra can be understood as one of a particular practitioner community evolving its own ethics of practice. The constitution itself defines the group in terms of the activities that it will pursue and develop through. That the constitution was subject to rewriting and revision during the time of the group's existence indicates there was an ongoing evaluation of this definition in relation to that evolving practice. One of the

and self-critiques from within traditions of protest and political action such as Christopher Linebaugh's 'history from below', Bookchin's critique of 'lifestyle anarchism' (Murray Bookchin, Social Anarchism or Lifestyle Anarchism: An Unbridgeable Chasm, Seattle: AK Press, 1996) and Jo Freeman's 'Tyranny of Structurelessness' (Jo Freeman, 'The Tyranny of Structurelessness', 1970, http://flag.blackened.net/revolt/hist_texts/structurelessness.html). Similarly, Italian Autonomism re-articulated Marxist practice by drawing from the history of worker's action gathered in the Autonomia magazine and films such as Manuela Pellarin's Porto Marghera: The Last Firebrands, 2004. For a fuller discussion of 'history from below' in the context of British radical history see: Anthony Iles and Tom Roberts, All knees and elbows of susceptibility and refusal, http://caughtlearning.org/all_knees_and_elbows. Stewart Home's critique of 'Anarchist Integralism' is also important in this regard: 'Anarchist Integralism: Aesthetics, Politics and the Après-Garde', http://www.stewarthomesociety.org/ai.htm. Recent discussions of anarchist practice in the UK have largely moved away from the integrational model criticised by Home towards clearer forms of self-definition, see: Benjamin Franks, Rebel Alliances: the Means of British Anarchisms, Edinburgh: AK Press, 2007.

[63] Richard Stallman, 'The GNU Project', Free Software, Free Society: Selected Essays of Richard M. Stallman, 2nd edition, GNU Press: Boston, 2004.

[64] Richard Stallman, 'The GNU Manifesto', Free Software, Free Society: Selected Essays of Richard M. Stallman, 2nd edition, GNU Press: Boston, 2004, p.35.

[65] Ibid., p.35.

[66] Stallman, 'The GNU Project', 2004, op. cit., p.18.

[67] See: Benjamin Franks, Rebel Alliances: the Means of British Anarchisms, Edinburgh: AK Press, 2007.

[68] The four freedoms are listed in 'The GNU Project' but not in the General Public Licence itself.

[69] Eric Raymond, The Cathedral and the Bazaar, http://catb.org/~esr/writings/cathedral-bazaar

[70] Kropotkin's concept of 'mutual aid' is referred to in Raymond's How To Become A Hacker, http://catb.org/~esr/faqs/hacker-howto.html

[71] MacIntyre, 2007, op. cit., p.74.

texts Cardew wrote in the period leading up to the formation of the Scratch Orchestra suggests ways in which the practices of the Orchestra might be understood in relation to a conscious form of virtue ethic. The essay is titled 'Towards an Ethic of Improvisation' and opens with the sentence: 'I am trying to think of the various kinds of virtue or strength that can be developed by the musician.'[75] It ends with an outline of seven 'virtues that a musician can develop', these include 'simplicity', 'selflessness', and 'preparedness'. The virtue of 'forbearance' is described in terms that echo something of Sun Ra's attitude: 'Overcoming your instinctual revulsion against whatever is out of tune (in the broadest sense).'[76] One of the most significant aspects of the essay is its emphasis upon improvisation as a form of 'active life'. It is in this that it connects most strongly with the later activities of the Scratch Orchestra and in particular their stated aim to 'function in the public sphere'. Virtue, Cardew tells us, 'is viewed to best advantage in action'[77], whilst improvisation is only purposeful when 'it occurs in a public environment' for 'its force depends to some extent on public response.'[78] Improvisation, like virtue, depends on a social context and both have value only when realised through actions within such a context. It is on this basis, as Paulo Virno explores, that improvisation exemplifies virtuosity.

## The Praxis of Virtues

Like MacIntyre, Virno's exploration of virtuosity derives from a reading of Aristotle via Marx.[79] Virno defines virtuosity in terms of two particular qualities. The first is that of 'an activity which finds its own fulfilment (that is, its own purpose) in itself' and therefore has no end product and, like improvisation, no 'object which would survive the performance.'[80] The second quality is that it is 'an activity which requires the presence of others, which exists only in the presence of an audience.'[81] For Virno, this relates virtuosity to Aristotle's notions of political action, to *praxis* rather than *poesis*. *Poesis* aims towards the making of an end product 'separated from action', whereas in *praxis* action is an end in itself.[82] This in turn is related to Marx's distinction between an 'activity-with-end-product', such as conventional manufacture, and an 'activity-without-end-product', such as that of the performer, the waiter, the teacher, and the medical doctor.[83]

Virno argues that such 'activity-without-end-product' is a *poesis*, a way of making, that tends towards the condition of *praxis*. For Aristotle, the action which finds fulfilment in itself is also the virtuous action, and following from this, MacIntyre describes those who pursue a practice in terms of furthering its internal goods as those who similarly find fulfilment in the activity itself.[84] Virtuosity then could be defined as 'the performance of a practice at the height of its virtues' and a form of *poesis* that is realised as *praxis*. This is clearly exemplified in Cardew's ethics of improvisation and carries through into the Scratch Orchestra as the conscious creation of a practitioner community based around such an ethic.

This can also be seen to apply to hacking, which similarly demonstrates how a form of production-through-notation may relate such virtuosity to an ethic of distributiveness. Whereas commercial software production emphasises the creation of distinct software products, hacking emphasises code as part of a ongoing dialogue between practitioners. In the accounts of the UNIX oral history project, Ken Thompson, one of the developers of UNIX, recalls his surprise at seeing how Bell's marketing people took the UNIX operating system which to him was 'part of a continuum' that could be adapted and extended as required, and packaged it as a discrete product to be consumed as a fixed entity.[85] In the LOGO Labs coding was pursued as a means of enquiry that found satisfaction in itself but which was directed towards collective dialogue between students and through the performance of the turtle.[86] Similarly, FLOSS projects today are primarily presented through their code repositories which foreground the project as a continuum of production and act as the 'public' context in which the activity of hacking finds an audience. Commercial software production is acquisitive in that firstly it acquires the labour of others, that is then sealed under employment contracts and copyright, and secondly demands that it is consumed as an acquisition whose disposition is similarly restricted. Copyright became significant to the emergence of commercial software as it is the application of copyright, used in its conventional restrictive sense, that is used to define the code as a fixed product. Free Software, in contrast, emphasises the code as something that enters into a continuum of production. So whilst there is an 'output' in the form of written code, it enters into circulation in a way that is distinct from a conventional

[72]
It would be wrong to suggest that Free Software developed through a conscious application of Marxist principles to software production, although Eblen Moglen for one has argued a conscious connection both to Marxist and left anarchist ideas of production: The dotcommunist Manifesto, http://emoglen.law.columbia.edu/publications/dcm.html, Anarchism Triumphant: Free Software and the Death of Copyright http://emoglen.law.columbia.edu/publications/anarchism.html

[73]
MacIntyre, 2007, op. cit., p.150.

[74]
For critiques of how Web 2.0 and 'long tail' capitalism has developed from Open Source models, see Dmytri Kleiner and Brian Wyrick, InfoEnclosure 2.0, Mute Vol.2 #4, Web 2.0 - Man's best friendster?, available online: http://www.metamute.org/en/InfoEnclosure-2.0, and Martin Hardie, FLOSS and the 'crisis': Foreigner in a Free Land?', Sarai Reader 04: Crisis/Media, edited by Shuddhabrata Sengupta, Monica Narula, et al. Delhi: Sara Media Lab, 2004, available online: http://www.sarai.net/publications/readers/04-crisis-media

[75]
Cornelius Cardew, 'Towards an Ethic of Improvisation', Treatise Handbook, London: Edition Peters, 1972, p.xvii.

[76]
Ibid., p.xx.

[77]
Ibid., p.xvii.

[78]
Ibid., p.xx.

[79]
Paolo Virno, A Grammar of the Multitude: For an Analysis of Contemporary Forms of Life, translated by Isabella Bertoletti, James Cascaito and Andrea Casson, Los Angeles: Semiotext(e), 2004.

[80]
Ibid., p.52.

[81]
Ibid., p.52.

[82]
Ibid., p.52.

[83]
Ibid., p.54.

[84]
MacIntyre, 2007, op. cit., p.197.

[85]
See Ken Thompson's contribution to An Oral History of Unix, http://www.princeton.edu/~hos/mike/transcripts/thompson.htm. This is also discussed in Martin Hardie, Time Machines and the Constitution of the Globe, http://openflows.org/%7Eauskadi/time;achines.pdf and http://auskadi.mjzhosting.com/ip.html

[86] The idea of performance is quite explicit in Papert's own account of the LOGO Labs, he cites the instruction methods of the Brazilian Samba Schools, as one model for how the labs worked.

[87]
Coleman, 1982, op.cit, p.117.

product. Free Software is an 'activity-without-end-product' not in the sense of having no output, but rather in the sense of constantly creating the capacity for production elsewhere. The fact that the knowledge of production can be expressed in notation, in the form of source code, is integral to this. This is echoed in the Scratch Orchestra with its emphasis upon the production of notation as both an ongoing and public activity. The notationally based improvisations of the Scratch Orchestra are therefore significantly different from those performed without a score. For whilst the actual performance itself may never be repeated the capacity for its production elsewhere remains. Notation therefore, not only contains the possibility of retaining the history of how a practice develops, thereby aiding its development towards its own internal goods, but also of enabling those internal goods to be expressed in a form that creates capacity for others, thereby becoming external goods.

## Black Notated Music

How a notation comes to be defined and how it is distributed are inherently political issues. This distribution extends beyond the publication of music scores and software code such as addressed through the copyleft mechanisms used by the Scratch Orchestra and FLOSS. As Ornette Coleman recalls, the very visibility of notation within the production process, how it is revealed and concealed, is itself dependent upon and expressive of particular relations of power and political context:

> *I once heard Eubie Blake say that when he was playing in black bands for white audiences, during the time when segregation was strong, that the musicians had to go on stage without any written music. The musicians would be backstage, look at the music, then leave the music there and go out and play it. He was saying that they had a more saleable appeal if they pretended to not know what they were doing. The white audience felt safer.*[87]

The denial of notation described in this episode is a denial of the black musician's self-legitimation. If the use of a notation may provide the basis for transcribing and re-coding the development of a practice, its own history of making and reflection upon that, then the denial of notation is a denial of such history and therefore a denial of the practitioner's basis for legitimation. It is from this perspective that Coleman distances his own practice from the idea of improvisation, for this form of 'virtuosity' became the basis of a denial of legitimation. The 'free playing' that he and other black jazz musicians promoted in the 1960s was not simply free in the sense of a break from conventional musical structure, but also free in breaking away from the condition of being 'improvisers in a compulsory situation.'[88] This led to the development of new performance venues, many situated directly within black communities, and of the conscious articulation of practice as a form of research. Lester Bowie of the Art Ensemble of Chicago adopted a scientist's white lab coat on stage to announce the performance itself as a site of radical experiment. As Sun Ra encouraged his Arkestra: 'You're not musicians, you're tone scientists'.[89] Ra followed this concept further through the creation in 1967 of Ihnfinity Inc, a research corporation intended 'to own and operate all kinds of research laboratories, studios, electronic equipment, electrochemical communicational devices of our own design and creativity...'[90] In St. Louis the Black Artists' Group set up a Training Centre to create a discussion forum for the local community that alongside performances, rehearsals, and workshops, hosted regular meetings and debates about local issues.[91] For Anthony Braxton the relation of notation to legitimation became the basis of research that has been the focus of his work ever since, the development of what he calls 'Black Notated Music'. 'Black Notated Music' goes beyond the simple description of sounds on a page and engages with the extended functionality of sound at a socially structuring level: 'notation can be viewed as a factor for establishing the reality platform of the music.'[92]

[88]
Theodor W. Adorno, 'The schema of mass culture', The Culture Industry: Selected Essays on Mass Cuture, edited by J.M. Bernstein, London: Routledge, 1991, p.76.

[89]
Quoted in Szwed, 2000, op.cit., p.112.

[90]
Quoted in Szwed, 2000, op.cit., p.241. Ihnfinity Inc had grown out of an earlier discussion group that had been setup alongside the Arkestra to explore aspects of mythology and science.

[91]
See: Looker, 2004, op.cit.

[92]
Anthony Braxton quoted in Lock, 1988, op.cit., p.317.

Whilst on the surface these may appear to mirror the pedagogic basis of projects like the Scratch Orchestra and LOGO Labs, they developed from an entirely different trajectory. Although the pedagogics of Cardew and Papert aimed, on the one hand, to break down certain established social structures determining acquisition of skills in music and programming, pedagogy was also the basis upon which they integrated their work back into existing institutional frameworks, thereby legitimating it in the terms of those institutional values. In particular this legitimated their 'non-commercial' status. A similar case could be made for Free Software's dependency on academia, and suggests a potential area of conflict of interest within artist-run workshops, or at least highlights the tensions under which self-valorising labour is forced to 'pay the rent'. For black musicians in the USA of the 1960s, for whom even basic access to education was an issue, such avenues were not available. The appropriation of 'white' lab coats and research culture did not seek accommodation within such institutions but rather questioned their very use as legitimising mechanisms. Eventually the Scratch Orchestra was to become aware of its own dependency on such external forms of legitimisation and the 'compulsory situation' within which it operated.

## Instrumentalising the Collective

In 1972 tensions began to emerge within the Scratch Orchestra. It was felt by some that the group was operating in a fashion that was becoming contradictory with its aims and a 'discontents file' was set up into which people could address these grievances.[93] In response, Cardew, Keith Rowe and John Tilbury established a Scratch Orchestra Ideological Group applying a practice of Maoist self-critique amongst the Orchestra members. Whilst a process of self-criticism within the Orchestra may have been beneficial, this approach merely exacerbated the situation. Many felt that it was the imposition of one self-appointed elite exerting its authority over the Orchestra as a whole and that the Ideological Group's dismissal of certain initiatives from other members did not properly recognise their own political basis.[94] Rather than finding a new clarity of purpose, the Orchestra fell apart. As one member, Eddie Prevost, was to later comment, the fundamental contradiction confronting the Orchestra was perhaps its dependency upon its own constitution 'legislating for noncomformity'.[95] Another member, Michael Chant, observed that the constitution was itself a 'score'.[96] The Orchestra was then the product of this score, a score that carried the name of only one author: Cornelius Cardew. From this perspective the setting up of the Scratch Ideological Group might be seen as an attempt to re-assert authorship over Cardew's 'composition', echoing the concern of his earlier writings that 'the score must govern the music'.[97] This may be a classic example of an ideological vanguard acquiring and instrumentalising the collective for its own ends, and the rebirth of the author in a group attempting to move beyond such notions of singular authorship. In refusing to succumb to such ideological and authorial acquisition, a

[93] Some of these problems are discussed by Eley in Cardew and Eley, 1974, op. cit. Hanne Boemisch's film, Journey To The North Pole (1972) documenting the Scratch Orchestra tour of Northern English towns, appears to illustrate some of this gulf and the growing tensions that were emerging in the group.

[94] Testimonies from different Scratch Orchestra members are given in Twenty Five Years From Scratch, op.cit., many of these comment on the issues surrounding the groups' break-up.

[95] Eddie Prevost in Twenty Five Years From Scratch, 1994, op.cit., p.38.

[96] Michael Chant, 'A Turning Point in Music History', in Experimental Music Catalogue, http://www.users.waitrose.com/~chobbs/chant.html

[97] Cornelius Cardew, 'Treatise: Working notes', Treatise Handbook, London: Edition Peters, 1972, p.iv.

necessary restructuring of the 'composition' of the Orchestra was taking place. The inherently distributive quality of the Orchestra empowered forms of self-actualisation that rendered the need for a single cohering group unnecessary. Many members went on to continue in different practices that extended the radical *praxis* that had developed within it. The breakup, therefore, represented not the failure of its members, but rather the breaking of the limit between the formal structure of the score/constitution and the people who were the 'substance' of the Orchestra. In words that Adorno used to describe an error of notation in one of Schoenberg's serial compositions, this represented

> *[...] the breakthrough of the substance to be structured, the point where it encounters the structuring process and but for which the latter could not be legitimated.*[98]

The imposition of ideological judgement upon the group may have had a similar effect as the recuperation of Free Software practice under the managerial aims of Open Source, undermining the evolution of the practice under its own internal good, and acting as an acquisitive force that separates the practice from the realisation of its accordant external goods.[99]

## Legislating for Nonconformity

There are parallels with Free Software's current reliance on copyleft and the GPL which can also be seen as a way of 'legislating for noncomformity'. The GPL may 'reverse' the normal restrictions created by conventional copyright, but it nevertheless depends upon their basic legal framework, and therefore upon a legalised notion of freedom that is realised through property ownership. Hence the attraction of copyleft for right-Libertarians such as Raymond. Indeed it may be argued that copyleft, as it is currently realised, rather than embodying a form of 'production in common' actually exemplifies something closer to Robert Nozick's 'just transaction'.[100] The problem with copyleft in its current form, and the notions of 'remix' culture and legalised 'appropriation' culture that have been developed from it, are that they merely present an alternative *within* proprietary, acquisitive production (capital) rather than an alternative *to* that. This is echoed in the active promotion of Jeffersonian 'liberty' amongst advocates

[98]
Theodor W. Adorno, Sound Figures, translated by Rodney Livingstone, Stanford: Stanford University Press, 1999 p.214.

[99]
The creation and impact of the Scratch Orchestra Ideological Group can be seen as the creation of a political vanguard within the Orchestra, in accordance with the kind of orthodox Leninist-Maoist politics of those who set it up. Benjamin Franks' critique of vanguardism highlights many of the problems that the Orchestra experienced through this, see: Benjamin Franks, 'Paternalism and Vanguardism' presented at the Civil Rights, Liberties and Disobedience conference, Centre for the Study of International Governance, Loughborough University, July 2007.

[100]
Robert Nozick, Anarchy, State and Utopia, London: Blackwell, 1978.

of Open Source and Creative Commons such as Eric Raymond and Lawrence Lessig. To place an emphasis upon copyleft as an end in itself, and upon the GPL as the key defining document of Free Software, is therefore potentially contrary to the aims of Free Software. This is borne out in a comment from Stallman:

> *Free software is a matter of freedom. From our point of view, precisely which legal mechanism is used to deny software users their freedom is just an implementation detail. Whether it is done with copyright, with contracts, or in some other way, it is wrong to deny the public the freedoms necessary to form a community and cooperate. This is why it is inaccurate to understand the Free Software Movement as specifically a matter of opposition to copyright on software. It is both more and less than that.*[101]

It is significant that this was given in response to Robert T. Long's promotion of copyleft as appropriate to the values of a right-Libertarian free market.[102] It is perhaps best to view the GPL and copyleft as tactics affording certain leverage in current circumstances therefore, and the proliferation of 'open' licences in recent years might be more a sign of the accommodation of resistant practices to an order of legitimation that they might best avoid, for under current law there is no magic licensing scheme that will bring an end to proprietary production.[103]

[101] Richard Stallman, http://www.gnu.org/philosophy/rms-comment-longs-article.html

[102] Robert T. Long, 'The Libertarian Case Against Intellectual Property Rights', originally published in the Autumn 1995 issue of Formulations, available online: http://libertariannation.org/a/f3111.html

[103] The Oekonux mailing list has provided a useful, and sometimes contentious, forum for the discussion of such issues: http://www.oekonux.org

## Distributive Production

The conflicts within the Scratch Orchestra and the conflicts between Free Software and Open Source illustrate the distinctions within forms of production between those that are collective and distributive, and those that are collaborative and acquisitive. A distributive practice enables the disposition of labour by others under their own direction, whilst an acquisitive one accumulates the labour of others without regard to their self-disposition. It also exposes the conflict that can emerge when a practice that has developed within a self-constituent community becomes subject to external forms of constitution and legitimation. Not all collaboration is inherently distributive, therefore. The nature of the power relations within it, and the disposition and legitimation of production they enable, may be subject to forces that operate in opposing ways.

*It is not out of the question that we consider these notations as a marketable product.*[104]

So wrote the composer Henri Pousseur in a description of his composition *Scambi*, composed in 1957, and presented as a key example in Eco's study of the open work. '*Scambi* is not so much a musical composition as a field of possibilities', Pousseur explains, 'an explicit invitation to exercise choice.'[105] His language anticipates that of Web 2.0 and the liberal market place in which, to use Eco's words, openness is 'the fundamental possibility of the contemporary artist or consumer.'[106] *Scambi* predicts the notions of personalised commodity and networked production in which the distinction between producer and consumer is diminished, not in a form that extends free disposition over capacities of creation, but rather operates acquisitively on the collaboration of the consumer. In some ways it points towards the legacy of Papert's 'potentially revolutionary instrument' becoming part of a consumer toy range in LEGO Mindstorms. *Scambi* provides an early example of how, according to Virno: 'Virtuosity becomes labour for the masses with the onset of a culture industry.'[107] The transformation from the factory-based production of the Ford era to the network-based production of the post-Fordist era that Virno addresses, is a transformation in the notation of production in general. All notations of production are inherently architectural for they all inscribe and interweave relations of power. This can be expressed in the sense of the archi-tectural as residing in an etymological family that links to terms such as hierarchy, monarchy and anarchy on the one hand and textuality and textile on the other. A notation proposes, and is taken up within, particular architectures of production and inscriptions of power. The history of notation is therefore integral to the history of the factory, the space in which production is physically marked out and performed. The significance of groups such as the Scratch Orchestra in the late 1960s to the emergence, nearly forty years later, of livecoding and a revival of interest in collective improvisation, can be related to the transition from the singular, coherent factory-within-walls of Fordist production-line manufacture to the polymorphic, unstable factory-without-walls of post-Fordist networked manufacture. As Martin Hardie argues, it is UNIX, with its networked, distributed filesystem, that created the basic notational inscription of the factory-without-walls.[108] Where once, Marx compared the factory manager to the conductor of a classical Orchestra, rehearsing a score set in machine and stone, now 'the tasks of a worker or of a clerk no longer

[104] Henri Pousseur, quoted in Eco, 2004, op.c it., p.168.

[105] Ibid., p.168.

[106] Ibid., p.174.

[107] Virno, 2004, op. cit., p.56.

[108] Martin Hardie, 'The Factory Without Walls', http://openflows.org/~auskadi/factorywoutwalls.pdf, see also: Martin Hardie, 'Change of the Century: Free Software and the Positive Possibility', Mute Vol. 2 #1, Underneath the Knowledge Commons, available online: http://www.metamute.org/en/Change-of-the-Century-Free-Software-and-the-Positive-Possibility

[109] Virno, 2004, op. cit., p.62.

[110] See for example: Brian Ashton, 'Factory Without Walls', MUTE vol. 2 issue 4, Web 2.0 - Man's best friendster?, available online: http://www.metamute.org/en/Factory-Without-Walls. Regus are one of the largest 'instant offices' providers offering services ranging from actual office spaces that can be rented by the hour to receptionists and 'on demand' call centres: http://www.regus.com

[111] Virno, 2004, op. cit., p.66.

[112] Virno, 2004, op. cit., p.85.

[113] Bourriaud, 2002, op. cit., p.30.

involve the completion of a single particular assignment, but the changing and intensifying of social cooperation.'[109] The factory has become an improvised collective ensemble composed of temporary contract workers, outsourced partners, 'instant office' providers, and consumers who are not even aware they are contributing labour to its production.[110] All performing what Virno describes as 'virtuosity without a script.'[111]

In the unstable environment of post-Fordist production, producers and consumers are caught in a condition of perpetual contingency. The agile responsiveness of the virtuoso hacker becomes the basic skill of the average employee:

> *Only one who is experienced in the haphazard changing nature of the forms of urban life knows how to behave in the just in time factories.*[112]

The social-networked pro-sumer becomes a catalyst to the combinatorial logic of late capitalist production, feeding the permutational offerings of personalised commodities and productised services that, in accordance with Bourriaud's aesthetic:

> *operate like a relational device... a machine provoking and managing individual and group encounters.*[113]

Virtuosity under post-Fordism compels us all to become 'improvisers in a compulsory situation.' This is virtuosity without virtue however. It directs practice towards 'external goods' set by managerial goals rather than arising from the 'internal goods' of those practices themselves. Collaboration becomes the dominant paradigm both of managerial control and everyday consumption. It constructs collaboration through relational mechanisms that are acquisitive rather than distributive. Contrary to Virno's claim, however, we are not performers *without* a script but rather enmeshed in endless small scripts and programs. Every aspect of our lives is notated to a degree not previously known and we are constantly challenged by new scores and scripts that we must perform in order to complete even the most mediocre task. It is through such notation that immaterial labour is valorised and managed. This is exemplified in the call centre worker who is the emblematic counterpart to the livecoder, performing actions and words composed in scripts and programs orchestrated on the computer screen they work from. These conduct a performance in strict tempo dictating duration of tasks and work breaks, a virtuosity like that of Sheherazade that must constantly justify and renew itself, trapped in an endless read-eval-print-loop. Through the interrupt mechanism of cold calling, this performance draws its audience into the collaborative labour of data acquisition, marketing surveys and sales support.[114]

The scores and scripts of these performances have been hidden and we are unable to narrate and legitimise our own actions withen them. In a wider sense, therefore, livecoding is emblematic of the demand that the scores be brought on stage, for only then can the problems of notation be properly addressed. Under a regime of acquisitive inscription, however, we may need to reverse Cardew's proposition: the problems of notation should not be solved by the masses, but rather the notations of production must be made constantly problematic.

In pursuing such a tactic we should be careful, as Cardew once warned, not to fall back on avant-gardist cliches of simply creating random noise and confusion as an end in itself, or into the spiralling solipsisms of post-modernism which have done so much to shape and inform the rhetoric and forms of personalised commodity culture.[115] Similarly, we should be wary in following Virno's call for 'unrestrained invention' that it may simply be the corollary of avant-gardist randomness, a permutational generator of lifestyle commodities and niche markets.[116] If Free Software, and related practices, are intended to realise a form of free-as-in-libre labour rather than free-as-in-unpaid-expropriated labour this can only happen in foregrounding and realising freedoms of production, rather than the 'bourgeois freedoms of circulation' promoted by Creative Commons and remix culture.[117] As enterprises such as Facebook and YouTube demonstrate, profits do not fall as the signal-to-noise ration of communication increases. Any noise, any unrestrained invention, that can be acquisitively channelled can be commodified. In such arenas it is circulation not content that counts, and as long as the 'mail gets through' the message is irrelevant.[118] In questioning a form of production in terms of its distributiveness we are asking questions as to how capacities and freedoms of production are articulated and enabled in relation to circulation, rather than cohering and channelling supposedly 'autonomous' labour

[114] For an analysis of call centre work see: Kolinko, Hotlines: Call Centre Inquiry Communism, Oberhausen: Kolinko, 2002. Aufheben use call centre work in illustrating some of the problems and limitations of 'immaterial labour' as outlined by Virno, see Aufheben, 'The Language of Retreat: Paulo Virno's A Grammar of the Multitude', Aufheben, issue 16, 2008, pp.36 - 48.

[115] For Cardew's criticisms of 'randomness' and 'confusion' as avant-garde strategies see: Cardew and Eley, 1974, op. cit., p.45 and p.77. For critiques of these aspects of post-modernism can see: Frederic Jameson, Postmodernism: Or, the Cultural Logic of Late Capitalism, London:Verso, 1992, and Michael Hardt, Anthony Negri, Empire, new edition, Cambridge MA: Harvard University Press, 2001.

[116] This is a key aspect of Virno's 'exit strategy', see: Virno 2005, op. cit., p.70. For a critique of Virno and the relation of his exit strategy to 'entrepreneurial Autonomism' see Aufheben, 2008, op. cit., p.31.

[117] Aufheben, 2008, p.29. The phrase is used by Aufheben in criticising Virno's concept of multitude rather than applied to Creative Commons. The conflicts between free-as-in-libre and free-as-in-unpaid labour are discussed in greater detail in

Tiziana Terranova, 'Free Labor: Producing Culture for the Digital Economy', Electronic Book Review, 2003, available online: http://www.electronicbookreview.com/thread/technocapitalism/voluntary

[118] The 'mail must get through' was one of Raymond's imperatives for Open Source. These forms of communications enterprise have been described by McKenzie Wark as 'vector capitalism', see: McKenzie Wark, A Hacker Manifesto, Cambridge MA:Harvard University Press, 2004, available online: http://subsol.c3.hu/subsol_2/contributors0/warktext.html. In regard to the use of such forums for radical dissemination, such as anarchist film archives on YouTube, or activist self-organisation through Facebook, the question remains as to whether these are unwittingly accommodating themselves through their own contribution to vectoralist commodification or are they exploiting the 'white noise' of Web 2.0 to spread content that might otherwise be blocked or more overtly appropriated?

under acquisitive 'collaboration' models. We should be careful, however, not to valorise distributiveness as an end in itself, for this would bring about a similar severing or misdirection between internal and external goods, and between means and ends, such as we see under the current conditions of 'collaborative' production.

# Autocreativity: The Operation of Codes of Freedom in Art and Culture

Olga Goriunova

*The role played by individual behaviour can be decisive. More generally, the 'overall' behaviour cannot in general be taken as dominating in any way the elementary processes constituting it.*

*– Isabelle Stengers and Ilya Prigogine, Order Out of Chaos: Man's New Dialogue with Nature*

Technical is political is aesthetic is cultural; every of these layers folds into the other and is fed back on itself; every layer informs, embeds and models the others, distributing the particular power patterns throughout the societal systems and their blurry zones of transfer. Free software and open source software are complex ideas, technologies, contents and cultures, however techno-determinist or purely instrumental manifestoes their ideologists might proclaim at times.[1]

Software is not bound to objects, it is social relations; and breaking away from the fetishism of proprietary software structures the commodification of social processes layered into software production and operation. Radical questioning of relations of ownership, of institutional architectures as a matter of modeling is linked into the proliferation of commodity logic into a variety of social relations. While Autonomist Marxism and liberal thinkers provide and promulgate such understandings via routes described below, the logic of these arguments and the premises they rest upon, as this text is called to demonstrate, do not exhaust the array of access points to this problematic and the excess of drives and capacities always at work.

[1] Throughout this text, 'free software' will be used to refer to the free software movement in its original undifferentiated pathos with its revolutionary rhetoric and a hope to transform society. 'Free software' as such is usually associated with the figure of Richard Stallman and the year 1983. 'Open source' will be used to refer to a more pragmatic business-oriented trend in free software development, started off by Eric Raymond in 1998 with the Open Source Initiative. FLOSS as a generic term comprising both 'free software' and 'open source software' was promulgated by Rishab Aiyer Ghosh. Ghosh explains that as an umbrella term, FLOSS originates from the titles of the project funded by the European Union's 5th

Framework Programme (IST), whose team comprised himself, Ruediger Glott, Bernhard Krieger, and Gregorio Robles. Though Ghosh currently contributes to the pragmatic shift in free software development, 'FLOSS' will be used in this text as a generic 'neutral' term, in places where there is no need to emphasize either revolutionary hopes or business plans.

[2] For one such attempt, see: Toni Prug, 'The Mirror's Gonna Steal Your Soul' in Marina Vishmidt et al., eds., Media Mutandis: a NODE.London Reader (Node.London, 2006).

Generally, adding a layer of abstraction upon the discussions of free software risks the danger of losing the coherence of American or European laws regulating ownership and defending property saturated with common sense regimes of bills, prices, costs, contracts, lawsuits, and imprisonment. But not doing so runs the risk of formal translations of certain principles to other regimes of culture, and summing up of points that easily turn into their 'opposites'. Since power and control are deeper and exceed the dichotomies, the questions that can be accessed via the discussion opened up by free software are complex and rooted in the histories of philosophy and discrimination, to name just two fields.[2]

Freedom and creativity are essential operators of neoliberal democracy and management jargon, but it is the concepts these strings of characters aspire to that are core to understanding current ways of happening of cultures and art, free and open source software, not the least, 'creative industries', and routes in-between. Freedom and creativity are the two horses that ride liberal thinking focusing on free software and creative industries, but also, under a different interpretation, post-Marxist thinking.

Freedom as a philosophical problem with a history dates back no earlier than to XIV century philosophy that enquired about the freedom of a human being in the Christian world model. Freedom, or, rather, autonomy, as an ability to think and act independently, e.g. thinking freedom in relation to determination and necessity is a speculative and conceptual operation that became prevalent to be addressed as a negative concept. From Hobbs to Schopenhauer, freedom was conceptualised negatively, through the lack of external determinants, through the limitation on the powers of laws and rules. Thus, freedom or independence is relative autonomy, e.g. functioning according to one's own logic while maintaining close connections with other actors.

Freedom also has a dimension of collectivity, collective experience, as it is linked into an understanding of a human being as a social and public being (thus, often moving the entire discussion into the field of ethics). And freedom is closely related to creativity.

A human being is an embodiment of the capacity for creation; and freedom is a quality of creativity (that is conceived as always free). Unlike freedom, creativity was discussed already in Greek philosophy; and for

Plato, human creativity is an imitation of divine creativity. In Christian philosophy, creativity becomes an experiment in changing the ontological status; for Descartes, creativity is reinvention. Creativity is, thus, a chance to render a human being autonomous. With the lessening importance of 'ideal' worlds, creativity becomes an actualisation of the real, a motor and an in-born character of life. While more will be said on creativity in the last parts of the text, for now it is important to point out that a common history of the related concepts of freedom and creativity gives rise to such opposed cultures of understanding of, for instance, FLOSS, as liberal and Marxist.

While Marxist interpretation of freedom as an opposition to constraint is not new, it developed in paying close attention to understanding a certain impetus to freedom as rooted in coercion and dominance (Adorno's and Horkheimer's principle of mastery) and focuses on the functioning of such mechanisms in culture (from Gramsci to Williams), whereas liberal theory adopts a concept of freedom as a self-fulfilling capacity for choice and action, assuming a human being is de facto rationally thinking, free and creative.[3] Autonomous individuals and free societies, according to Benkler, are those who win through property and common property (commons) that enforce freedom and knowledge (creativity).[4] Thus, a side of open source software propagators represented best by liberal and neoliberal prestigious American universities' law and economics professors, votes for enhancing democracy and knowledge through open source.

Certain labour process organisation aspired to by the 'creative class' and characteristic of the creative industries frames freedom and creativity in terms of opposition to factory, assembly-line or other previous forms of structuring and enforcement of labour.[5] In this respect, the FLOSS production model can be seen as a change in line with the overall transfer to new forms of labour in the First World and throughout global elites, and as such is a neighbour to the creative industries discussion. Though IP (intellectual property) regimes of creative industries are not very keen on freeing their products from copyright enforcement, autonomy and creativity of a liberal kind are the terms widely used in creative industries' propagation and also tend to replace the previous 'revolutionary' rhetoric of FLOSS.

The 'early believers' of free software built a 'romantic' picture of the free software movement at large, when aiming to describe its ideology, causation and economic model; although Eric Raymond and others, with

[3] Yochai Benkler, The Wealth of Networks: How Social Production Transforms Markets and Freedom (Yale University Press, New Haven and London, 2006), pp. 278–279.

[4] Ibid., p. 143 and elsewhere.

[5] Richard Florida, The Rise of the Creative Class (Basic Books, New-York, 2004), pp. 40–42.

the Open Source Initiative moved towards creating a more pragmatic rhetoric appealing to business from the point of view of efficiency, Raymond's seminal papers 'The Cathedral and the Bazaar' and 'Homestanding the Noosphere' continued to apply cultural and anthropological interpretations, describing free software development as a 'post-scarcity gift culture' with hackers creating software out of the possession of leisure time, and through artistic motivation.[6]

In recent years, a number of significant books released by major publishing houses have appeared devoted to the economics of FLOSS production, testing various existing presuppositions on the development models, motivation and economic challenges produced. Utopian leftist promises of the reincarnation of gift culture were tested with sociological surveys and a lot of empirical data.[7] Attempts were made to answer the question of whether FLOSS software presents a better model of software development in terms of quality, time and effort spent; and, especially in the work of Ghosh, to interrogate the motives, including altruism, pleasure, drive for recognition, self-education, desire to signal professional competency in the job market; to map the structure of the community and so on.

This new wave of analysis is related to the economic success of FLOSS. Reports demonstrate a great increase in the share of open source software usage in IT services and in economic revenues accrued, according to which,

> *FLOSS-related services could reach a 32% share of all IT services by 2010, and the FLOSS-related share of the economy could reach 4% of European GDP by 2010. FLOSS directly supports the 29% share of software that is developed in-house in the EU (43% in the U.S.), and provides the natural model for software development for the secondary software sector.*
>
> *... Firms have invested an estimated Euro 1.2 billion in developing FLOSS software that is made freely available.* [8]

The FLOSS development model proved to be a somewhat efficient business model for software development, and new research addresses

[6] Eric S. Raymond, The Cathedral & the Bazaar. Musings on Linux and Open Source by an Accidental Revolutionary (Revised edition, Sebastopol, O'Reilly and associates, 2001). Articles also available at: http://www.catb.org/~esr/writings/cathedral-bazaar/

[7] Joseph Feller et al., eds., Perspectives on Free and Open Source Software (MIT Press, 2005); Rishab Aiyer Ghosh, ed. CODE, Collaboration, Ownership and the Digital Economy (MIT Press, 2004).

[8] Rishab Aiyer Ghosh, 'Study on the Economic Impact of Open Source Software on Innovation and the Competitiveness of the Information and Communication Technologies (ICT) Sector in the EU'. Final Report (2006), http://ec.europa.eu/enterprise/ict/policy/doc/2006-11-20-flossimpact.pdf

such evolution by attempting to build working economic models that radically depart from the rhetoric of gift culture and volunteer labour of early explanations.[9]

Having divorced itself from revolutionary rhetoric, the Creative Commons incarnation of FLOSS led by Lawrence Lessig is not about transforming capitalist society, but is about enhancing liberal free democratic society and liberal individual autonomy by creating legal tools that would guarantee certain actions. Such freedom and autonomy, as described above, are assumed to be naturally given in liberal society and automatically preserved if certain instruments are applied, irrelevant of systems of conditioning, subjectivation, persuasion, coercion, profit, discrimination, distortion, control operating in such a society and in ones dependent on it.

Such a stage in the development of the FLOSS movement has been widely discussed in the free software world where it prompts angry and critical responses, such as the follows:

> *Lawrence Lessig is always very keen to disassociate himself and the Creative Commons from the (diabolical) insinuation that he is (God forbid!) anti-market, anti-capitalist, or communist. Where we would benefit from making space available for the political, the Creative Common's ideological stance has the effect of narrowing and obscuring political contestation, imagination and possibility. As a result, the Creative Commons network provides only a simulacrum of a commons. It is a commons without commonality. Under the name of the commons, we actually have a privatised, individuated and dispersed collection of objects and resources that subsist in a technical-legal space of confusing and differential legal restrictions, ownership rights and permissions.* [10]

Pristine liberal democracy advocates flatten the radical dissatisfaction with the capitalist, racist, patriarchal and other forms of historical societal organisation, whose iceberg tip is property and ownership in the age of information networks. An innate free ability to make informed rational choices as readymade 'subjects', conceptualised as a constant in liberal thinking, is as utopian an understanding of a human being as a robot. Criticising instruments and processes that the former work in without aiming to understand the planes the processes operate on and the problems structuring these planes cannot provide any exciting routes for

[9] Ibid.

[10] David M. Berry and Giles Moss, 'On the "Creative Commons": a critique of the commons without commonalty', Free Software, Issue 5, June (2005), http://www.freesoftwaremagazine.com/files/nodes/1155/1155.pdf

change. Distancing themselves from Stallman's obsessions that were parallel to the re-appearance of references to 'communism' within the digital domains, such accounts aim at explaining the routes to universal happiness through open source software, creative commons and, not least, flexible organisation and creativity at the workplace that can happily coincide with profits without endangering inherited properties.

At the same time, the concepts of freedom that Stallman's free software tried to put forward fit well into a dichotomous model of Marxist philosophy of history and society by their rather narrow and technocratic understanding of control, freedom and human beings and by building closed sets of oppositions between proprietary and free software. Freedom as an absence of constraint to adjust a program or learn from it couples with a belief that a universal tool is possible. It is of a little wonder that attempts to think free and open source software as principles applicable to cultures and arts often do not lead further than summarising free software production principles that culture and art shall assume without much translation.[11]

There appeared various Open Content licenses that concern music, art, text or any other kind of publication, sampling and many more forms of use, which attempt to describe the rhetoric of 'free culture' and 'open society'.[12] The GNU project and Open Source Initiative are built on an understanding of software programming that places emphasis on unrestricted access to program code for the purposes of education, use and modification for improvement or further application. Various license models, from the GPL[13] (General Public License by Free Software Foundation) to the 'legal toolbox' of Creative Commons are built on such an understanding of the source code, which is then directly applied to the fields outside of computer programming, to art.[14] 'Free culture' here is understood as freedom to distribute and modify creative works. Not least it is about communal creation organized horizontally, with participants adding on and improving each other's contributions by a self-evolved mechanism. Wikipedia is the best working reincarnation of 'open culture'. Here agreement seems to end and confusion starts.

If for software, functionality, minimization of bugs, safety and other points may stand as evaluation criteria and allow for an objective estimation of more and less successful projects, within the art field, such

[11] A lot has been written on how un-open, hierarchical, and gendered free software production is. See a dozen of articles in the 'Open Congress' section of Marina Vishmidt et al., eds. Media Mutandis, op. cit. Also, Francis Hunger, 'Open Source - Open Gender?' (2003), http://comamama.irmielin.org/

[12] See Lawrence Liang, Guide to Open Content Licenses (Piet Zwart Institute, Rotterdam, 2004); Lawrence Lessig, Free Culture. How Big Media Uses Technology and the Law to Lock Down Culture and Control Creativity (The Penguin Press, 2004), http://www.free-culture.cc/freeculture.pdf; Feller et al., 2005.

[13] GNU General Public License, http://www.gnu.org/copyleft/gpl.html

[14] Creative Commons, http://creativecommons.org/

objective evaluation is impossible. Value attributed to a particular artwork is symbolic and cannot be directly derived from expenses spent on its production, its momentary success, or any estimation of its 'quality'.[15] A desire to build on a certain work does not originate from its usefulness or functionality but is one result of a complex mechanism governing the construction of value in the cultural sphere. Besides, if open source code ensures the better development of both software and programmers' skills, the 'open source code' of artistic work does not work in the same direction, for the reasons mentioned above. If Wikipedia, in its role of encyclopedia, or Wictionary, an open dictionary, are useful for particular identifiable purposes, for instance, the pooling of actual information, it is impossible within their style of operation to identify a practical need to use, for instance, any particular 'artistic' video stills. When open content deviates from practicality and enters the realm of the symbolic, it meets inconsistencies.

[15] While philosophy of art has dedicated extensive thinking to this matter, it is probably worth referencing here a rather pragmatic approach by Pierre Bourdieu, in, for instance, The Rules of Art: Genesis and Structure of the Literary Field (Polity Press, 2005).

[16] Nicolas Malevé, 'Creative Commons in Context' in Miren Eraso et al., eds., The Mag.net Reader. Experiences in Electronic Publishing (Italy, Arteleku-Deputación Foral de Gipuzkoa, 2006), p. 64.

Let us consider the License Art Libre. LAL is a product of the group of French activists, Copyleft Attitude, trying to apply the General Public License to the artistic field. Nicolas Malevé explains:

> *The world of art (the dissemination of culture) was perceived as being entirely dominated by a mercantile logic, monopolies and the political impositions deriving from closed circles. Copyleft Attitude tried to seek out a reconciliation with an artistic practice which was not centered on the author, which encouraged participation over consumption, and which broke the mechanism of singularity that formed the basis of the processes of exclusion in the art world, by providing ways of encouraging dissemination, multiplication, etc. From there on, the LAL faithfully transposes the GPL: authors are invited to create free materials on which other authors are in turn invited to work, to recreate an artistic origin from which a genealogy can be opened up.*[16]

LAL is an excellent demonstration of the contradictions inherent in this discussion: while attempting to serve as a legal tool, adhering to principles of communal creation and open access to and modification of the source code, it at the same time makes one aware how difficult it is to frame cultural and artistic processes and products as 'source code' and to set up the 'shallow bugs' process.[17] The latter is particularly evident in the discussion of centeredness on 'authorship' (which often means 'ownership') cited above, which has to deal with the ups and downs of the history of subject and author in western cultures.

[17] The law 'Given enough eyeballs, all bugs are shallow' meaning 'enough beta-testing and co-developing will allow identify and fix most problems quickly' was formulated by Eric Raymond in an article mentioned above.

[18] Karl Marx, Comment on James Mill, Éléments D'économie Politique (written 1844), http://www.marxists.org/archive/marx/works/1844/jamesmill/index.html

[19] Matthew Fuller, Media Ecologies. Materialist energies in art and cultures (MIT Press, 2005).

Any serious discussion of 'free culture' turns out to be a discussion of the bottomless pool of questions, on the institutions and subjectivity, control and production experiments, on altering what artist and art means to force these spheres into the open and unknown; it departs from looking for the match for the category of source code in art and searches, as does Simon Yuill's text in this volume, for experiments with notation, improvisation, live performance, 'noise', contingent, collaborative and 'distributive practices' – all core politically informed and informing elements of contemporary production, to unfold the dimensions of the alternative at the borderlines of art, open source principles, code, and change.

Stemming from the history of thinking transcendence described above, Feuerbach and Hegel through the interpretation of Marx, are often the basis for contemporary leftist understanding of operations of freedom, control, and creation in the contemporary social and cultural settings. The conceptualisation of freedom through negation, as an absence of capitalist alienation via exploitation, which thus, can never be experienced while the capitalist order remains a constant is still a living tradition. Such a framework assumes the existence of the universal principles, be it Absolute Spirit, authentic consciousness or naturally given pleasure of life, able to serve as a legitimate foundation for everyone to build on. [18]

Marxists fix on capitalism as a system of exploitation, freedom is impossible while the mechanisms for deriving surplus value remain in place. It is an either/or system to be solved in a Hegelian fashion by a synthesis in a future transformation (revolution). As Matthew Fuller noted, Marxist dissatisfaction with prevailing society is only one among a history of inabilities to accept the given systems of relations and processes of individuation, among which feminist theory and studies of the oppressed can also be mentioned.[19] While generally ignoring patriarchy or colonisation, Marxists focus on mechanisms of capitalist domination that supposedly drain every area embraced of naturally given juices of life (freedom).

With the success of the *Empire* by Michael Hardt and Antonio Negri, and also with work of Maurizio Lazzarato and Tiziana Terranova, the Autonomist Marxist trend of analysis became widely accepted in the last decade. Originated in the Italian struggles of the '60s and '70s, current versions of Autonomist Marxism suggest critical accounts of contemporary forms of labour and exploitation and address not only creative industries but the entirety of creative labour, including FLOSS production.

Members of the Workers' Autonomy (Autonomia Operaia) movement, such as Antonio Negri, Paolo Virno, Mario Tronti and others at different stages of the development of their theory introduced the concept of the socialized worker, social labour power, immaterial labour or the social factory that describe facets of the same changed reality of labour character and class composition. Initially, Tronti in an essay 'La fabrica e la società', interpreting the potential of the working class as an agent of change of the capitalist system, suggested that the field of antagonism is transferred to a more socialised level, so that, to cite Tronti in a translation by Wright, 'the social relation becomes a moment of the relation of production'.[20] Moreover, the factory extends to the whole of the society that becomes a site of production, with capital extracting value from the entirety of social relations.

Wright suggests, that while today this analysis is assumed to be describing the process of the broadening of productive labour beyond the point of immediate production into the entirety of society and human life, none of these meanings 'were to be forthcoming' in Tronti's work of the 1960s.[21] However, the category was established and further enriched by multiple developments. The social factory as a category signifies a new understanding of labour power and the process of production. The figure of the socialized worker, and the mapping of social labour power represents a new working class no longer limited to a 'paid proletariat', which is controlled by capital through the entire span of life.[22] Terranova, for instance, brings attention to the fact that within the conceptual framework of 'immaterial labour' developed by Maurizio Lazzarato (as 'labour that produces the informational and cultural content of the commodity'), specific or classic class formation does not have a meaning.[23] Immaterial labour is not confined to the elite of skilled workers, but is applicable to describing any productive subject within postindustrial society.[24] Immaterial and

[20] Steve Wright, Storming Heaven: Class Composition and Struggle in Italian Autonomist Marxism (London, Pluto Press, 2002), p. 38.

[21] Ibid., pp. 40-41.

[22] Antonio Negri, Revolution Retrieved. Selected Writings on Marx, Keynes, Capitalist Crisis and New Social Subjects (London, Red Notes, 1998), p. 209.

[23] Paolo Virno and Michael Hardt, Radical Thought in Italy: A Potential Politics (Minneapolis, University of Minnesota Press, 1996), p. 133.

[24] Tiziana Terranova, 'Free Labor: Producing Culture for the Digital Economy' In Social Text, 63, Vol. 18, No. 2 (2000), http://www.btinternet.com/~t.terranova/freelab.html

[25] Paolo Virno, A Grammar of the Multitude (Semiotext(e), 2004), p. 64.

[26] Terranova, 2000.

[27] Ibid.

affective labour rooted in human communication and relationships serve as a source of surplus value in the new process of production. For Virno, 'thought becomes the primary source of the production of wealth'.[25] Contemporary production, thus, includes linguistic competence, knowledge, imagination, and social interaction as its core sources of surplus value.

It was just a matter of time before someone applied this analysis of labour-power and production to free and open source software production. Tiziana Terranova suggested an Autonomist analysis of FLOSS at the point when the movement was undergoing major conceptual (and economic) transformations. Terranova maintains that FLOSS production and, more broadly, cultural production on the internet, does not only always originate and occur within the capitalist system but also is functionally and economically central to its development. In a rare cultural critique of FLOSS, Terranova suggests that the 'gift economy' of networks represents an important element, a basis of the digital economy that is in turn an essential part of late capitalist economy at large. Terranova's central claim is that while internet cultural networks or FLOSS production depend on a vast amount of continuous work, most of which is 'free', it can only mean that such free labour is immanent and central to late capitalism, rendering the 'gift economy' merely an important economic tool.[26] Thus, there is no struggle with and no appropriation of an authentic moment, but a mutual constitution working towards an advancement towards more developed forms of capitalist production:

> *...there might be more productive ways of looking at the increasingly tight relationship between an 'idealistic' movement such as open source and the current venture mania for open source companies. Rather than representing a moment of incorporation of a previously authentic moment, the open source question is exemplary of the overreliance of the digital economy as such on free labour, both in the sense of not financially rewarded and willingly given. ...*
>
> *Late capitalism does not appropriate anything: it nurtures, exploits and exhausts its labour force and its cultural and affective production. ... Especially since 1994, the Internet is always and simultaneously a gift economy and an advanced capitalist economy'.*[27]

In her book published in 2004, *Network Culture: Politics for the Information Age* Terranova omits the detailed analysis of the open source movement as an avant-garde form of capitalist production she gave in her article, that is reworked and included into the book, but she still mentions that any utopia of autonomy equals a new method of late capitalist production.[28] Terranova uses the term 'free' in the sense of 'free beer' or free labour, as unpaid, not financially compensated labour and interconnects it with pleasure and desire (for affective labour).[29] Thus, that labour is 'free', not something imposed, but its meaning, for Terranova, does not have a nuance of processual freedom in the sense of 'liberation'.

Describing digital cultural production as a process, taking place always within a capitalist system of relationships, nurtured and exhausted within it, Terranova happens to build a picture of the passage of capitalism as a smooth, seamless, monolithic process. She mentions that it would be a mistake to take such coexistence for an unproblematic equivalence, though she does not develop this point further anywhere.[30] If there are no contradictions and ruptures, no potentials and struggles, no excess, no gaps, no 'liberation', 'emancipation' in 'free', then what kind of action and practice is possible today, and what the potential could be?

For Terranova, every field she focuses on becomes interpreted as a zone of experimentation for late capitalism. The digital economy is an experiment with production models and new kinds of value[31], network culture is a political experiment[32], and new forms of production and cooperation are experiments with new technologies of control.[33] Her analysis of these models amounts to a totalizing picture with no excess, no exit, except for a 'catastrophe'.

Despite the fact that Autonomist Marxism sees the changes within the capitalist system as an outcome of struggles, Terranova's work is demonstrative of the general dynamics of Marxist thinking as it adds up to the history of the impossibility of thinking multiplicities and conditionalities within a dialectical system of categories. 'Catastrophic' Nietzsche wrote about freedom as an affect, but these references do not provide routes out of Terranova's absolute capitalism. Somewhat reminiscent of Adorno's deadend of negative dialectics, such a method builds up sets of mutually exclusive and interlocked oppositions. It is a project (to paraphrase Jameson) to

[28] Tiziana Terranova, Network Culture: Politics for the Information Age (London, Pluto Press, 2004) 79, p. 84.

[29] Ibid., pp. 83-84, p. 91

[30] Ibid., p. 94.

[31] Ibid., p. 79.

[32] Ibid., p. 153.

[33] Ibid., p. 108.

desubjectify the analysis of labour and power while committing to prolong the traditional framework of Marxist understanding of capitalism as a 'totalitarian' system, which is the Grand Narrative by the Subject, and which thus can only move to collapse (for aesthetics, Adorno chooses the 'unsayable').[34]

[34] In a book on Adorno, Jameson suggested that the charge of Adorno's aesthetic theory is the tension between 'his formal project of desubjectifying the analysis of aesthetic phenomena' and 'his commitment … to prolong the traditional framework of philosophical aesthetics to the description of aesthetic experience: some last remnant of absolutely subjective categories …' Fredric Jameson, Late Marxism: Adorno and the Persistence of the Dialectic (Verso, London/New York, 2007), p. 123.

Whilst Marx envisaged the intensification of the proletariat's exploitation to the extent of its absolute impoverishment, that would advance its self-liberation through the revolution, Autonomist Marxists see the plane of production blown open to the whole of the society as a totality of subsumption (Terranova's subsumption as a pre-requisite of any action), which would intensify the domination and exploitation of the finest and most intimate human capacities, rendered productive forces (biopower for Virno), to its highest peak from where it would slide into the revolution. Again and again freedom is seen as an exclusive category, transcendent of any political, cultural, bodily, household reality that could only be achieved through the complete destruction of the existing order of production, ownership and valorization. Radical action, experiment, slow motion microchange, a moment of freaking out, a potential have no immanent presence in this plane of transcendent values.

Autonomist Marxism does not only provide tools for Terranova to suggest a cultural critique of open source software as a mere path for lucky advancement of digital economies of late capitalism, but also becomes a source to draw from in addressing network cultures, digital media art and creative production critically. Participatory and social platforms, network cultures become labeled as machines of exploitation and subsumption, deformation of freedom, communication and desire by approaches essentially Marxist, which see the social plane as a totality.

If for Marxist thinking the register of production that allows the surplus value to be extracted from communal efforts become conflated with the entirety of production and become an unconquerable proof of pre-subsumption, thus, the radical lack of freedom, for free software ideologists and for many hackers the construction of systems on open source software become the unconquerable proof of their freedom. In this re-conceptualisation of intellectual property, open source gets on one side of the barricades with peer-to-peer networks. So, if Autonomist Marxists focus on value and labour force, free software ideologies focus on what sometimes get rather erroneously termed just 'tools' and sometimes 'means of production'.[35]

For classical Marxism, means of production refer to tools and technologies and are a subset of productive forces, while the relationships of property, control and law, and the relations among people are united in relations of production. Software taken, it can hardly be referenced as a tool, for as its embedding of general intellect[36] and social relations at the least. Moreover, it seems that to understand what means of production would signify today means to include human capacity for thought and communication, brain cells and networks.[37] In this sense, comprising both, free software is more likely a mode of production, and has to be taken beyond its mere functionality or reference to ownership. In this manner, software conflates productive forces and relationships of production, building nets of human bodies invested in codes, waves and enquiries. It is a historical subset of modes of production operating in society, if we are to adhere to these categories, and in this sense Terranova's analysis is understandable in its attempt to conceptualise free software as key to a new kind of labour organisation and value production.

[35] See, for instance, a mail from Jaromil, on 22/01/2008, Subject: Re: [spectre] content vs. tools (was: Sharing is Sexy.org is live), to Spectre mailing list, http://www.mail-archive.com/spectre@mikrolisten.de/msg03340.html

[36] See Matthew Fuller, Softness: Interrogability; General Intellect; Art Methodologies in Software (Media Research Centre, Huddersfield, 2006).

[37] See the transcript of a lecture by McKenzie Wark and a following discussion in Piet Zwart Institute, http://pzwart.wdka.hro.nl/mdr/Seminars2/DesDocTrans/wark.html/

But maybe to return to the discussion at the beginning of the text, there is no need to adhere to these categories if new realities conflate base and superstructure, relations of production and productive forces, if these categories do not anymore provide mechanisms of access to the principles of organisation and core problems; if the 'organic totality' they build is thankfully not total. Maybe stepping outside of these modalities of analysis would allow for new actors to come on stage and to extend the closed circuits of Marxist nurturing-production-subsumption-extracting value or set-free – harvest-the-results of liberal free creative-work into more inspiring labyrinths.

Hence, whereas any complete and consistent system always contains within itself its own inconsistencies and incompleteness, grains of difference (a loose interpretation of Gödel theorems of incompleteness in relation to society and culture), bringing about ruptures and bursts within the seeming 'totality' of social relations of productions (here equals culture), the free software seems a more complex phenomenon than the mere 'means of production', 'tools' to build with, 'architecture' to work inside of, principles of openness to build 'free culture' on, or free pre-subsumed labour to extract value from.[38] It can be discovered on many layers, as social relations, self-organisation, creation, metaphor, fight, passion, enquiry, way of living, way of learning how to live, identity, way of speaking, hierarchy, techno-discrimination mechanism, interaction design pattern, and many more.

[38] This part builds on the lecture by Matthew Fuller at Art Oriented Programming 2, Symposium by Laboratoire des Arts et Medias [LAM], l'Université Paris 1 (Sorbonne), October 2007, which is in turn based on his article on code elegance in Matthew Fuller, ed., Software Studies: A Lexicon (MIT Press, forthcoming in 2008).

Finally departing from dichotomies and entering the multiple domains of operation of metaphors, symbols and concepts should help us imagine how free software can be played out and how it can be fed back into the society, how it can proceed in patterns operating in other registers, sometimes referred to as art and culture.

Such an operation would demand some mutation done to the principles constitutive of free software. As a reaction of expansion of the ideology of free software, they are neutralised in open source and moreover in 'free culture' having little to do with the starting incentives. If freedom has got to be rethought in software, culture and art, one should start not from adopting the principles of free or open source software production and distribution to culture but from energies and mutations that answer the current modes of domination.

A conceptual pair to address the scale and modes of operation of modelling power in a society is composed by the Foucauldian disciplinary society updated by the Deleuzian society of control. Foucault is a central figure in designing a concept of power that operates in modes that are non-hierarchical, not based on direct repression and not owned. For Foucault, power is manifested rather then possessed, it resides in networks of relationships, which are immanent to every scene, in which they are performed and which are constitutive for the scene itself. Power is not simply prohibitive or coercive; it plays a productive role, it is invested in, generated and reproduced by the very processes of education, everyday life, through institutional and disciplinary techniques of individuation.

Building bridges between Foucault and feminism Jana Sawicki notes that if power is not an objective force that can be possessed then the enquiry shifts from questioning the bodies of authority on the basis of their legitimacy, which means searching for certain authenticity (i.e. found in the proletariat) that might permit the exercise of power to thinking the subjectivities that are formed through power relationships.[39] If powers of resistance, for Foucault, are inbuilt and constitutive of the exercise of disciplinary power, then resistances should be site-specific, should be practiced on microlevels reinventing new forms of subjectivity. Relationships of resistance break the singularities into multiplicities, cause re-groupings, and change processes of individuation, trespassing upon various levels of apparatuses and institutions without being localised in any of them.[40]

Sawicki cites an interview with Foucault who maintains that power cannot possess the ability of capturing in an absolute trap; there is always an option of altering its passage. Moreover, 'power reveals itself only in relation towards free subjects, only if those are free'.[41] (Note, that these 'free subjects' are radically different from liberal free subjects and, certainly, from late Marxist unfree biopower). For Sawicki, it means, firstly, that power only happens in relation to resistance, and secondly, that those relationships of resistance are capable of altering the vectors of power saturation.

In a short text published in 1992, Deleuze departs from the Foucauldian disciplinary society to draft newer emerging paradigms of power operations within what he calls a control society. Whereas Foucault studied the roles of institutions in modeling subjectivation, Deleuze allows for a new concept to appear, to that of a 'free-floating' control, operating at miniscule levels. Testing this forthcoming kind of control against Foucault's disciplinary powers, Deleuze describes it through a metaphor of modulation whose nature is numerical (he states it does not necessarily mean binary) instead of 'molds' whose nature is analogical. To trace the metaphor Deleuze makes use of would mean to draw from telecommunications engineering, where modulation refers, roughly speaking, to a process of transfer of a nonstandard (free structure) signal through standard means (through a signal of clear structure). Modulation works both in analogue and digital technologies. In two main kinds of analog modulation methods, amplitude and frequency modulation, either the amplitude of a sinusoidal carrier wave is altered while it keeps the same frequency or a sinusoid is varied in frequency while the amplitude remains constant. In digital technologies, modulation relates to a conversion of data from analog to digital form (modulation and demodulation). Digital modulation, describing an analog signal

[39] Jana Sawicki, Foucault and Feminism, Politics of Difference [in Russian, Foucault i feminism: k politike razlichija] in Mary Lindon Shanley and Carole Patemon, eds., Feminist Interpretations and Political Theory (Polity Press, 1991) [in Russian, Feministskaja kritika i revisija istorii politicheskoj filosofii, Moskva, Rosspan, 2005] Russian edition, p. 301.

[40] Michel Foucault, Volia k istine. Po tu storonu znanija, vlasti i seksualnosti (Moskva, Magisterium - Kastal', 1996). In Russian, Michel Foucault, Power/Knowledge: Selected Interviews and Other Writings, 1972-1977 (Pantheon, 1980), pp. 191-195.

[41] Sawicki, ibid., p. 305.

through a digital bit stream, has its own techniques, but what is central here is not the differences between analog and digital modulation, but the principle of modulation as a fundamental principle applied to any signal. That is what allows Deleuzian control-as-modulation to be described as never finished, individually customised, atomised and, nevertheless, a 'universal system of deformation'.[42]

Now, what can be done with such an understanding of power and control, as horizontal, immanent, feeding on resistance, continuous, limitless and mutating, a 'self-deforming cast', acting as a principle, as a denominator, as individual 'codes'? Which, to return to *Postscript on the Societies of Control*, 'new weapons' or 'lines of flight', or sites and strategies of resistance can be made palpable, can be opened up and discovered as already put into practice by coders, artists, agents of cultural practices?

Tracking the mutual constitution of power and resistance, control as a prerequisite for freedom is a recurrent motive that Gayatri Chakravorty Spivak exemplifies with birth control as a basis of sexual freedom. Wendy Chun, referring to this example, writes about control in networks as a basis of their freedom, but also about freedom as something exceeding control.[43] For Tiziana Terranova, modern forms of control are more akin to setting up a system and letting it develop freely to either milk its results if they are desirable or abandon to self-annihilation if undesirable catastrophic mutations have taken place.[44] Control makes freedom possible, but also freedom, openness and self-evolution is the condition of control. Thus understood, control and freedom are interlocked in specific relationships, not to say dependencies, and diffused into each other. However, specific distribution of these forces and their processual change are unpredictable as well as found beyond mutual exclusion and exhaust. If we talk of FLOSS and proprietary software, we shall not forget to include the discussion of internet protocols, and hardware; and to capture these systems in terms of openness and closures would mean talking about combinations and dispersion rather than oppositions and concentration.

These modalities of freedom are best described through art, software art and practices that would not describe themselves through such figures but which share some essential vectors, attitudes, aesthetics, and principles. Fuller called it 'interrogability' in software, and talks about the proliferation of 'art methodologies' of which interrogability is one.[45] Such

[42] Gilles Deleuze, Postscript on the Societies of Control (Originally published in the journal October 59, Winter 1992, MIT Press, Cambridge, pp. 3-7), http://libcom.org/library/postscript-on-the-societies-of-control-gilles-deleuze

[43] Wendy Hui Kyong Chun, Control and Freedom. Power and Paranoia in the Age of Fiber Networks (The MIT Press, 2006) p. 272, pp. 290-291.

[44] See the section 'Soft Control' in Terranova, 2004.

[45] See Fuller, 2006.

occurring questionability that is a happening rather than a quality gives a key to various events and living objects. Such a concept provides a smooth path to the key argument of this text, the question of creativity.

In the recent years the concept of creativity (and, remember, freedom, as inseparable from it) gained an amount of attention and usage that made it acquire readings charged with opposing drives and affects and linked it to the discourses of changing labour organisation, neoliberal markets, new economies, life quality and self-realisation, child labour and ecological collapse, increasing inequality and subsumption, and many more.

Creativity is researched in the history of science, education, economic theory, aesthetics and many other domains, which are largely isolated in their attempts.[46] However, for now, we can roughly describe, traditionally two (for this text) camps of thinking on creativity: a neoliberal 'creative class' vector, which is rooted in economic and psychological analyses and leftist 'anti-creative' vector, focusing on either creativity as a source of surplus value and/or on the reliance of the creative individuals for their endeavours on the shipment of hard labour to Asia.[47]

Psychology and other cognitive sciences research individual mental processes, building models of creative process, analysing creative individuals, creative products and creative environments, focusing on creativity as production of something new and useful.[48] Such studies are applied in developing 'techniques of creativity' and in working out the organisational aspects that would allow for increasing number of employers to discover and apply their capacities for innovation.[49] In 'leftist' thinking, creativity is, first, something that was naturally given and alienated (in industrial society) or nurtured and subsumed (in information society), with the latter building on top of the former transferred to the poorer regions of the world.

While the fallacies of the liberal approach were critically addressed in the beginning of the text, the second camp as, not least, more sympathetic, deserves closer examination. For those having an experience of living under various kinds of totalitarian rule, such large critical gestures of pointing towards hard living conditions (including political, physical,

[46] Robert Sternberg, ed., Handbook of Creativity (Cambridge, Cambridge University Press, 1999).

[47] See, for instance, a mail from Brian Holmes, 'Subject: Year Zero Amsterdam Creative City', on 06/03/2008, to Nettime mailing list, http://www.nettime.org/Lists-Archives/nettime-l-0803/msg00009.html

[48] Keith Negus and Michael Pickering, Creativity, Communication, and Cultural Value (London, Sage, 2004); Mihaly Csikszentmihalyi, Creativity: Flow and the Psychology of Discovery and Invention (New York, Harper Collins, 1996); Dean Keith Simonton, Origins of Genius: Darwinian Perspectives on Creativity (New York, Oxford University Press, 1999).

[49] Raymond Nickerson, 'Enhancing Creativity' in Sternberg, 1999.

[50] Henri Bergson, Creative Evolution (Dover Publications, Mineola, New York, 1998), p. 250-251.

[51] Scott Lash, 'Life (Vitalism)' in Theory, Culture & Society, Vol. 23, No. 2-3, 2006, pp. 323-329.

[52] Alfred North Whitehead, Modes of Thought (The Free Press, New York, 1968), p. 46.

[53] Bergson, 1998, p. 237.

mental, etc) as a counterweight to 'privileged' life forms has little meaning. Nietzsche's creativity loudest by the side of tyranny, creativity as an affect; creating and memorizing poetry as a means of survival in a Stalinist camp; 'inner immigration' in the Soviet Union are all different faces and layers freedom/creativity is sensed and lived under conditions radically different from those experienced by the 'creative' class of the first world. A reference to a suffering unknown Chinese 'Other' does not help to understand what are the central problems in the concepts of creativity and freedom, and what can be done to understand a variety of contemporary practices in light of this problematic.

Creativity, though initially very different from the ones described above, most convincingly stems from the 'vitalist' philosophers, from Bergson to Deleuze, to name two. This route is also to be taken if we are to depart from dichotomies this text was arguing against for much of its length. To understand the radical multiplicity of flights we need to attend to the vitalist school.

While it is not my aim in this text to unfold the genesis of the vitalist ontologies, creativity as a general characteristic of life under various masks is present in all of them. Bergsonian impetus of life is found in a need of creation, and it struggles to introduce into matter the largest possible degree of freedom.[50] For Bergson, creation is becoming itself, not from possible, but from actual; it is unceasing life, experienced in action, a perpetual growth, vital current loaded with matter. To imagine such an ontology, redeveloped at a different level, for instance, by Deleuze, and to understand the roles assigned to creativity in it, one has to carry in mind that vitalism is not a humanist philosophy per se. As Lash notes, vitalists are interested in plants and animals, in non-human ecologies, unlike humanist branches of thinking, which counterpose a human being and non-human materiality.[51] For vitalists, understanding a human (or microbial colonies) means understanding the passage of nature[52]; and the core concepts to such endeavour are being-made (and not ready-made)[53], becoming (not being), continuous (indivisible), multiple, actual found in becoming (real becoming possible and not possible becoming real), exploding actuality which is immanent. Here, creative activity is the major characteristic of life, whatever diverging conceptualisations of it are provided by different vitalist philosophers.

For Bergson, as mentioned, creativity/invention is found in nature, as an instance in the variation on the routine. However, creation, which is a need of vital impetus, is confronted with matter. The movement of matter and the movement of life (creation, vital impetus) are opposite.[54] 'The vital impetus is neither pure unity nor pure multiplicity', it is the matter the vital impetus communicates itself that chooses. The movement of life is opposite to the movement of matter, and it creates a vortex, a flexion; it is where it moves freely carrying the weight of obstacles that do not terminate it and it is where there is humanity.[55] In humans, creation becomes an instrument of freedom, a triumph of the machine over mechanism (organism as a machine for action that rebuilds itself for every new act).[56] Life, vital impetus is an 'immensity of potentiality', and those manifold tendencies are individuated, actualized in matter, therefore created by the potentialities.

[54] Ibid., p. 251.

[55] Ibid., p. 269.

[56] Ibid., p. 252 and p. 264.

[57] Isabelle Stengers and Ilya Prigogine, Order Out of Chaos: Man's New Dialogue with Nature (Flamingo, London, 1985), pp. 93-96

[58] Whitehead, 1968, p. 151

[59] Ibid., p. 151

While Bergson is seen as one of the first philosophers to protest against 'noumenal' thinking and positivism as well as classical physics to find a way to disregarded questions, such as of duration and time, Whitehead is one of the first to construct a system that would bridge the gap between science and philosophy, building a new philosophy of nature. For Whitehead, two centuries of failures of science and philosophy to communicate and appreciate each other, were over with new discoveries in physics and biology, which allowed to understand human experience as physical existence, as a process belonging to nature with its constant reconciliation of permanence and change.[57]

> *For Whitehead, process, activity and change are the matter that has no instants, no primary entities, but where the essence is the transition itself, the realisation in the 'creative advance'. Creative advance, to cite Whitehead, lies in discriminating the actualised data presented by the antecedent world, the non-actualised potentialities which lie ready to promote their fusion into a new unity of experience, and the immediacy of self-enjoyment which belongs to the creative fusion of those data with those potentialities.* [58]

The doctrine of the creative advance of the evolving universe implies that creative activity is found in the very essence of each occasion of experience.[59] Nonetheless important for us is that for such a constant transition of a 'community of the actualities' of the world, every emerging

[60] Ibid., p. 146, p. 164

[61] Stengers and Prigogine, 1985, p. 175

[62] Manuel DeLanda, Intensive Science and Virtual Philosophy (Continuum, London, New-York, 2005), pp. 9-26

[63] Gilles Deleuze and Felix Guattari, Kafka: Toward a Minor Literature (Theory and History of Literature, Volume 30, University of Minnesota Press, Minneapolis, London, 1994), p. 7, p. 10.

[64] Such wording can be found throughout ibid., for instance, p. 26, p. 36

factor makes a difference in the nature of every other happening.[60] Whitehead laid the ground for an understanding of human experience in terms of self-organising processes in complex systems existing in conditions far-from-equilibrium as well as the entire biosphere.[61] Deleuze was the one to radically continue such an enterprise.

Manuel DeLanda introduces his book on Deleuze by characterizing the project of Deleuze as striving to get rid of, to put it mildly, certain philosophical habits and routines, in particular, by replacing the concept of an 'essence' with the one of 'multiplicities', from which a major change follows. To replace an essence with a multiplicity means to get rid of 'unified and timeless identity', 'eternal archetypes' and 'external forms', of opposition, category, resemblance, direct causation, hierarchy and many more, and to start building a different, 'realist' ontology and epistemology.[62] Certainly, no index in the back of books by Deleuze or Deleuze/Guattari would list 'creativity' or 'freedom', but there are concepts developed/problems addressed in his/their work that are sources to draw from when discussing creativity (and freedom). For Deleuzian ontology, 'creative' or 'free', with traditions of their own described in the beginning of this text, savour too much of categorial sense, and are too eager to get locked into oppositions with uncreative and non-free. However, if 'freedom' is replaced with finding a route out (as Kafka states and Deleuze/Guattari take on in their book on Kafka: 'the problem is not in liberty but of escape'), these lines of escape are being found in becoming-animal, undergoing metamorphosis, body without organs, deterritorialising, decoding, intensifying, creating and taking lines of flight, counter-actualising, and undeciding, not to conclude the ever-growing list.[63]

For Deleuze (and his coauthor) an escape from an actualised assemblage, territorialised functions and forces, from lines of segmentarity and stratification, from forms done, from denumerable sets, from axiomatics is not only possible, but always happening, and is constitutive for segmentary structures; these 'creative lines of escape' are what interests Deleuze and his coauthor in much of their writing.[64] Minor literature, producing a continuum of intensities in a nonparallel and asymmetrical manner, involution, dismantling machinic assemblages, always going farther in the movement, symbiosis, and non-equilibrium are among many happenings that are called to help grasp what it is to think multiplicities, critical transitions and their trajectories.[65] To give one example of this story that never terminates, let me cite the finale of the '7000 B.C.: Apparatus of Capture' plateau out of *A Thousand Plateaus:*

> *At the same time as capitalism is effectuated in the denumerable sets serving as its models, it necessarily continues non-denumerable sets that cut across and disrupt those models. Coexistence and inseparability of that which the system conjugates, and that which never ceases to escape it following lines of flight that are themselves connectable. The undecidable is the germ and locus par excellence of revolutionary decisions. Every struggle is a function of all of these undecidable propositions and constructs revolutionary connections in opposition to the conjugations of the axiomatic.*[66]

[65] Ibid., p. 13, p. 48

[66] Gilles Deleuze and Felix Guattari, A Thousand Plateaus. Capitalism and Schizophrenia (Continuum, London, New-York, 2004), p. 522

[67] DeLanda, 2005, pp. 174-175

A few issues following from the above are core to rolling this text further. First of all, for Deleuze as well for all vitalists, self-organisation is core to materiality. If re-problematised matter under non-linearity is not passive and exercises its own powers, it is capable of behaving in new ways, of self-assembly.[67] Self-organisation (via collaboration) in arts or in software production is widely discussed these days; linked into it is a discussion of a new type of an institution, site-specific and processual, which is always a discussion of power, desire and authorship. Intensiveness of various 'catalytic agents' (Whitehead) that divert the flow of energy are key to understanding such operations of art and culture.

What I would like to do now is to re-read the concepts of creativity and autonomy (and self-organisation, collective, 'amateur' production, linked into those), all three widely discussed with polar opposite estimations, to demonstrate which other routes can be drawn to re-create, reclaim them and adjust for grasping current pathways of culture, society and art, FLOSS is a component of. Such an attempt is rooted in a need to add a level of abstraction and conceptualise numerous practices, current and recent, which do not subsume to the feeling of powerlessness and directly practice the difference, however difficult it might be to provide a non-utopian and non-nihilist account of themselves.

Attempted throughout the entire text, this endeavour is based on an understanding of 'molecular' control and multimodalities of resistances to it and routes out, which suggests that the same routes can simultaneously function as modeling trajectories and vectors of leakages, passages of excess and 'lines of flight'. Creativity, openness, inclusion, flexibility, self-organisation, collaboration all need to be made more thick, chaotic, 'dirty', and conflicting.

Since all these concepts are interconnected, we can pick up any to approach the other ones.

Self-organisation is a line of change, of intensification, that allows accumulation and metamorphosis, to use the Deleuzian lexicon, or creation of an environment, of a 'site' where certain tendencies, work, desires are connected to acquire a new dimension, a different 'nature', to mutate. Assembling such a milieu or a trajectory is based on creative action, much in a vitalist sense, on creativity as an impetus, flux, action, symbiotic and multiplying, changing the horizon of what is possible. Self-organisation deals with superfluous creative powers that splash out of the stratified.

At this point self-organisation links to grass-roots, DIY, amateur, folklore, vernacular, silly, bedroom production. Self-provision and self-dependency, (geek) craftsmanship – these powers and desires feed self-organisation. Amateur creation is always linked to collective production and as such is always a political action.

Such creativity is superfluous and abundant and cannot be 'subsumed', but defines the state of the system. Such creativity is machinic, self-evolving, dissimilar and heterogenic. Self-organisation grows from such powerful and excessive creativity; it acts through accumulation and mutation, and is rooted in openness and inclusion.

Self-organisation is necessarily open and flexible, as it is a state of non-equilibrium. Qualitative differences, mechanisms of mutation, symbiotic, and found always in transition are central to its logic: these mechanisms can lead to its homogenisation and stabilisation, to increased randomness, to other transitions. Self-organisation, like turbulence, is not chaotic. Self-organisation occurs when a catalytic effect takes place.

As a 'self-valorising, self-empowering, self-historicising social and productive force', self-organisation (collaboration, exchange, opposition, emancipation are its bullet points) is one of the concepts to think free software / culture on a more abstract level without losing its coherence.[68]

[68] Anthony Davies, Stephan Dillemuth and Jakob Jakobsen, 'There is no Alternative: The Future is Self-Organised. Part 1' in Nina Möntmann, ed., Art and its Institutions Current Conflicts, Critique and Collaborations (Black Dog Publishing, 2006).

Through the autonomy and dynamism of self-organisation we can also approach creativity; possibly, this could in part be done through the concept of autocreativity; as autonomous, autopoetic, automatic, and self-organising creativity.

Autocreativity is an action that is impossible to localize or subjectify. In digital networks, it is a dynamic process occurring in the relationship between network systems, technology and human beings; autocreativity appears as an explosion within a particular combination of forces. This self-unfolding creativity is not entirely dependent on people, on grassroots or 'official' institutions causing it to happen or on technologies that resonate in the right special way with humans' efforts.

[69] Rosi Braidotti uses this Lacan's formulation in her lecture 'Rosi Braidotti, A transcript of a lecture' (2003); REK IAK/IBK 09/03: Rosi Braidotti en Matthew Fuller, met Stefan Decostere. Posted at Cargoweb forum, http://www.cargoweb.org/forum/viewtopic.php?t=128 128

[70] Virno, 2004, p. 84.

Autocreativity is a micro catastrophe, setting up a myriad of spaces of possibility rather than, like Terranova's, annihilating. It is a process, an explosion creating the valuable, creating, like love, something that we do not possess and giving it to someone who does not need it.[69] This absence of need for it and inability to assume possession of it means this autocreative explosion is essentially excessive. The catastrophe, excess spreads out an extra space, a dimension where construction of value is enabled within a different logic. Autocreativity gets systematized but it happens as an explosion, as an excessive event that cannot be pre-subsumed, a force that establishes a possibility of difference. Autocreativity provides for inventiveness, intuition, open creation, self-organisation. In this explosion, the dynamics of the unfolding of an excessive, additional space is the basis of autonomy.

It certainly does not mean that every user is creative and autonomous or every creative act or project is 'free'. Autocreativity cannot be pinpointed and located in human beings, objects, projects or machines, it is found in their interrelationships, in-between. Autocreativity is dynamic; it is an explosive process that cannot be frozen. It is a potential that can be realised into moments of autonomy.

The potential of autocreativity is not simply located on the biological level, as a potential of labour-power, inseparable from a living body, a potential that acquired a status of a commodity.[70] The potential of autocreativity is distributed within technical systems, human beings, the fields of culture and of society. This potential cannot be exhausted. Moreover, autocreativity functions as a catalyst, intensifying processes,

[71] See, for instance, Merijn Oudenampsen, 'Back to the Future of the Creative City: An Archeological Approach to Amsterdam's Creative Development' in Geert Lovink and Ned Rossiter, eds., MyCreativity Reader. A Critique of Creative Industries (Institute of Network Cultures, Amsterdam, 2007).

accumulating the potential. The freedom of autocreativity means its superfluity, its existence in ruptures, in events, in intensification, in uncontrolled catastrophes.

The catastrophes of autocreativity, the autonomy of self-organisation produced by such catastrophes may be realised in the creation of alternative hierarchies, meanings, discourses, assemblages. By means of autocreativity, these self-unfolding self-directed practices exist within additional, excessive contexts, new dimensions built on principles that are autonomous or dislocated from that of the dominating monetary, gender, symbolic, and other orders. Such attempts are sets of elements, contexts, manifestations of creativity which are self-unfolding actions, functions and models, which besides enclosures and usages provide some possibilities of revolutions at the level of the self, of context, of the social, of aesthetics – provide a space of the construction of different value. Such circulation, simultaneity, multiplicity are the right context for understanding the potential for another cultures and societies which are both impossible and existent.

When typing out such a reading of autocreativity, hands reach out to type the inverted commas to frame the word with, so much 'annoying' content 'creativity' is usually loaded with. There are excellent critiques of neoliberal, post-Keynesian 'creativity', as translating areas of human life previously considered thoroughly personal, communal, intimate into the sphere of economic transactions.[71] Creative class, creative cities, creative industries are all actualisations of new economic and political orders, social layouts, mechanisms of subjectivation. However, these do not construct a mechanistic totality, explainable through a clear set of laws, like the universe in the times of classical physics.

For Autonomist Marxist theory 'creativity' is an engine of 'total subsumption'. As explained above, creativity as a free dynamic act is seen as a force of the multiplying and changing life itself, immanent, free and lasting, and as such is milked by late capitalism. Psychological theories and trainings of creativity, programs of development and 'creative labour' organisation stratify and territorialise, commodify 'creative impetus' immanent to most individuals and non-human forms of life. The expansion and mutation of modes of production is conceived to devour all living energies in order to transform them into denominated flows feeding capitalism. Though such poetic pictures fit apocalyptic ecological prospects well, there are unknown or unpredictable factors or behaviours to influence the balance of complex systems, as well as the mode of production is not the only way to explain the genesis of social formations to those discontented with a rich variety of injustices and horrors of our societies (for Deleuze/ Guattari, it's machinic processes that modes of production depend on).[72]

[72] Gilles Deleuze and Felix Guattari, A Thousand Plateaus. Capitalism and Schizophrenia (Continuum, London, New-York, 2004), p. 480

The question remains of pathways to imagine certain diversions, change and difference. It might possibly be the excess and exit points at the same time, as with creativity. Capitalism today as a system (in theories) of total 'real subsumption', is grasped as stretched beyond nature. Capitalism for today's leftist theory is vitalist itself, as micro- and macroscopic, fluid, affective, inconsistent, but also seamless, with no gaps and ruptures, with no chance. Within Marxist tradition, the development of capitalism is traditionally aimed at stretching to completely exhaust human potential and control bodily remaining (as with Adorno/Horkheimer's concept of the culture industry); however, it always turns out there is more and more to exhaust and control. However creative, 'self-organised', and effective capitalist channeling becomes, every factor is able to influence and misbalance the system of effects, and the leakages of the system are its central characteristic.

Perhaps the course of this text might seem to have digressed from its topic, free software and art. But free software, as mentioned, is not simply a set of objects or an organisation of production. Free and open source software provide not only means of thinking and speaking about software publicly, as Matthew Fuller once mentioned, but it also provides ways of access to a set of, on the one hand, ever-bothering and, on the other hand, newly assembled combinations of questions, such as: what is freedom, what is 'open society', how can 'free culture' work and how is a human constituted to function in these systems? Free software destabilised existing definitions of property and threatened certain forms of wealth because it touched upon the transformation of agents involved in the constitution of relationships, subjectivities, and experiences linked into the sphere of production and maintenance of the society. Free software is not a metaphor in this text used to talk about a different set of problems, but a leap onto the grain problematic of today, the core struggles and weapons. Here what comes on stage is the question how freedom, autonomy, openness operate at different layers? What are moments, strategies, bursts of autonomy, what are the layers at which these catastrophes of autocreativity, the struggles can unfold some dimensions of difference? If human potential is essentially excessive, what are the vectors at which we can find possibilities of emancipatory action?

Hierarchical, direct and repressive forms of power are not undone today, but complemented by horizontal, everyday refusal and deprivation. Free software is usually described to work at an architectural level, while it generates rich questions at other layers, modes, affects, and actions. And what we witness is not a revolution and restoration, but a dynamic open change, affecting the ecology it is born within.

Acknowledgements

I would like to thank Matthew Fuller for feedback on various versions of this text and Aristarkh Chernyshev for excursions into physics and mathematics.

# Who Done It? Ethico-Aesthetics, the Production of Subjectivity and Attribution

Sher Doruff

## art: Situating Ethico-Aesthetics

> *To tend the stretch of expression, to foster and inflect it rather than trying to own it, is to enter the stream, contributing to its probings: this is co-creative, an aesthetic endeavour. It is also an ethical endeavour, since it is to ally oneself with change: for an ethics of emergence.*
> *– Massumi, 2002, xxii*

> *We are faced with an important ethical choice: either we objectify, reify, 'scientifise' subjectivity, or, on the contrary, we try to grasp it in the dimension of its processual creativity.*
> *– Guattari, 1995, p. 13*

1. To enter a streaming stretch of expression, such as a shapeshifting expanse of collective code, to nourish and inflect it through the differential dynamics of participation, foregoing authorship as ownership, is to enter an ethico-aesthetic practice. It is to enter a processual field as a force, as a modulator. One clear example of the transversal tendencies of an ethics of emergence is in the movement(s) of open source collaboration; specifically and importantly, in FLOSS+art praxis.

2. Transversality, which can be described as a processual subject's movement through and beyond an existential domain through mobility, creativity and self-engendering (Genosko, 2002), is a concept articulated in the work of Felix Guattari. Transversality accentuates the interplay of three ecologies – environment, social relations and the production of subjectivity – from which an ethico-aesthetics emerges. In the FLOSS+art context, these Guattarian ecologies correspond to the network environment – on and offline, relational dynamics/affective tonalities and processes of individuation respectively. Transductive forces between these

vibrant relational fields induces a resonance that generates a felt dynamic in the artistic encounter.

3. The 'production of subjectivity' or the ontogenesis of the subject, is a continual process of becoming. It disrupts an existential 'I' and moves beyond the static grid-positioning of identity politics; leaps the liberal humanist pretext of absolute/sovereign freedom for the self-affirming production of autonomy. As Brian Holmes has clarified in an earlier Mute article:

> *Guattari tried to understand how people can displace their embodied routines, their existential territories, by transiting through a machinic assemblage capable of producing collective enunciations. (2006)*

Guattari's project, mapping an ethico-aesthetic paradigm, mutates and radically 'opens' Francesco Varela's earlier (re)formulations of cellular autopoiesis[1]. Guattari offers a refreshed notion of autopoietic, self-referencing, self-organizing systems:

> *Autopoiesis deserves to be rethought in terms of evolutionary, collective entities, which maintain diverse types of relations of alterity, rather than being implacably closed in on themselves. In such a case institutions and technical machines appear to be allopoietic, but when one considers them in the context of machinic Assemblages they constitute with human beings, they become ipso facto autopoietic.' (Guattari, 1995, pp. 39-40).*

Guattari's ethico-aesthetic is a *chaosmos*, a compositional chaos, an 'open', autopoietic, metastable system.

4. In an ethico-aesthetic paradigm, artists produce *toolkits* comprised of 'concepts, percepts and affects' for diverse publics' (Ibid, p. 129). Artistic production has no monopoly on the creative, but it can provoke the unpredictable through processes of creation pushed to mutational extremes. For FLOSS artists, this transversal movement – the affirmation of affective modulations between social, technical and political ecologies is akin to what Varela has called *ethical know-how*, an immanent expertise whose only requirement is 'full participation

[1] With Humberto Maturana, Varela helped define autopoiesis in second wave cybernetics: An autopoietic system is a system organized (defined as a unity) as a network of processes of production (transformation and destruction) of components that produces the components At this time, the components have the following characters: (i) through their interactions and transformations continuously they regenerate and realize the network of processes (relations) that produced them; and (ii) they constitute it (the system) as a concrete unity in the space in which they (the components) exist by specifying the topological domain of its realization as such a network.' (Varela, 1979)

in a community' (1992, p. 24). This commitment is evident in the toolkit approach to creative production that FLOSS artists have fostered.

5. Guattari dramatically appeals to creativity as the means of extending homeostatic, closed self-referential systems to becoming-open, novel and imaginative. This appeal correlates with the shared tools produced by artists that enable transductive experiments in transversal networks. A transductive, ontogenetic process as outlined by Gilbert Simondon, temporally restructures disparate forces, energies, across an interface that resolves and integrates 'information' while the original terms remain part of the new network. Integration in a transductive sense isn't homogeneous but multiplicitous, differential. Guattari again:

> *The future of contemporary subjectivity is not to live indefinitely under the regime of selfwithdrawal, of mass mediatic infantilisation, of ignorance of difference and alterity [...] Beyond material and political demands, what emerges is an aspiration for individual and collective reappropriation of the production of subjectivity. (1995, p. 133)*

6. Fast-forwarding from the 'mass mediatic infantilisation' of the late 20C propagation of the spectacle, an evaluation of contemporary creative toolkits in the manner of Web 2.0 social networking surely casts an eyebrow-raising shadow of runaway capital on the toolkit format and clearly demonstrates the lucrative allure of distributed affectivity. Yet the raison d'etre for socially invigorated technical tools that enable individuating regimes of power through the production of subjectivity is clear. It is in and through the ethico-aesthetic of collective individuation that the complex polyrhythms of transversality and the affective relations between FLOSS and art resonate. The creative event supersedes a mere development process; it is the emerging force of emergence.

7. If individuating systems with emergent potential are autonomous, how might they belong together, co-operate? Within these networks, the relational glue is ontogenetic and autonomous. Referencing the positive and negative feedback mechanisms that both sustain life and generate change in autopoietic biological systems, one can imagine similar negotiations in human-machine networks; the transductive phase-shifts between homeostatic sustainability and mutational difference. One can comfortably situate within the ethicoaesthetic paradigm the implicit understanding that 'situating' is not positioning, that it is dynamic and self-varying – non-rigidifying a passing through.

[2]
The quasi-cause according to Deleuze, haunts its effect: [...] it maintains with the effect an immanent relation which turns the product, the moment that it is produced, into something productive. (p. 95)

8. The initial conditions of 'free' and 'open' that generated an arguably unapologetically ideological movement in software production in the 1980's are in themselves quasi-causes[2], elusive, non-definitive fields of potential that actualize variant systems through coding, recoding and overcoding. These virtual-yet-real quasi-causes imbue enough expressive force to rouse and challenge a sector of artists that meld the instrumental with the performative and the political; function with affect. To use a popular Spinozan soundbite: FLOSS ecologies effectively 'affect and are affected by.' They exact the ethical know-how of participatory engagement with the unstable dynamics of change.

## Another Part: Situating the Detournement Remix and Share Alike

36. Ok. Situating FLOSS+art as an ethico-aesthetic practice is all well and good. It syncs with the Guattarian profile. But beyond the trendy ontological hype, beyond the theoretical cheerleading, what are the realities of the genre? Is the production of subjectivity a true collective enunciation in a FLOSS ecology? Are collaborative skills evolving? How is the recognition of effort, expertise and sharing acknowledged in peer-to-peer economies and how has the politics of collaborative arts-related authorship changed with FLOSS and Creative Commons communities?

28. Drifting through an urban landscape, guided by the shifting rhythms of random and selective attraction and disoriented provocation is a well-known subversive aesthetic of everyday life - the *dérive.* It was one mode of artistic practice catalyzed by artist/activist groups in France, Belgium and The Netherlands in the 1950's. They merged to become the Situationist International (SI) in 1957, contentiously disbanding in 1972. Their diagrammatic mesh of theory and practice, through the *dérive, détournement,* written word and political activism, remains viable today. The *dérive* for example, like the mathematical derivative (the rate of change in a function with respect to one of its variables), inflects a relational differential, an a-signifying affectivity as aesthetic production.

29. Guy Debord, a key contributor to the Paris faction of the SI speculated on a now infamous social paradigm – the spectacle – the self-generating image of capital at an extreme degree of accumulation. Ultimately, the spectacle feeds on itself, consuming its antidote, all protest, all critique, to adapt mutate and thrive. (An altogether inglorious example of open autopoiesis). The playful expression, advocated by the SI,

attempts to trump the representational content of the spectacle, the image of the image. This may be accomplished through the détournement, a diversionary appropriation of one aesthetic for another more playful and subversive one. The Situationists conceived a double-sided aesthetic event in the *détournement.* On one side: the devalued meaning of an appropriated cultural object or concept. On the other: the reorganization of that devalued material to create a new aesthetic genre; to re-appropriate something 'aesthetic' to differentiate, to remix. *Détournement* is a processual method, a tool. In the words of the SI:

> Détournement *is thus first of all a negation of the value of the previous organization of expression. It arises and grows increasingly stronger in the historical period of the decomposition of artistic expression. But at the same time, the attempts to reuse the 'detournable bloc' as material for other ensembles express the search for a vaster construction, a new genre of creation at a higher level. (SI, 1959)*

Seen as a 'negation' rather than a modification, the *détournement* is reflective of its political epoch. Yet as a means of affective modulation, it prefigures contemporary remix culture, FLOSS sensibilities, and ethical know-how.

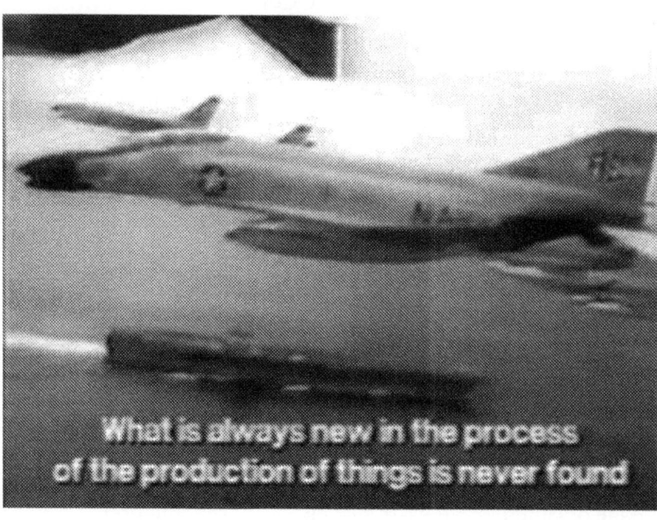

[3]
In: In Girum Imus Nocte et Consumir Igni – The Situationist International (1957-1972), Stephan Zweifel, Juri Steiner and Heinz Stahlhut for Musuem Tinguely and Centraal Museum, JRP/Ringier press, 2007.

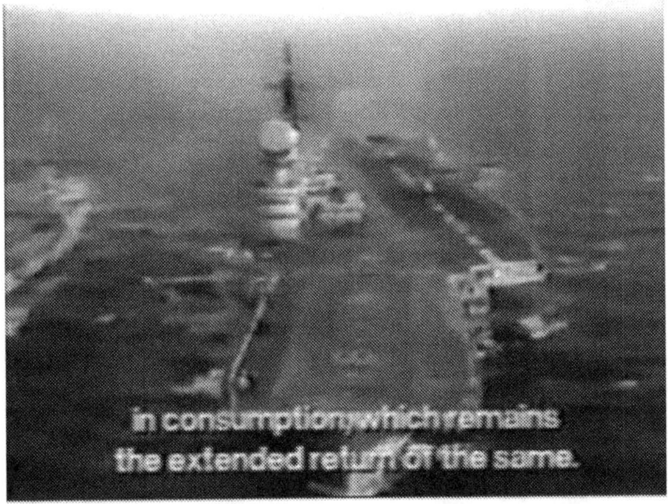


22. FLOSS tendencies, the sharing and distributing of open code, content and resources, makes sense. This type of collaborative co-creation challenges the degrees of difference between authorship and ownership, as have others...

23. The subjectivity produced in the collective enunciation of an Open Source framework where functional code is shared and distributed is not peculiar to digital practice. An interesting historical case-in-point proffered here is from the Situationist Internationale. It exemplifies a complex ethico-aesthetic expressed in the following quote, which directly reflects issues of attribution, ownership and remix/share alike from a pre-digital era:

> *The meaning of a text on unitary urbanism, written by Debord and published by a gallery in Essen on January 9, 1960, turned out to be greatly altered by several editorial cuts. Is it really necessary to remind everyone that when we declare ourselves uninterested in any notion of private property when it comes to ideas or phrases, it means that we let absolutely anyone publish part or all of such and such a Situationist writing without any reference or even attribution, as long as our signatures are not included? It is completely unacceptable for our publications to be reworked – unless it is done by the SI as a whole – and still be presented as the responsibility of their authors. Our signatures should be removed after the smallest modification.*
>
> *–trans. Reuben Keehan, Internationale situationniste, no. 4, June 1960.*[3]

24. Working out how the above proto-licensing statement from Debord and the SI in 1960 might comply with contemporary Creative Commons categorizations of distributed sharing, remixing and the tweaking of creative stuff is not so straightforward. There seems to be no current, equivalent CC license for the SI point of view regarding attribution and its derivatives. One the one hand the SI is saying that if their work is attributed to individuals in the collective it must NOT be edited or partially extracted (de-contextualized) in any way. Clear enough. It's similar to a standard:

Attribution No Derivatives (by-nd) Creative Commons licence. That the SI agreed to 'let absolutely anyone publish part or all of such and such a Situationist writing without any reference or even attribution...' confounds the non-commercial aspect of their would-be CC licensing strategy. Therefore the addition of the

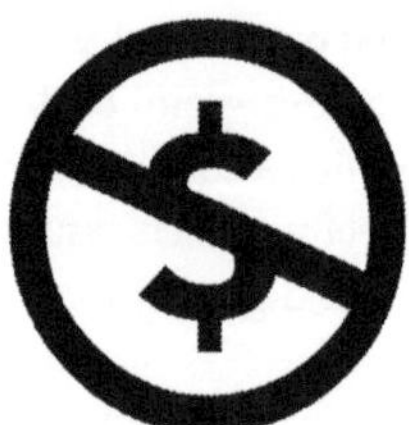

non-commercial (nc) clause is highly speculative and provocative. Nonetheless, as the material is freely and openly distributed then, if remixed or tweaked, in keeping with the détournement ethico-aesthetic, it must NOT be attributed. It is interesting that current Creative Commons licensing does not allow for this sentiment. Such a CC license icon might look like this:

[4] The non-attribution icon in this example is 'hypothetically' posited. For a full description of the CC License possibilities see: http://creativecommons.org/about/licenses/meet-thelicenses

Either: Attribution, No Derivatives

Or: Non-Attribution, Share Alike [4]

Insert the

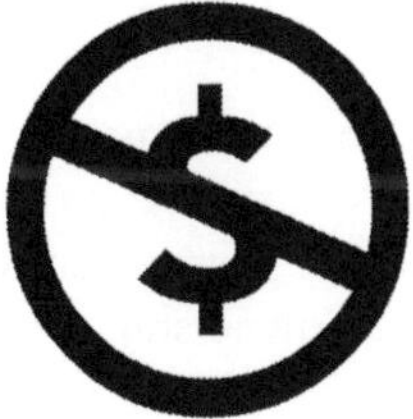

(nc) Non-Commercial clause if appropriate. In other words, it's free and open content but if you change the work it's no longer the 'responsibility' of the original author(s) in which case the author's name or 'signature' should not be identified with the material.

25. This begs interesting questions. A slew of questions:

Has the proto-ethico-aesthetic of the Situationists been *détourned* by the FLOSS and CC movements of 21C? Is there a substantive shift in ethical aesthetics in that seeking attribution for collaborative effort, now takes, indeed demands, taking responsibility for that effort? Is this an ethical quantum leap or the sleight-of-hand of ownership hoarding in an economy of recognition? That the SI distanced itself from 'the smallest modification' of the original that jeopardized a perceived integrity of identity itself bodes a strong hold on ownership in terms of reputation. So to problematize: Is then 'reputation' the juggernaut or the liberation of an ethico-aesthetic? Is responsibility-linked reputation hyperidentity-driven (think of the new wave of celebrity philanthropy) or does it allow the production of subjectivity á la Guattari to flow freely?

44. And more questions: Ethically, when should the work of the SI appear un-attributed due to 'the smallest modification' as per their request? Looking to the language of the Creative Commons as a guide, one wonders what constitutes a 'remix' and a 'tweak'? Remixing and tweaking, as verbs, are more easily construed in a processual aesthetic than the thingyness of remixed and tweaked artefacts-cum-products. Do quotation marks alone protect the integrity of a decontextualized phrase? Do citations grabbed from longer texts and inserted in new texts such as this one constitute remixes? Arguably, might not all creative production be classified a remix: stream of past in future, of sensation with memory, of knowledge with process? Guattari nearly answers this:

> *[...] the work of art, for those who use it, is an activity of unframing, of rupturing sense, of baroque proliferation or extreme impoverishment, which leads to a recreation and a reinvention of the subject itself. (1995, p. 131)*

As that recreation and reinvention is movement itself, a process of individual and collective subjectivity, it synergizes with OS practice and distributed information networks of the peer-to-peer variety which neutralize authorship and 'eviscerate' ownership, which has no landing site in the processual. However...

45. to eviscerate: to disembowel, to expose a body without organs, a field of intensive flows, zones of production, which ironically, proliferate an apparently irrepressible capitalism.

References

Gilles Deleuze, The Logic of Sense , trans. Mark Lester, London, Athlone press. First French edition published in 1969. Reprint Continuum 2004.

Gary Genosko, Felix Guattari: An Aberrant Introduction, London, Continuum, 2002.

Felix Guattari, Chaosmosis: an ethico-aesthetic paradigm , trans. Paul Bains and Julian Pefanis, Bloomington, Indiana University Press, 1995.

Brian Holmes, 'Coded Utopia' Mute, January 2006.

Brian Massumi, 'Introduction: Like a Thought' in: A Shock to Thought , Brian Massumi ed, London, Routledge, 2002.

Gilbert Simondon, 'The Genesis of the Individual' in: Incorporations , eds., Jonathon Crary and Sanford Kwinter; trans. M. Cohen and S. Kwinter, pp. 296-319, 1992.

Situationist International, 'Détournement as Negation and Prelude', 1959, http://library.nothingness.org/articles/SI/en/display/315

Francisco Varela, Principles of Biological Autonomy, Elsevier, 1979.

Francisco Varela, Ethical Know-How: Action, Wisdom and Cognition, Stanford, Stanford University Press, 1992.

# The Creative Common Misunderstanding

Florian Cramer

Lately, the growing popularity of the Creative Commons licenses has been accompanied by a growing amount of criticism. The objections are substantial and boil down to the following points: that the Creative Commons licenses are fragmented, do not define a common minimum standard of freedoms and rights granted to users or even fail to meet the criteria of free licenses altogether, and that unlike the Free Software and Open Source movements, they follow a philosophy of reserving rights of copyright owners rather than granting them to audiences. Yet it would be too simple to only blame the Creative Commons organization for those issues. Having failed to set their own agenda and competently voice what they want, artists, critics and activists have their own share in the mess.

In his paper 'Towards a Standard of Freedom: Creative Commons and the Free Software Movement', free software activist Benjamin Mako Hill analyzes that

> *despite CC's stated desire to learn from and build upon the example of the free software movement, CC sets no defined limits and promises no freedoms, no rights, and no fixed qualities. Free software's success is built upon an ethical position. CC sets no such standard.*[1]

In other words, the Creative Commons licenses lack an underlying ethical code, political constitution or philosophical manifesto such as the Free Software Foundation's 'Free Software Definition' or Debian's 'Social Contract' and the Open Source Initiative's 'Open Source Definition'.[2] Derived from each other, these three documents all define free and open source software as computer programs that may be freely copied, used for any purpose, studied and modified on source code level and distributed in

[1] Benjamin Mako Hill, Towards a Standard of Freedom: Creative Commons and the Free Software Movement, http://www.advogato.org/article/851.html

[2] http://www.gnu.org/philosophy/free-sw.html, http://www.debian.org/social_contract, http://www.opensource.org/docs/definition.php

[3] http://www.linuxp2p.com/forums/viewtopic.php?p=10771

[4] Ibid.

[5] http://www.fsf.org/blogs/rms/entry-20050920.html

[6] http://lists.debian.org/debian-legal/2004/07/msg01193.html

modified form. The concrete free software licenses, such as the GNU General Public License (GPL), the BSD license and the Perl Artistic License, are not ends in themselves, but only express individual implementations of those constitutions in legal terms; they translate politics into policies.

Such politics are absent from the Creative Commons. As Mako Hill points out, the 'non-commercial' CC licenses prohibit use for any purpose, the 'no-derivatives' licenses prohibit modification, and the CC 'Sampling License' and 'Developing Nations License' even disallow verbatim copying. As a result, none of the user rights granted by free and open source software are ensured by the mere fact that a work has been released under a Creative Commons license. To say that something is available under a CC license is meaningless in practice. Not only does the CC symbol look like a fashion logo, it also isn't more than one. Richard Stallman, founder of the GNU project and author of the Free Software Definition, finds that 'all these licenses have in common is a label, but people regularly mistake that common label for something substantial.'[3] Yet some if only vague programmatic substance is expressed in CC's motto 'Some rights reserved.' Beyond being, quote Mako Hill, a 'relatively hollow call', this slogan factually reverses the Free Software and Open Source philosophy of reserving rights to *users*, not copyright owners, in order to allow the former to become producers themselves.

While Mako Hill embraces at least a few of the CC licenses, such as the ShareAlike License under which his own essay is available, Stallman finds it a

> *self-delusion to try to endorse just some of the Creative Commons licenses, because people lump them together; they will misconstrue any endorsement of some as a blanket endorsement of all.*[4]

According to an entry on his weblog, Stallman had 'asked the leaders of Creative Commons privately to change their policies, but they declined, so we had to part ways.'[5] The Debian project even considers all CC licenses non-free and recommended, in 2004, that

> *authors who wish to create works compatible with the Debian Free Software Guidelines should not use any of the licenses in the Creative Commons license suite*[6]

mostly because their attribution clause limits modifications, because of restrictions on the Creative Commons trademark and ambiguously worded anti-'Digital Rights Management' (DRM) provisions that could be interpreted as prohibiting distribution over any encrypted channel, including for example PGP encoded email and anonymizing proxy servers.

[7] http://www.sourcelabs.com/blogs/ajb/2006/02/creative_commons_is_broken.html

Whatever stance one may adopt, the name 'Creative Commons' is misleading because it doesn't create a commons at all. A picture released, for example, under the Attribution-ShareAlike license cannot legally be integrated into a video released under the Attribution-NonCommercial license, audio published under the Sampling License can't be used on its soundtrack. Such incompatible license terms put what is supposed to be 'free content' or 'free information' back to square one, that is, the default restrictions of copyright – hardly that what Lawrence Lessig, founder of the Creative Commons, could have meant with 'free culture' and 'read-write culture' as opposed to 'read-only culture.' In his blog entry 'Creative Commons Is Broken', Alex Bosworth, program manager at the open source company SourceLabs, points out that 'of eight million photos' posted under a CC license on Flickr.com

> *less than a fifth allow free remixing of content under terms similar to an open source license. More than a third don't allow any modifications at all.'*[7]

The 'principle problem with Creative Commons', he writes, 'is that most of the creative commons content is not actually reuseable at all.'

While these problems may at least hypothetically be solved through improvements of the CC license texts – with the license compatibility clauses in the draft of the GNU GPL version 3 as a possible model – there are farther-reaching issues on the level of politics as opposed to merely policies. CC's self-definition that 'our licenses help you keep your copyright while inviting certain uses of your work – a "some rights reserved" copyright' translate into what the software developer and Neoist Dmytri Kleiner phrases as follows: 'the Creative Commons, is to help "you" (the "Producer") to keep control of "your" work.' Kleiner concludes that

> *the right of the consumer' is not mentioned, neither is the division of 'producer' and 'consumer' disputed. The Creative 'Commons' is thus really an Anti-Commons, serving to*

*legitimise, rather than deny, Producer-control and serving to enforce, rather than do away with, the distinction between producer and consumer.*[8]

[8] Dmytri Kleiner, The Creative Anti-Commons and the Poverty of Networks, http://info.interactivist.net/article.pl?sid=06/09/16/2053224

[9] http://creativecommons.org/images/find.gif, http://creativecommons.org/license

Citing Lessig's examples of DJ Dangermouse's *Grey Album* and Javier Prato's *Jesus Christ: The Musical* – 'projects torpedoed by the legal owners of the music used in the production of the works' – Kleiner sharply observes that 'the legal representatives of The Beatles and Gloria Gaynor could just as easily have used Creative Commons licences to enforce their control over the use of their work.'

The distinction between 'consumers' and 'producers' couldn't be more bluntly stated than on CC's home page. It displays, on its very top, two large clickable buttons, one labelled 'FIND Music, photos and more', the other 'PUBLISH Your Stuff, safely and legally', the former with a down arrow, the latter with an up arrow in its logo.[9] The small letters are no less remarkable than the capitals. Upon first glance, the adverbs 'safely and legally' sound odd and like material for a future cultural history museum of post-Napster and post-9/11 paranoia. But above all, they name and perpetuate the fundamental misunderstanding artists seem to have of the Creative Commons: Free licenses were not meant to be, and aren't, a liability insurance against getting sued for use of third-party copyrighted or trademarked material. Whoever expects to gain this from putting work under a Creative Commons license, is completely mistaken.

Artists are desperately looking for a solution to a problem that ultimately resulted from their own efforts of redefining art. When art was granted, in Western cultures at least, an autonomous status, artists were – to a moderate degree – exempt from a number of legal norms. Kurt Schwitters was not sued for collaging the logo of German Commerzbank into his 'Merz' painting which yielded his 'Merz' art. Neither did Andy Warhol receive injunctions for using Coca Cola's and Campbell's trademarks. As long as these symbols remained inside the art world, they did not raise corporate eyebrows. Experimental artists embraced the internet just because it did away with the separation of white cubes – in which logos and trademarks were safe from being mixed up with the original ones – and the outside world. Mainly thanks to the internet, artistic simulations of corporate entities were believable for the first time. The Yes Men could pose as the World Trade Organisation and get invited to World Economic Forum as WTO representatives, 0100101110101101.org could tactically disguise themselves as the Nike company. Older artistic simulations like Res Ingold's 'Ingold Airlines' were not only transparent and clumsy in comparison, but also on the safe grounds of an art system with little or no interference of corporate lawyers. But ever since the world wide web, file sharing and cheap or free authoring software tore down walls between art and non-art practice, producers and consumers, former consumers were held liable as producers, and artistic production became subject to non-art world norms, as obvious in the FBI investigations of Steve Kurtz and ubermorgen.com for bioterrorism and tampering with the U.S. presidential elections respectively.

Previous artistic critiques of corporate and intellectual ownership were much less efficacious even where they were programmatically more radical. Between 1988 and 1989, a series of countercultural 'Festivals of Plagiarism', organized by Stewart Home, Graham Harwood and others, struggled with wide gaps between radical anti-copyright rhetoric and an artistic practice limited mostly to photocopied mail art work. John Berndt, a participant of the London Festival of Plagiarism, left with the impression that

> *a repetitive critique of 'ownership' and 'originality' in culture was juxtaposed with collective events, in which a majority of participants [...] simply wanted to have their 'aesthetic' and vaguely political artwork exposed*[10]

making fellow Neoist tENTATIVELY, a cONVENIENCE conclude that 'Festivals of Recycling might have been more accurate descriptions' for the events:

> *By virtue of calling the act of reusing and changing previously existing material (not even always with the intention of critiquing said material) 'Plagiarism' the appearance of being 'radical' could be given to people whose work was otherwise straight out of art school teachings.'*[11]

Today, similar gaps and misunderstandings exist between copyleft activists and artists who just seek to legitimize their use of third-party material. When Lawrence Lessig characterizes the Creative Commons as "fair use'-plus: a promise that any freedoms given are always in addition to the freedoms guaranteed by the law'[12], this is technically correct, but nevertheless misunderstandable, especially for people who aren't legal experts. Putting a work under a CC license – or even a non-ambiguously free GNU or BSD license – means to *grant* rather than to *gain* uses in addition to standard fair use. The Creative Commons do not solve the

[10] John Berndt, Proletarian Posturing and the Strike that Never Ends, SMILE magazine, Baltimore, 1988.

[11] tENTATIVELY, a cONVENIENCE, History Begins where Life Ends, self-published pamphlet, Baltimore 1993.

[12] http://creativecommons.org/weblog/entry/5681

problem of how not to get sued by Coca Cola or Campbell's at all. Non-free copyrighted material cannot be freely incorporated into one's work no matter what license one choses. Even worse, the opposite is true: copyright owners are most likely to categorically refuse clearance for anything that will be put into free circulation because the license of the work incorporating theirs would effectively relicense the latter. If, for example, the Corbis corporation would permit the photograph of Einstein sticking out his tongue – for which it holds the rights – to be reproduced in a freely licensed book, it would free the picture for anyone else's use as well. Since this can hardly be expected from the Bill Gates-owned company, free licensing often restrains rather than expands one's possibilities of using third-party material.

This example reveals a crucial difference between software development and artistic practice: Programming can sustain itself on its own, self-built library of reusable work, art hardly so. The GNU copyleft works on the premise that modifications are also contributions. If, for example, a company like IBM chooses to modify the Linux kernel to run on its own servers, the GNU license forces it to give back the added code to the development community. And the more code is available as free software, the higher the incentive for others to simply build on existing free code libraries and give back changes rather than building a new program from scratch. This explains why even for computer companies, free software development can make more economic sense than the close source commercial model. In addition, free software development profits from a difference between source code and perceivable appearance that doesn't have an exact equivalent in most artistic work: Programs can be written that look and behave similarly or identically to proprietary counterparts as long as they don't use proprietary code and do not infringe on patents and trademarks. This way, AT&T's Unix could be rewritten as BSD and GNU/Linux, and Microsoft Office could be cloned as OpenOffice. Even patents which could spoil such borrowings aren't as internationally universal and not remotely as long-lasting as copyright. In other words, free software development could be an 'appropriationart' without copyright infringement.

The same isn't possible for most artists, however. It makes little sense for them to restrict their uses to material whose copyright has either expired or that has been released under sufficiently free terms. The Coca Cola logo can't be cloned as a copylefted 'FreeCola' logo, and it would be pointless for the Yes Men to pose as an 'OpenWTO' or for 0100101110101101.org to have run as 'GNUke' instead of Nike. If even harmless collaging, sampling and quoting becomes risky because of media industrial internet copyright paranoia and whole business models based on injunctions and lawsuits, this is a political matter of fair use, not of free licenses. In the worst case, free licenses, all the more fluffy and pseudo-free ones like the Creative Commons, could be used to legitimize new restrictions of fair use legislation, or even its abolition altogether, with the alibi that the so-called 'ecosystem', or ghetto, of more or less freely licensed work provides enough fair use for those who bother to care.[13]

It is not hard to bash the Creative Commons for being an organization run with little understanding of the arts, and not even a good understanding of open source and free software philosophy. On the other hand, artists themselves have failed to voice what they want. The exceptions are few and rather marginal: the anti-copyright philosophies and politics of Lautréamont, Woody Guthrie (who, according to Dmytri Kleiner, released his songbook with the license that 'anybody caught singin' it without our permission, will be mighty good friends of ours, cause we don't give a dern. Publish it. Write it. Sing it. Swing to it. Yodel it'), Lettrists, Situationists, Neoists, Plunderphonics musicians and some internet artists including the French artlibre.org collective whose 'Free Art License' predates the Creative Commons by two years.[14]

A team of lawyers whose work consists of creating, as Bosworth puts it, 'low cost legal templates', the Creative Commons organization has simply listened to all kinds of artists and activists, trying to do justice to diverse and sometimes contradictory needs and expectations, with licenses 'designed to give artists choice' (Mako Hill) rather than prioritizing free use and reuse of information. In contrast, Free Software and Open Source are, like any human and civil rights effort, universalist at their core, with principles that are neither negotiable, nor may be culturally relativized.

If someone is to blame for the fact that artists, political activists and academics from the humanities have largely failed to recognize those essentials, then it is Eric S. Raymond, founder of the 'Open Source Initative' (http://www.opensource.org), the group that coined the term 'Open Source' in 1998. The main advantage of the term 'Open Source'

[13] This scenario isn't too far-fetched considering Lessig's recent advocacy of the non-open file format Adobe/Macromedia's Flash which he calls a 'crucial tool of basic digital education in a free culture' (quotation translated from the German article, http://www.heise.de/newsticker/meldung/78278/, see also http://lwn.net/Articles/199877/) Since proprietary file formats cannot be universally accessed and lock information into technology whose availability is at the mercy of a single vendor, they restrain fair use.

[14] http://artlibre.org/licence/lal/en/

[15] It is not coincidental, for example, that the term 'Open Content' and the web site http://www.opencontent.org was launched in 1998 only a few months after the first propagation of 'Open Source', until its founder David Wiley abandoned the initiative in 2004 in order to - ironically or not - become a director of Creative Commons.

over 'Free Software' is that it doesn't merely refer to computer programs, but evokes broader cultural connotations.[15] For most people with artistic backgrounds, GNU's 'Free Software' sounded too confusingly similar to (closed-source) 'freeware' and 'shareware.' 'Open Source' sparked an all-the-richer imagination as Raymond didn't simply pitch it as an alternative to proprietary 'intellectual property' regimes, but as a 'Bazaar' model of open, networked collaboration. Yet this is not at all the Open Source Initiative's own 'Open Source Definition' says or is about. Derived from Debian's 'Free Software Guidelines', it simply lists criteria licenses have to meet in order to be considered free, respectively open source. The fact that a work is available under such a license might enable collaborative work on it, but it doesn't have to by definition. Much free software – the GNU utilities and the free BSDs for example – is developed by rather closed groups and committees of programmers in what Raymond calls a 'Cathedral' methodology. Conversely, proprietary software companies such as Microsoft may develop their code in distributed 'Bazaar' style. Nevertheless, the homepage of http://www.opensource.org states that the 'basic idea behind open source' is about how 'software evolves', 'at a speed that, if one is used to the slow pace of conventional software development, seems astonishing', thus producing 'better software than the traditional closed model.' Regardless which position one takes in the philosophical and ideological dispute between 'Free Software' and 'Open Source', the self-characterization of Open Source as a development model mixes up cause and effect, being inconsistent with what the Open Source Definition, on the same website, qualifies as Open Source, i.e. software whose licenses fulfill its criteria of openness.

Given how 'Open Source' has been propagated as a model of networked collaboration instead of user rights or free infrastructures, the gap between the lip-service paid to it in the arts and humanities and the factual use of free software and copylefts comes as little surprise. 'Cultural' free software conferences whose organizers and speakers run Windows or the Mac OS on their laptops continue to be the norm. With few exceptions, art education hardly ever involves free software, but is tied to proprietary software tool chains. Yet – often vague or ill-informed – 'Open Source' references abound in media studies and electronic arts writing.

The problem is not so much that people do not use free operating systems, but that software-political correctness anxiety prevents a more honest critical discourse. A debate on 'why free software doesn't work for us' would be more productive for free software development than the current hypocrisy. Recent discussions on why, for example, free software culture involves disproportionally few women – even in comparison to proprietary software development – have at least begun to tackle some of those issues.

Productive critique, after all, is needed. Eight years after the coinage of 'Open Source', Raymond's Hegelian claims of superior development methodologies sound increasingly hollow. Free software hasn't displaced proprietary software at all. Despite its success on servers and in embedded systems, it is unlikely to take over mainstream personal computing any time soon. Free software, it seems, has its strength in building software infrastructure: kernels, file systems, network stacks, compilers, scripting languages, libraries, web, file and mail servers, database engines. It lags behind proprietary offerings, for example, in conventional desktop publishing and video editing, and, as a rule of thumb, in anything that isn't highly modularized or used a lot by its own developer community. The closer the software is to the daily needs and work methods of programmers and system administrators, the higher typically its quality.

Similar rules seem to apply to free information, respectively 'Open Content' development. The model works best for infrastructural, general, non-individualistic information resources, with Wikipedia and FreeDB (and lately MusicBrainz) as prime examples. Similarly, the cultural logic of sounds and images circulating under CC licenses is largely that of stock music, stock photography and clip art, regardless the fact that current CC licenses mostly fail to permit their 'mashups', boiling down to little more than 'Web 2.0' lifestyle logos. Beyond software, infrastructural information and publishing that waives reproduction rights, the value of free licensing is somewhat doubtful. Experimental, radical art and activism that does not play nice with third-party copyrights and trademarks can't be legally released and used under whatever license anyway. Its work should rather – and explicitly – be released into the public domain with, quote jodi, 'all wrongs reversed' and, quote Kleiner, 'all rights detourned under the terms of the Woody Guthrie General License Agreement.' For professional artists, this simply means to acknowledge the reality of contemporary art economics: that artists, with the exception of a handful of stars, no longer live from producing material goods (for which copyright granted lifetime monopolies, or at least the illusion of continuous revenue streams), but like 17th century project entrepreneurs from commissioned projects whose material products have little or no market value by themselves.

Copyright, having turned from regulation into subsidy of publishing industries, is the 21st century equivalent of drug legislation. Everyone knows that it is obsolete, dysfunctional, and depriving people of their rights; absurd wars are fought in its name. The simple fix is to abolish it.

# Copyright is for Copying

Hans-Christoph Steiner

*This song is Copyrighted in U.S., under Seal of Copyright #154085, for a period of 28 years, and anybody caught singin' it without our permission, will be mighty good friends of ourn, cause we don't give a dern. Publish it. Write it. Sing it. Swing to it. Yodel it. We wrote it, that's all we wanted to do.*

Never before have artists and performers been so well versed in copyright law. In the past decade, there has been a big push for media creators to explore what copyright means, and how they want to use it. Creative Commons and other organizations are putting a lot of work into making copyright law more understandable and usable. At the same time, copyright law is being used to try to enforce new kinds of stipulations which the creators of copyright law never would have thought of, like enforcing sharing and attribution. In this paper I argue that using copyright to enforce attribution provides little benefit to creators, and that such licenses do in fact cause harm. Additionally, there is already a well-established code of ethics in the realm of creative work that long predates copyright which is in fact the most useful mechanism for ensuring that creators get credit where credit is due.

### Experimenting with Copyright

Starting in the '70s, hackers kicked off a new era of experimenting with copyright licenses. The Tiny Basic Copyleft is an early, informal example. Starting with the Emacs General Public License[3], Richard Stallman and the Free Software Foundation (FSF) began to explore using copyright law to enforce concepts that are not commercial in nature. This lead to the GNU GPL, which is a copyright license that encourages people to freely modify, copy, and distribute the copyrighted material, with only one caveat: that if they distribute any modifications to that work, they must grant the same freedoms as the original work did. A crucial point here is that the FSF has laid out a code of ethics[4], and uses the license as a tool to enforce them. Copyleft licenses like the GNU GPL were designed to use the copyright system as a means to

[1] Tort is the area of law dealing with wrongful acts that cause damages.

[2] AKA Digital Rights Management (DRM).

[3] R. Stallman, 'Emacs General Public License', http://www.freesoft.org/gplhistory/emacs gpl.html

[4] Free Software Foundation, 'The Free Software Definition', http://www.gnu.org/philosophy/free-sw.html

[5]
Art Libre, Free art license, http://artlibre.org/licence/lal/en/

[6]
B. M. Hill, 'Towards a Standard of Freedom: Creative Commons and the Free Software Movement', Advogato, July 2005, http://www.advogato.org/article/851.html

work against it, aiming to enforce freedom and disallowing as many restrictions as possible. Many authors even ascribe their copyright to the FSF to further circumvent the copyright system. In order to take a copyright issue to court, you must have the permission of all of the relevant copyright holders. Instead of the typical view that owning the copyright means owning the creation, these authors trust that the FSF will enforce their code of ethics, leaving the creators free to work on their creations.

Since the creation of the GNU GPL, a wide variety of licenses have been created with a wide variety of terms included in them. The Free Art License[5] was an early effort, designed to bring the freedoms of the GNU GPL to art. One of the most prevalent licenses in the art world is the Creative Commons suite of licenses. Creative Commons aims to make copyright law accessible to ordinary people since they believe that copyright law is the central tool for managing creative work. Creative Commons licenses are organized into license 'modules' which the user can mix and match in order to put together a set of restrictions they want to place on their work. While they were directly influenced by the GNU GPL, an essential difference between Creative Commons and the FSF: Creative Commons has not established a code of ethics to guide their work, and the licenses do not demonstrate a unifying code of principles[6]. Creative Commons has deemed their attribution clause so important, it is not optional. Every Creative Commons license now includes the attribution clause.

## Copyright Was Created For Publishers

To start out, I should point out that this article has a strong bias towards British and American copyright systems based on what came out of Britain. These systems of copyright law have evolved into the international standards, whether or not they are broadly accepted domestically in every country or whether a given country had its own system beforehand. Many countries have very different legal structures related to publishing creative works. For example, the French *droit d'auteur* and German *Urheberrecht* systems give moral rights to creators in addition to the property rights of copyright.

An early example of copyright started with the monopolies, usually known as patents, that some monarchies would grant to specific publishers or creators. Only a handful of authors and composers were ever granted this right, more often it was publishers who received these royal monopolies. In Britain in the 1550s, the Stationers' Company, a publishers' guild, was granted a monopoly on all publishing. In 1710, the Statute of Anne was an attempt by Parliament to limit the timeframe and scope of these publishing monopolies, which by then had been established in the common law outside of statutes. This was the beginning of copyright as we know it now. While it introduced language framing copyright in terms of the author, it was in fact the publishers that were lobbying for the enactment of such a law. Although copyright laws are often framed around the idea of creator's rights, they have always been enacted due to the lobbying of publishers. The very name 'copyright' explains very well what it aims to protect.[7] It is interesting to note that the first copyright in China, introduced in 1068, was also a protection for printers.[8] Copyright did not apply to other creations like performances, drama, paintings, sculpture, and drawings until much later.[9] After all, these did not involve a publisher copying them. New laws extended copyright to cover these starting in the mid 19th century. For example, rules covering performance of music were added in the 20th century at the behest of music recording industry once people starting playing their recordings in public.

[7] K. Fogel. 'The Promise of a Post-Copyright World', http://questioncopyright.org/promise

[8] F. Zhang and D. Xie, 'Chinese Copyright Protection has Storied History, Strong Future', http://www.sourcetrix.com/docs/Whitepaper-China Intellectual Property.pdf

[9] E. Samuels, The Illustrated Story of Copyright, chapter six, Thomas Dunne Books, St. Martin's Press, December 2000, http://www.edwardsamuels.com/illustratedstory/isc6.htm

[10] L. Lessig, Interview with Jim M. Goldstein, EXIF and Beyond, 2008, http://www.jmg-galleries.com/blog/2008/01/02/exif-and-beyond-lawrence-lessig-interview/

## The Law is Expensive

> *...[H]ere's the fundamental design flaw of the copyright system. It was architected imagining that it would be implemented by about 150 lawyers around the United States, who would be living in relatively large institutions and able to manage the intricacies of the system. Because of digital technologies, this extremely arcane, complicated system of regulation now gets extended to everybody who wants to express themselves using creative work.*[10]

Creative Commons believes it is possible to use copyright law to benefit creators despite being created for publishers. The key question here is: do you believe that the legal system is accessible to artists? Lawrence Lessig, who spearheaded the creation of Creative Commons and its licenses, is a lawyer who believes in copyright law as a useful tool. Lawyers generally believe that the law works while overlooking how expensive the law is. For lawyers and entities with

[11] A. C. Engst, Creative Commons License Upheld in Dutch Court. TidBITS, 2006, http://db.tidbits.com/article/8469.

[12] Capitol v. Thomas, http://arstechnica.com/news.ars/post/20071004-verdict-is-in. html

substantial resources the law works well, they can represent themselves effectively within the legal context. For basically everyone else, we have to pay a lot of money to get effective representation in court (unless we are fortunate enough to get someone to volunteer their services).

Adam Curry, of MTV and podcasting fame, recently sued a Dutch newspaper for using one of his Flickr images, marked with a Creative Commons noncommercial clause, without permission. While technically, he won the suit since the court found some merit to his claims. But the ruling was so weak that it is hard to call a win: the court ordered a fine of €1,000 only if the newspaper violated Curry's copyright license again, there were no damages or other requirements of the newspaper.[11] What the press did not mention is how much money Curry spent on lawyers fees. Facing the experienced lawyers of a tabloid newspaper undoubtedly requires a good lawyer spending many hours of billable time. So when it comes down to it, are you going to spend thousands of dollars suing someone who didn't give you attribution? If it was free content, they would still be able to distribute and use it for free.

When using copyrighted materials, a creator had best understand copyright law. Misusing copyrighted materials can cost you dearly in damages and lawyers fees if you tangle with a vindictive organization like the RIAA. Normally in torts[1], the person bringing the lawsuit must prove that they were harmed by the wrongful acts, it is not enough to show only that the were wrongful acts. Copyright law is unusual because it includes statutory damages, meaning that the person suing only has to prove infringement in order to receive a payment for damages. For example, in the United States, these damages are set out in the law, and can range between $200 and $150,000 per work. Even if someone had no intention or idea that they were infringing on a copyright, they could still be required to pay these damages. A recent example of large, statutory damages can be seen in the US case Capitol Records v. Jammie Thomas. Jammie Thomas was ordered to pay $222,000 in damages for sharing 24 songs via KaZaa, in addition to her substantial legal bills.[12]

To avoid getting penalized, you have to keep up with copyright law, and make sure that you are aware of the license terms for every bit of material you are using. Creative Commons licenses are fully part of the copyright system. That means that even if you use material with the most liberal license, the Attribution license, these statutory damages can still apply. Additionally, since Creative Commons started releasing licenses in 2002, it has released new versions every year and a half (1.0, 2.0, 2.5, 3.0) of its core license modules. While it is admirable that Creative Commons is trying hard to make the law more accessible, it is still approaching the law from a lawyer's perspective. Frequently tweaking the license means that artists have to do even more work keeping up with the changes to make sure they are operating legally. In comparison, the FSF has just released the third version of the GNU GPL after 18 years. The previous version was in use for 16 years. Additionally, share-alike clauses regulate copying, which copyright law was designed to do, there is a clear, general understanding of this. This means it is rarely necessary to go to court to enforce such clauses, unless the violator is uncooperative. If you use the GNU GPL, the FSF will help to represent your claim.

[13] Free Software Foundation, 'The BSD License Problem', http://www.gnu.org/philosophy/bsd.html, 1998

[14] Creative Commons, Attribution 3.0 license, http://creativecommons.org/licenses/by/3.0/legalcode.

## Using Copyright for Attribution has Unintended Consequences

There are many arguments in favor of giving attributions, a key attribution can help launch the career of an artist. The key part of my argument is not whether giving credit can be beneficial. Instead it is a question of whether creators benefit more from copyright than they lose. Attribution clauses have been widely discredited in the free software world. In the late '90s, people began to realize that the attribution clause in the original BSD license was causing problems with projects that involved large collections of packages, such as GNU/Linux distributions.[13] Basically, the attribution clause required them to have hundreds of attributions on any advertisement they published. Imagine trying to include hundreds of attributions on a banner ad and you get the picture. Then factor in the amount of work that someone would have to do just to keep track of all these attributions. The new BSD attribution clause is harmless because it ties attribution only to distribution: just include the license file with the files that you distribute. Similarly, the GNU GPL requires that the name of the copyright holders of any included work are listed only where a copyright notice is listed. On the other hand, the Creative Commons attribution clause is very broad, creating more work than the original BSD license (see section 4(b) of Attribution 3.0 Legal Code).[14]

[15] Freesound, http://freesound.iua.upf.edu

[16] Creative Commons, Sampling plus 1.0 license, http://creativecommons.org/licenses/sampling+/1.0/

Imagine that you are making a new piece and you sample some other video and audio sources. If these sources don't include other sources, then the job of managing attributions shouldn't be too difficult. Since many artists are sampling, you will have to track the attributions of the works that you are sampling, since you might be including parts of those secondary sources in your new work. As people sample more and more, this will only compound, and soon you will be dealing with exponentially increasing attributions. Even if everyone involved just sampled from five sources, through five generations of sampling, then you will have to track down and manage 3,125 attributions. That means your album cover, your web page, your video credits, etc. will need to have an additional 3,125 credits added. Not only is this a lot of work, but those attributions lose value as their numbers compound. Who is going to bother reading through thousands of credits?

Take the example of Freesound[15] which uses a Creative Commons Sampling Plus 1.0[16] license throughout. If I create a work of my own using samples from Freesound, then I will have to manage those attributions, making sure I have all the details correct, and that they are everywhere they need to be. If I make a mistake in those attributions, then I could be liable for the statutory damages of copyright and the associated legal fees. If I use any of the standard commercial sample libraries such as Sound Ideas, there is no such requirement. Once you have bought the sample library, I can use the samples without worrying about attribution. Considering all of the license grants and restrictions, Sound Ideas seems to provide more freedom than Freesound.

On top of this, someone has to track down the authors and find out how they want to be attributed, unless the attribution is very simple and clearly defined. Imagine if RedHat had to manage attributions for all of the packages that it includes in its distribution. Now consider new uses, what if scientists start releasing data sets using licenses with vague attribution clauses, then an artist working on visualizing data searches a database of these data sets, getting 50,000 useful results. That artist would then have to track 50,000 attributions. That takes real and substantial effort. Some argue that this could be automated so 50,000 attributions would not be hard to handle. That begs the question, how would you display 50,000 attributions, and more importantly, would some collection of 50,000 attributions be a useful thing that people would actually look at? If no one ever bothers to wade through those 50,000 attributions, then it seems quite clear that it was not a useful exercise. The project would need to be extended to visualize its attributions! We are immersed in a world of copyrighted material. When making art that documents the real world, like movies or photographs, it is inevitable that copyrighted work will get included in these documentations.[17] Even if all this material was covered by a Creative Commons attribution license, all of the copyrights will still need to be managed, from figuring out the attributions to handling noncommercial terms.

[17] K. Aoki, J. Boyle, and J. Jenkins, Tales from the Public Domain: BOUND BY LAW? Duke Center for the Study of the Public Domain, 2006, http://www.law.duke.edu/cspd/comics/

It is possible that such an attribution might get you high profile attention that you might not otherwise get. The license might also dissuade people from using your work, leaving it unused. As long as you can show that the work originates from you, something the internet makes much easier, then the more your work spreads, the greater the possible effect on your reputation. Adding restrictions can hinder the spread of your work. This is actually quite common in commercial design. If a major corporation wants to use your work, and it does not like the fees or license, it will pay someone else to imitate it, and therefore own the copyright entirely. This is a major activity of sound design firms, especially for music used advertising. They then need to give no attribution for this imitation, and you have gained neither money nor a greater reputation.

### Reputation Works Separately from Attribution and Copyright

When copyright was created, it was never intended to be a 'creditright'. Through practice of using licenses and a concerted effort by the publishing industries, most people now believe that copyright is intended to be a right to attribution. Attribution is often confused with reputation, they are not interchangeable concepts. While attributions like album credits definitely can help to build a reputation, they are only one of many ways to do so. On web forums like Freesound, download counts and number of comments are a visible way of seeing someone's reputation; the identity of the original author of a useful addition to a program is often spread via email lists while very few people bother to read the copyright statement where the author's name is listed; working at a highly esteemed magazine such as The Economist will carry a journalist far, even though The Economist does not have bylines on its articles. What is most important to someone working as a creator is their reputation. A reputation is built up by doing good work and people

[18] K.-E. Tallmo, 'Copyright Alert', The Art Bin, January 1996, http://art-bin.com/art/acopyalert.html

recognizing it. Strictly enforced attribution is rarely how people get recognized.

The movie business is well known for providing detailed listings of attributions, also known as 'credits', that appear at the end of movies. It is not because of any rule of copyright that the credits are included. They are the product of contracts, union agreements, and a code of ethics. The standard free software licenses, like the new BSD license the GNU GPL, and others, do not require attribution anything like movies have. Writing software is much like any other creative work, reputation is an essential part of earning a living. Yet even with the vast amount of free software out there, it is extremely uncommon to find people plagiarizing software. It would be a simple matter of downloading the source code of a program, renaming it in the key places, and putting it out there on its own website. There are many other things that make it difficult to get away with plagiarism: it is very easy to find code thanks to search engines, free software users expect to see forums, lists, and a browseable source code repository. Imitating these takes a substantial amount of work, and discovering a fraudulent version it not difficult.

For a new artist starting out, it is more useful to use extra means of proving authorship. If someone plagiarized this new creator's work and gets a lot of attention from it, this new creator can then demonstrate that they were the actual author in one of many public forums and therefore lay claim to the credit. There will be a trail of proof on websites, blogs, peer-to-peer networks, and even timestamping services like [http://signedtimestamp.org/]. '[T]he Internet is also one gigantic detective machine, for one finds stolen material much more readily here than in the real world.'[18] When a creator has a reputation, then people who are seeking the works of that creator will want to make sure that they are getting the original versions. This impulse exists outside of copyright. The distribution of media on peer-to-peer networks is a clear example of this. The vast majority of illegally shared files are accurately labeled, even when the copying is illegal. The success of the creator is based on their reputation. If a creator just rips off people's work and tries to claim it as their own, they can easily be discredited and their reputation will damaged or destroyed.

There are a wide array of occupations where reputation plays a crucial role, yet those involved collectively ignore copyright and attribution:

> *Most judicial opinions nowadays are written by law clerks but signed by judges, without acknowledgment of the clerks' authorship. This is a general characteristic of government documents, CEO's speeches, and books by celebrities.* [19]

Business contracts are a similar case, lawyers involved in mergers and acquisitions freely use sections of contracts, often verbatim, without any acknowledgment of original authorship or their copyright.

Before copyright became dominant, the vast majority of composers and musicians made their living from other means, and they built their reputations outside of copyright, often outside of any system of attribution. Before widespread copyright, the most famous composers were known for their musicianship more than their compositions, and were expected to play regularly. Many published pieces of music where not attributed to a composer since it was deemed irrelevant. Composers like Mozart, Haydn, and DuFay relied on a patron to sponsor their entire livelihoods.[20] J.S. Bach and Couperin were organists in the employ of churches for large portions of their lives. While Bach is now known most of all for his compositions like the Brandenburg concertos, he wrote them as an application to be the church organist in Brandenburg. (He did not get the job, and the concertos were forgotten in library of the margrave of Brandenburg-Schwedt for over a decade.) Making money from publishing music and recordings did not become widespread until well into the 20th century, and still the vast majority of musicians make the bulk of their earnings outside of copyright and publishing.

Radiohead experimented with removing copyright law, in effect, with the distribution of their new album In Rainbows. People could download the whole album from Radiohead while paying as much as they wanted. Radiohead earned a substantial amount not because people felt they were required to pay, but rather because of their reputation. Radiohead has an excellent reputation with fans and critics alike, and people are willing to give them money in order to ensure that they continue to make music.[21] Another classic example is the Grateful Dead bootleg scene. The band explicitly allowed people to record, distribute, and even sell bootleg recordings of live concerts. Whenever they were touring, they were consistently one of

[19] R. Posner, 'Plagiarism', http://www.becker-posner-blog.com/archives/2005/04/plagiarismposne.html, April 24 2005

[20] P. G. Downs, Classical Music: The Era of Haydn, Mozart, and Beethoven, chapter Musician in Society, pp. 17-21, W.W. Norton, 1992.

[21] J. Pareles, 'Pay What You Want for this Article', New York Times, 9 December 2007, http://www.nytimes.com/2007/12/09/arts/music/09pare.html

[22] L. Harrison, 'Stephen King Reveals The Plant Profit, The Register, February 2001, http://www.theregister.co.uk/2001/02/07/stephen king reveals the plant/

the top grossing concert acts, they even had good record sales, so it is hard to imagine that this voluntary suspension of copyright did them any harm.

Say a new writer publishes a novel under a free license with no broad attribution requirement, and puts it on her website, people download it, read it, and spread it so her reputation builds. Then a publisher takes this novel and prints books out of it and sells it. This publisher now has invested time and money into selling your book, and will want to promote it as much as possible in order to sell more books. They would be foolish to avoid capitalizing on the author's reputation, which would provide them with free promotion, so they would want to be sure her name is on it. Any money they spent on promoting the book would add to her reputation, perhaps they would even hire her to promote your book. On the other hand, if such a printer was publishing the work of a well known author, not much promotion would be needed. But most readers will want to read the author's recommended version. With internet search engines that is becoming ever easier to find, so such a publisher would want the author's recommendation. That said, there will always be unethical copying, but such is the case now, even with draconian copyright laws in place. If copyright was an effective means of deterring people, the RIAA would not have to sue many of its customers. And even with their huge litigation budget, they are only having limited success.

The writer Stephen King provides an earlier example of using the internet to cash in on reputation while working outside the normal realms of copyright. In 2000, he began to publish chapters of The Plant serially, asking downloaders to pay $1 for the download, either before or after downloading it. He said he would keep on releasing new chapters as long as 75 percent of downloaders paid. After a few installments, the percentage of payers dropped to 46 percent, and King stopped the project. Many called the project a failure, and publishing companies breathed a sigh of relief. After a few months, King revealed that he made a $463,832 profit on this half-finished novel.[22] That figure seems quite hard to label a failure, especially since the majority of writers never make that much money on all of their writing.

As it is, attribution in the art world is widely abused and ignored. Consider for example the sculpture of a famous artist like Louise Bourgeois. When you look at the attributions, her works only ever have one: 'Louise Bourgeois'. But when you consider how they were actually made, there are numerous interns and employees making the sculptures that she signs her name to. This is far from unusual; big name media artists basically always have lots of people giving substantial contributions, who rarely get specific attributions. Yet you will find that many people can build a reputation from this kind of work, it is enough to demonstrate that you worked on well regarded projects in order to boost your reputation.

[23] M. Maar, The Two Lolitas, Verso, Sept. 2005, http://www.versobooks.com/books/klm/m-titles/maar_m_two lolitas.shtml

**Building upon the Creativity of Others**

The commodification of creative work has created the artificial idea that the work of art is purely the work of the artist who produced it. This flies in the face of millennia of human endeavor, we are all standing on the shoulders of giants. Art is built upon the works of others, like all of human creativity, it does not exist without being firmly implanted into the context of human communities. If you believe that artists can create great works completely of their own minds, consider the humans who have grown up in complete isolation, such as the legendary Kaspar Hauser. Sadly, they are never able to contribute or even generate much, and even have trouble with the basics of communications. Even if they were to produce substantial works, those works would lack any cultural reference and would be incomprehensible to the current culture. It follows that in order for human creativity to flourish, there needs to be a large body of material for people to draw upon. And if this material is freely available and unencumbered by restrictions such as licenses, then creativity will flow more freely.

Sampling and remixing are natural whenever people are creating. Nabokov's *Lolita* is widely regarded as a excellent work of art, but few remember Heinz von Lichberg's story of a 13-year old seductress called Lolita from just a few decades earlier.[23] Could it be that Nabokov was a rip-off artist? Or perhaps he sampled from or even remixed the earlier work to make a more compelling work. This is especially ironic when you consider the copyright infringement lawsuit that Nabokov's family brought against Pia Pera for writing *Lo's Diary*, a similar story told from the girl's point of view.

The idea of authorship needs to return to its roots, the author is the person who is responsible for the current incarnation of the ideas taken from many people. When we pretend that authorship is

[24] J. Lethem, 'The Ecstasy of Influence: A Plagiarism', Harper's Magazine, pp.59–71, February 2007, http://harpers.org/archive/2007/02/0081387

complete and total, that every single idea and detail of a work sprung forth purely from the author's mind, then explicit attribution is necessary to counteract that total claim of credit. Whenever we ask, 'who are your influences?', 'where did you get that sample?', or even 'what software did you use?', we are assuming that authorship is not a sweeping totality, but rather the remixing of our experience into a new form.

Now, free software provides an excellent example of freely building upon the work of others. But it is important to note that these ideas did not originate in the world of computers. While academic traditions are often cited as the root of these ideas, there are many other examples. Before recording and the widespread use of copyright, music was also firmly rooted in this method of development. Musicians freely lifted and used other people's music, playing it, modifying it, passing it on. These ideas are present throughout the development of human civilization, you can see it in storytelling traditions, recipe swapping, traditional house designs, painting, and on and on.

> *[I]t becomes apparent that appropriation, mimicry, quotation, allusion, and sublimated collaboration consist of a kind of sine qua non of the creative act, cutting across all forms and genres in the realm of cultural production.*[24]

## The Internet Removes the Middleman, No More Publishers Needed

Up until the past few decades, creative works had to be distributed in physical form. Now, with computers becoming ubiquitous and interconnected, it is no longer necessary to distribute anything tangibly physical in order to reach an audience. There is an essential difference between the world of digital media and the physical world: as the digital world develops, scarcity becomes closer and closer to nonexistent. Making and distributing physical media requires substantial resources, and there are huge gains in efficiency in economies of scale. Creators were not able to reach large audiences without the aid of the publishers and their established distribution networks.

Now, anyone with a computer can readily copy digital media with insignificant cost. A number of developments are drastically reducing the costs of distribution: the widespread adoption of peer-to-peer distribution technology like bittorrent and the ever increasing bandwidth of network technology. Even the cost of promotion is going down as people get their information from a wider array of outlets, like blogs, netlabels, etc. Once you buy into this system of digital media distribution, the cost of distribution is so minimal that it is no longer an economic factor in the creation of the work.[25] When lobbying for the original copyright laws, publishers often said these laws would ensure that buyers were getting an accurate copy of the author's original work. After all, for another printer to start printing a book, they would have to typeset the whole thing, a laborious, manual process fraught with errors. Karl Fogel outlined an essential difference in the digital world:

[25] J. P. Barlow, 'The Economy of Ideas: Selling Wine Without Bottles on the Global Net' http://homes.eff.org/barlow/EconomyOfIdeas.html

> *To make a perfect copy of a printed work is actually quite hard, although making a corrupt or abridged copy is very easy. Meanwhile, to make a perfect copy of a digital work is trivially easy, it's making an imperfect copy that requires extra effort.*[7]

We are entering a world where all media ever created will be able to fit inside your pocket, distribution is getting easier and easier, media search technologies are getting better and better. This drives the cost of media down to the point where media will have to become a service rather than a commodity. If someone wants a particular piece of media they cannot find, they will pay someone to produce it. The internet has proven very useful in allowing people to communicate directly, eliminating all sorts of middlemen. Physical media, the whole basis of existence for publishers, is fading away as means of disseminating creative works. Even many publishers are losing faith in copyright law, and are now attempting to bypass copyright law by implementing digital restrictions management.[2] All this points to one inevitable conclusion: publishers are rapidly becoming obsolete. Copyright was designed around physical media at the behest of the publishing industry. Since the internet is freeing creators from publishers, creators should be freed of the harms of copyright at the same time.

**Free Software, Free Hardware, Free Culture, Free Art!**

It is widely established that monopolies generally suppress innovation and drive costs up, yet copyright terms have been continually extended over the past century. Due to the massive benefit of free access to the body of human creativity, new standards

[26] Public Library of Science, http://www.plos.org

[27] Elephants Dream, http://www.elephantsdream.org

of funding artistic work are emerging. Media artists are leading this push since digital media resists the easy commodification of traditional arts. So how then will artists earn an income? Here are a few examples that have nothing to do with copyright: festivals pay for the 'performance' of the work, not for the work itself; commissions and grants pay to develop a work; more and more people are making direct donations to artists; and of course, the biggest source of income for artists will likely remain teaching.

Sharing and collaboration are essential human traits, especially when it comes to intangible things like ideas, stories, music, and knowledge. Until recently, existing technology has largely worked against this impulse by turning knowledge into marketable chunks, like recordings, books, etc. Now we have the technology to re-enable this innate human trait on a broad scale. Digital media and the internet basically eliminate scarcity, the costs of copying and distribution in this realm are miniscule compared to the cost of production. Therefore everything that can work within the realm of digital media, can, should and will follow the direction demonstrated by free software.

If you believe that freedom generates the most innovation, then use free licenses. If you want to gamble in the lottery that is the commercial art world and recording industry, then you will most likely be required to restrict freedom and suppress innovation. As more and more of human endeavor can be packaged up into digital formats, it starts to behave like models of software development. Chunks of sound, image, and text can be woven together to form a new work with no more difficulty than it takes to use other people's code in your program. If we believe that open source methods provide more efficient production, as free software has clearly demonstrated, we must allow all human creativity to be as free as free software. Free software is well established and is growing ever more in adoption. Free hardware is making inroads into the broader public's consciousness. The idea of open source is also spreading beyond computers, with free scientific journals such as *PLoS*[26] as well as free movies like *Elephants Dream.*[27]

## Rely on the Creative Code of Ethics

Hopefully by now, I have begun to make clear that the creator's reputation is what is most valuable, not where she is credited, or the copyrights she owns. In the world of art, music, writing, and creative pursuits, there is a code of ethics that exists. It may not always be clearly defined or communicated, but it is present nonetheless: give credit where credit is due, do not rip off the work of others, support art that you enjoy, to give a few examples. Many organizations have codes of ethics which they require their members to obey. Most unions, including actors and writers guilds, also require their members obey a code of ethics. Academics and doctors follow strict codes of ethics, as do lawyers. If a DJ becomes known for 'biting', that can kill any future prospects. Being known as a rip-off artist or a fraud can rapidly kill a creative career. Remember Milli Vanilli? They went from selling tens of millions of albums to almost nothing once people found out that they did not sing any of their songs. If a legal remedy is the only thing that will suffice, then there are plenty of well established laws to rely on, from libel to slander to fraud.

The law is expensive, slow and cumbersome, and requires armies of highly trained people to navigate, support, create, and manage it. The law is a very useful tool for many problems, but in an ideal world, we would not need the law. Societies and communities have all sorts of rules and codes in many different forms. Compared to the law, social mores and codes of ethics are a lightweight way to establish agreed-upon standards of behavior. It is only when certain people consistently violate these mores and codes of ethics that society needs to have them codified into law.

The law is very much like any other facet of humanity, it is developed to solve problems at hand. Developments in technology and changes in society regularly render things obsolete, think of professions like blacksmithing, technology like oil lamps, and rules about handling horses. Why should the law be any different? Now that people are embracing free culture, they are removing restrictions on copying and distribution. Since copyright was designed around copying and distribution, removing those stipulations means that the core reasons for the existence of copyright have been removed. Free culture therefore needs to move beyond copyright.

Notes

# Common(s) Issues for Digital Art Libraries: From Open Licensing to Open Collaboration

Prodromos Tsiavos

## Introduction

Copyright has been an issue of concern for the art world since its inception (see e.g. McClean and Schubert, 2002; Rosenmeier and Teilmann, 2005; Stokes, 2001). In its original form, Copyright has purported to be an instrument of protection of the artist from the unauthorized exploitation of his work. Most importantly, Copyright has been perceived as an instrument of liberation of the artist from the limitations of patronage (Sterling, 2003). This latter conceptualization has identified Copyright with notions of freedom of artistic expression and unhindered creative endeavour. However, in the past decade, for a series of reasons primarily related to the introduction of digital means for the production and dissemination of artwork, the role of Copyright has been excessively debated and disputed (e.g. Boyle, 1988). Broader social changes that have undermined the romantic concept of authorship have had a tremendous impact in the way we view creativity, art and the relationship of the artist with her audience (Rose, 1994; 2003; Rose, 1993). We have consequently seen a polarization of the debate concerning digital art and Copyright and art, one camp arguing that they are inherently incompatible and a second one lobbying for the expansion of both protection and enforcement instruments (Rosenmeier and Teilmann, 2005). The core of the dispute between the two streams of thought has been the way in which the concept of originality is perceived in art and in law and the kind of protection it entails (Rose, 1993). Very recently, a series of initiatives like Creative Commons (Creative Commons, 2005) or the Creative Archive Licence Group (Creative Archive Licence Group, 2006) have suggested a middle ground solution, acknowledging the need to protect the creative contribution and the autonomy of the creator, while allowing subsequent uses of the work by other creators. In this process of explicitly acknowledging the role of collaborative development of artwork and the increasingly growing involvement of the audience in art's life-cycle, the role of art libraries becomes progressively more important. They operate as the cultivators of the necessary associations between existing and future creators. In such a capacity, they also have to make a choice concerning the kind of licensing scheme they are to adopt in order to achieve their educational role and facilitate the expansion of the common creative domain.

This paper explores the role of art libraries in relation to digital art forms and Copyright. It further seeks to investigate how the availability of different open licensing schemes has affected the policy and strategy of such libraries.

In the following section we explore three fundamental issues in relation to Copyright , the commons and art: first, Copyright as an instrument for the protection of free artistic expression; second, issues of authorship for the legal and creative worlds; and third, the notion of commons in relation to Copyright and art. Section three deals with the role of art libraries in environments of great complexity and intense digitization. We also make a brief overview of the British experience with such licensing schemes particularly in relation to three technologies: Flickr, YouTube and Podcasts. Finally we explore the possibilities for further employment of peer-to-peer technologies, particularly torrent communities, as a way to decentralise the digitization and indexing process. The paper concludes by presenting the current, often conflicting, trends in the realms of art libraries in relation to licensing and different forms of collaboration.

## 2. Art, Copyright and the Commons

The discourse around the way in which Art and Copyright relate is primarily concerned with the concepts of authorship, originality and the idea/expression dichotomy (Litman, 2001; McClean and Schubert, 2002). All three are closely related to each other and may provide us with a link to the broader issue of art and the commons. In the Anglo-American Copyright tradition, the original Copyright holder is deemed to be the creator of the work. The way in which such a creator has been conceptualized in Copyright law, is to a great degree the result of what by various authors has been described as the 'romantic' notion of authorship (Rose, 2003; Rose, 1993). Such a conceptualization views the author as an individual creator that is to be rewarded for her original expression of an idea. The author is hence rewarded for the 'added value' she provides to an existing body of knowledge and in that sense she is awarded a limited property right. The problem with such a concept of authorship is that it is very often the case that the creative practices of contemporary artists do not conform to such a model. As art becomes increasingly reliant on existing works rather than ideas, and indeed works that are still under Copyright protection, the creative process becomes extremely difficult or expensive. This is particularly true in relation to the use of works that have been particularly successful in the sense of them becoming part of our popular culture and in that sense reference points for other artists. The problem with such reference works is that a number of subsequent artists are willing to use them and the permission obtaining process is either cumbersome or in certain cases not even possible. Originality as non-copying is also problematic beyond the issue of popularity of the works of reference. For a great number of contemporary works the need to copy or alter pre-existing works constitutes an intrinsic part of the creative process. At the same time, work that is more conceptual than expressive seems to be falling outside the scope of Copyright protection causing distress to the relevant artists. The idea/expression dichotomy that assumes protection of the form rather than the underlying idea is not always suitable for artistic forms that are of a more conceptual nature.

Returning to some of the original arguments of granting Copyright protection to artistic works may provide us some useful insights regarding the current trends in the protection of artistic works. As mentioned in section one, the protection of artistic works under Copyright has been argued to provide a greater freedom to the individual artist that could thus produce her work free from the limitations of patronage. This argument is further reinforced by the operation of the idea/expression dichotomy as a heuristic that allows new ideas to freely flow whereas the expressions are protected on an individual basis and on the assumption that they have not been copied. However, both assumptions seem to be under increasing strain in recent times. First, the financial autonomy of the creator is increasingly threatened by the broader market trends that may render only particular types of art as commercially viable. Inversely, the artist may choose to finance her work not through direct appeal to an open art-market but through accepting commissions for his work or funding the production of a certain work in advance. Second, as we have shown above, the idea/expression dichotomy is increasingly either not relevant to the creator or - even worse – may operate as a hindrance of creative activity. Third, a combination of the above two trends, indicates that Copyright , instead of supporting the free artistic creation it constrains financially and thus artistically the creative expression: if in order to produce a derivative work the creator needs to spend increasing amounts of money to clear rights on pre-existing works, it is very likely that her creative output is to be reduced. Such clearance would involve the identification of existing rights holders, the negotiations with them, and finally the paying of the relevant fee. The existing exceptions or Fair Use provisions in various Copyright laws could be said to operate in such a way, but practice reveals that this is not really the case. Exceptions are very narrowly drafted in many national jurisdictions or if they have a broader scope and ambit, then expert legal advice would be required in order to be used in order to avoid the risk of Copyright infringements (Boyle, 1996; 1997; Boyle, 2003b).

The commons literature has greatly emphasized the problem of extensive Copyright protection on forms of derivative creativity (e.g. Lessig, 1999; 2001; 2002; 2003; Boyle, 1997; Boyle, 2003a; Samuelson, 2001; 2003; Benkler, 1998; 1999; 2000; 2001; 2003; Litman, 1990; 1994; 2004). This stream of literature has concluded that the fostering of the public domain is essential for the production of works drawing from our existing cultural environment. While the relaxing and reform of Copyright laws has been repeatedly suggested as a means for achieving a rich public domain, the institutional costs for such a reversal has been so great that a second solution was suggested more in tune with notions of private property and less costly in terms of regulatory reform. Such a solution has been based on the assumption that the commons could be reinvigorated through the application of licensing schemes supporting copying and reuse of existing copyrighted material. Three different streams of literature seem to be coming to the same conclusion: first, the Creative Commons literature; second, the Copyright and Art literature; and third, the European Free Speech literature.

Starting point for the Creative Commons project has been what is described by its founder as the notion of 'Fair Use Plus'(Lessig, 2005). The latter is an expression of the Fair Use or Fair Dealing principle in contractual or licensing terms. As indicated above, Fair Use principles seem to be the mechanism within the existing Copyright system that comes closest to solving the problems appearing in relation to contemporary creative practices. We have also seen how such provisions suffer from problems of limited clarity and as such they cannot really provide the desired solutions. The CC licences are targeted to such problems and constitute 'Fair Use Plus' in the sense of providing a clear set of allowed uses that are both more extensive and more limited than the classic Fair Use provisions. They are more extensive in the sense that they are applicable in a much wider set of uses of the work and are not limited by what is known in the Copyright literature as the three step test (Sterling, 2003). At the same time they provide a more limited form of protection than Fair Use provisions since they are not obligatory limitations of the rights of the creator conferred by Copyright law but rather are the result of the will of the creator: if the latter is not willing to licence her work under a CC licence, then there is no application of the 'Fair Use Plus' concept.

The Copyright and Art literature has also concluded that besides Copyright reform, the possibility of licensing instruments that could allow such users could be a solution. Though the idea of using a licensing instrument is the same as in the case of Creative Commons, there are some differences between this second solution and the 'Fair Use Plus' concept. The idea here is that the licences are compulsory in the sense that the creator is not able to negotiate their granting or not with a potential licensee, that they require the payment of a certain fee and that they are – in all probability – collectively administered through a collecting society. An example of such a case would be the DACS licences that allow secondary uses of creative works provided they fit under the definitions of the licences it provides (McClean and Schubert, 2002).

Finally, the Copyright and free speech jurisprudence seems to be conferring a similar solution. There is a relationship between free speech concerns and Fair Use provisions or Copyright exceptions, which in the US literature and jurisprudence has been expressed in the doctrine that a free speech test is virtually non applicable if the Fair Use test has not been applied first. In the relevant European literature, free speech concerns are primarily satisfied 'internally' by national Copyright laws through the requirements of originality and the idea/expression dichotomy (free circulation of ideas) or the limited term of protection of the copyrighted work and the Copyright exceptions (amounting to the US fair use and UK fair dealing). However, most interestingly in a recent French case (France 2 case, EComHR, 1997) when the court was asked to decide whether the prohibition of use of material in a broadcast that involved the reproduction of copyrighted artistic works fell under the free artistic expression exceptions, it gave a negative answer. The reason behind the adoption of such a stance has been that a licence existed and that the user of the material could have paid a pre-fixed amount to use the relevant material. Such a decision indicates that for those uses that are not covered by Fair Use provisions or Copyright exceptions, the existence of a licensing scheme renders any expansion of the relevant provisions in the Copyright law unnecessary.

While licensing undoubtedly constitutes a practical and hence attractive solution to the problems appearing as a result of new creative practices, it is far from clear the specific manifestation that such solutions could or should have and is even more doubtful the degree to which they could further disturb the ecology of Copyright regulations (see e.g. Elkin-Koren, 1997; 1998; 2005; Dusollier, 2006). Voluntary individual open licensing schemes such as Creative Commons or the Free Documentation Licence are appealing but are still at the early stages of their life-cycle and hence, as many commentators have noticed, could fragment the commons: by having more than one mutually incompatible licence, it is likely that artists will again face the problem of individually having to negotiate the use of pre-existing works or sets of data. Voluntary or compulsory collective licence schemes such as the DACS licences, require that the relevant collecting societies agree with the secondary uses of the works of their members. This is highly unlikely to happen, other than in the case of very standard cases (such as broadcasting) as it is not possible that all members will consent to secondary uses of their works. What seems to be more likely in the future is a merger of the two models as we have seen in the case of the Dutch collecting societies: the provision of licensing instruments that allow standard secondary uses and the provision of the possibility to the members of a collecting society to use standardized public individual licensing schemes such as creative commons.

In the following section we examine the implications of this trend to move towards the use of licensing schemes for supporting the increasingly diverse creative practices for the art libraries.

## 3. The Changing Role of Libraries in Complex Creative Environments

The use of licences as the preferred instrument for the regulation of creative activity is the direct result of an increasingly more diverse set of creative practices supported by digital networks. Four aspects of digital technology are most relevant to this paper that all relate to the lowering of costs: (a) technologies allowing the production of digital works; (b) technologies allowing the reproduction of existing digital works and digitization of analogue works; (c) technologies of decentralized dissemination of digital content and communication between individuals sharing common interests (social networks software); (d) the embedding of digital networks into analogue environments and hence the creation of hybrid environments.

Most of the relevant literature emphasizes the lowering of costs of reproduction and dissemination technologies, often ignoring the importance of social networks software and the emergence of hybrid environments possibly because the latter two are a far more recent development. However, in order to appreciate the challenges that art libraries are likely to face we need to take all four factors into consideration.

For the purposes of this research we take as the primary purpose of any library to be not merely the storage of the relevant material but rather the provisions of the associations that make it relevant to its users. In that sense the library and particularly the specialized art library constitutes a portal which provides access primarily to creators rather than end-users. In the face of a creative process that becomes increasingly referential to or makes direct use of pre-existing works, the role of the art library is to facilitate such access while ensuring it remains within the realms of legality. While this may appear as a trivial task to the non-expert, it is in fact a much more complex endeavor. As noted by the copynorms (Schultz, 2007) and charismatic code (Strahilevitz, 2003) literature, the librarians often have to explore the limits of Copyright law in order to conform with their professional norms that advocate the free flow of information and open access to knowledge. Thus the objectives of Copyright law and the librarians norms may often appear as inconsistent. While in practice this is often true, in terms of a Copyright justification analysis it should not be so.

At least in the Anglo-American tradition, Copyright is a limited property right that is granted to the creator for a specific duration and which does not cover a wide range of creations that should remain in the public domain. In section two we have seen different instruments of ensuring that the public domain or the commons remains wide enough so that the artists could draw from it for their subsequent creations. We have also seen how current creative practices render existing Fair Use provisions not appropriate for what the artists need in order to continue their creative work. It is not a coincidence that some of the early open content licences such as the Open Publication Licence or the BBB Open Access declarations came from the archive and library area.

Similarly to the approach followed by the French court as described in section 2 the librarians are conscious of the situation where copyrighted material is increasingly required to be used by subsequent authors and in that sense they are interested in licensing schemes that expand the possibilities provided by the Fair Use type provisions.

The role of librarians in relation to licensing is particularly important if we consider the role of the library both as a consumer or intermediary and as a producer of cultural goods. As a consumer or intermediary the library needs to acquire the relevant rights from the relevant rights holders or the entities that are entrusted with the collective management of such rights, i.e. the collecting societies. This is the case with the majority of the material held in a library, which are made available to the library patrons through a series of channels. For instance a library may make available the physical copies of material for use or limited reproduction. The same is valid for digital copies of content that is made available to the users of the library through a series of arrangements ensuring that the owners of such rights are duly compensated. Such a role presupposes that the libraries have developed capacity in two respects: first, that they are able to choose those licensing schemes that are most suitable for the needs of their patrons; and second, that the librarians themselves in their daily professional contacts with users of material are able to instruct them in the way in which the material should be used. The latter is not such a trivial task as the librarian has to on the one hand ensure that the maximum amount of information is made available to the user of the library and that all lawful possibilities of using such material are encouraged, while ensuring that the libraries abide by the relevant laws. As the users of the library have increasingly access to a variety of material that is governed by different rules which are not always self-evident, the library plays the role of an educator regarding the kinds of rights that the user of the library has in relation to the offered material.

Libraries in the past have predominantly dealt with publishers or collecting societies in relation to the procurement of the physical artifacts and the relevant rights; however, technological and legal developments have pushed libraries and art schools and universities libraries in particular to a new realm where they increasingly have to deal directly with the artist. This is the case when the library is located within a certain educational institution where members of the staff and students are encouraged to systematically deposit their works under what is commonly known as digital repositories. These contain material that is normally conferred by the educational institution within which the library is placed and it could range from PhD thesis or dissertations to art work produced during courses offered by such an institution. Besides, the material that is found in such repositories, each educational institution produces a variety of other material that is contained in its website without a homogenous system of indexing and consequently sharing the relevant material. The role of the library being one of associating material and ensuring that it is made accessible to its users, it has now to face a series of new challenges in relation to these new creators: (a) first the relevant material has to be somehow categorized and indexed so that it is easily accessible; (b) the libraries have to work together with the academic staff of the relevant institution in order to set a series of policies that define the terms under which material produced by the members of the staff and the students will be made available to the academic community of the specific institution and the broader users of the relevant libraries. Thus the library has now not only to explain to its users the kinds of rules governing the material made available, but also to suggest licences which are likely to serve the creative community in the best possible fashion. This latter function is again an especially tenuous one: the library in collaboration with the relevant educational institution has to ensure that on the one hand the creator is provided with a range of options regarding how she is to make her work available; on the other hand it should also suggest policies about the preferred mode of licensing of the relevant material and make sure that such licences are most convenient for the objectives of maximum knowledge dissemination and availability. It is in this stage that libraries should and are actually encouraging open forms of licensing to the institutions they are placed within.

The second role of the library is that of the creator. This may be seen broadly speaking in relation to types of works: First, in the process of indexing material the libraries produce a huge amount of metadata that are in themselves protected under Copyright Law and in EU under the *sui generis* database right. There is an ongoing discussion about such metadata and the standards used for their development that is primarily focused on issues of interoperability and the production of a single standard that is made available to everyone so that libraries may further collaborate with each other. What is interesting in relation to such metadata and standards is that there is a general consensus on keeping them open, however there is no specific set of licences or agreements governing their production. This is to a great degree related to the fact that the relevant licences are rather new. In addition most of the standards are de facto open or are covered by specific FLOSS licences. Second, art libraries in particular have in their possession old manuscripts, drawings or books that are now gradually digitized. In this digitization process, though the library initially holds only physical property, it could potentially become the right holder of the digital version of the book or the manuscript or the artwork. In that sense the licensing agreement that allows the digitization of the relevant physical artifact when assigned to a third entity, which is very often the case, it has been given extra care, so as to ensure that the copyrights or database rights that could emerge out of such a process remain with the library. Again the library as an institution has to have developed the relevant capacity to ensure that: (a) the library and not the contractor retains the copyrights; (b) the licence to the contractor to potentially use the digitized material is non-exclusive and allows the open licensing of the same material by the art library. In these last two cases (metadata production and digitization) where the library appears to be the creator of copyrighted works its role is not to educate either users (as in the case of library as a user of copyrighted material) or other authors (as in the case of the library as repository of internally developed material) bur rather to make conscious decisions about how it will retain its digital assets and to make them openly available.

An interesting twist in the narrative of library digitization is provided by the way in which such digitization is perceived and organized. Digitization by the libraries tends to be a systematic, centrally organized and either publicly or privately funded function that needs to be thoroughly managed in order to produce a result. Art libraries in particular are primarily focused on the digitization of older artwork or books and film libraries with the digitization of rare copies of early cinema. However, a great part of popular culture that has been produced in analogue audiovisual media, particularly on the internet is not deemed as relevant to such libraries, cannot attract funding for its realization or requires complex processes of clearing rights that are both costly and require expertise that art libraries do not have and they cannot afford to acquire. At the same time a great part of such content is increasingly reproduced without permission in torrent trackers that are devoted to particular types of content either in terms of type (e.g. music) or nationality (e.g. Greek) or area of interest (e.g. political works). Digitization is occurring in a very decentralized, not properly governed but increasingly systematical fashion by such networks that operate as archives of popular culture or specific genres or artistic production. Unfortunately, research in this area is still at its nascent stages and with few exceptions (e.g. the Internet Archive which however stores web pages and specific types of content in a fairly centralized fashion) it has not caught the attention of any of the art libraries or art schools.

In all three roles of the libraries presented above (user, facilitator, creator) we have assumed that the art library operates within a closed institutional setting, as indeed was the case until very recently with most of the libraries. However, this is increasingly not true, especially for art libraries that operate not in an educational institution but rather within a museum or a gallery. The latter often invites as users, individuals that are neither as specialized as the patrons of e.g. a university library nor necessarily inclined to produce new works on the basis of the ones they have access to, nor do they have the training to access the material without some prior experience. Such an audience presents different types of challenges and accordingly has invited the extensive use of digital technologies to tackle such issues.

Such museum-based art libraries, for instance the Tate Galleries library, or the British Museum or the Victoria & Albert National Art Library also have to produce material that is provided to the audience in a really simple and easy fashion. V&A has been one of the most interesting cases. Podcasting technologies are currently used by V&A in order to produce sound recordings explaining different aspects of their exhibitions and attract a wider audience. Podcasts are particularly easy to handle as copyrighted material because they tend to include material to which the provider of the podcast owns the Copyright s. In most cases they are in the form of talk-shows including interviews with relevant artists or descriptions of items of the V&A collection by its curators. Unfortunately the use of podcasts is still fairly limited and their content is not licensed under any open licence. V&A has also made use of social networking technologies, mainly Myspace in order to encourage V&A resident artists or students to made their work available to the wider public. Again there are still no clear licensing guidelines and there is no conscious policy for licensing such material under open licences. It seems that to a great extent there is reluctance by the libraries or museums themselves to follow such approaches as a result of the less than clear legal status of artifacts they hold in their collections or the exact ownership structures in the case of digitized material. The vast amount of art items held by such institutions makes the situation even worse.

However, the most interesting technology currently used in order to engage the audience of V&A, British Museum or the Tate Galleries has to do with the use of the Flickr application. The latter allows the users to upload their own photos and also decide on the licence under which they are to be disseminated. A similar service is offered by YouTube where videos by users may be also uploaded and then streamed by other users. There is a growing interest particularly by the Tate Galleries to use such devices in order to get the audience to participate in art events or even art creation. The most recent example has been the 'How We Are' at Tate Britain, where users were invited to offer their own version of contemporary Britain and these pictures were then used for the relevant exhibition that took place in Tate Britain this summer. Again no strict licensing policy has been employed in order to govern the use of the relevant images other than that the Tate Galleries had the permission to use such pictures in their exhibition and actually charge for that. While the Tate example is a clear case of involving the audience in the production of an artistic work or in the realization of an exhibition, the norm is not for the art venue to organize the audience and engage them in its artistic activities, but rather the audience to use the art venue, whether a gallery or a museum, as the locus where they produce their own works and then share them with each other. This is the case with a series of groups and communities in Flickr where users share photos they have taken in parts of some of the major London galleries and museums. One of the most interesting cases is again that of Tate Modern: the users that have uploaded photos on Flickr have wondered about the limits of their ability to take pictures and publish them on the net: which were the physical areas in which picture taking was allowed, which exhibits were allowed to be photographed and which limitations were set on the use and dissemination of the relevant material. As one is informed by the site itself, one of the uploaders of photos in the Tate Modern group has actually contacted the responsible Tate representative who explained that while taking pictures in the turbine hall (Tate Modern's main hall) was allowed for non-commercial purposes, this was not allowed for the exhibitions hosted in the rest of the building. These rules aside, this still remains an unexplored area for a series of reasons: first, there is no clear set of rules all uploaders may adhere to. Second, these groups of uploaders that are at the same time visitors to the relevant art spaces have constructed communities on their own and without the guidance of the owners of the art spaces themselves.

Nevertheless, the latter are now starting investigating the capabilities of the medium as well as of other social networking software to further interact with such audiences. Third, there is no clear understanding by galleries of how the interaction of digital and physical space takes place or how the roles of creator and audience actually interchange and what the implications primarily for the creative process and secondarily for the ownership and licensing of the relevant material are.

## 4. Conclusions

In this paper we have explored a series of issues related to art production, art libraries, licensing and collaboration that all revolve around a common pole: the general trend towards more open forms of licensing and more collaborative models of artistic production and dissemination. In section 2 we have seen how creativity is increasingly dependent on the reuse of existing works and how this trend is the result both of the technological developments that have substantially reduced the costs of production, reproduction and dissemination of material but also of the broader cultural trend of creating art through the reproduction of existing works. Such creative practices may be accommodated by the existing legal framework only through the extensive use of different forms of licensing. This is a conclusion reached by three streams of literature and practice: First, part of the Fair Use jurisprudence holds that in cases of secondary uses of creative works, if some form of licensing scheme is available the Fair Use defense is not applicable; second, the

Creative Commons is based on the assumption that for a series of secondary creative uses of a work which are not covered – or are not clearly covered – by Fair Use provisions, standard open licensing is the solution; finally, the contemporary Art and Copyright literature has emphasized the importance of using collective licensing as a potential solution to the problem of unauthorized secondary uses of an artistic work.

Though the need for some form of licensing and particularly open licensing (the Creative Commons solution) or at least non-discriminatory licensing (the contemporary Art and Copyright or the Fair Use jurisprudence and theory) is established, the way in which such licensing schemes, even where existent, are to be applied by the arts libraries is less than clear. In section three we explore the way in which technological change has changed the role of arts libraries. In particular, we examine how they are positioned in relation to the issue of licensing use as they may adopt (often simultaneously) three roles: First, that of being a licensee (user); second, that of suggesting a set of licences to creators (facilitator); and third that of choosing a set of licences for its own use (creator). While most of the literature regarding digital Copyright focuses on problems raised by the lowering costs in the production, reproduction and dissemination of protected content, this paper also introduces two more elements: first, the emergence of social networks that view cultural or content production as part of their core functions (such as community based torrents); and second the blurring of the boundaries between the physical and the digital and of the concepts of the audience and the artist (such as is the case with the uploading of pictures by galleries), the use of social software networks by arts students or the participation of the audience in the setting of an exhibition).

Overall, we have seen two complementary trends over the last ten years: on the one hand the sector of libraries, museums and archives is concerned with integration, synergy and standardization and on the other hand the same sector is interested in increasingly more decentralized and bottom up approaches both in the way the works are disseminated and the way in which some of their core functions take place. Surprisingly, both trends may be facilitated by licences belonging to the broader family of open licences: standardization of metadata and broader collaboration between libraries may be achieved through open standards and open data licences; at the same time decentralization, radicalization of production and collaboration between the artists is possible through FLOSS, open content licences or collective and non-discriminatory licensing of secondary uses of work.

In conclusion, though licensing plays an indisputable role in the way in which artistic works are enjoyed and created, it is still far from clear even to organizations playing a key role in artistic production such as the libraries, which are the most appropriate licences for each particular set of circumstances. Furthermore, collaborative creative practices are far ahead of any legal expression of their organizing elements, such as is the case with real and virtual environment interactions in the case of Flickr or – even worse – are considered as against the current legal regime, as in the case of torrent trackers. This paper does not purport to provide any final answers to the issues identified. It is rather a call for further research on these issues aiming at understanding the creative practices and organizational norms before attempting the imposition of any regulatory model.

Bibliography

Y. Benkler, 'The Commons As A Neglected Factor of Information Policy', 1998, http://www.law.nyu.edu/benklery/commons.pdf [Accessed, 20/05/06]

Y. Benkler, 'Free as the Air to Common Use: First Amendment Constraints on Enclosure of the Public Domain', New York Law Review, 74 (354), 1999.

Y. Benkler, 'From Consumers to Users: Shifting the Deeper Structures of Regulation Towards Sustainable Commons and User Access', Federal Communications Law Journal, (561), 2000.

Y. Benkler, 'The Battle Over the Institutional Ecosystem in the Digital Environment', Communications of the ACM, 2 (44), 2001, p. 84.

Y. Benkler, 'Freedom in the Commons: Toward a Political Economy of Information', Duke Law Journal, 52 (April), 2003, pp. 1245-1276.

J. Boyle, 'The Search for an Author: Shakespeare and the Framers', American University Law Review, 1988, p. 27.

J. Boyle, 'Shamans, Software and Spleens: Law and the Construction of the Information Society', Harvard University Press, Cambridge, Mass.; London, 1996.

J. Boyle, 'A Politics of Intellectual Property: Environmentalism for the Net', Duke Law Journal, 47, 1997, p. 87.

J. Boyle, 'The Second Enclosure Movement and the Construction of the Public Domain', Law and Contemporary Problems, Winter-Spring (66), 2003a, pp. 33-74.

J. Boyle, 'Foreword: the Opposite of Property?' Law and Contemporary Problems, Winter-Spring (66), 2003b., pp. 1-33.

Creative Archive Licence Group, 'BBC Creative Archive Pilot has Ended', BBC, http://creativearchive.bbc.co.uk/news/archives/2006/09/hurry_while_sto.html [Accessed 31/10/07]

Creative Commons, 'About Us: "Some Rights Reserved": Building a Layer of Reasonable Copyright', Creative Commons, 2005, http://creativecommons.org/about/history [Accessed, 07/07/06]

S. Dusollier, 'The Master's Tools v. the Master's House: Creative Commons v. Copyright ', Columbia Journal of Law & the Arts, 29 (Spring), 2006, pp. 271-293.

N. Elkin-Koren, 'Copyright Policy and the Limits of Freedom of Contract', Berkeley Technology Law Journal, 12 (1), 1997, p. 93.

N. Elkin-Koren, 'Copyrights in Cyberspace - Rights Without Laws?', Chicago Law Review, 73, 1998, p.1115.

N. Elkin-Koren, 'What Contracts Cannot Do: The Limits of Private Ordering in Facilitating a Creative Commons', Fordham Law Review, 74 (November), 2005, pp. 375-422.

L. Lessig, 1999, 'Code and Other Laws of Cyberspace', Basic Books.

L. Lessig, 'The Future of Ideas: The Fate of Commons in A Connected World', Random House, 2001.

L. Lessig, 'Innovating Copyright ', Cardozo Arts and Entertainment Law Journal, 20, 2002, pp. 611-623.

L. Lessig, 'The Creative Commons', Florida Law Review, 55 (July), 2003, pp.763-777.

L. Lessig, 'CC in Review: Lawrence Lessig on CC & Fair Use', Creative Commons, 2005, http://creativecommons.org/weblog/entry/5681 [Accessed 02/11/05]

J. Litman, 'The Public Domain', Emory Law Journal, 1990, 39, 965.

J. Litman, 'The Exclusive Right to Read', Cardozo Arts and Entertainment Law Journal, 1994, 13, 29.

J. Litman, 'Digital Copyright : Protecting Intellectual Property on the Internet', Prometheus Books, Amherst, NY, 2001.

J. Litman, 'Sharing and Stealing', Hastings Communications and Enterprise Law Journal, 2004, p. 271.

D. McClean and K.Schubert, Dear Images: Art, Copyright and Culture, Ridinghouse/ICA, London, 2002.

C. M. Rose, 'Property and Persuasion: Essays on the History, Theory, and Rhetoric of Ownership', Westview Press, Boulder, Colo.; Oxford, 1994.

C. M. Rose, 'Romans, Roads, and Romantic Creators: Traditions of Public Property in the Information Age', Law & Contemporary Problems, 66 (Winter/Spring), 2003, pp. 89-110.

M. Rose, 'Authors and Owners: the Invention of Copyright ', Harvard University Press, Cambridge, Mass.; London, 1993.

M. Rosenmeier and S. Teilmann, 'Art and Law: the Copyright Debate', DJF Pub., Copenhagen, 2005.

P. Samuelson, 'Toward a New Politics of Intellectual Property', Communications of the ACM, 44 ((March) 3), 2001.

P. Samuelson, 'Digital Rights Management {and, or, vs.} the Law', Communications of the ACM, 46 (4), 2003, pp. 41-45.

M. F. Schultz, 'Copynorms: Copyright and Social Norms' in Intellectual Property and Information Wealth: Issues and Practices in the Digital Age, Ed. P. K. Yu, Praeger, Westport, Conn.; London, 2007, pp. 4 v.

J. A. L. Sterling, 'World Copyright Law: protection of authors' works, performances, phonograms, films, video, broadcasts and published editions in national, international and regional law: with a glossary of legal and technical terms, and a reference list of Copyright and related rights laws throughout the world', Sweet & Maxwell, London, 2003.

S. Stokes, 'Art and Copyright ', Hart, Oxford, 2001.

L. J. Strahilevitz, 'Charismatic Code, Social Norms, and the Emergence of Cooperation on the File-Swapping Networks', Virginia Law Review, 89 (May), 2003, pp. 505-595.

# From Open Circuits to Open Distribution: Can Video Artists Adopt FLOSS Strategies as their Own?

Ross Rudesch Harley

*The cassette will diversify the video culture. Now there is only one television structure in the United States, one-way communication from three major networks. You get their kind of television, or you must cut it off. But in the future world, you will have cable TV, video cassettes, and picture phones... Why move, why drive somewhere in your car, if you can do everything right at home?*

*– Nam June Paik, 1973*[1]

[1] Nam June Paik, quoted in David Joselit, Feedback: Television Against Democracy, MIT Press, Cambridge, 2007, p. 46.

[2] Mark Pesce quoted in J.D.Lasica, Darknet: Hollywood's War Against the Digital Generation, Wiley, New Jersey, 2005, p. 162.

While the history of video art is presently being be re-told in books and journals, and its presentation in museums, galleries and art events is more widespread than ever, video art is in danger of becoming disconnected from the far-reaching changes underway in today's networked media world. The 'future world' Nam June Paik imagined may not have actually arrived exactly as he envisaged it, but he wasn't that far off. The trouble is I'm not sure the video art world agrees.

This chapter argues that the most radical proponents of video art were always concerned with establishing alternative networks of communication based on the principle of 'open circuits' and 'participation TV'. An understanding of this historical context is helpful in highlighting the potentials to be found in today's web-based networks that privilege 'sharing', 'participation' and 'openness'.

While we should not be too hasty in declaring a victory for open source, we should note – as Mark Pesce reminds us – that 'as broadband succeeds, broadcasting will fail.'[2] The open source movement and Creative Commons protocols represent the best distributed, shared and non-proprietary tools we have at our disposal to achieve the alternative networks of distribution envisaged since the 1960s and now mutating into their broadband offspring.

[3]
[empahasis added]
Kate Horsfield, 'Busting the Tube: A Brief History of Video Art', in Horsfield, K and Hilderbrand, L, (eds) Feedback: The Video Data Bank Catalogue of Video Art an Artist Interviews, Temple university Press, Philadelphia, 2006, p. 9.

That said, there are many stumbling blocks to be overcome before we will see the widespread distribution of video art according to FLOSS principles. Today, the biggest opponents of free and open distribution for video art are often the artists and distributors themselves, who are struggling to come to terms with the immense changes happening in the alternative media universe – largely emerging as a result of digital networks and technologies (from web-based platforms to peer-to-peer networks). The difficulties lie in very real concerns to do with the assignation of rights and the control of distribution that earns income for both artists and organizations alike. As emerging artists find new ways to sell limited editions of their work through gallery and museum circuits, what does it mean to make their work 'freely' available via the web?

I want to suggest that solutions to these challenges can be found in FLOSS principles, and that these approaches will 'diversify the video culture' in new and unexpected ways. The radical challenges to television, art and culture made by video artists in the 1960s and 1970s find their echo today in the principles of FLOSS, Creative Commons, Open Content and other emerging principles of participatory culture.

When artists first took to making video in the 1960s, its radical form and function was often predicated on the ease of access to the means of production. For a couple of thousand dollars anybody could buy a portapak and start making videos. The same is true today, as the barriers to entry-level video equipment tumble. But making work is only ever one small part of the production-distribution-exhibition circuit. As Kate Horsfield argues in 'Busting the Tube: A Brief History of Video Art', groups such as the Radical Software collective of the 1970s saw beyond the means of production to another immense shift in politics and culture:

> *Power is no longer measured in land, labor, or capital, but by access to information and the means to disseminate it. As long as the most powerful tools (not weapons) are in the hands of those who would hoard them, no alternative cultural vision can succeed. Unless we design and implement alternate information structures which transcend and reconfigure the existing ones, other alternate systems and life styles will be no more than products of the existing process.*[3]

Forty years ago, video artists proposed a radical approach to the rise of the 'information society'. They saw the potential for far-reaching changes to mainstream media models. With their focus on process over products, their 'alternate cultural vision' was squarely aimed at disrupting the easy fit between the one-way communication networks of broadcast television and the circuit of commodity-consumption. In the 1970s and '80s, it was the one-way tube of commercial television that was reconfigured by video art practice. And while the dissemination of video art in alternate information structures has certainly been growing and transforming over the past thirty years, distribution has remained the Achilles heel of all video art movements.

As interest in the past and present of video art increases, it remains almost as difficult to access and view these works today as it was in the 1970s. If you can't access a reasonable viewing copy of a work online, what chance is there of tracking down a copy anywhere else? But what would it mean to establish a distributed, networked archive of video art – one that is based precisely on the viral principles of peer-to-peer sharing, the democratic protocols of open archives and the powerful technics of open source codecs? It is my contention that the current conditions of digital media provide significant opportunities to create globally distributed archives that extend and develop the early vision of video art radicals. Video artists and their representative organizations should therefore embrace and adopt the culture of open source as an extension of the 'original' video art project.

The problem of inadequate distribution has existed for video art since its inception. Make as many videos as you like, but who was going to keep them and where could you show them? The rise of the video festival circuit and the organizations devoted to the preservation and distribution of video art made perfect sense in this context. But despite all these significant efforts to distribute alternative videos by alternate means, their impact has been necessarily stunted by the physicality of the networks. The video image may have been wrenched from its commercial televisual framework, but the objects [tapes] and viewing contexts remained.

Of course it's not going to stay that way for much longer. The technical possibilities for the distribution of video art and experimental film are rapidly changing, and there are many opportunities to make work that has been hard to see freely available via open systems. I want to argue that the question of video distribution has been crucial for artists since the inception of video, and that open means of distribution lie at the heart of alternative uses of video. Historically, individual artists and representative organizations have worked hard to ensure their work is seen and disseminated to the largest possible audience, without disrupting the integrity of the work. FLOSS is an important cornerstone in the development of this crucial aspect of video art – it's wide dissemination.

[4] Stoffel Debuysere, 'Culture Intercom Redux: Audiovisual Media in a Network Culture', in Ramon Coelho (ed), Content in Context: New Technologies for Distribution, Netherlands Media Art Institute, Amsterdam, 2005, p. 51.

In this chapter, I want to underscore the differences between FLOSS platforms and proprietary ones. Although there are many issues surrounding the rights of works to be resolved, an open archive approach presents a broad set of possibilities that will help contribute to the expansion of video art to wider audiences. Creative Commons licensing practices and the open source ethos offer new ways of brokering the relationship between video art and new (and old) audiences.

From the point of view of user experience, there is simply little or no difference now between the technical/aesthetic characteristics of proprietary systems and open systems. While proprietary formats such as Windows Media, Quicktime and RealVideo have developed their own competing and incompatible formats and codecs, a plethora of high quality open source solutions to digital video are finding widespread utilization – witness OGG Vorbis/Theora, MPEG-4IP, VideoLAN or FFMPEG. The sustainability and growth of any distributed archive or online video art channel is better served by subscription to the FLOSS model, which allows for a greater uptake of 'agnostic' technical systems that are not in the service of particular corporate constraints (cost and licensing).

Open content management systems assign very different sets of rights along Creative Commons lines. This can leave the copyright with the originator of the work, assign it to another agent or person, or vary the extent to which a work may circulate. The standard Creative Commons licenses have a significant impact on the assignation of copyrights, allowing for a variety of flexible (though legally binding) agreements that benefit publishers, audiences/users, and most of all, artists.

As Stoffel Debuysere has pointed out in a recent article entitled 'Culture Intercom Redux: Audiovisual Media in a Network Culture', the convergence of television and video art strategies finds its expression in the FLOSS ethos:

> *This becomes clear in practices such as 'broadcatching', in fact a variant of 'Podcasting' but in relation to video and other media files, by which with the aid of RSS feeds digital image fragments can be called up and downloaded via BitTorrent. Independently developed software such as the video download program Videora and open source, build it yourself InternetTV applications such as MythTV demonstrate that the restraints built in by the industry can be gotten around or overcome with little difficulty. Recently various communities launched a call to hack and modify the PSP ... which resulted in countless brilliant hybrid applications.*[4]

The open source and participatory media community represent forward-looking bottom-up initiatives that challenge the conventions of broadcast networks and corporate media ecosystems. It seems natural that the video art community would align itself with these 'movements' and new paradigms.

The efforts of organizations like Montevideo in Amsterdam, the Video Data Bank in Chicago and Electronic Arts Intermix in New York have championed the collection and distribution of artist's works for decades. It is thanks to their efforts that many video works have any distribution at all, and that more and more artists' videos find their way into more general circulation.

The Netherlands Media Arts Institute has played a major role over a number of years in attempting to provide structure and consistency for databases and processes that are needed to make any online system easily adopted by anybody. A number of viable models and tools have already been introduced by the Capturing Unstable Art project. And most promising of all, the OASIS project has also made significant advances in this direction. It is an open source collection management system that is well-suited to the needs of an open content video art system.[5]

Recent moves to make parts of their collections available online (i.e. A Kinetic History: EAI Archives Online and REWIND | Artists' Video Collection at the Visual Research Centre, Dundee Contemporary Arts and CARTE in central London) point towards a future where archives will become less repositories for dead content and more like a living, expanding database that will link past and future media arts.

What would be the impact of such a system for the institutions who have been trying to archive and distribute such material for decades?[6] My question is really to ask what would it mean to put this model of user-generated content, distributed viewing, and exhibition networks in the service our institutions and individual video artists?

What would happen if we could dynamically bring together our geographically distant and fragmentary histories of video art using the participatory and user-centric technologies of the peer-to-peer web? Perhaps a FLOSS view of the internet can offer new possibilities for stitching these 'immaterialities' together into new relations in a mashable, hyperlinked, electronic universe. Under such conditions, it is possible to

[5] http://www.oasis-archive.eu/index.php/En:Metadata:Model [accessed 4 April 2008]

[6] By asking this I suggest that we need to respond to the conditions surrounding the rise of YouTube, today's most popular video service on the web. According to Greg Sterling of the Search Engine Journal, YouTube presently contains 6.1 million videos with 1.73 billion total views taking up an estimated 45 terabytes of storage. Almost 70 percent of the online population has watched online video and the average consumer watches 73 minutes of online video a month.

create a multi-way read-write web of connections, links, videos, writing, biographical data, images, comments, debate and other important documents (and not a unified giant that takes ownership and control).

Unlike physical archives that must house objects and place them in a single location (an object can't be in two places at once), digital archives don't need physical space. They need server space. They chew bandwidth. Driven by metadata that allows an enormous amount of flexibility for classifying, sorting and browsing, these digital 'objects' (i.e. video) can exist in many places (by way of hyperlinks) and in many categories and subcategories at once (by way of tags and folksonomies). Videotapes and DVDs, along with index cards and library stacks, just can't do that.

The explosion of video on the web also coincides with a renewed interest in the re-tracing and re-telling of the history of video from different perspectives to the North American-European axis which has tended to have a monopoly on the grand narrative of video art. We are all familiar with the official accounts of well-known global celebrities, founding fathers, protagonists, subcultural groups and influential organisations that form important nodes in the bigger story of Video Art. But the problem with these histories is that they're often monolithic and bounded by national boundaries. They miss the large waves of video art activity happening everywhere all at once all around the world. They leave no room for contestation. Forty odd years after the emergence of video art, it's only natural that people everywhere would want to account for their own particular local history and to want to relate it to the broader history. As those early video tapes begin to disintegrate, the imperative to collect, preserve and interpret this output becomes more pressing. The need to tell the stories surrounding the making and circulation of these tapes becomes even more compelling.

Individual mavericks such as Jonas Mekas are also establishing the presentation of their oeuvres online, and sites such as UbuWeb provide an ever-expanding assortment of digital files of hard-to-see material by key avant garde film and video makers. UbuWeb insists that the digital videos on the site are presented for educational and non-commercial use only and that copyright of artists is respected. Though this may not be altogether entirely legal it's hard to argue against the fact that

> *most of us don't live anywhere near theatres that show this kind of fare and very few of us can afford the hefty rental fees, not to mention the cumbersome equipment, to show these films. Thankfully, there is the internet which allows you to get*

*a whiff of these films regardless of your geographical location. We realize that the films we are presenting are of poor quality. It's not a bad thing; in fact, the best thing that can happen is that seeing a crummy shockwave file will make you want to make a trip to New York to the Anthology Film Archives or the Lux Cinema in London (or other places around the world showing similar fare). Next best case scenario will be that you will be enticed to purchase a high quality DVD from the noble folks trying to get these works out into the world. Believe me, they're not doing it for the money. Please support these filmmakers and their distributors by purchasing their films. Please support the presenters of these works by going to see them in theatres whenever you can.* [7]

[7] www.ubu.com/film [accessed 20 November 2007].

While not everyone is in agreement with this free-wheeling approach to copyright, there is something about the open and expansive spirit of projects like this one that makes it hard to deny the value of ad-hoc online video archives such as this. As Lawrence Lessig would have it, the more you share something the more valuable it becomes. UbuWeb is more than mere promotion for artist's work: it is indeed a global digital distribution outlet that increases the cultural value of work included on the site.

A number of isolated projects are emerging spontaneously from their own unique conditions of existence. There are groups in Brazil, Australia, Japan, Hungary, Germany, Holland, France, Canada, the US and the UK working on their own local histories, many of which challenge and supplement the dominant histories of video art. And while conferences such as this one (together with the Refresh conference in Banff in 2005 or the Future History of the Moving Image symposium in the UK late 2007) seek to make links across the boundaries of national histories, our projects remain fragmented, disconnected and looking very much like unconnected silos – not because we want them that way, but as a result of our of pre-information society organisational structures and distribution infrastructures. A globally moderated FLOSS system for video art archiving, scholarship and presentation is needed to address this situation.

So how might all these things come together in the age of peer-to-peer networks and the sharing of digital files across time and space? Videos circulate and are remixed, mashed up and broadcast over the web at an ever-increasing rate. They are being blown-up, torn apart, ripped, mixed and burned to such an extent that there is no going back. Images and sounds are coming unstuck, opening up a new space for the renegotiation of their associated history, archival context, and critical commentary. And

[8] YouTube Terms of Use, http://www.youtube.com/

in the process, innovative new ways of making, exhibiting, circulating, annotating and supplementing digital video works are emerging.

If the old televisual models have indeed been totally busted by the movement towards user-generated video inaugurated by video art of the 1960s, then I want to propose that we continue this process and hack the archives and the histories we are responsible for. A FLOSS distributed network should allow us to collectively annotate, post, and grow video art cultures – and to provide links to other new media and electronic arts cultures.

In this context we can assert that FLOSS and Creative Commons may provide answers for archiving artworks, maintaining them and making them accessible to students, scholars and the public.

It is clear from this brief description that we are not talking about replicating YouTube, with its restrictive user agreements and monolithic structure. Whatever the platform is for our new model, we need to link it, open it up, blow it apart – as that's what is necessary to avoid the creation of yet another proprietary walled garden and individualised silo. YouTube's restrictive license agreement has been much commented upon in this regard, and is an excellent case in point. It represents the type of agreement that would be avoided by the adoption of FLOSS and Creative Commons systems:

> *by submitting ... to YouTube, you hereby grant YouTube a worldwide, non-exclusive, royalty-free, sub-licenseable and transferable license to use, reproduce, distribute, prepare derivative works of, display, and perform the User Submissions in connection with the YouTube Website and YouTube's (and its successor's) business, including without limitation for promoting and redistributing part or all of the YouTube Website (and derivative works thereof) in any media formats and through any media channels.* [8]

Beyond the restrictions of YouTube, a large number of internet TV models are implementing a wide variety of promising alternatives for a very different approach to the digital networking of video. One of the most important of these is the Participatory Culture Foundation, a non-profit organization whose mission is to enable and support independent, non-corporate creativity and political engagement. Its primary project is a free and open-source internet television platform, Miro (previously known as Democracy Player), a free open-source desktop video application designed to make mass media more open and accessible for everyone.

There are a number of obvious links that can be drawn between the aims of the PCF and those involved with Radical Software in the 1970s:

> *Television is the most popular medium in our culture. But broadcast and cable TV has always been controlled by a small number of big corporations. We believe that the internet provides an opportunity to open television in ways that have never been possible before. Miro is designed to eliminate gatekeepers. Viewers can connect to any video provider that they want. This frees creators to use the video hosting setup that works best for them – whether they choose to self-publish or use a service. It's the kind of openness that the internet allows and that we should all demand.[emphasis added]*[9]

[9] participatoryculture.org [accessed 10 November 2007].

If just a few companies such as YouTube dominate online video, creativity will be restricted by their corporate terms and conditions of use. If the most popular video tools rely on closed, proprietary distribution systems, creativity and innovation will suffer. FLOSS video platforms are specifically designed to give video creators and viewers more freedom in the way they aggregate, browse and distribute video. Because they are open, they work with as many video hosting sites and video search engines as possible. Rather than being forced to use a few monopolistic services, the developers of FLOSS platforms believe that the future of media depends on creators being able to choose the publishing services that work best for them.

A number of other projects are worthy of mention here, including Wikimedia, OurMedia, Archive.org, BlipTV, Metacafe and OhTV. Another is Videoart.net, which highlights the problem of the intersection between local and international concerns. Founded by video artists and filmmakers based in New York City, Videoart.net provides a searchable online archive and connects artists with curators, producers, and the public. The Videoart.net archive is open to all genres, from short films, video installations to interviews. We could well adopt their mission as our own:

– To establish an international hub of video artists, filmmakers and audiences.
– To expand video arts into public spaces accessible to a wider audience.
– To create an online community of filmmakers and artists.

If we can imagine a growing collection of digitised work with large 'metadatabases' and tag clouds associated with the collection, we start to see how we can preserve, distribute and contextualise video art material in a recombinatory history/archive project. Using web interfaces we can sort, aggregate and recombine elements into multiple histories and new relations. In order to achieve this we need to use new open tools that help us grasp the power of the growing digital disorder.

An example from the field of literature may be instructive here. Project Gutenberg (a volunteer effort to digitize, archive, and distribute cultural works) was founded in 1971. It is one of the oldest digital libraries, and most of the items in its collection are complete texts of public domain books. The project tries to make these as free as possible, in long-lasting, open formats that can be used on almost any computer. Unlike some other digital library projects, Project Gutenberg does not claim new copyright on titles it publishes. Instead, it encourages their free reproduction and distribution. Since December 2006, Project Gutenberg has more than 20,000 items in its collection, with an average of over fifty new e-books being added each week.

A similar distributed network of intelligence could be initiated for international video art. While there is clearly a need to address questions of rights (Creative Commons style), value (originals and copies don't make any sense in the digital world, but in the artworld they do), and governance, success in other fields of endeavour suggest that these obstacles are surmountable. Indeed, the active negotiation of these issues has led to the most successful and innovative systems of the moment.

Although the rise of YouTube and other proprietary video services have offered us a glimpse into the extraordinary possibilities of globally distributed user-generated video networks, it also alerts us to the issues that video artists have been challenging for decades. As a loosely connected network of interested curators, researchers and artists, we have a powerful new means of distribution at our disposal.

Network television has been consistently challenged and diversified by video art and user-generated content. The challenge remains to organise our diverse ideas of what constitutes video art in the age of digital networks, and to collectively develop a distributed open content system that will build upon the rich history of open circuits and participatory cultures of video art.

# The Shrink-Wrapped Design Process

Michael van Schaik

## Preface

It takes us years of education to learn to read, write and talk as ways of interacting with our environment. Isn't it strange, then, that one receives barely any kind of education in interacting with computers (as a modern communication environment)? Instead most computer programs are built to use interfaces as translators from computer to human. Although this is meant to help, in many cases this also makes users less powerful because they can only consume set functions within the program. You can only compute what the software lets you compute, and only manipulate what you see.

This is especially the case in the world of graphic design; due to the global monopoly of big firms like Adobe (which recently even bought it's only real competitor Macromedia), all graphic designers seem forced to use the same software to produce their work. Strangely enough, the lion's share of designers don't really seems to care. Looking at my own education (in the Netherlands), a reason for this could be that the discourse here seems to be focused on ideas more than actual products (and the tools used to create them). Though there seems to be a growing interest in alternatives such as open source software as a means to a more independent design practice, the problem with these is that the few packages that are currently the killer apps in this field are often just free-er copies of existing software, not much different from their proprietary counterparts.

What if designers actually learned to use the real power of the computer and computational media instead of the ready-made physical workspace that it currently tries to represent? There is an interesting opportunity here for designers to start using the computer as the universal machine that it really is instead of a shrink-wrapped special purpose machine modelled on analogue tools, locking them away from new

[1]
Friedrich Kittler, 'There Is No Software', 1995, http://www.ctheory.net/articles.aspx?id=74 [Accessed 12/04/2006]

[2]
JODI, http://en.wikipedia.org/wiki/Jodi

creative possibilities specific to the field of computational media. Why learn to use only the Adobe tool-chain if one can build one's own production-environment tool by tool?

## Current Situation

The main software tool-chains used in the field of graphic design can be divided in to 'digital' and 'print' oriented. Since most classically educated graphic designers (like myself) are primarily educated in the field of print production, it shouldn't come as a surprise that this is also the main focus of most software. The main, widely used print-production software can be classified under three categories: vector based (Illustrator, Freehand), bitmap based (Photoshop, Fireworks) and software to gather and combine the two for prepress (X-press, inDesign). The software that focuses more on digital-design such as design for websites and CD-roms/DVDs generally tries to represent these media in a way designers are already familiar with from the world of print. What these software programs have in common is that they are an interface between a technical system and the visual workspace of a designer. So placing an image on a website works in just the same way as placing it in a book; the designer just imports the image and it's there. What actually happens beneath the surface of the Graphical User Interface stays hidden. This might be considered a good thing, since it saves the designer from having to learn a whole new way of working for any new technical system, it's just a matter of learning it once and then using the same techniques throughout all media designs. And who wants to know what's 'under the hood' anyway? – that's the world of programmers, which is generally not of much interest to graphic designers.

Without advocating Friedrich Kittler's suggestion that computer users learn to read the true (hexadecimal) language of the computer, hiding the real (raw) material of a medium from the user is indeed an important paradigm common in most software engineering.[1] It can be considered the reason for the sort of fear of programming code that seems to exist among designers (and lots of computer users in general). Code is equal to problems. Code is where you see the actual computer break through the graphical skin, like in the art of JODI, or the field of glitch art, which is about errors and other things you'd like to prevent.[2] Take a look at, for example, the Macintosh OS X operating system, where the 'engine' of the computer is almost invisible for the common user. You just do whatever you want to do as if you were in the physical world, and, invisibly, the system takes care of the technical layer. One never sees any program code, or even a glimpse of how the system is built up, while the fact that this system is based on Unix is considered one of its main advantages (The Unix-philosophy typically means having simple applications doing their job as well as possible, instead of wasting CPU power on things like dynamically resizing screens and using a 'genie effect' on hiding them).

The fear of program-code may originate from the first desktop systems, which introduced this shrink-wrapping of program code in a nice GUI (Graphical User Interface). And this fear is also very much there among graphic designers. It is considered their job to work in the visual field, the field of texts, nice fonts and images, and the computer is supposed to generate the appropriate code, say postscript (for print) or html or actionscript etc. (for digital media). This way the designer has the feeling of staying 'above' the medium, calibrating it to their needs, unaffected by its actual individual (technical) capabilities and way of working. However, if we look at the historical context designers have worked in, things weren't always like this. On the contrary, well known designers such as Piet Zwart or Wim Crouwel, for example, were actually working with new techniques (photography and photographic typesetting) and challenging, changing and creating the possibilities of these techniques. Through their knowledge of these new media, they also learned their intrinsic qualities. Thus, photography introduced the photographic image into design, but instead of taking that for granted, Piet Zwart re-appropriated these images as design elements. And while photographic typesetting was invented to easily reproduce existing type, Crouwel instead invented type specifically for the capabilities and restrictions of this technique. These are things that wouldn't have been possible without a thorough (technical) knowledge of the medium.

So, taking fear of the actual medium of the computer, program code, as a given, it is interesting to look at how this fear in fact restrains the designer nowadays. As mentioned, artistic education is focused mainly on the development of the self, and of original ideas. There is less interest in or time for studying the digital media used to communicate them. Because of the fear of being restrained by (the absence of knowledge of) program code, instead of the freedom this knowledge might give, the focus (at least in the Netherlands) is much more on concepts and physical or visual techniques. But what is forgotten is the importance of the medium in constituting part of the message. The computer is therefore, mistakenly, seen as just a meta-medium. One that reproduces all earlier media without changing them. Think also here of how metaphors like the paper folder in the desktop or the term 'web pages' in the internet are used. And this last example is also one of the more obvious illustrations of the constraint this disinterest in/fear of the technical produces. The internet is, obviously, a totally different medium from print but by applying this metaphor of a page as a piece of paper,

[3] http://www.microsoft.com/windowsvista/features/default.mspx [Accessed 12/04/2006]

[4] http://badvista.fsf.org/

designers become its captive, in turn producing ideas such as websites that one can flip through like pages in a book (next, previous). This places a huge restriction on the actual 'hyper-' quality of the web.

In order to understand the media we work in, there should be much more focus on learning and understanding at least the basics of their intrinsic technical layers. This way designers may acquire more of an insight into the constraints GUI programs impose on the way they design our messages/media.

## FLOSS vs. Proprietary, or: Why it is Important to Study Our Software

The importance of knowledge for fully understanding and using or even designing the medium may seem quite obvious. It is also important, however, for less obvious reasons. If we consider graphic design a form of communication, or even a cultural activity, it is highly important for it to be totally free. Free to question, challenge and form critical opinions, free to question authority, free to protest and free to question and shape the media it works with. Therefore, knowledge of technology should also be considered an important way to gain insight into how political choices in software may invisibly inhibit a truly free and critical stance. To give an example, according to Microsoft the new Windows Vista operating system

> *introduces a breakthrough user experience and is designed to help you feel confident in your ability to view, find, and organize information and to control your computing experience.* [3]

The last part of this claim in particular can be seen in a totally different light if combined with the claim the Free Software Foundation makes on badvista.org:

> *Among other harms, BadVista.org will focus on the danger posed by Treacherous Computing in Vista. Commonly called Trusted Computing in the industry, it is an attempt to turn computers from machines controlled by their user into machines that monitor their user and refuse to operate in ways that manufacturers don't authorize.* [4]

Though the last claim (as well as the first) should be considered an opinion, their combination gives a nice insight into how at least some technical knowledge should be considered a necessity to gain insight into the political choices forming the bases of software.

Another way software can constrain its users may be found in the example of big software companies 'donating' computers to schools or institutes and thereby implicitly forcing them to learn, use and thus buy their specific products. Or as Jaromil put it: ‘teaching them to use Sony cameras.’[5]. The strange thing is that while there exist excellent alternatives to most proprietary software in the form of Open Source software, this doesn't seem to catch on very well. Open Source software is free (libre) software because the source code of the software is publicly available (or available after one has purchased the software). It is often free (gratis), created and maintained by networked communities of hackers and programmers. The importance of this software lies in the fact that it makes the user free to study or change it without being dependent on the original creators. Another important paradigm in this field is Open Standards, meaning the file formats used are documented and can be freely studied and implemented. An example of Open Standards can be found in the Open Document Format, which originates from the xml-based file format used by Open Office. Open Office is nowadays a fully working, Open Source alternative for closed proprietary software suites like Microsoft Office. The Open Document Format is a freely implementable file format that, because of its Open Standards, can be studied without restrictions. The value of the transparency and freedom that comes with these kinds of formats is underlined by the decision of the Dutch government to fully adopt open source software and open standards by 2006 (the ‘Motie Vendrik’, accepted in 2002). In June 2006 the Belgian government even decided to prohibit closed formats in official government documents by 2008.

[5] Jaromil, personal conversation, November 2006.

Though change takes time, this is also caused by the historic policy of deterring uptake of Open Source and Open Standards by those companies currently holding the biggest market share. Much of the history of free software is about circumventing restrictions put in place by companies. For example, at the time of writing Microsoft Office still does not support Open Document Format, which may be an important reason why the Dutch government’s progressive plans decided back in 2002 have yet to be realised.

And if, for example, Adobe, nowadays the publisher of Flash and the Flash-player, were to implement support for the (open standard) Scalable Vector Graphics format, the viewer-coverage for this Open Standard file format would instantly be about 100 percent. Instead they have decided to cease development of their svg plugin which was one of the few ways people using Internet Explorer were able to view svg content (since IE, surprisingly, is the only browser which hasn't got any sort of basic native

[6] Marshall McLuhan, 'The Relation of Environment to Anti-Environment', 1966, in Marshall McLuhan-Unbound, Gingko Press 2005, pp. 6-7.

svg support). Luckily most other browsers have some form of native support for svg graphics built in, it's just too bad that about 70 percent of computer users are still using Internet Explorer.

The same story, by the way, goes for support of the (24-bit) png format (indeed, also an open standard), which all browsers except IE support natively. With the release of IE7 this seemed to have improved, except that this version is built not to install on systems older than Windows XP which, in turn, will not run on older hardware.

**Software is the Message**

To get an insight into how software shapes our message, it might be nice to take a look at linguistics, for here the influence of the computer is quite remarkable. 'Browsing' as a word for finding information (as in a library), 'system crash' for not being able to remember something or even 'ctrl-z' for undoing a mistake. These terms have not only become part of the wider language, their influence reaches far further. The software we use determines how we think. I personally noticed this phenomenon when I once tried to use sticker-remover to remove some traces of tape on a coffee-machine. The tape dissolved just fine, but so did the plastic of the coffee-machine. The first thing that popped into my mind was to press Cmd-z (I 'Think different').

According to Marshall McLuhan,

> *The new medium of TV as an environment creates new occupations. As an environment, it is imperceptible except in terms of its content. That is, all that is seen or noticed is the old environment, the movie. But even the effects of the TV environment in altering the entire character of human sensibility and sensory ratios is completely ignored. The content of any system or organization naturally consists of the preceding system or organization, and in that degree acts as a control on the new environment. It is useful to notice all of the arts and sciences as acting in the role of anti-environments that enable us to perceive the environment.*[6]

However, according to media theorist Arjen Mulder, while computers are indeed often said to also remediate the preceding media, they actually are a 'metamedium', a combination of all previous media:

*Only in this case, it is not so much a matter of remediation of all old and new media, as it is a hybridization, a melting of unequal media to a new unity.*[7]

[7] Arjen Mulder, Over Mediatheorie, V2_/NAi Uitgevers, Rotterdam 2004, p. 207. (My translation from the Dutch).

Another example, which a friend with a background in architectural studies recently pointed out to me, is that with the introduction of each new software used in architecture, a new trend is born. For example, the release of Maya 3D sparked blob-architecture, whose shapes were specific to this software and could easily be traced back to the lines of software code from which they were generated.

This leads to another interesting question: who is the producer and who is the consumer in this software setup? In a way the software companies are the producers of the environment in which certain ideas develop. One could argue this by saying software is just a tool in the process of developing and communicating ideas, but in the case of Maya, the generative algorithm is created by a software developer. Isn't it true that the 'designer' is actualising a potential form generated by the software developer's algorithm?

Of course this comparison might be seen as an exaggeration, but it illustrates the basic point very well. What a user/consumer of software is actually doing is placing his ideas in a preset environment. This works both ways, so (unconsciously) he is also conforming his ideas to this set environment. If we look at the example of Maya, the ideas of blob-architecture might well be developed according to a certain 'zeitgeist', but by elaborating them with this software the resulting physical shape becomes far from universal and is, as mentioned, sometimes very specific to the software used. In this instance we might even wonder who the actual producer of the blob-building is.

Software always (in a certain way) influences your thinking. Analogous to 'the medium is the message', the software has become the medium (and thus, the message).

**Software Filters the Message**

With the invention of the private computer, its developers started searching for ways to make it understandable to non-scientists. Maybe the most important development in this field has been the desktop metaphor. So far it has seemed to work fairly well; developers started to put all kinds of these metaphors into software and they made people understand computers better because of the references to existing physical objects. But the problem is that this imposes the idea of the computer as meta-medium. As a result the computer as medium in itself has become invisible behind all kinds of brush-metal windows and 3D-push buttons, and we tend to forget to question their logic. We often take software as a given fact, something that's just there.

But software, apart from influencing messages because of it's logic, has another layer of influence, which is now becoming more obvious every day; politics. If we communicate using a software structure like the internet, aspects of the wider world such as free speech become an important issue here, too. That's why it is so striking to see software companies functioning as an extension of less free regimes, such as Google for the government of China. Here Google is developing ways to filter the content of the 'free' web, so that its Chinese users will not find results that are considered harmful by the Chinese government. (It should be mentioned here that Google was one of the last search engines to submit to these demands from the Chinese government, which is both admirable and an index of the companies' power).

Without necessarily passing judgement on Google or the Chinese government in this situation, it is a good example of why it is important for us to be able to look 'through' software, to study the environments that manipulate our thoughts and that manipulate the information that is at the basis of formulating these thoughts. The inner-workings of Google are a big secret and can therefore in no way be objectively monitored. Hypothetically, what would prevent them from filtering results on, say, a person-to-person basis, or on an ip-location basis? These examples might seem far-fetched, but if I search using the term 'test' on google.nl I get different and fewer results using the Safari browser than if I use Firefox (806 million results in Safari vs. 843 million in Firefox). This can be interpreted as at least some sort of browser-specific filtering already going on. It's also no big secret that companies offering gratis services on the internet often generate money by selling the data they gather through their services.

A friend gave me another recent example of software filtering of the message that is fuelled by politics: part of his practice as an artist involves researching new media. Another part involves photography, occasionally containing artistic nudity. So when a new system like Flickr appeared, he became an early and extensive user. It offered a very interesting way of combining two of his interests. But when Flickr was acquired by Yahoo and so became subject to its rules he was asked to remove his photos because they were considered sexually explicit content.

Though internet companies haven't at present much to do with the software we use to create graphic design, the situation is a strong example of the problem of relying completely on proprietary software. We have no way to monitor how they work, nor are we able to check what the major software companies might be planning in the future for their services. Some nowadays repressive regimes started out as 'Don't be evil' revolutions (e.g. China) but power seems to have strange effects on people.[8] We should never blindly rely on a particular software as our main let alone our only platform.

[8] Google's corporate philosophy, http://investor.google.com/conduct.html

[9] http://www.kde.me.uk/index.php?page=fosdem-interview-scribus [Accessed 12/01/2006]

## OS / Free Software vs. Free Design / Libre

In the field of graphic design Open Source development can be regarded as a healthy alternative to proprietary software because it offers the possibility of studying / changing the source code, thereby disclosing how the program works, and how it may influence its user. This makes users less dependent on the original developer to make changes or solve bugs. Also, because most open source software uses Open Standards for saving files, users will not likely 'buy in' to a specific software but are free to exchange files and projects between different applications. At least, that is the idea of Open Standards.

These are interesting times in the development of Open Source possibilities for graphic designers. For quite a lot of proprietary software a fairly developed open source alternative can be found. In the case of inDesign that would be Scribus, for Photoshop, The Gimp and for Illustrator, Inkscape. Then there are a whole bunch of less familiar but equally interesting software developments. For the purpose of giving an overview of the basic design software, however, these three examples should suffice.

Without wanting to deny the political and philosophical impact of these projects, a practical issue is that they actually aren't much more than a 'free/libre' clone of existing proprietary software. The reason for this is simple, as Craig Bradney, part of the Scribus development team says:

> *Our aim is not to replace wholesale other applications, but to provide the best DTP experience for Linux users – to provide the same kinds of tools users have had on other platforms and to use the inherent strengths of 'Open Source Software' and Linux/Unix to Scribus' advantage.*[9]

Though this is a perfectly legitimate reason for developers to create their software, the problem is twofold: firstly, the focus on 'free as in libre', is easily displaced to 'free as in beer'. What is the importance of these developments, beside the fact that it doesn't cost money to use them? Of course there is the advantages of it undermining the monopolistic landscape of (design) software, and that users are not made dependent on big companies. Although most Linux users are aware of this, and it may be a key consideration when they choose whether or not to use a particular piece of software, I have my doubts about how important this aspect really is to other users. Running Open Office on Windows is a lot less about being 'free' and probably a lot more about being 'gratis'. Though that's as good a reason as any, this can in some ways be compared to using a black market reproduction of a product that has taken years of research and development. It looks the same, it works the same, but it's Open Source. This comparison opens up another discussion in which one could argue that the way big companies have been able to become this big and rich is by underpaying their workers and patenting (other) peoples' ideas. Here, a motive could also be found for pleading for the right to take this knowledge back and make it public property. This is, however, something which will probably remain a point of contention for a long time, and is certainly not something I want to pass judgement on here.

The second problem, which is actually more important to me, is that as a clone of existing software, these open source alternatives also copy the traps and mental models of their properietary counterparts. Therefore, in my opinion, for 'free software' to be a valid term, the open sourcing of closed software by reverse-engineering should be seen as only a beginning; a way to make software available as a field of study in order to discover its inner logic; to redevelop it in order to be really 'free as in free speech', or even thought. This doesn't seem to be the aim of the free software movement at the moment. Just as much as the proprietary software it resembles, it focuses on making computing understandable by hiding it behind metaphors. These metaphors might actually be where the real problem lies.

If we take a look, for example, at Pure Data, a software developed as an open source project intended to work with any data, we see that there is much less hiding going on. The data is 'wired' around by simple lines (like a pipe in the Unix command line environment), resembling nothing other than a line. Data flowing around can be manipulated in any conceivable way, if it don't exist yet, it can be programmed. This same kind of openness or freedom can also be found in another open source project: Processing. As the website explains:

Processing is an open source programming language and environment for people who want to program images, animation, and sound. [...] It is created to teach fundamentals of computer programming within a visual context and to serve as a software sketchbook and professional production tool. [10]

[10] http://processing.org[ Accessed 12/04/2006]

This description also suggests a shift that seems necessary in current design education. In order to develop the design profession further in an interesting way instead of the constant spiral of visual sampling that it is now, a better understanding of media should be developed. Now that everybody can use software, and the pragmatic (theoretical) technical skills can be coded into computer systems, it becomes more and more important to develop this software further. Because, if software is the medium, it will be this software (digital media) that is part of the future subject of design.

I'm not trying to say here that the formal study of conceptual thinking, or theoretical and technical knowledge, will become obsolete. Merely that, by getting a better understanding of our media, we will be able to design them better and to develop the design field further. To enable this understanding, it will be necessary to stop superimposing physical metaphors on everything computer related. This, as I have said, is causing an incorrect understanding of our media. This is the reason why, when constructing a website, designers often fail to use the potential of hypertext and hyper structures. They are trained to create an all inclusive conceptual idea and to communicate that within the technical possibilities of the medium (print). This might be why a website is often called a 'page' and why designers often design them as if they were printed (preferably including kerning and all kinds of custom typefaces). In the digital media this attitude can only be seen as a dictatorial obsession, because part of (the strength of) digital media such as hypertext is that it can look different on any computer. Users get a say in how they would like to use the information you have designed, and therefore the design should focus more on structure and route than on punctuation. This obsessive focus on detail might be inherited from the physical world whose design and printing processes have been reproduced in computers. New media are much more modular.

With the emerging generations of designers having been surrounded by computers all their life, it's time to step out of representing the physical media within the computer. Designers should be trained in (at least the basics of) the underlying codes that make up the digital media in order to be able to really understand and use them. As Florian Cramer states:

[11] http://www.nettime.org/Lists-Archives/nettime-1-0610/msg00025.html [Accessed 12/07/2006]

*The closer the software is to the daily needs and work methods of programmers and system administrators, the higher typically its quality.*[11]

This shows how important it is for designers to start taking a more critical stance toward their software and to study it. The best Open Source software has been written in the field of programmers, simply because they found things missing or not working the way they wanted it to. Just as designers have been able to study and develop their processes and methodologies for years, now software (/programming) has become one of these processes and should be studied and developed the same way and with the same understanding. Maybe that way designers will learn to develop their own, really 'free', processes and escape the physical metaphors.

Other Sources:

Don Genter & Jakob Nielsen, 'The Anti-Mac Interface', http://www.acm.org/pubs/cacm/AUG96/antimac.htm

Marc de Bruijn, 'Designer Dictator', Rotterdam, 2006.

Jeff Raskin, 'Down with GUIs!', http://www.wired.com/wired/archive/1.06/1.6_guis.html

'Open Source Publishing - Design Tools for Designers', http://www.constant.irisnet.be/~constant/ospublish/

# Appropriation and Type – Before and Today

Ricardo Lafuente

Appropriation has been a recurring and accepted strategy in defining typography as an activity and a business. We can pinpoint four cases where appropriation has been key in defining landmarks in the history of type, not only aiding the breaking of technical and creative boundaries but also helping to question legal and moral ones.

A brief analysis of the current situation in typography will follow, focusing on the approach to the subject by corporations, users and designers. The current business model (digital foundries, font files with copyrights) is, as we'll argue, a remnant of a time where a typeface filled a whole drawer and fails to account for the necessary changes that the information age demands.

Finally, we'll conclude with the definition of an essentially contradictory business model that has a very strong stance against 'font forging' and copyright issues, although it has historically – and now, more than ever – thrived on constant, and often uncredited, appropriation of ideas and designs.

## Appropriation in Type through History

We could certainly identify many more instances of inspiration or downright copying of ideas in typography, but these four cases will suffice to demonstrate the different uses of copy, inspiration and appropriation in general. Our focus here will be on the issue of creative appropriation (inspiration) on one hand, and corporate business models and copyright issues (plagiarism) on the other.

### The Gutenberg Press

In 1450, Johannes Gutenberg produced the first commercially viable model of his printing press, which was widely used for centuries until the advent of the Linotype machine, the first way to automate, though only partially, the type setting and printing process.

Gutenberg's press was the result of the combination of five key methods and processes, three, possibly four, of which were not original:

- The screw press, which was already used by the Greeks and Romans to process olive oil and wine.
- Block printing, present in China since 594 AD. Gutenberg's innovation was to use metal cast types (instead of the Chinese traditional woodblock printing technique), although metal typecasting was already developed in Korea around 1230 AD.
- Letter punches, which were a goldsmithing technique – Gutenberg was a goldsmith – used to engrave letters in metal pieces.
- Letter replica casting, a method to quickly create new individual characters, along with a particular metal alloy that made for durable pieces. This method has been attributed to Gutenberg but recent studies shed doubts on this fact.
- Metal-adherent ink, devised by Gutenberg.

This shows that originality, in a time before copyrights and patents existed, is not a straightforward issue. It was not before 1700 that the first copyright statute appeared in Britain – the protection of ideas could have changed the fate of this invention and the combination of methods made. The point here is that they were combined in a way that made typography as we know it possible, and there seems to be absolutely no question regarding the legitimacy of this invention made possible by appropriating previous methods and processes. Gutenberg's model of printing stood firm for centuries until the Linotype machine introduced partial automation of the printing process.

## Stanley Morison and Monotype

In 1886, the Linotype machine began to be produced by the Mergenthaler Printing Co. in the United States. This machine revolutionised the printing process by introducing a degree of automation, allowing for quick composition of lines of text. It wouldn't take long (a year) for Lanston Monotype to begin production of their own fully automated typesetting machine, devised by Tolbert Lanston, which could typeset whole pages from a mechanical keyboard input.

In 1922, Stanley Morison was appointed as typographic advisor of the Monotype Corporation (the British branch of the Philadephia company), a post he would keep until 1967. The Monotype Corporation built an extensive catalogue of cuts made by Morison from classic references, such as Bodoni, Bembo, Baskerville, and several others. These revivals helped bring general interest to the old masters' works They were also a key marketing strategy to try to push up the value of the Monotype machine – the faces available would definitely determine the decision of a buyer who fancies a particular style, and thus the Monotype Corporation had no qualms about recruiting all the classics, which were by then in the public domain.

It is tremendously unfair, though, to portray Morison as a hijacker – he was one of the hallmarks of 20th century type, being responsible for the creation of the Times typeface and hugely influencing the field of typography to the present day through the efforts he dedicated to bringing the classics to the general public – legitimately appropriating other designs. Without Morison's endeavour, our legacy would no doubt be poorer today.

[1] Friedl, Ott and Stein, Typography: An encyclopedic survey of type design and techniques through history. London: Black Dog & Leventhal, 1998. p. 409.

[2] Arial is now a 'standard' font of web typography, being part of a very limited set of fonts that most browsers can read.

**Arial, Monotype and Microsoft**

1982 is the year in which the Arial typeface was released by Monotype Typography, Monotype Corporation's type design division. Designed by Robin Nicholas and Patricia Saunders, this typeface had a remarkable impact. Not only does it have obvious similarities to other modern sans serifs (sharing features with Helvetica, Univers and Akzidenz Grotesk), it exactly mirrors the glyph width tables from Helvetica, which is the data included in a font file that describes each character's dimensions – an exact match that gives little chance of coincidence.

Microsoft licensed Arial from Monotype instead of the more expensive Helvetica, and in 1990 it was bundled with Microsoft Windows 3.1. It has been a staple of Windows systems until today. This is a specific case where a typeface was chosen not for its genuine creative and/or practical value but based upon external reasons, in this case driven by financial motives. Type designers are almost unanimous in shunning Arial as a lesser typeface: it is notably absent from Robert Bringhurst's typeface selection in *The Elements of Typographic Style* (the current all round reference on type design from the designer's perspective), and is also only mentioned as a passing remark on Robin Nicholas's entry on the typographic encyclopaedic survey by Friedl et al.[1] This is pretty much a clear indication of type designers' consensus on the Arial issue; it's also worth noting that there has been, to date, no attempt to replace Arial as a standard font in operating systems.[2]

In strict law and copyright terms, it's appropriate to compare the Arial case to a cheating student who argues that the fact that his exam has exact passages from his nearest classmates' exams owes to coincidence. It is equally reasonable to argue that borrowing from three sources rather than just one does not make the situation more acceptable.

So Arial stands in mixed principles: the type community is almost unanimous in calling shenanigans, but it has still made its way into our current operating systems despite that fact – it didn't face any legal actions as of 2008.

**Segoe**

In early 2006, Microsoft announced a significant effort to dignify type design in their upcoming Vista operating system: six type designers – Lucas de Groot and Robin Nicholas figuring among them – were commissioned to design appropriate typefaces for screen and print. The result was six very attractive fonts that not only could appeal to general uses by less savvy people for simple word processing tasks, but also suit the type designers' fancy.

Another font included in Vista is Segoe, a revival of Frutiger Next (which in turn is a revival of Frutiger) that Microsoft licensed from Monotype and altered. It's not the first case in which Adrian Frutiger's work has been remade, Adobe's Myriad and Apple's Podium Sans also bear a striking resemblance to Frutiger's structure. When Microsoft registered Segoe in Europe in 2004, Linotype sued for copyright infringement since European law, unlike the American one, recognises the rights to font designs (although patent law is often used to circumvent this legal void in the U.S.).

The most significant fact is that Microsoft based their defence not on the issue of originality – stating the differences between Segoe and Frutiger Next, but on the fact that Linotype wasn't selling its typeface in Europe when the request was filed. This situation could very well be interpreted as an admission by Microsoft's part that the font in fact owes credit to Frutiger's design.

This case becomes all more revealing in that it is both a high profile and current example of an attempt to settle the authenticity of a type design in courts. Unlike Arial, it didn't sneak past the critics and found serious hurdles while Microsoft tried to implement it in its Windows OS. The EU ended up rejecting Segoe's application, prompting the release of a modified version that bore less resemblance to the Frutiger typeface. The plaintiff, Linotype, was acquired by Monotype Imaging – the designers of Segoe – in 2006.

## The Digital Typography Paradigm

Typography, and type design in particular, is historically defined by a constant recursion of past themes and trends, be it as inspiration, revivals, or as a way to question them – as in postmodern type examples, such as Emigre's or David Carson's work. Nevertheless, modern designs still owe heavily (with or without credit) to a tradition of arts and crafts spanning five centuries.

Meanwhile, during the last two decades, the type world hasn't ceased discussing the issue of rights and plagiarism, a discussion that was sparked by the digital revolution and the introduction of the personal computer as an all purpose design and production tool. This shift implied that the tools used in typography and book production ceased to be the sole domain of type makers, printers and book publishers – the only ones who could afford the initial investment of a type foundry, workshop or printing press and manage it effectively. Designing type soon became cheaper and cheaper, as the physical and financial burden of the new tools gradually became less and less significant. Nowadays, a computer and a printer can do in minutes what a huge phototypesetting equipment would have taken a lot of time, effort and money to produce ten years ago.

The key effect of the digital revolution in type design is that typefaces became fonts – a radical change in that they were no more lead blocks but data – files that describe how each glyph should be drawn on screen or on a printer. A free software solution to type design, FontForge, was released in 2004, doing away with any software costs involved in font creation and editing, meaning the only overhead for a type design business would be a PC, paper, drawing tools, an image capture device (scanner or camera) and eventually an internet connection. This change has serious repercussions in the whole typography market: now type design wouldn't, in theory, require any kind of intermediaries between the typographer/designer and its audience. Reality developed otherwise, as we will see from three standpoints in typography usage and creation.

## Corporate Type

The digital revolution made a deep redefinition of most areas of study possible. We will show, though, that the field of typography has been lagging behind when it comes to taking advantage of the digital medium. Moreover, the corporate business model has failed to account for the specific needs and features of information technology, sticking to an artificial market sustained by an inflated value attributed to digital files as if they still were physical objects that are owned.

Nowadays, there are three major players in the type business: Microsoft, Adobe and Monotype Imaging.

Apple Computer hasn't been a key figure in the type market (concentrating on developing font technology for its operating system), but it had an essential role in developing the actual playing field. Apple heralded the personal computer era in with their original Macintosh and has intermittently collaborated and competed with Microsoft and Adobe, being responsible for the development of the TrueType font format along with Microsoft as a response to Adobe's expensively priced PostScript Type I font description format. The release of TrueType in 1991 forced Adobe to gradually reduce prices and eventually follow suit, releasing the PostScript specifications so that software developers could implement it in their programs without limitations.

Adobe Systems Inc., besides being responsible for a highly successful suite of imaging and DTP software, has a very strong position in the type market: not only is it a type vendor (through its typography division, Adobe Type) but also the most influential company in the sense that it owns most digital design solutions, especially after acquiring its main rival Macromedia in April 2005 and facing no significant competition in its market.

Microsoft is responsible for creating the most widely used operating system in personal computers, as well as the most popular office suite. Along with Adobe, Microsoft developed the currently dominant OpenType file format, which is freely available to developers as long as they agree to its rather restrictive licensing terms. Adobe converted its entire type collection to OpenType in a move to spread the new standard.

Monotype Imaging is now a distant remnant of Tolbert Lanston's original creation. It has adjusted technical breakthroughs in the 20th century and claimed a staunch position in today's digital type market. It was acquired by Agfa in 1999 forming Agfa Monotype, which in turn was acquired by T. A. Associates, a North American investment firm, changing its name to Monotype Imaging and developing a position in font software and rendering engines. It also secured a strong standpoint in the font vendor market after acquiring its rival Linotype, along with the rights to their entire type collection.

**User Type**

Most people get introduced to digital type by means of text editors. The digital revolution would be the perfect reason to finally open typography to everyone and make it a mainstream subject instead of a limited access craft. Things have happened otherwise, though, and the inability to create a suitable interface for allowing basic experimentation with type has severely crippled the possibilities of the new medium.

The font selection paradigm has changed little during the years, offering a whole collection of typefaces in a drop down menu. Such is the immediateness of digital type: It's just there, no need to open drawers with thousands of lead characters. Users are encouraged, by means of a simple GUI, to just pick their font and get to work on their document. Even more: you don't even need to choose, just stick with the default choice the software maker has made for you. Word processing interfaces also assume the user doesn't want to be bothered with layout choices such as margins, structure – and they also make the choice for us (incidentally, they also made it quite awkward to change these defaults). In short: the standard word processing interface tells users not bother to with type.

This paradigm helps to build the general perception that a font is a finished, shrinkwrapped and untouchable product – pretty much like pre-packaged software. Although font files can be opened and edited as long as we have an appropriate editor, most typeface editors are either crude or catering exclusively to the type designer market. The user usually isn't able to reach the underpinnings and intricacies of type, instead being expected just to understand that the default template is more than enough.

Such an approach to software designing effectively discourages any kind of interest in typographic issues by the general public, and helps to fuel the thought that fonts are 'just there'. It's worth noting that there is still no easy and streamlined way to buy, install and use fonts, unlike most other digital markets – iTunes would be a good example of that kind of market strategy. There's an obvious reluctance to develop alternative business models for type design.

## Designer Type

The type designer community is centred on the study of classical and modern examples and making attempts to postulate theory and practical guidelines for the craft of type design, sitting somewhere between the methods of architecture and those of poetry.

Fred Smeijers, a highly regarded Dutch type designer, analyses the type designer's duty quite straightforwardly in his manifesto *Type Now.* On the issue of the responsibilities of type designers and commitment to specific guidelines, he states that

[3]
Fred Smeijers, Type Now, London: Hyphen Press, 2003. p. 25.

[4]
ibid. p. 40.

*a type designer cannot escape this responsibility of judgement (...). In the end, people – the society – either accept it or they don't'*[3].

Society, it seems, would be the ultimate judge of whether a typeface is a hallmark of craft or doomed to failure.

On the other hand, we find a curious account on Smeijers's description on Fontana, a typeface by Ruben Fontana inspired by Meta: he describes it as 'uncomplicated', '*tres sympathique*', 'sunny' and 'open minded'.[4] This certainly sounds more like a description of a person or a song than of an object, and indeed sheds some doubt on the much touted objectiveness of good type design. It seems impossible to find serious and objective terms to classify a typeface's features. Historical categorisations of design tendencies vary from author to author, and although there are some widely used terms to describe historical periods and typeface features, such as 'transitional type' or 'slab serifs', there's a tendency to borrow from poetry and music to identify a type family's 'soul' (which, though relevant from an artist or a historical point of view, is rather unscientific).

This is not a contradiction, though, since we can distinguish between type as a creative activity (in which there would be no problem with this kind of analogy) and type as an industry and commodity (where profit, market tendency, shareholder demands and legal requirements imply that things have a definite value and purpose). Naturally, Smeijers's interest is in the craft and art of typography, and not the market and the economic relationships that it spawns. On the other hand, our interest is definitely that which Smeijers doesn't care for.

We must assert that defending the status of type as a functional solution to practical problems requires an objective set of rules that derive from the way we read and write. We cannot yet account for matters of objective legibility while we do not possess all information on our mental processes and the mechanisms in the brain involved in acquiring and processing written information – this is the responsibility of cognitive psychology and neuroscience.

We know, from history, that a text with generous line spacing will certainly read better than other with no line spacing at all. The German blackletter used by Gutenberg in his Bible, however, is almost unreadable to a contemporary westerner's eyes and definitely alien to someone from a non-Western background. In the fifteenth century, though, it was certainly the norm. History can help to avoid repeating our mistakes, but it also shows the relative importance of our current standards.

In short, we still cannot objectively define type, and won't be able to before a major breakthrough in neural science. However, copyright issues and legal matters impose formal specifications on what a font is and what it is not. Whether a typeface is a tweak, a revival or a work of art is left to the courts.

[5] ibid. p. 32.

[6] Robert Bringhurst, The Elements of Typographic Style, Vancouver: Hartley & Marks, 2002. p. 309.

## Tweaking and Reviving

In order to explain the type designer's first reluctance to embrace the digital alternative, and also to understand how design processes are not as straightforward as they are presented to us, we'll concentrate on Fred Smeijers's account on the current state of events in typography. Specifically, we'll borrow his term font tweaking.[5] This process consists of loading a font, 'tweaking' it – altering small details – and releasing it with different names, thereby circumventing copyright laws, since U.S. Law protects font names as trademarks, but not font designs. Smeijers is clear in pointing that font tweakers have nothing to do with type design at all, reinforcing the distinction between doing type as a labour of love and doing it for a profit.

Font revivals, on the other hand, are reinterpretations of existing designs, and our best example would be Morison's effort in bringing the classical designs into the Monotype type library. Revivals matter to us because they aren't original productions (as they draw inspiration from existing designs) but aren't copies either (because no rights over them could be warranted otherwise, since there would be no original idea).

Digital type foundries and vendors still maintain the tradition, digitising and redoing the old masters' work. It's worth noting that even if a certain typeface, such as those with expired copyrights, resides in the public domain, anyone can make a digital version – a revival – and claim the rights to it.

Digital type catalogues are rife with revivals: In Bringhurst's inventory of digital foundries, we can find 14 that issue revivals, and 4 that only release original designs.[6] This interest in resuscitating previous designs also has motives that stand apart from simple typographic archaeology. Revivals are routinely issued by vendors and foundries to protect the rights of the rights holder when a typeface's copyright is about to expire. Such is the case with Avenir LT, Adobe Garamond and Frutiger Next – which is what allowed Linotype to retain the rights to the original design and be able to sue Microsoft in the Segoe case.

Revivals reside in a kind of legal no man's land – some, like Arial (which is more a tweak than a declared revival), manage to stick around while others, like Segoe, raise copyright lawyers' eyebrows.

Given these two aspects, one cannot but wonder that a type designer wouldn't be thrilled with this perspective. One has also to question why there is such a rift in reactions between font tweaking and font revivals, which can be interpreted as no more than corporate font tweaking. A practical example of this is MyFonts.com's description of the Avenir LT font (link, down the page) – a 'recut version of Avenir', stating that 'The 'LT' was added to the name as the metrics differ from the original version'. This definitely corresponds to Smeijers' description of font tweaking, despite the fact that the name change wasn't intended to avoid legal troubles, but to assert the brand of the author of the revival. What is a revival, then, other than a corporate sanctioned font tweak?

**Free software and Type Design**

So far, we've kept our focus on corporate approaches to type design. As of 2008, the digital design tools field is dominated by Adobe Systems Inc. with its Creative Suite bundle of applications targeting photo, video, vector and sound editing. Adding to that the fact that Adobe software is the staple in most design courses in Europe and the United States, it can be stated that we are, indeed, faced with stifled possibilities when choosing digital creative tools, a monoculture of sorts. Although there have been parallel efforts from the free software and open source world to create alternatives, Adobe's sole dominance in this market remains unquestioned.

Going back to type design, we could point Donald Knuth's TeX and METAFONT as the best examples of an alternative approach to designing type on computers.

Having come from the UNIX crowd, and hailed as one of its most highly regarded representatives, Donald E. Knuth reflected this background in his efforts to create a simple system for dynamic typesetting. TeX was first released in 1989, with several new versions being introduced during the '90; its most recent update was released on 2002. It is still very popular among the academic and scientist audience for typesetting papers, since TeX excels at accurately setting and displaying mathematical formulae and including them in book layouts.

For an Adobe software user, TeX will definitely look alien, not least because of its lack of a graphical user interface, instead relying on command line input for operating. Instead of the mainstream point and click, drag and drop way of laying out and manipulating text and image boxes, TeX is meant for processing specifically crafted plaintext files, in turn outputting a printer-ready, typeset document. While requiring a rather steep learning curve, TeX introduced a model of digital typesetting that would be mostly put aside by the software houses that produced GUI page layout editors.

METAFONT was designed to be the font handling backend for TeX. It is based on a modular method of generating letterforms, based on instructions fed to the METAFONT processor, which outputs valid font files for use in TeX documents. Computer Modern, the hallmark font of TeX, was created by Knuth using METAFONT, and sports variable parameter such as stroke thickness, serif dimensions and shape contrast. Thus, by tweaking the parameters, one could create endless variations on letterforms, treating them as data to be manipulated, in contrast with the commercial model of fonts as unique authored pieces.

Due to its lack of a GUI – an absence that a seasoned hacker would see as a good feature – TeX and METAFONT presented little appeal for business opportunities. As such, these two programs remain largely unknown to the non-computer scientist audience since, among other reasons, you won't easily find a book introducing TeX as you would a book on Adobe InDesign.

Still, the METAFONT model can be the foundation of a new model of regarding typography and type design. Because of its simple input/output architecture, it is only missing a proper interface for easy operation, along with compatibility with existing formats. Other projects, such as MetaType1 or LiveType – not the Apple product, but a parametric approach to typeface construction, presented in 1997 at SIGGRAPH – show that a modular, open-ended approach to fonts is possible and has definite advantages over the manual creation process that's the norm in applications such as Fontographer, FontLab or its comprehensive free software alternative, Fontforge.

### Technology on Arcane Standards

The current terminology used in typography is also a clear signal of how it still depends on former traditions instead of adapting to its new medium.

Digital typography's rules and terminology have been determined by its physical counterparts, and that still hasn't changed. For example, we still talk about 'leading' – a term for the spacing between lines that takes its name from the lead strips used for that purpose – although the term 'line spacing' is gradually replacing it in user oriented applications such as Microsoft Word.

Another example – while type foundries got that name because of their heavy use of metal, single person studios with Macs are still referred to as 'foundries'. And fonts are described as being 'cut' or 'cast', more than 'digitised'. We talk about 'digital versions' instead of digital copies, perhaps to preserve their history and soul and not treat them as just another file in a user's computer.

Although we can forgive this persistence in using traditional typesetting terms, it also is a symptom that the type activity and business have failed to redefine themselves for the digital medium. On the other hand, these examples can actually be interpreted as quite an artificial and linguistic way to value the work of the typographer, probably with the aim of distinguishing between 'true' type designers and mere font tweakers, and not let 'true' typography be contaminated by the creeping tweaker threat.

**What Now?**

Given that digital type has been hanging around for thirty years, the progress in improving on font technology and taking advantage of the digital medium has been rather low. On the other hand, type designers in general (with the exception of rare cases such as Emigre or Letterror) have not tried to get to grips with font technology, rather limiting themselves to drawing and tracing their designs in Fontographer and selling them on major font vendors (MyFonts, Monotype) or independent ones (such as T26 and Veer). Worse still, issues of originality and plagiarism have been discussed in type design circles, but corporate entities break them routinely while trying, at the same time, to assert their rights in courts.

The difference between major and minor vendors is not substantial: though distributors like Veer try to create a community and improve on the users' and designers' experience through research, designer spotlights and support. Despite these efforts, digital typefaces are still regarded in an esoteric limbo between metal characters and abstract data. And though the price tags have steadily declined (and recently stabilised around the 20 dollar range in general), it is revealing that despite business models such as iTunes or Flickr, collaborative methods in producing typefaces (many typographers are still lone workers) haven't yet developed, and file formats have changed so little in the face of recent, sleeker solutions like XML and SVG. There's little hope for innovation: the Adobe-Macromedia and Monotype-Linotype mergers have paved the ground for a corporate monoculture ruled by software and typeface vendors and distributors, with very little margin for competition.

We can also point a mutual apathy between commercial developers and designers as a possible reason – type designers try to adapt to outdated ways – file formats and type tools – to create their works, while developers lag in keeping up to date to new breakthroughs. Limiting the tools is limiting the imagination.

On the other hand, font vendors have an incredibly contradictory stance regarding font rights, using copyright law to protect their products while violating it to borrow from others'. The different fate of Arial and Segoe begs the question: are the vendors and distributors handling this as it should be handled?

This model's obvious contradictions definitely invite serious questioning as to the legitimacy and validity of the current type market and business model, which cannot effectively release its standards and technology because of the threat of competition. It is therefore left to users, designers and independent developers to shape a new way of defining type and creating effective communication channels between providers and users, be it through online communities or real world discussion in type designer's circles and colleges.

If type design takes the free/open source route – and the wheels are already in motion – how can type vendors sustain their profit margins and their markets? With open fonts and free font editing software around, there would be little doubt that typography can take a very interesting turn. Could we also see the open approach and the business approach coexist, catering to specific users' needs, whether amateur or professional? And, finally, will the type world come to terms with the fact that appropriation and use of other's ideas have defined the activity since its beginnings, and that it implies a serious rethinking of concepts such as authorship, plagiarism and author's rights?

Bibliography

Robert Bringhurst, The Elements of Typographic Style, Vancouver: Hartley & Marks, 2002.

Fred Smeijers, Type Now, London: Hyphen Press, 2003.

Friedl, Ott and Stein, Typography: An encyclopedic survey of type design and techniques through history. London: Black Dog & Leventhal, 1998.

S. H. Steinberg and John Trevitt, Five Hundred Years of Printing (4th Revised edition). London: Oak Knoll Press, 1996.

Online references

'The Scourge of Arial' by Mark Simonson (background and critical account on Arial).

Brian Livingston, 'Is Microsoft's Vista Font Just a Copy?' (news article on the Segoe legal case).

Brian Livingston, 'Designer Says Vista Font Is Original', (follow up on the previous story).

Ulrich Stiehl, 'The Funny Font Forging Industry - A Report for Legal Authorities', (an aggressive take on font tweaking and appropriation).

LiveType - http://tinyurl.com/2fscfv

MetaType1 - http://www.nowacki.strefa.pl/

# Linux for Theatre Makers: Embodiment & Nix Modus Operandi

Nancy Mauro-Flude

Author's note: This is a text I wrote during my MA in Media Design at Piet Zwart Institute, in response the Thematic Project 'Command Line Culture' September - December 2006 led by Florian Cramer (the course director). From the perspective of a performing artist, and as a developer of the /Eclectic Tech Carnival [http://eclectictechcarnival.org/] I discuss my observations on how using the command line interface may be seen to possibly co-constitute one another in everyday life, operating as fields of embodied reflection.

## Introduction

*The overriding desire of most children is to get at and see the soul of their toys, some at the end of a certain period of use, others straight away. I do not find it in me to blame this infantile mania; it is the first metaphysical tendency. When this desire has implanted itself in the child's cerebral marrow, it fills his fingers and nails with an extraordinary agility and strength. The child twists and turns his toy, scratches it, shakes it, bumps it against the walls, throws it on the ground. From time to time he makes it re-start its mechanical motions, sometimes in the opposite direction. Its marvellous life comes to a stop. The child, like the people besieging the Tuileries, makes a supreme effort; at last he opens it up, he is the stronger. But where is the soul? This is the beginning of melancholy and gloom.*

*– Charles Baudelaire, 17 April, 1853*

My central thread in this text is the Linux computer operating system (OS) and more specifically the use of the command-line interface within this OS and its relationship to embodiment.[1]

Since bodies and machines are often seen in opposition, I suggest that they are better perceived as complementary in nature rather than antagonistic. For people who have never worked with command line computing on a standard *nix machine[2], especially people who are already conditioned to point

[1] Hereafter, I will refer to the computer operating system as OS.

[2] For the rest of the essay I specifically refer to Linux, one of the many Unix operating systems. I also am a user of the terminal on the Mac OSX based on Open BSD, so I talk from both perspectives. Although both of these operating systems are different from Linux, which is a kernel wrapped in one of the many distributions, there are numerous similarities between Unix and Linux systems. For an account of the genealogy of the Unix machine and its offsprings of *nix derivatives i.e. Linux, BSD see 'An alternative history of *nix - machine(s) = person(s) | dev/*nix' by Martin Hardie, http://www.openflows.org/~auskadi/nix1.pdf Linux is specific because it is not proprietary, i.e. the source code is

and click methods cultivated by Graphical User Interfaces (GUIs)[3] such as Windows OS or Mac OS, this involves sensitising procedures (such as one may endure with any new instrumental skill acquisition) for the operation of code as a series of interrelated programmes. I will discuss how using the command line interface may be seen to possibly co-constitute one another in everyday life, operating as fields of embodied reflection.

I propose that the body, like any organism, is a protean reality in constant flux and it is in this sense that I'd like to consider some of the OS applications from the GNU/Linux community, I am specifically referring to the non-proprietary tools that are developed to use in a command line interface.[4] I position myself along the same vein as Martin Hardie who reads 'Unix as consistent with more philosophical descriptions of thinking or of living life itself.'[5] Indeed the spreading development and use of Linux operating systems and free software has political implications. As Alan Sondheim (1999) writes:

> *linux is, if not art, at least fashion, wearable, at problematic variance with capital (punk for example), useful for intruders, the mouth and tongue for some.*

I hope to elucidate how the regular use of a computational interface, command line or GUI, has deep physiological effects. I question why it is mostly the case that the GUI is presented as a *given* to the regular computer user. Since information feudalism affects not only information society and subsequent issues of ownership, privacy, sharing – clearly seen in the over-abundance of patents and agreements to *harness the user*, which in my view, is an attempt to strip humanity of all civil freedoms; what products to use, what plants to grow and consume, what seeds to cultivate, and to an extent our ability to even engage with molecular living matter is being restricted.[6]

## Long Live the Amateur and Eclectic Hacker!

> *Custom, that obscure crossroads where the constructed and the habitual coalesce, is indeed mysterious.*
> *– Michael Taussig (1993)*

made available for users to modify and extend upon. Finally, I am required by Law to write *nix, instead of UNIX as Calum A. Selkirk (2004) writes: '...I used the term '*nix' to denote Unix, or more precisely Unix-like operating systems, this is due to the fact that "Unix" is a trademark, and as such cannot be used in this way. However, as the operating systems we are discussing owe their historical roots to AT&T's "Unix", we will describe them generically as "*nix"'.

[3] Hereafter, I will refer to Graphical User Interfaces as GUIs.

[4] For a description see 'GNU's Not Unix! – Free Software', GNU General Public License, http://www.gnu.org/copyleft/gpl.ht.ml http://www.nettime.org/Lists-Archives/nettime-1-0506/msg00042.html 'Free software is a matter of liberty not price ... Free Software Foundation, established in 1985, is dedicated to promoting computer users' rights to use, study, copy, modify, and redistribute computer programs. The FSF promotes the development and use of free software, particularly the GNU operating system, used widely in its GNU/Linux variant. The FSF also helps to spread awareness of the ethical and political issues surrounding freedom in the use of software.' http://www.fsf.org

In light of Merleau Ponty's method of phenomenological description and dealing with experiences in raw reality, I choose to write this paper in a personal register, because general divides between practice, theory and the self-referential, replicates harmful objectifying, and empirical models.[7] I'll also acknowledge my own corporeal complicity in the way in which I view the subject, as Kathy Acker so aptly stated 'Politics don't disappear they take place inside my body'[8], *political* for me always comes through the personal. A critique I have is that a large majority of people who contribute to the discourse about *nix have a desire to produce totalising accounts without any regard to cultural difference. As in all situations, I believe there are varying ways or modes of participation. In the following section I shall trace out some of the more salient benefits in relation to approaching learning in the spirit of an amateur.

I consider whether Linux tools can instigate, as well as create, represent and respond to intuitive working methods for a broader community – outside the field of free software developers and end-users and not as a way of living or being separate. I will also propose that engagement in thought, as in any repeated action where the body is foregrounded, the regular use of technology both hardware and software, has physical effects on who we are and how we consider our sense of self. I focus upon the inter-corporeal and sociological aspect of 'the user' rather than the cybernetic debate.[9] My basic premise is, if we consider that genuine and meaningful communication with other humans is a necessary and gratifying part of life, as computers begin to take the centre stage of many of our daily lives (for those of us in the metropoles), I emphasise we may want to be aware of the consequences of the decisions that we are (perhaps not) making, in our choice of OS as communication apparatus.

Is humanity in great danger of losing its diversity? It has never been so possible to speak so convincingly of global civilization as it is today. For those of us in the metropoles are we becoming unable to discern with any clarity the manner in which our own perceptions and thoughts are being shifted by our sensory involvement with consumer electronic technologies?

For more on the FSF and a definition of Free Software see, http://www.fsf.org/licensing/essays/free-sw.html and philosophy http://www.gnu.org/philosophy/philosophy.html

[5]
Martin Hardie, 'Time Machines and the Constitution of the Globe', 2005, http://www.nettime.org/Lists-Archives/nettime-1-0506/msg00042.html

[6]
A local example is when I went to the dentist and got my wisdom tooth taken out, I wanted to keep it, since it had a large curl on the root of the bone, like my curly hair, that I was curious about, but the dental institute would not let me keep it due to sterilization laws. I felt it was an infringement on my private body since I cultivated the raw material myself who were they to keep and inscribe a law regarding my own flesh!? ... A broader example of how artists (especially in the USA) are vulnerable is the PATRIOT Act which has made freedom of speech questionable. For instance, see the ongoing debate about Critical Art Ensemble who by simply communicating corporeal experience in a performance installation, are persecuted for alleged involvement in acts of bio-terrorism.

[7]
The idea behind this is to safeguard the phenomenological moment of analysis whilst juxtaposing a

If this combination is insupportable to some readers, pray let him/her stick with my explanation, rather then we should part company here, as I explain how the infusion of different fields of discourse can create new ones. Opening up normally closed circuits can create a myriad of new parameters, which may presage an emergent paradigm shift...

I write here as a *nix machine neophyte or *newbie* although for at least a decade I have been involved with human machine interaction, for example, inter-mixing dance theatre pieces with software for live and/or online telematic performance situations, or circuit bending[10] electronic toys in punk bands to push the instruments into other dimensions.[11] This could be called *hacking* because I feel the need to extend materials (and situations) beyond their particular given limitations.[12] Usually this action is an improvised reaction that unfolds itself as a sensual process and spontaneous desire rather than a reverend discipline, so therefore I am not a geek.[13] Probably, I do not deserve to define myself with the term *hacker* since I did not discover circuit logic in a sophisticated way, nor do I look for how connections complete their loops in order to then break them or think in terms of 'problems' that need to be solved. I usually just start playing, wasting a lot of time dreaming and aimless wandering, until someone with that knowledge points out the fundamentals to me and then I try and absorb the information whilst continuing in my own idiosyncratic experiential manner.

I am enchanted when I look inside machines and I like to touch their inner parts, I guess this stems from my childhood, as when someone would turn the TV off, I'd run to see if I could catch the people leaving from behind, curious and mystified. According to Baudelaire, 'This is the first metaphysical tendency.' In his 'Philosophy of Toys' he suggests that 'In their games children give evidence of their great capacity for abstraction and their high imaginative power.' I come from a cultural tradition where personal creative practice is done for the eventual benefit of society to maintain the prosperity and health of all of the people, not just the atomised individual (your profession here...) artist, or movement, so it is mainly in meaningful collaborative contexts I find such acts profoundly thrilling.[14]

Foucauldian genealogical perspective, for a discussion of this in relation to Merleau-Ponty's work read Perspectives on Embodiment: The Intersections of Nature and Culture, G. Weiss and H.F. Haber (eds), Routledge, New York, 1999.

[8]
Karen Brennan, 'The Geography of Enunciation: Hysterical Pastiche in Kathy Acker's Fiction' in Boundary 2: an international Journal of Literature and Culture, Summer 21:2, 1994, pp. 243-68.

[9]
For writings in this area see N. Katherine Hayles, My Mother Was a Computer: Digital Subjects and Literary Texts, Chicago: University of Chicago Press, 2005.

[10]
Circuit Bending is the creative implementation of audio short-circuits.

[11]
Most obviously in Toydeath where I performed under the name of s.g.ballerina, 'Picture a hyper band of aliens channelling through a broken AM radio, and someone's playing with the speed control. But the Hendrix-worthy feedback wails are actually the sirens of toy fire engines. The spastic beats courtesy of model helicopters. Toydeath proves that punk ain't dead, it's just moved into the toy box.' http://minorkeys.tripod.com/reviews.html

Apart from the black box in the theatre, I did not ever expect there to be another vessel deep enough to hold all these moments and abstractions of experience and potential until I experienced the dark magic space of the shell. However, first and foremost, I must claim I find much of Linux geek rhetoric far from affable, my own conviction is that such a revision in attitude carries concrete and far-reaching implications beyond our understanding of the *nix operating system. Calum Selkirk (2004) in a concise and elegant description of 'shell basics' admits that 'These concepts are often difficult to grasp for someone completely unfamiliar with programming.' He continues:

> *It is for this reason I spend probably more time than is perhaps necessary explaining them, often with the most simplistic of examples.* [15]

Does this explanation ensure to the reader they must be a moron if he/she should not understand his detailed simple explanations of the command line interface? No – these are regular humorous antics of the field, as hacker Eric Raymond (2003) reminds us: 'To do the Unix philosophy right, you have to value your own time never to waste it'.[16] A most extreme case of tech-humour (or is that megalomania?) we can witness here in an interview with Radia Perlman, an expert at networking protocols and distinguished engineer at Sun Microsystems, tells us of her stringent desire to abolish an intimate social custom that extends back to 6th century BC; Frauenheim (2005) recounts:

> *Thinking about smart communication strategies is something that comes naturally to Perlman. She even sees room for improvement in the way people clink glasses during dinner toasts. 'That actually drives me crazy', Perlman said, 'because it's an inefficient protocol'.* [17]

Steeped in superstition and self-preservation, a toast for many people is a spontaneous and congenial tradition, which binds us to each other. It is outrageous to overplay the intellectual aspect of collective human experience, and define knowing as strictly a function of the rules and categories appealing to the cognitive mind, to the exclusion of sensory

[12]
http://en.wikipedia.org/wiki/Hacker_definition_controversy

[13]
I am involved in various projects that suggest that when women-centred activities are foregrounded people usually expect me to subscribe to the rules or often identify me with a geek, because some of these focus on Free Software based workshops. My desire is driven by sharing information with people who don't get access to it or cannot afford it, and with those women who do not have the confidence or even think they deserve to learn anything because they were brought up in extraordinary, challenging environments. See: http://eclectictechcarnival.org http://genderchangers.org;
To see if you are a geek you need to take 'The Geek Test', http://www.innergeek.us/geek.html

[14]
As opposed to physical conditioning, disciplines that became techniques to generate rules and exercises in order to produce functional escalation in the army and finally in civil society.

[15]
Calum A Selkirk, 'Shell Basics.v1.1', 2004, https://pzwart.wdka.hro.nl/mdma/staff/cselkirk/Documents/shell_basics.Pdf
I want to confess that it has taken me 1.5 years to fully understand this

factors. The body is not a programmed machine but an active and open form, continually improvising its relation to things and the world. Moreover, as Matthew Fuller (2003) states:

> *Free Software is too internalist. The relation between its users and its developers is so isomorphic that there is extreme difficulty in breaking out of that productive but constricted circle.* [18]

I advocate that geeks should leave these structures of discourse behind them! Otherwise by now all of the experiences with command line tools and all their responses in the shell would already have been anticipated from the beginning, already programmed, as it were into the initial Unix kernel.

What fascinates me is that for a significant amount of us, which is a massive majority of the world population who actually use computers, do not even know that a spectrum of OS choices are even available! Let alone about the GNU/Linux or free software foundation (FSF), which exists to insist people should have the freedom to choose and modify the technology they use in the way they see fit and not be restricted by economics or reductive proprietary laws. If people are talking about greatly enhancing our communication models, I suggest that users and/or creators of free software, or *nix developers, who until now habitually operate in isolation, need to appreciate different modes of being, in order to share the potential of human development in regard to embodiment, language, information and communication technologies. Why are users and/or developers of x etc, involved in totalising accounts of human interaction? – whereas we might expected them to be more open-minded. The teleological attitude, conventions and the allocation of roles, of some hardcore technocrats is intimidating and in regard to optimizing smart communication strategies it seems rather disingenuous (and also a total come down).

## The Shell vs Terrestrial Gravity, and Inertia

The rubric of GNU/Linux is a vista of permissive, open-ended media as the source code is free to be used, developed and extended. Specifically, users of command line tools have

text. However, should my confession prove me low in intellect? I am a graduate of the University of Sydney obtaining first class 1:1 honours, which placed me in the top 5 percent mark of Australian Universities for the year 2000. I could not possibly have destroyed all my brain cells since then, so this might then perhaps give some kind of legitimate proof that I am considered, not only by myself, to possess adequate mental ability. The point I am trying to make is -- if I give this text to a person who has never even heard of *nix, and only grew up thinking Windows machines are available and was to be introduced to the world of free software rhetoric they have no way to enter such discourse.

[16] Eric S. Raymond, 'The Art of Unix Programming', 2003, http://www.faqs.org/docs/artu/

[17] Ed Frauenheim and Gilbert Alorie, 'Opening doors for women in computing: Harvard president's comments re-ignite debate over women in computer science, with reformers trying to reverse guy-centric patterns', 2005, http://news.com.com/Opening+doors+for+women+in+computing+-+page+2/2100-1022_3-5557311-2.html? tag=st.num

[18] Matthew Fuller, Behind the Blip, Essays on the Culture of Software, Autonomedia:New York, 2004.

endless variables, executed by programmers inhibited by and impatient with the limitations of the GUI. Martin Howse suggests:

> *Alternatively living coding at the command line; that horizontal prompt proving a horizon for contemplation... And thus to the application of a new discipline, expanded software; endophysical interface and Alice in Wonderland. (another beginning marked)'.*[19]

[19] Martin Howse, 'Version Control 1.6' in [the] xxxxx [reader]xxxxx, OpenMute Print-on-demand services, 2005, http://openmute.org

[20] In response I made a /dev/null Doll, see: http://sistero.org/devnull/doll/

When I first discovered the power to delete the file in my OpenBSD terminal that the OSX finder could not trash I felt was no longer a prisoner inside my machine, only possessing knowledge of a GUI, I was formerly stuck in a holding pattern. Using x you keep moving all the time, discovering always new executable codes sensitive to commands.

In the shell I find a marvelous mess of constellations, nebulae, interstellar gaps, awesome gullies, that provokes in me an indescribable sense of vertigo, as if I am hanging from earth upside down on the brink of infinite space, with terrestrial gravity still holding me by the heels but about to release me any moment. An example is /dev/null – a special *nix file where you pipe your unwanted data flow through this output. When I first experienced viewing data disappearing into this file, I immediately had an epiphany about the black hole and how the theory of the event horizon might function in an every day context.[20]

Sondheim (1999) has a similar perspective on the abyss-like nature of the shell,

> *2. The graphic interface opens to shells as well, and since the inter-face devolves from a blank screen, there is simultaneously potential (click anywhere on it) and absence (nothing visible), reflecting upon the human operator / monitor interface as well.*

The experiential in the *nix world is truly an unvalidated mode. I believe that the meaning of life is to be uplifted, to be in a euphoric state and make art that reflects this experience of traveling through the manifold of time. All you need is humility and imagination for the 'baroque protocol' as Howse (2006) suggests:

*All patches, software encodings, algorithmic elaborations for either space should prove readily extensible (in the codified realm, heavily abstracted and based on message passing, in the social realm driven by baroque protocol) and concerned with an extreme escalating overmapping of expanded and reduced software domains. The problem states itself as that of the practical and the experiment. Substance.*

In the *spirit* of the awe-inspired or amateur, a very particular experiential learning aspect and protocol is set in motion, especially in the mode and register of collaborative communication when you working at this level you have a massive advantage, not only do you enjoy a certain level of freedom – when you don't *really* know what you are doing – but you do things with tools that other people would not do, whereas a professional attitude has all these constraints. Ironically x experts or in general technocrats who have certain defined methods and formulas, end up becoming completely unintelligible to people outside the Information *Communication* Technology culture.

**Vessels of Infinite Veracity**

*You seek for knowledge and wisdom as I once did; and I ardently hope that the gratification of your wishes may not be a serpent to sting you, as mine has been.*
*– Mary Shelly Frankenstein (1818)*

Perception is precisely about this reciprocity, the ongoing interchange between the body and the entities that surround it, and can be seen as a form of 'expanded software script (human)'. (Howse, 2006) Therefore, I am curious about the development of the human form in regard to long-term computer usage. We experience our world as fabric woven together out of inextricable sensory threads, not as individual sensory media, nor as individual data. Whatever account we give of experience not only must take this synaesthetic motif into consideration, but also begin with and from it. As Howse explains:

*On the other side, the human, and within a narrow context the meta, the xxxxx/PLENUM experiment attempts a simultaneous overmapping of both realms using operatic, logical and holographic technique dressed up in the emperor's new clothes; the expanded software script (human) translated into machine and meta-human-machine operation. We would rather view interface in terms of a Gunter Brus incision than a question of design and GUI.*[21]

When operating a computer we are connected to the machine by means of our human body, including its movement and skills as well as the senses and linguistic activity. As a Linux user we are a creator, engaged in a dynamic, symbiotic dance with the computer. In *Matter and Memory* Bergson confirms the process of affect with all that we encounter, he writes,

> *...we have to take into account the fact that our body is not a mathematical point in space, that its virtual actions are complicated by, and impregnated with real actions, or, in other words, that there is no perception without affection. Affection is, then, that part or aspect of the inside of our body which we mix with the image of external bodies. (1911: 38)*

[21] PLENUM was a project in March 2006. As audience you are also part of an emerging expanded exchange where the interaction via the software is reflected during the dialogue itself, http://kop.kein.org/plenum/html/documentation.html The software used was Pure Data. As Howse writes, 'We could begin to unravel expanded software (the realm of PLENUM) using the example of a network to be mapped within our software; mapping the connections of Alice (in Wonderland, through the Looking Glass)...' Howse, Op. cit.

From the perspective of the actual machine, Sondheim (1997) affirms the uncanny nature of Linux referring to its physical like form:

> *Beyond the traditional division of graphic user interface (GUI) and text-based interface, the Unix and Linux system/s create a unique environment problematising machine, boundary, surface, and structure.'*

Linux engages in a dimensional model, it leaks, each programme is bound up within the other. The vast amount of command line tools and *nix concepts, file names, paths, wild cards, input and output redirection, regular expressions apply to many different commands. The recurring concepts seem to transcend most kinds of simple breakdown. As my command line experience grows, I find myself returning to these. Slowly I delve deeper into the possibilities, specific tasks and commands seem more like membranes, because they define a surface of metamorphosis and exchange. The entire system can be controlled and tweaked by the user, in this sense; the OS has a subjective aesthetic by its very substance, which blurs the line between two self-contained realms of human and machine.

This is why I advocate that the GNU/Linux shell should be approached as an OS in flux responding to the output and needs of a living community, for if the user's awareness is not locked up in the density of a

[22]
Loss Peqeño Glazier, 'Jumping to Occlusions' in Digital Poetics, 1997, http:// epc.buffalo.edu/authors/glazier/essays/occlusions/

[23]
I first heard the concept 'operating system as process' in the 2006 Thematic Project Command line Culture at Piet Zwart Institute lead by Florian Cramer.

[24]
The Wings, an area of the stage not visible to the audience.

closed and bounded object, the ability for the machine to extend itself to a network is also open and indeterminate. Hence, change and transformation in every aspect of human life is imminent, to such an extent that life itself is being transformed. As Loss Pequeño Glazier (1997) has remarked, 'The language you are breathing becomes the language you think'.[22]

This is the inter-corporeal level of using a networked computer, since I even begin to experience myself in an expansive networked or socio-centric sense rather than an individual egocentric sense. If the human intellect is rooted in, and borne by our contact with the multiple shapes that surround us, what is the impact of the computer, becoming more embedded in our daily lives, upon our bodily membrane?

You need to approach the Linux OS as a continual learning process[23], as such, (for the command line *nix user), you need to initiate the system maintenance operations, it requires the constant need to monitor and intimately understand the functioning of the machine. Under the surface of the computer's interface, processes seethe with undiscovered activity. Since an OS runs many daemons and services, many of these processes merely wait for actions to occur – one example is a cupsd process, which is a background daemon of the CUPS printing system. This process waits for you to call it to work, it lies back stage in the wings just watching to see if it is needed, and this is passive activity that uses very little processor time or memory.[24] But only the Linux command line will show you the actual parsing of these processes and at least with my experience with the Gentoo distribution it will not spoon feed the user informing them when updating their world needs to be done.

Therefore I believe that the constant need to monitor and intimately understand the functioning of the Linux machine also deepens our kinaesthetic awareness about our own anatomy, physiological and kinesiology systems. Further, Hofstader in *Gödel, Escher, Bach: An Eternal Golden Braid* recounts a moment when he was showing some friends the PARRY programme, when some of the OS information came up in the terminal after a mistyped mistake, they asked 'why are you over-typing what's on the screen?' To which he explained,

> *The idea that 'you' know all about 'yourself' is so familiar from interaction with people that it was natural to extend it to the computer – after all, it was intelligent enough that it could*

> *'talk' to them in English! Their question was not unlike asking a person, 'why are you making so few red blood cells today?' People do not know about that level – the 'operating system level' – of their bodies.' (1979: 301)*

I propose that after prolonged use of Linux, people will begin to develop more sensitivity to their own need for inner maintenance because of its labyrinthine architecture; this is 'expanded software, a timed response'. (Howse: 2006) This information can be experienced as dwelling within the body apparatus. Having awareness of our inter-cellular processes leads to a change in physical experience, a change in sensation.[25] No doubt from my experience in experiential movement techniques, such as Laban Movement Analysis, ideokinesis, Alexander Technique, I am more open to this.[26] But what I am implying is that this is the sort of silent conversation that we carry on with things with our proprioceptive facilities, a continuous dialogue that is a proto-linguistic state, for instance, when the hand readily navigates the space between the fingers and the keys on the computer.

With Linux I begin to understand and have an idea of the most important processes and how to manage them, for example, with 'top' command I can get information on my system and its operations. When Sondheim (1997) writes in point 4 in his tenets:

> *Phenomenology of Linux / Unix: 4. It is easy to assume that source code is equivalent to bones and operable binaries to flesh; or the kernel as fundament, and file structure as slough. I would rather argue for a system of cubist plateaus of intersecting information regimes, with vectors / commands operating among them. In this sense it is information that is immanent within the operating system, not any particular plateau-architecture.'*

An understanding of these processes will no doubt help me to practically manage my Linux OS, but perhaps it also may help me relate to my own physicality. After a while, I suspect I may find potential problems that vampirize my machine's processing speed, runaway processes, broken sessions which never properly terminated, and I may

[25] The feeling of such change is then reported back to the central nervous system by the proprioceptive apparatus. Nancy Udow (1977) refers to psychological research studies by Washburn (1916) and Schilder (1950) which, through 'the use of electromagyograms and electroencephelograms have shown the presence of muscular activity and brain waves during a mental motor image which are similar to those activities and waves during overt movement'. Theatre Papers Archive, 1977 – 1984, Dartington College of Arts, UK, http://www.spa.ex.ac.uk/drama/research/exeterdigitalarchives/main.html

[26] After much experimental research and training in touch and repatterning techniques learnt at the Institute for Somatic Movement Studies I can access my own and other bodily cellular tones. The tone can be explained in how the intercellular and extra cellular fluid is flowing in and out of the cell's membrane; this can be reflected at many levels e.g. low (not enough intercellular fluid), high (too much fluid inside the cell) of the organ, http://www.somaticmovementstudies.org/

[27] Laurie Anderson also questions this strange phenomena, http://www.droppingknowledge.org/bin/media/list/commercial.page#media_65

simultaneously detect blockages in cell movement in my body – which slows down my nervous system's ability to provoke or control the release of hormones and in turn may diminish nerve impulses.

Understanding the internal micro-choices and actions our automated nervous system performs every moment of our living existence, the same as the instrumental process of learning tools, writing scripts for managing programs and processes; getting information on process and shutting down processes, just as there are kinetic techniques that are often used for longevity. Neil Stephenson (1999) observes this complexity:

> *Many Hackers have launched more or less successful re-implementations of the Unix ideal. Each one brings in new embellishments... Thus Unix has slowly accreted around a simple kernel and acquired a kind complexity and asymmetry about it that is organic, like the roots of a tree, or the branching's of a coronary artery. Understanding it is more like anatomy than physics.*

Delving deeply into the myriad tools available in Linux and exploring possibilities of the entire file system, this concentration and imagination can actually stimulate and facilitate material, physical change in the human body. I advocate this may have more benefits then just powerful processor speed, script automation and multitasking. As it seems at the moment, prevalent is a strange sort of vanity based on identity, form and high end graphics, which is becoming more and more removed from the actual living human organism.[27]

Perhaps over the years the g-term use of GUI's may see its end-users becoming like the pathetic monster's of Mary Shelley's *Frankenstein*, their walk staggering and jerky, their reach clumsy and inaccurate, reflexes spasmodic; unaware of his labyrinthine space of the middle ear, careening about the environment, every movement a source of danger to himself and others. As regular computer users I fear we are losing our ability to sense our own inner communication and physiological processes and, I conjecture, using Linux OS might be a way to return to this. So early in history Mary Shelley recognized this danger and predicted the perils of the technological society and the GUI!

Perhaps her fiction was not about the easy Hollywood version of the uncontrollable man-made monster, I have a hunch that this great work was about the horror of a human who didn't have the capacity to imagine realms of abstraction or even their very own inner veracity. The body I here speak of is very different from the objectified body where the emphasis is on the Skeletal-muscular system, that complex machine whose broken parts or stuck systems are diagnosed by westernised medical doctors. Underneath the anatomized and mechanical body that we have learned to conceive, dwells the subjective body as it actually experiences things, this poised vessel that initiates our projects and suffers our passions.

[28] http://www.cryptonomicon.com/beginning.html

**Protect Me from What I Want...?**

> *You said it, my good Knight! There ought to be laws to protect the body of acquired knowledge. Take one of our good pupils, for example: modest and diligent, from his earliest grammar classes he has kept a little notebook full of phrases. After hanging on the lips of his teachers for twenty years, he's managed to build up an intellectual stock in trade; doesn't it belong to him as if it were a house, or money?*
> *– Paul Claudel, Le soulier de satin, Day III, Scene ii*

If bodies are complex systems embedded in the environment, what does this mean when we experience a saturation of media images on a daily basis? In fact I often feel my communication has been so corrupted, to that extent that I hardly ever watch television, yet its sound bites have infiltrated my own speech. Here Stephenson (1999) makes a connection between the mass media and the GUI:

Disney is in the business of putting out a product of seamless illusion – a magic mirror that reflects the world back better than it really is. But a writer is literally talking to his or her readers, not just creating an ambience or presenting them with something to look at: and just as the command-line interface opens a much more direct and explicit channel from user to machine than the GUI, so it is with words, writer, and reader.[28]

The Graphical User Interface (GUI) is the most commonly used OS and for most people perceived as an efficient and effective tool because of its point and click interface. However, according to Nielsen & Gentner (1996), if people opt for the GUI it ultimately limits human communication and even our ability to imagine the intangible:

> *The see and point principal states that users interact with the computer by pointing at the objects they can see on the screen. It's as if we have thrown away a million years of evolution, lost our facility with expressive language, and have been reduced to pointing at objects in the immediate environment. Mouse*

*buttons and modifier keys give us a vocabulary equivalent to a few different grunts. We have lost all the power of language, and can no longer talk about objects that are not immediately visible...*

Internalising enough of what seem inscrutable and cryptic commands that can be used quickly at appropriate times, is indeed an arduous initiation process; especially after the seemingly decadent but limiting life of the GUI. In due time as in any learned routine, working with the command line, or so I am told, the keystrokes will become hard-wired in my fingers and I will learn to automate maintenance and do backup commands with cron, or combine commands in hundreds of shell scripts. The material limitations one faces in any instrumental process and indeed when using the notoriously powerful *nix core, is certainly unapproachable for most of us, especially when one encounters a black hole when syncing and updating or then having to unemerge blocked packages.[29]

After about three years of listening to 'distro wars', the multiple and vexed opinions about which Linux distribution to actually install and use, in general, most people tried to 'protect me' from installing Gentoo Linux, which arguably, brings one closer to understanding the OS intimately than most other distributions (that is, apart from Linux-from-Scratch).[30] Eventually the installation, even with experienced support people guiding me, felt similar to that of a rite-of-passage, or making a pact with the Devil. However, no learning is easy, and in fact it should be frustrating, as when things are frustrating, that means we are learning – frustration is a necessary part of the learning curve. As I have said, the operation of Linux is a continual process, which, like most developmental patterns gives rise to new situations with each new stage of sensory information and language integration.

However, it is common that people now want things to be neatly packaged with a snazzy logo. Even education is catering more to the rules of economic rationalism, than to a deep pedagogical function. Nielsen Gentner (1996) suggests the inevitability of computers in our daily lives, and how this idea of time investment should be reflected in the educational system:

*Today's children will spend a large fraction of their lives communicating with computers. We should think about the trade-offs between ease of learning and power in computer-human interfaces. If there were a compensating return in increased power, it would not be unreasonable to expect a*

[29] People may be familiar with other installation terms, this description is specific to the Gentoo distribution [http://www.gentoo.org/ Linux] which is a kernel wrapped in one of the many distributions.

[30] http://www.linuxfromscratch.org/

> *person to spend several years learning to communicate with computers, just as now we expect children to spend 20 years mastering their native language.*[31]

[31]
Jakob Nielsen and Don Gentner, 'The Anti-Mac Interface', http://www.acm.org/pubs/cacm/AUG96/antimac.htm

[32]
Jef Raskin, 'Down with GUIs!', 1993, http://www.wired.com/wired/archive/1.06/1.6_guis.htm

[33]
Samuel Weber, 'Texts/Contexts', in Institution and Interpretation, Minneapolis: University of Minnesota Press, 1987, pp. 3-17.

What skills are OS users prepared to learn, what contexts are they prepared to situate themselves in, really? Indeed end-user alternatives are easy to propose, but difficult to put into practice, especially when they are presented as natural but exist by force of habit. Jef Raskin (1993) writes:

> *GUIs have become so pervasive (or is it perversive?) that many computer users can't even think about anything else as a human-computer interface ... But GUIs are modal from the get-go. Now that you've read this you know that interfaces which are far less modal are possible, but you should be warned they are habit-forming, even addictive. Start to use them and you are hooked forever...*[32]

In general, the actual shifting of inertia, of habitus, that is entailed in asking people to make perceptual shifts, is something we have to come to fully understand and work through. Weber describes this resistance:

> *because such fixed habits become, by virtue of their very fixity and hence inflexibility, incapable of dealing with changing and infinitely variable circumstances (1987: 14)*[33]

I find it remarkable that there has been hardly any research into the changes wrought by the massive use of particular computer OS's, nor has there been consideration of the long term impact and benefits of everyday usage.

In the wake of increased computational usage, it is an important moment for people to want to actively continue to reinvent language. Yet even in spite of their severity, computer languages have caused a tremendous creativity because there was, so far, no power to discipline them, as Sondheim (1999) has noticed: 'for some of us, Linux *has* changed the language'. If I consider the paranoia and the will to fix forms by software patent acts and extend this to the people who make their source code protected by copyright laws and international treaty provisions, it's clear that the compulsion for this finds its origin in a very particular and limiting view of the world. It is among other things, also handing over control to a fixed conceptual discourse of the Law.

[34]
Graham Harwood, 'Cartography and the Technologies of Location', http://www.scotoma.org/notes/index.cgi?CartoTech (Accessed 12 December 2006).

[35]
http://www.medienkunstnetz.de/themes/generative-tools/read_me/

Language as such has long been seen as simply a copy of a world and not something that is proto-linguistic, heteroglossic, and constantly adapting, changing. Some of this is due to the unfortunate result of mandatory schooling and the introduction of a national grammar. Much of our natural ability to acquire languages (which we might well say is in fact the essence of language) has already been lost. As the relation between so-called dialects and the 'core-language' show, the dialects are primary, not the core-language, rather, the standardized language is the derivative. All groups of people inevitably are from a language specific to them. This was something mis-understood about sign-language for a long time. However, place a number of deaf people from different sign-languages together and they will soon be speaking a new sign-language. But hope springs eternal, standardization of language/code is always trailing behind the current state of things.

As I have explained, language and code are not fixed or ideal forms, but an evolving medium we collectively inhabit, a vast topological matrix for which our bodies are generative sites. While individual speech acts are guided by the structured lattice of the language, that lattice is nothing other than the sedimented result of all previous acts of speech, and here we can see how Linux code itself is altered by the very expressive activity it now guides. As Harwood comments,

> *It seems software exists in some form of invisible shadow world of procedure ... Software is establishing models by which things are done yet, like believing the objectivity of maps, we forget that software is derived from certain cultural, historical and economic trajectories.*[34]

In 'Read_me, run_me, execute_me: Code as Executable Text: Software Art and its Focus on Program Code as Performative Text', Inke Arns specifically attributes code work to an economic class: 'These works use the poor man's medium, text, which also appears performative or executable in the context of the command line.'[35] Language and implied rules and protocols have always been principal instruments of the control process and unrestricted creativity is considered to be dangerous. According to Clive Phillpot, it is preventing any major social revolution when he reminds us:

> *There is no need to ban books since a significant percentage of the population – usually the most deprived, who have the most to gain from reading and changing the status quo –*

> *cannot read them. Instead we have to try to ban pictures and music because even the illiterate people can read pictures and understand lyrics.*[36]

[36] Clive Phillpot 'Art, Anarchy and the Open Library', 1991, in Art Libraries Journal, 4: 10. p. 9.

If we are to take real-life social stratification into consideration, although it costs nothing (except the price of a computer, lots of time, a certain education), for the moment, code work and understanding Linux is definitely not a 'poor man's' tool or 'modus operandi'.

**If you Make a Mistake with a Wildcard the Consequences are Serious...**

The embodiment process in Linux is relational and interactive, in *[the] xxxxx [reader]*, Howse (2006) writes 'Code leaks both ways across a broken-world interface.' I hope it is clear why above I advocate a revision of the discourse in general, since I believe this knowledge is necessary to understand in order to extricate the discussion of the cognitive from the limitations inherent within this text's presupposition of *simply asking everyone to switch to command line computing.*

To have a noticeably wider participation in the new developments in the language influenced by Linux, is to be fully aware of the current problems of this language and convinced of its extreme importance, notwithstanding more awareness. Ultimately the human capacity for reflection, planning and manipulation of our environment brings with it the responsibility of choice, but first and foremost, we need to be open and inform people that there is a choice. Above all, it seems important to recognise differences within, as well as beyond the borders of the Linux community or people will continue to fall into corporate traps of people like Bill Gates' idea of what a personal computer is, and Disney's limiting idea of what constitutes entertainment.

Furthermore, when source code is made available I think of it more as having reverence for other people's work. To be able to acknowledge, then copy that work or code and then try to understand how that person thought and felt – but always bringing in my own idiosyncrasies and vision to that, in the understanding that all these efforts are related, and have a larger common purpose. We are always faced with the problem of getting on with our own necessary process of self-discovery, which for regular users of computers, should also entail finding out how their operating systems work, discovering their internal system, language and power.

Our ability to create, plan and code our environment makes us responsible for what we create and for how we choose to live in that creation. Since all of us are, always-already, living on the edge of our own destruction, as Howse (2006) writes,

> *too much knowledge of programming. We can see this clearly in programming terms such as continuations, stack and, of course, memory. Yet such simple facts bear repetition; past and future are inherent within computation. The Turing tape moves backwards and forwards, according to specific instructions on that tape... And finally, it's not for nothing that Turing and indeed the entire field of computation is obsessed with the halting problem. When will it end?*

Because I keep wondering what happens if these entire systems continue to process even though basic human understanding has broken down.

# Live coding for free

Alex McLean

## Live Coding

Live coders write programs on the fly. They program in conversation with their machine, playing with instructions while a computer follows them. Here, there is no distinction between creating and running a piece of software – programs run while they are being created, gaining complexity via source code edits. We can think of coding live in the sense of working on electricity live, re-routing the flows of control around a program with the real danger that a faulty loop will get activated, causing the program to crash in sparks of logic.

Live coding environments make it possible to write code to generate music and video in real-time without having to restart any processes. Every adjustment to the code such as adding analgorithm to modulate a rhythmic back beat, or adjusting the inner workings of a video filter is immediately reflected in the audio or video output with no break.

It is not only the relationship between programmer and code that defines live coding, but also that between programmer and audience. Live coding can be a performance art, where an audience watches an artist write code while enjoying the output. As with all improvisations some preparation is necessary, but for many the aim is to begin with an empty text editor and live code their performance from scratch.

It can be difficult to pin down the definition of live coding. For example, what is the real difference between changing a number in a piece of source code and moving a slider in a graphical interface? The following points clarify some misconceptions underlying this kind of confusion.

*Rules must be explicit.* We may be inventing and changing rules all the time in our heads, but unless those rules are written down and modified while they are being followed by a computer (or other agent), that is not live coding.

*Higher order functions must be defined and manipulated.* A human musician could be described as an intricate, perhaps beautifully composed function that live codes itself. Here however we are interested in live coding within formal languages, with support for abstraction and composition.

*An audience is not required.* We can live code on our own, with a few friends or in a stadium, it is up to us (and our publicists).

Live coding is not an island. Live coders often perform with other kinds of musicians and indeed most live coders have musical training wider than only computer music.

## Mechanics

Live coding of music, video and other time-based works presents a technical problem – how to dynamically change a running program without unwanted discontinuities in the output. There are many different solutions, with a few described below.

In Object Oriented Programming (OOP), *hot swapping* methods are common. A method is a responder to some kind of message, so it is quite straightforward to arrange for a message to arrive at an alternate, newly coded method.

In lisp-like languages, *temporal recursion* is a common form of live coding, for example as described by Sorensen and Brown (2007). These are functions which call themselves with some temporal delay, where functions may be replaced for the next call.

In the pure functional language Haskell, live coding is made possible through *state injection* (Stewart and Chakravarty, 2005). Here state is managed by monadic computations, and passed back to a static core during the reload of dynamic parts.

In SuperCollider there is something more like a a contemporary form of *conversational programming*, where an object oriented language is used to manipulate and communicate with synthesis graphs.

Source code feedback is an technique whereby a live coded program may make edits to its own source code (McLean, 2004). This is most useful in inserting comments to give the programmer feedback on the running of the program.

## Live Coding Culture

> *Computers're bringing about a situation that's like the invention of harmony. Sub-routines are like chords. No one would think of keeping a chord to himself. You'd give it to*

*anyone who wanted it. You'd welcome alterations of it. Subroutines are altered by a single punch. We're getting music made by man himself: not just one man.*
*John Cage (1969).*

A number of fully fledged environments designed for live coding music and/or video have emerged in the past few years. The most well known are SuperCollider (McCartney, 2002), ChucK (Wang and Cook, 2004) and Fluxus (Griffiths, 2008), all three of which are FLOSS (Free/Libre/Open Source Software). The scheme-based Impromptu (Sorensen and Brown, 2007) is gaining traction, with freeware binaries available. We should also add Pure Data Puckette (1996) to the list; while the syntax is in the form of a graph, it remains a language with textual identifiers where live edits are the norm. The use of home brew environments is also common, often built around general purpose languages such as Perl, Python, Ruby and Haskell.

The communities around live coding environments are strong, with commonplace swapping of synthesis unit generators, scripts and patches. Here there is no clear line between software and music; by using someone else's synthesis library, you are in collaboration with them, making an audio collage of their technique and your own. The code sharing goes beyond synthesis libraries however. The snippets of code passing by email, demonstrating some technique or sharing a pleasing pattern, are perhaps equivalent to an oral tradition where nothing is fixed, just modified and passed on. By participating you contribute towards a cultural evolution of music.

Informal sharing of code is lifted into live improvisation in the performances of powerbooks unplugged (Rohrhuber et al., 2007). The players, of which there may be six or more, play together by passing SuperCollider patches over a wireless network. The code is shared via a simple chat system like interface, where themes may be collaboratively developed and call-response games played through source code edits. They avoid what they see as problems of artistic ego by rejecting any stage and playing as audience members, with the only sound emitting from their laptop speakers.

Instead of being reduced to commercial product, live coded music places human activity in focus. According to Small (1998), music is defined by all human activity around a performance, and the focus on music as a product rather than an activity itself is only a very recent aberration. Powerbooks unplugged can therefore be seen as returning live coding to the roots of musical activity, and indeed the group themselves see their laptops, unplugged from any central sound system, as acoustic folk instruments.

## Live Coding History Before Computers

Linguistically performative statements include 'I apologise', 'I promise' and 'We find the defendant guilty as charged.' Saying is literally doing. If the speaker has sufficient power, for example as an elected official, they may use performative statements to make rules which others must follow. To prevent things getting too messy, they will make rules about how future rules are made. The result is a system of law which includes how laws are made and changed, perhaps with the unchangeable nucleus of a constitution. Yes, we can view parliament as hardware, the law as software and politicians and voters as live coders.

However, examples within the realm of music are elusive – it does seem as though live coding of music began after the invention of computers. The experimental musicians of the 1960s explored rule based composition but even then did not, as far as we have heard, improvise those rules during performances.

## Dynamic Programming

Outside of the context of time based arts, live coding is generally termed dynamic programming. It began in the form of bit twiddling – modifications of low level machine instructions while they were being followed. This was done for debugging, experimentation, and hackerly fun, although in the early days of computing, hands-on access to computers was hard to come by. The demand for dynamic edits continued with arrival of the classic languages Lisp, FORTH and Smalltalk, which are indeed still used for live coding today.

The term conversational languages (Kupka and Wilsing, 1980) gained some traction in the late 1970s, where a computer operator worked by typing a line of code, getting a response, and then typing a further line. It seems a shame that this term has fallen into disuse, but the idea is very much alive as what we now know as command line languages or shells. Indeed, the standard shells found on UNIX based operating systems are fully fledged programming languages.

## Live Music

There are claims that The Hub were early live coders, although band members themselves do not make this claim. They performed with early networked computers from the mid 1980s, but did not make substantial live edits to running source code. They did, however, allow audience members to walk around them and see their screens, a position which has relevance as we will see.

Nonetheless, dynamic interpreted languages such as Lisp, Forth and HMSL were used to improvise music around this time, the earliest known example being by Ron Kuivila at STEIM, Amsterdam in 1985. Further work in establishing a historical record of live coding of this era is badly needed.

Live coding as a cultural movement grew from the release of SuperCollider 3 and ChucK. In Europe, the Changing Grammars meeting in 2004 was a particular turning point, where practitioners met to explore new possibilities of live coding. The attendees where largely from the SuperCollider community but members of slub where also present, including Adrian Ward who demoed his Map/MSG and PureEvents live coding software. An international link up of sorts was made with Ge Wang of ChucK, and so the cross platform live coding community was formed. All it needed was a name, later plucked out of the smoky air of a late night bar; TOPLAP (Ward et al., 2004).

## Show Us Your Screens

In contrast to musical instruments directly plucked, struck and bowed by a human performer, the movements of a live coded performance all happen inside a computer. The live coder may be typing furiously, but it is the movement of control flow and data inside the computer that creates the resonances, dissonances and structure of music.

It is no surprise then that many live coders choose to project their screens, so that the audience may see something of the music production. This live freeing of software as part of an improvised performance might itself be considered avant garde.

Whether the audience is expected to follow the projected code is an open question. We may see a guitarist move their fingers across a fret board, and feel closer to the music as a result, but do we need to follow and understand what these movements mean? Absolutely not. But there remains a strong sense that the performance is opened up to us by being able to see the movement behind it.

No wonder then that we hear anecdotes of audience members feeling alienated by laptop performances where screens are hidden. They could close their eyes, but couldn't they then have stayed at home, listening to a recording? However, many question whether projection of screens distract from a musical performance. If an audience can see the code behind a performance they may feel obliged to read it, moving their attention away from the sounds produced from it. Worse, if they do not know the programming language in use, then they may end up feeling just as alienated.

There is a logic then behind overlaying, where several screens are projected on top of one another, for example as practised by the live coding band slub. This amounts to obfuscation, where the audience can see fragments of code but no overall picture. They can observe the music being made, but their attention is directed away from the detail and instead to more important things such as the music, their neighbour or their drink.

Another alternative is to try to make the language more understandable to a lay audience, for example by using language with a simplified syntax, choosing highly descriptive variable names and so on. Griffiths (2008) takes this approach to artful proportions, making highly colourful miniature live coding environments embedded in his 'Fluxus' live coding language, controlled entirely from a gamepad. One example is 'Al-Jazari', where on-screen musical robots are controlled from a set of instructions specified using icons, including jump instructions for Turing completeness.

**Licensing**

These projected screens allow ad-hoc software distribution. We can compare live coding culture to the hacker culture around early computers as characterised by Levy (2002), in that freedom is the unchallenged norm. No thought is given to licenses of performance code, instead permissive and respectful sharing of algorithmic ideas and techniques is assumed. That an audience member could photograph the screen, download a interpreter that night and play with the algorithms themselves adds something to the atmosphere around the music.

Whether this free atmosphere will persist, or will be tempered by future commercial involvement is unsure. However, even within free culture, issues of copyleft will undoubtedly rear their head. Projecting a screenful of code constitutes 'propagation' in the terms of licenses such as the GPL. Indeed producing live music via the 'fixed form' of source code could have wider ramifications for copyright . Perhaps we should enjoy the free sharing idealism while it lasts.

## Coder Creativity

The practice of programming is informed by the corporate world of business software, with its talk of formal design, unit testing and ISO quality assurance. This all attempts to drive the creativity out of programming so that software may be as predictable as possible. The result is a cultural role of programmer as implementer and facilitator rather than creative individual.

This can lead to the bizarre situation where programmers make commercial software which practically generates music, and yet somehow the users of the software are seen as being more creative than the programmers. Here the programmers encode their musical style in the software, and the users do little beyond guiding the software to a destination pleasing to them. This can be seen in filters and plugins of music studio software as well as explicitly generative commercial applications such as Sseyo Koan Pro. The creativity of programmers is tapped into flattery of paying users.

It has to be said that this commercially-driven culture at times influences FLOSS music software culture, where programmers work to produce musical interfaces non-paying users. There are dark moments when free software is accused of mimicking commercial software with some justification.

With live coding, everyone is a programmer. There is understanding and respect that end user programmers have for those developing live coding language environments that is very different to that users have for anonymous brands of closed source software.

Perhaps this is an area where live coding can contribute something back to FLOSS culture in the form of alternative role models. Instead of stifling early enthusiasm of young programmers with vocational training, ad-hoc human creativity with all the mess of dynamic, serendipitous explorations can be encouraged and supported.

Bibliography

John Cage. John Cage: Writer, chapter Art and Technology, Cooper Square Press, 1969.

Dave Griffiths, Fluxus - a rapid prototyping, livecoding and playing/learning environment for 3d graphics and games. online; http://pawfal.org/fluxus/, 2008.

Kupka and Wilsing, Conversational Languages. John Wiley and Sons, 1980.

Steven Levy, Hackers: Heroes of the Computer Revolution. Penguin Putnam, January 2002.

James McCartney, 'Rethinking the computer music language: Supercollider', Computer Music Journal, 26(4):61-68, 2002.

Alex McLean. 'Hacking perl in nightclubs', 2004, http://www.perl.com/pub/a/2004/08/31/livecode.html,

Miller Puckette. Pure data: another integrated computer music environment. In In Proceedings, International Computer Music Conference, pages 269-272, 1996.

Julian Rohrhuber, Alberto de Campo, Renate Wieser, Jan-Kees van Kampen, Echo Ho, and Hannes Hölzl, Purloined letters and distributed persons, 2007.

Christopher Small. Musicking: The Meanings of Performing and Listening (Music/Culture). Wesleyan, June 1998. ISBN 0819522570.

Andrew Sorensen and Andrew Brown, 'Aa-cell in practice: an approach to musical live coding', Proceedings of the International Computer Music Conference, 2007.

Don Stewart and Manuel M. T. Chakravarty. Dynamic applications from the ground up. In Proceedings of the ACM SIGPLAN Workshop on Haskell. ACM Press, September 2005.

Ge Wang and Perry R. Cook. On-the-fly programming: using code as an expressive musical instrument. In NIME '04: Proceedings of the 2004 conference on New interfaces for musical expression, pages 138-143. National University of Singapore, 2004.

Adrian Ward, Julian Rohrhuber, Fredrik Olofsson, Alex McLean, Dave Griffiths, Nick Collins, and Amy Alexander, Live Algorithm Programming and a Temporary Organisation for its Promotion 2004.

# Expression and Time: the question of strata and time management in creative practices using technology

Thor Magnusson

Let us rewind to the late 1990s. In the West the internet had become ubiquitous and artists were drawn to the new potentials of artistic expression through the medium of the computer, allowing for interactivity, collaboration and connectivity across time and space. This resulted in the emergence of various fields such as net art (where the HTML code is used as artistic material), software art (where software is re-interpreted or commented on from cultural and political standpoints) and robot art (where computers are used to control hardware bodies, often through telepresence). It also injected new life into fields such as interactive installations, video art and sound art. The problem here was that of tools. There were not many tools that allowed for sketching or fast generation of ideas and producing complex works that both look good and work well. The artist could either learn languages like C/C++ or Java and try to code their own engines for artistic creation or decide to use higher level environments such as Macromedia Director that provides a graphical working environment for multimedia production. Director contains a scripting language (Lingo) for more complex interaction or networked data communication. The limitations of Lingo defined the aesthetics and the nature of the work that could be produced.

Fast forward to the middle of next decade. We are now faced with a panoply of free open source tools and programming environments that have been created by artists-technologists for other artists-technologists to use. The explicit aims of these environments are to function as open toolboxes that do not limit or direct the artist regarding form or content (Puckette, 2002; McCartney, 2002). From the level of analogue input into the machines (Arduino, Wiring) to operating systems (pure:dyne, Planet CCRMA), to programming languages and frameworks (SuperCollider, Pure Data (PD), ChucK, Processing, OpenFrameworks, etc.) to distribution media formats (flac, ogg), we are seeing proliferation of environments made by artist-technologists to create and distribute their work. The aim here is not only to create free and open source (thus collaborative and sharing in nature) production tools, but more importantly to allow for tools that do not necessarily limit the artist's expression in rigid ways. For example, when a user stumbles into an expressive limitation of Director, 3D Studio Max or Cubase, there is no way of getting around that limitation. Even when a bug is found, the user might have to wait two to three years before it is fixed, although updates to the software have happened in the meantime. In the situation of free open source software, the user can fix the bugs and extend its scope with very little effort. Often a mail to the mailing list describing the problem situation will have it solved within few days. Most importantly, open source tools give the user the feeling of really owning their creation, as they are able to understand and relate to the tool they are using.

This is a true paradigm shift and a very positive one for people using the computer for creative work, whether it is music, graphics, video, multimedia, installations or robotics. However, there are a few drawbacks, typically those related to the effort required to learn the environment. Working in open source programming languages can be time consuming and lead to diversions from the creative process where the production of the artwork sometimes becomes tangled up in working on the environment in which the artwork is made. The relationship between work and its foundations blur. This is not necessarily a negative. The problem is that of time-management and how artists manage to situate themselves at a level of code that benefits their work. In this paper we will look at the reasons why working with open source programming environments for artistic production is a meaningful and rewarding activity, despite its dangers regarding the expenditure of time.

## Why Open Source Programming Environments

Above I described the situation in the mid 1990s, where there were few alternatives for art practitioners to create their works unless working in quite time consuming and unfriendly programming languages like C/C++ or Java. The computer had become fast and cheap enough for use in interactive installations, algorithmic composition, real-time synthesis of audio and video, and powerful digital signal processing for manipulation of sound and graphics. As artists are normally inquiring people who want to know why someone designed the tool to perform certain ideas and not others, there was a need for environments where artists could explore the cogs and wheels of programming as artistic material which cannot be done if the source is hidden.

This need is expressed by Jaromil the creator of dyne:bolic: a Linux distribution that includes all the main tools a media artist might need:

> ***dyne:bolic*** *is shaped on the* needs *of media activists, artists and creatives as a practical tool for* ***multimedia production****: you can manipulate and broadcast both* ***sound and video*** *with tools to* ***record, edit, encode*** *and* ***stream****, having automatically recognized most device and peripherals: audio, video, TV, network cards, firewire, usb and more; all using only free software! [my italics] (Jaromil, 2007)*

We read from the creators of pure:dyne, also a Linux distribution with a specific focus:

> *The development of pure:dyne can be traced back to the inclusion of Pure Data in the dyne:bolic liveCD distribution. As this addition became increasingly popular, there was suddenly a* demand *to increase its support for Pure Data in a more serious production context... Today pure:dyne gathers a growing user community and has been used in numerous workshops and performances. [my italics] (Mansoux, Galanopoulos & Lee, 2007)*

And the maintainer of Planet CCRMA (a Linux distribution including all the main tools for sound and video production) describes how users outside the Stanford University CCRMA centre began to use the Planet CCRMA as the link to the system circulated and search engines pointed people to its existence:

> *This changed the nature of the project. As more people outside of CCRMA started using the packages I started to get* requests *for packaging music software that I would not have thought of installing at CCRMA. The number of packages started to grow and this growth benefited both CCRMAlites and external Planet CCRMA users alike. [my italics] (Lopez-Lezcano, 2005)*

All three operating systems – dyne:bolic, pure:dyne and Planet CCRMA – respond to certain needs and demands in the general culture. All three have become immensely popular and are used all over the world. The situation has changed dramatically: whereas a decade ago an artist working with computers would probably work on a proprietary operating system and with expensive software – for example, Director, where a three year old version of the software sets you back by over £1000 – users now have incredibly cheap hardware, free operating systems and many of the best creative environments are open source and free. The impact is huge and more so for cultures whose currency exchange rate is not favourable to the Western valuta, rendering the chance to pay legally for software all but impossible.

Many of the people working in the field today started using computers when, in the middle of the 1990s, they became available in an affordable price range and interesting enough for creative purposes.[1] They either had to learn the hard way with low level languages that required too much time operating on a level that was more computer science than art. Or they would be stuck in the constraints of high level packages that limited their creativity. They began to collaborate on projects, distribute code and very often this resulted in environments that allowed others to jump the step of computer science and get involved creatively straight away. Here is how the creators of the Java-based programming language Processing construe the *raison d'etre* of the software:

[1] The precise timing here is obviously debatable: some might say with the Atari computer and the invention of MIDI but others would argue that it was when one could perform real-time manipulation of audio and video in high resolution.

> *Processing relates software concepts to principles of visual form, motion, and interaction. It integrates a programming language, development environment, and teaching methodology into a unified system. Processing was created to teach fundamentals of computer programming within a visual context, to serve as a software sketchbook, and to be used as a production tool. Students, artists, design professionals, and researchers use it for learning, prototyping, and production. (Casey & Fry, 2007)*

As this book attests, the FLOSS (Free Libre Open Source Software) movement in the arts has become strong and functional. There now exists free and open source software for almost everything one would like to do and often it is impossible to find the equivalent tools developed in the commercial sector. Tools like SuperCollider, PD, CSound, Ardour and Audacity for music; Processing, openFrameworks, Fluxus and Mirra for graphics; Wiring, Arduino and MUIO for hardware interfacing and countless open game engines for 3D gaming, film-making or interactive narratives are all providing the artist with highly professional, expressive and focussed tools for the task.

But things are not so simple. If we look at the fields of music or the fine arts (at least up until modernism) we see that much art involved the development of fine motor skills, a craftsmanship where the trained body would produce works of virtuosity. Today, when working with automated and intelligent machines, we do not train our bodies any longer. The training consists in the comprehension of the underlying systems of the media we are working with and their modes of production, distribution and consumption. It becomes a question of understanding the field of software and their multiple cultures, of choosing an environment at the right level in which to work. Yes, the media arts are quite cerebral by nature, but much of modern art since Marcel Duchamp is. Virtuosity has taken on another meaning: it now involves a deep understanding of computer science and the science of digital signal processing and mathematics with regards to sound, visuals or 3D spaces.

Learning a programming language is not an easy task. One can become conversational in a month or two, but fluency of expression is something that might take over two or 3 years, with many hours put into the practice every day. Further, the logic of programming is not the only thing that has to be mastered: working at this level means that the artist has to understand the nature of sound and visuals from both physical and psychological perspectives. (In the case of music one would learn the physics of sound, digital signal processing and psychoacoustics). This takes roughly as much time as mastering an acoustic instrument. The problems here are often related to the power of the computer as a medium. The computer and the programming paradigms that exist for it are strong conceptual models that prime the mind of the student into particular ways of thinking, perhaps altering the cognitive style of the student. The question becomes: what is the nature of the tools that we are currently using and how well do they reflect the demands of artistic practice? Does the artist-technologist create the tool or does the tool create the artist-technologist? To what degree will the artist develop a different cognitive style through studying computer science?

**Time and Expressivity: how/why does this equation work in practice?**

Developing an operating system, programming language or a sketching environment for creative work is time consuming. For one creative person this can be too much sacrifice for what the initial idea involved. For another, programming is a mode of thinking and as art is essentially about thinking it becomes the tool *par excellence* for artistic creativity.

Above, we talked about the strata of programming abstractions and how each artist chooses his/her tool for expression with regards to what he/she wants to do and how. For the sake of pseudo-science and from an urge to have an equation in this chapter, an illustration of this problem might look like this:

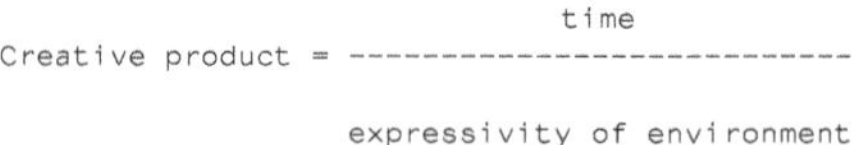


That is, the more expressivity we have through the capabilities of the environment, the more time it takes to make the creative work. This has nothing to do with the aesthetic quality of the works, as that cannot be defined by the technology used to produce them.

In order to understand the question of time management and expressivity, i.e. the question of making the tool itself versus making something using the tool, I decided to go beyond my own personal experience of these things and ask a few colleagues who are already practitioners – developers, programmers and artists all at once – about their work patterns and attitudes towards time and expressivity. How do creative people justify their spending time on building tools and not the artwork itself? Why the fascination with code? How can this technology represent our thinking? From the replies to the survey, we can detect a few threads originating in the idea of code as creative material.

## Coding as Self-Understanding

*What I cannot create I do not understand – Richard Feynman*

One of the participants in the survey quoted Feynman as above. This is an illustrative idea that most of the participants seemed to subscribe to. The desire to learn about one's music or visual art through building the tools is a common characteristic of all the practitioners. A crucial distinction is whether one is building the tool for a personal or public use. The latter seems to be time-consuming on an exponential scale.

> *Tools have such a strong impact on the artistic process that I like to know mine well and there is no better way to know a tool than to build your own. Paul Lansky once said that he didn't really distinguish between building the tools and making the artwork. I have a lot of sympathy for this idea. [AS]*

> *Where this question becomes tricky for me is in relation to developing tools for other users. On the surface this really is a black hole. You end up spending a lot of time supporting other users needs and this generally has little to do with your own artistic practice. However, end users are really good at forcing you to do the bug fixing, stability and performance improvements that you would probably not do on your own, but which you are really glad you did! [AS]*

## No Distinction of Building a Tool and a Artwork

Most actions require creativity unless one has incorporated some skills for rote activities. A recent survey (Magnusson & Hurtado Mendieta, 2007) showed that many musicians actually thought playing an acoustic instrument was a cliché-prone activity as it was so practised and so inscribed in a cultural tradition. Building one's own tool is a highly creative activity that forces a self-awareness in the artist and which often cannot be separated from the process of making the art.

> *In software art... It is impossible to dissociate the creation from the process, to the point where using the words 'tool' or 'environment' becomes completely irrelevant. [AM]*

> *Programming for music is a part of music-making, just as ruling bar-lines on manuscript paper can also be a modest part of music-making, all distinctions less important to my mind than whether or not one is concentrated when working. [TH]*

> *I rarely use a piece of software I've written for more than one thing, so use and development are the same in most cases. I'm not really even that bothered about the 'music' as I don't really see it as the primary goal or validating factor. [TB]*

## The Artwork as a Process

Software art fits well with the modernist tradition of seeing art as a *process* rather than a finished piece as software is not written in stone. Software is never finalised. Only the material constraints of older art forms reinforce our habit to see art objects as completed works of art. These are constraints that were introduced mainly with the Gutenberg press and the phonograph. Before these media technologies, texts and music would normally change every time someone wrote another copy of the text or played the song. Code as immaterial, abundant, copy-able, omnifunctional and executable text is never dead. Instead of concluded pieces of art 'frozen' in time, we have versions.

> *If the art is truly living in the process, then developing it will not only change the guts but also influence the output as they are the same and sole object. [AM]*

## Coding as a Conceptual Practice

Art can be highly formal, mathematical or scientific. Music is a good example of an art form where practitioners have investigated formal and mathematical relationships in harmony, melody, timbre and meter. Programming as a means of formalising one's thought, externalising them and testing them in performance using a logical machine is therefore a tempting method of working for many artists.

*Programming problems can be an interesting thing to pursue while musical problems (as defined by Schoenberg and others) are being turned over in one's mind. Especially so as programming problems thus encountered are usually simpler than the accompanying musical problems. [TH]*

*For me art is not so much about expression, but more about reasoning, so the process is maybe a different one. The environment is not separate from the work, neither as a work of art nor as a work of theoretical research. [JR]*

## Creating the Tool for Originality

The modernist demand of originality in our art is still with us and many people consider the highest form of creativity to be artistic creativity where the artist transforms the cultural space in which he or she works in (Boden, 1990). For many, it is by necessity that they build their own tools, as using other people's tools might lead to less thought and original design solutions to both aesthetic, formal and technological problems.

*Inevitably tech issues intrude. But I guess you want to come up against difficulties; else you're not pushing the boundaries? [NC]*

*Knowing that I'm using an obscure programming language that very few are using makes me excited, as the language allows me to think and compose in certain innovative ways. [AN]*

## Coding as an Artistic Practice

Many of the participants in the survey see coding as an artistic practice in itself. In fact some of them see it as a performative act and 'live-code' in front of audience with their screens projected on the wall (Toplap, 2007; Nilson, 2007). Coding is here seen as a way of externalising thoughts, in a manner similar to sketching by drawing or model building. When programming is seen as a performative action, a choreography of thought, it ceases to be a means to an end and becomes an end in itself.

*I see programming as a part of my creative practice, just like playing the piano or studying books on composition. As such I try to be as fluent at it as I can afford to be so that my creative ideas can be realised as efficiently as possible. This is not at all to say that programming is transparent to the creative process – like any tool it has an impact on the work. [AB]*

## Coding as Craft: An Inscribed Skill

Any search engine will show countless books and articles on the topic of coding as craft; a skill that has to be mastered through time with lots of practice. The programmer learns to think in the language that he or she works in and formulate the problems in the terms of that language, often conceptualising the world through the means of programmatic paradigms. But coding is not only a craft: it is a performance as well, as the case of live-coding exemplifies. Live-coding requires that the practitioners are good at their trade, which involves fast thinking, fast typing, practised algorithms and good knowledge of the material (programming environment) they are working with. (Nilson, 2007; Sorensen & Brown, 2007).

> *I find my expressiveness is limited by the 'gestures' my environment can support. I prefer to be able to express things in my library very tersely, so I see working and thinking about changes to the performance environment as relevant part of my time spent. Much as an instrumental performer must spend time learning new techniques, the live-coder must take time to extend their library of musical gestures. [GC]*

> *A virtuoso computer musician needs to be a decent programmer... [AB]*

## More Fun Building the Tool Than the Work

The concept of art is famously narrow and defined by cultural practices. Most of the participants of the survey were not concerned with 'art' as an isolated cultural phenomenon and saw creativity as a ubiquitous human behaviour. For some there was not only the absence of distinction between the tool and the work, but building the tool itself was more important... and fun:

> *Building sequencers rather than sequences seemed to be more fun. [IZ]*

> *For me, the software itself is what I'm focusing on and what I like to present as my work. I sometimes perform with it and have released some recordings of the tool in practice but those almost have the status of a 'demo'. I find that some people don't understand this attitude, but that's not really my problem. [AN]*

However, some wanted to draw a distinction between making the tool and the work that could be made with the tool. In fact this seemed to be related to the level of coding in which the artist is working. For example in

PD one could write an external (an object encapsulating more complex and lower level code) or in SuperCollider one would write a Unit Generator. This is a stratum down from patching in PD or coding in sc-lang (the native programming language of SuperCollider) as it involves more debugging and, most annoyingly, having to compile the code before putting it to use.

*I think it is what it is. If you develop a UGen, you develop a UGen; you shouldn't kid yourself that you're making music, though you might be making an essential technological component. But things blur again, for example, in testing the UGen, which is suddenly so very exciting, musically... [AN]*

**The Danger of Spending Time on the System not the Art**

Most participants acknowledged in some way the danger of forgetting oneself in building the ultimate creative system and never have time to use it for creative work.

> *Creating your own ultimate dream system to make art is a dangerous game as most of the time the focus is attracted by the building of the environment itself, developing it, updating it, documenting it and never ending adding features to it. It can become so important that the art produced with it becomes a minor manifestation or demonstration of the system. [AM]*

> *Sometimes I rehearse every week, but this is perhaps for 3 hours, vs. 30 hours working on the environment. [RB]*

This distinction however is rather superficial as there is as much creative thought put into the design of an environment as the design of a musical piece for example. People have started seeing the building of tools as an artistic endeavour and Linus Torvalds getting first prize in Ars Electronica 2003 for the kernel of his Linux operating system is good proof of this.

> *It is not easy to give an artistic statement about an operating system, because while an operating system can be a work of art (I certainly feel that there is an artistic component to programming), it's not in itself very artful... In more 'artistic' terms, you might consider the operating system to be the collection of pigments and colours used to create a painting: they are not the painting itself, but they are obviously a rather important ingredient – and a lot of the great painters spent a large portion of their time on making the paint, often by hand, in order to get their paintings to look just right. (Torvalds, 2003)*

## Coding Takes Time

[2] http://www.signwave.co.uk

Most of the participants seemed to have a stoic attitude towards the time they put into their work. They see this as the nature of art itself; in order to make good art, you have to work a lot whether that is through reading, preparing materials, learning, exercising or talking to people. Programming and learning the skill is no different than learning how to play an acoustic instrument or train the hand in freehand drawing.

> *Well I am still using up the mileage to be gained by convincing yourself that all the time you spend screwing around with open source software trying to get it to work makes you learn things you wouldn't have learnt otherwise. [MYK]*

> *When preparing for a piece, there is always a trade off between what is possible within the environment, what do I need to add, and what am I able to implement (and debug!) before showtime. [MB]*

> *In a way, the 24h to the day limit seems like an inconvenient constraint; but the again it is good preparation for the limited lifetime constraint we all face at some point, and trying to spend that time well. [ADC]*

## Programming as Meta-Art

Creating something that creates something else is on the meta-dimension. Many software artists, such as Adrian Ward, see themselves as creating meta-art, i.e. art that is used by artists to create more art.[2] It varies how the programmers see their role, from being participant in the creation of the end object (as Ward claims) to rejecting all co-authorship and clearly separating the software as meta-art and the product that it creates when an artist uses it.

> *As I see it, if I create a tool that is used by artists in their work, I have created something that is of value to them as a product. I see this as an object of art and the artists using my tool not only as users but also as aesthetic 'actors' or 'perceptors' for lack of better words. (Basically for what 'listener' is to music, 'viewer' to film, we need a word for the person that engages with software art). [AN]*

[3] http://makezine.com/04/ownyourown/

## What I Cannot Take Apart, I Don't Own

Much commercial music software sets up the whole structure of the music by default and the process of composing is more a question of removing presets than composing from an empty plate. Many people find that what they cannot take apart and understand the bits of, they cannot claim is their own creation. This idea can be found in circles of people working with hardware just as software.[3] But the question is not only that of understanding, but also of archiving as commercial formats are often closed. An artist that produces work in a closed source format or software might not be able to revisit that work in the future.

> *I feel I need to understand the technological foundations of my music, what cogs and wheels I am using to implement my ideas and how they in turn change through using the tool. Therefore open source software is important to me, if not I'd be stuck in a situation where I feel I am a mere consumer of the software and not an active participant. Of course, this has to be taken with a grain of salt, as there is obviously code 'all the way down' and I'm not interested in looking at machine code or processor design. [AN]*

## Oh, Where has the Body Gone?

The problem of embodied skill, the trained musical/artistic body, is something that is ingrained in the question of coding as artistic practice. This feature of the man-machine relationship has been dealt with in recent survey (Magnusson & Hurtado-Mendieta, 2007) but it is something that comes up repeatedly when talking about the digital arts. For live-coders, the haptic interface of the computer (such as mouse and keyboard) might just be an unnecessary interruption between the thought and the implemented algorithm (hopefully to be solved soon), but for other artists, the body is an integral part of the creative process. The pre-linguistic or unconscious mind might be better expressed through bodily movements than as linguistic thoughts after all.

> *Also sometimes I find it quite cumbersome to have to program everything, rather than being able to just play, like I can on a piano or an analogue synthesizer; i.e. instruments that have behaviour in themselves. [MB]*

## The Question of Strata and Location

As seen from the preceding chapter, programming is a craft, an inscribed skill that involves complex relationships of an environment and its logic expressed in a programming language; the programmer and his/her integration of the environment's logic; the programmer and his/her embodied relationship to the hardware used; and various other threads that connect the finer elements of the human-machine network. The question for the artists is where to locate themselves in the strata of expression through code. Where in the machine building process do they want to work?

Here it can be useful to think of software as strata: as concrete layers or sedimentations of varied abstractions. Assembler is an abstracted machine language; Java compiles into a virtual machine that is machine language; SuperCollider is a language written in C++ that is a level above assembler, etc. These are all strata that function on their independent level, but allow for modifications across the spectrum (or belts of abstraction) if we are working in open source.

> *The strata are extremely mobile. One stratum is always capable of serving as the substratum of another, or of colliding with another, independently of any evolutionary order. Above all, between two strata or between to stratic divisions, there are interstratic phenomena: transcodings and passages between milieus, intermixings. Rhythms pertain to these interstratic movements, which are also acts of stratification. Stratification is like the creation of the world from chaos, a continual, renewed creation. (Deleuze & Guattari, 1987. p. 502.)*

If we look at software as the phenomena that Deleuze and Guattari describe, it becomes fundamentally wrong to sacrifice your freedom of thought and action to a closed source environment, and we will see why in the third section of this chapter.

We have already seen from the threads above, how some people enjoy the building of a tool even more than performing or composing with the tool itself. The focus ranges from working on operating systems, the source of an expressive language (like creating the source code of SuperCollider, PD or Processing) or working with code as expressive means and try to shy away from computer engineering tasks. Each programming language has its own characteristics and for some it might be better to work in a high level language like Lingo or ActionScript where others click with Processing or SuperCollidier. For yet others, thinking in a graphical programming language like PD is easier and more intuitive, and switching to writing objects for it (at a lower level) is only done by necessity. An important question here is that of the economy of time vs. expression. Many people are ready to invest more time in the building of their expressive environments to acquire in return personal, unique and aflexible methods of production.

[4]
Here we should read HCI as literally as possible, i.e. not as a field concerned with how a button should look or function, but as a field that should study the more philosophical questions related to what it means to be a human that deals with a symbolic machine created by the human itself implanted with its creator's symbolic logic

[5]
Amazingly little has been written about the way commercial software companies effectively run a new type of Western imperialism with their way of representing thought and activities through their interaction and interface design. (but see Sardar, 2000)

However, this is not the whole story. Choosing to work with PD rather than Max/MSP or Processing rather than Flash or Director is also a political decision. It relates to the freedom of individual expression; who is in power; relations to the capitalistic market; the question of open formats for future archiving; and a clear awareness of what it means to be a user of software.

## Ideologies in Software Environments

An extensive cultural critique of software as expression is yet to be written although Matthew Fuller (Fuller, 2008) and a few others have done excellent job in trying to create the discipline of software criticism in the way such discipline exists for literature, film and music. The history of Human Computer Interaction (HCI) has gone through various phases and a few of them are relevant here.[4] The initial and naïve way we saw the functionality of software was that of a neutral symbolic parser that would take data input, perform some logical calculations and then output some other data. The basic assumption here is that the mind and its processes are independent from any material manifestation or embodiment. Actions are seen as logical, pre-planned and well definable in the context of the task to be performed. There is a separation of the internal world of the subject from the external world of objects. The agent is always a rational agent that moves in a world of logical laws. All representation of the world or understanding of it can be expressed in logical formulas of which the computer is the machine par excellence. The early Wittgenstein would be a good example of this way of construing the world.

But as the later Wittgenstein discovered, this world-view is a simplistic portrayal of the human situation and forgets about the embodied nature of our thinking and perceiving our environment. The fields of hermeneutics and phenomenology bring us a clearer understanding of what it means to be a human in the world and interpret the signals around us. Nothing is neutral any longer. As designing a programming language or a tool necessarily involves taxonomic design, it becomes an ontological endeavour. This is a question of transformation: how an individual system designer interprets the world and represents it in a cultural computational engine that is necessarily political as well as aesthetic.[5] For an artist, the idea that someone has looked at the world and categorised it into sections that are represented in the functional aspects of a software can be simply uncanny. To what kind of ideology am I subscribing when I use this particular operating system, this software or this interface? These are complex questions with no clear-cut black-and-white answers, but they are questions that many people deal with albeit in an indirect manner when they choose their tools.

We now understand some of the political implications of software design (Bodker, 1991); i.e. how software design largely influences and structures the work patterns of information workers sitting in their offices all over the world. This has resulted in solutions such as 'participatory design' where the software designers collaborate with the people that will use the software in its design. However, these studies are mainly concerned with people working with productive tools such as spreadsheets or text editors or recreational software such as games. One thing is to create a survey as a software designer that focuses on office work-patterns or the logic of a gameplay, but another (and theoretically impossible) is to try to build a model of how artists want to work, what they want to express and by what means. This is precisely the area where artistic open source software situates itself, allowing users to define their own agendas and aesthetic values by resisting a closure in the design of the software environment.

## Conclusion: Creators vs. Consumers of Expressive Tools

The FLOSS tools mentioned above are practically all commentaries of the question of software consumption. As they are open source, they invite the artist-technologist to modify and transform the tool by collaborating in its design either privately or as part of the culture around the tool. The idea of collaborative artist-made operating systems, programming languages/frameworks and creative tools makes sense. They are the people that know and understand how and what is required in the process of making computational art. They are the people whose work involves the reinterpretation of the social ontology of our culture through re-categorisation. The situation where artists are forced to buy closed source software and thus constantly being pushed into ergonomic patterns or conceptual boxes by the companies that made them is now over. The 'software consumers' of the commercial world become 'software co-designers' in the FLOSS world – users who have the freedom to choose the form of their expression and the manner they express it.

## Bibliography

Margaret A. Boden, The Creative Mind: Myths and Mechanisms. London: Wiedenfield and Nicholson, 1990.

Susanne Bodker, Through the Interface: A Human Activity Approach to User Interface Design. Hillsdale, NJ: Erlbaum, 1991.

Gilles Deleuze & Félix Guattari, A Thousand Plateaus: Capitalism and Schizophrenia. London: Continuum, 1987.
Matthew Fuller, (ed). Software Studies: A Lexicon. Cambridge: MIT Press, 2008.

Casey Reas & Ben Fry, Processing: A Programming Handbook for Visual Designers and Artists. Cambridge: MIT Press, 2007.

Thor Magnusson & Enrike Hurtado Mendieta, 'The Acoustic, the Digital and the Body: A Survey on Musical Instruments', in Proceedings of the NIME 2007 Conference, New York, USA, 2007.

Aymeric Mansoux, Antonios Galanopoulos, & Chun Lee, 'pure:dyne' in Proceedings of the 2007 Pd Convention. Montreal, 2007.

James McCartney, 'Rethinking the Computer Music Language: SuperCollider' in Computer Music Journal, 26:4, pp. 61-68, Winter 2002. MIT Press.

Click Nilson, 'Live-Coding Practice' in Proceedings of the NIME 2007 Conference, New York, USA, 2007.

Miller Puckette, 'Using PD as Score Language' in Proceedings of ICMC 2002, 2002. pp. 184-187.

Ziauddin Sardar, 'ALT.CIVILIZATIONS.FAQ: Cyberspace as the darker side of the west' in The Cybercultures Reader, Bell, David & Kennedy, Barbara M. (eds.). London: Routledge, 2000.

Andrew Sorensen & Andrew Brown. 'aa-cell in Practice: An Approach to Musical Live Coding' in The Proceedings of ICMC 2007, Copenhagen, 2007.

Toplap, http://www.toplap.org - accessed 3 November, 2007.

Jaromil, http://www.dynebolic.org - accessed 3 November, 2007.

Linus Torvalds, 'Linux' in Ars Electronica, 2003, http://www.aec.at/en/archives/prix_archive/prix_projekt.asp?iProjectID=2183

Fernando Lopez-Lezcano, 'Surviving on Planet CCRMA, Two Years Later and Still Alive' in Proceedings of the 2005 Linux Audio Conference. Karlsruhe:ZKM, 2005.

## Notes

This text draws on a survey polling artist-technologists exploring the time/creativity question and interpret their answers into 13 traces of thinking about tool use. We look at the question of strata in production environments and the question of finding a platform where the focus is on the enabling of general production (the time factor) with as minimum limitations as possible. Finally, we discuss the status of open source artist-created software environments as meta-art, i.e. expressive platforms that necessarily embody aesthetic ideas and purpose.

## Acknowledgements

Many thanks to Anonymous, Marije Baalman, Ross Bencina, Tom Betts, Andrew Brown, Graham Coleman, Nick Collins, Alberto di Campo, John Eacott, Tom Hall, Enrike Hurtado-Mendieta, Aymeric Mansoux, Click Nilson, Julian Rohrhuber, Andrew Sorensen, Matthew Yee-King and Johannes M. Zmoelnig for their brilliant answers to my simple question on time and expressivity in open source production environments. The opinions in this article (outside of italic quotations) are my own and I apologise if I have misrepresented the contribution of the respondents.

# On free software art, design, communities and committees

Dave Griffiths

Free software has more to offer artists than cheap tools. It brings with it powerful new production methods and vibrant communities, which challenge artists to change the ways things of all kinds are made. However, there are limits to this approach which need to be acknowledged. These limits highlight a difference between the development of software and art, and also help clarify the difference between software art – code written for artistic purposes, and artistic software – code written to create an environment for making art in.

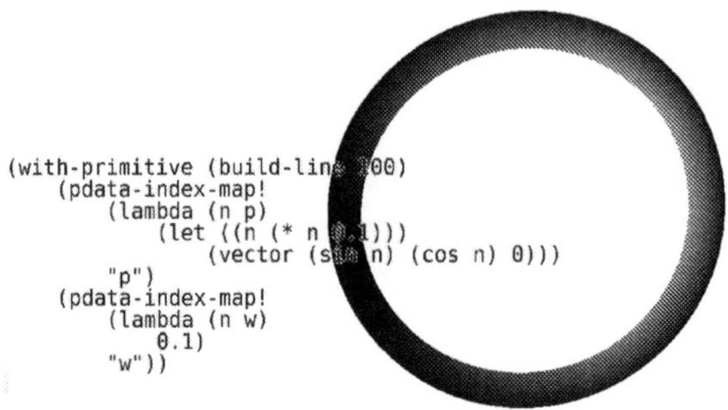


## Software is People

The value in a piece of software is the group of people who are involved in it's design, construction, documentation and use. Good software forms a shared goal, and a shared way of working and communicating, so the community is of great importance to both those using, and constructing a piece of software.

Software with a good community surrounding it is more useful than software which is engineered well, but lacks a community. Engineering alone is not enough to get most people's attention or continued interest, and doesn't guarantee people investing time learning and using it.

It's a mistake to separate the executable product from it's community when discussing software. The community dictates the future of a piece of software.

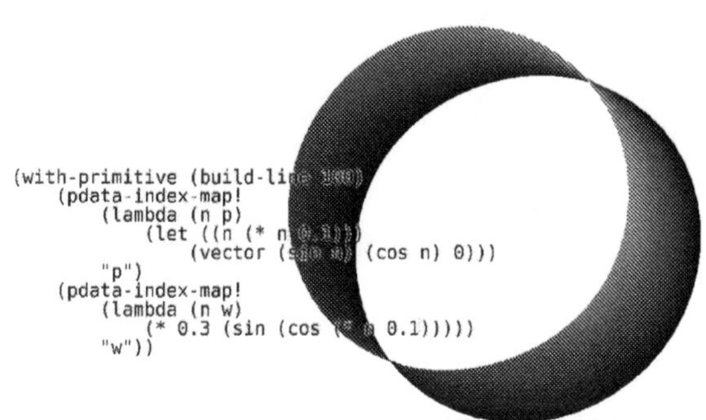


## Software isn't Source Code

Source code represents a fixed point in time in a continuing succession of decisions which form the process of software development. Finished software is software which is not used any more.

The loss of the community surrounding some software can be more drastic than the loss of it's source code, since new people taking up the initiative will have to learn why decisions were taken in the design of the software. The source code can only tell you with certainty ‘what’ decisions were taken. The ‘why’ is generally found in comments and version control commit notes – but there is no compiler or interpreter to enforce the provision of this information, and it is generally inadequate to form a good understanding. The usual result of the loss of a group surrounding a piece of software, is starting again, which means rewriting, and retreading old ground – remaking the decisions.[1] In a commercial setting this is usually a very bad idea.[2]

One kind of free software is worth special mention, when source code is released which is not considered to be in the process of open development. Such projects are usually developed in a closed form, and

[1] Development on SpiralModular, a software synthesiser, ceased, contributing to the initiative for Om/Ingen which was started on a new codebase, http://www.pawfal.org/Software/SSM/, http://wiki.drobilla.net/Ingen

[2] Things You Should Never Do, Part I, Joel Spolsky http://www.joelonsoftware.com/articles/fog0000000069.html

are released when they have been completed, or when other development has come to a halt. Such 'single release' projects are a weaker form of free software, but are still very important as they can be learned from, experimented with, or, in some cases, picked up by new communities and turned into full open source developments.[3]

[3]
See Blender http://www.blender.org/ and The Mozilla project http://www.mozilla.org/

[4]
Some examples are Supercollider http://www.audiosynth.com/, GIMP http://www.gimp.org/, Fluxus http://www.pawfal.org/fluxus/, Maya http://www.autodesk.com/maya

[5]
Some examples are Pure Data http://crca.ucsd.edu/~msp/software.html, MAX/MSP http://www.cycling74.com/, Houdini http://www.sidefx.com/

```
(with-primitive (build-line 100)
    (pdata-index-map!
        (lambda (n p)
            (let ((n (* n 0.1)))
                (vector (sin n) (cos n) 0)))
        "p")
    (pdata-index-map!
        (lambda (n w)
            (* 0.1 (sin n)))
        "w"))
```

## Three Classes of Software

We can break down software development into three broad categories based on the intent, or the nature of the goals it is designed to fulfil. These categories are gross simplifications, as most software is comprised of a blend of these types.

### 1. *Classical 'tool' – Simple goals*

The conventional idea of a piece of software is that of a tool for achieving some clear goal. This is not a matter of software complexity – there may be many different competing goals, and a very complex implementation required. However, with this type of software, the goals are clear, even if there are many of them. Examples of classical tools range from the 'ls' command to a web server.

### 2. *An environment for working in – Complex goals*

When the nature of the goal is more complicated, and involves more human issues – software often ends up providing functionality through an environment. This is usually a text or graphical user interface. In software designed for artistic use, programs often have to go one step further, enriching their environment with a scripting interpreter[4] or a visual programming language[5]. These are needed because artistic goals are

[6]
RunMe software art repository http://www.runme.org

[7]
Ben Fry & Casey Reas, Processing: A Programming Handbook for Visual Designers and Artists, MIT, 2007.

[8]
TOPLAP http://www.toplap.org

[9]
Frederick P. Brooks, The Mythical Man-Month: Essays on Software Engineering

much harder to predict, and the solutions need more flexibility to be useful in the long term.

3. *Artistic – Ambiguous goals*

A lot of software is written in a situation where goals are difficult to define in any way. Someone may write a program to exercise the use of a new language or try out something new. The goals for game play code in computer games and software written to produce generative art are very difficult to pin down. Software art is strongly ambiguous, as it comprises programs which are written to express something by merely existing, it's not even required that they run, or do anything at all.[6] Sometimes software is the only way to express something. At other times the writing of software is an artistic process of exploration, such as sketching code[7] or livecoding.[8]

## Design by Committee

A recognised problem with software development is that it is difficult to scale. Brookes Law states that 'adding manpower to a software project that is behind schedule will delay it further'.[9] With added people, there is a danger of losing the direction made possible by one or a small number of dedicated people with a clear vision. Successful software projects are often those which are headed by individuals with a very clear philosophy, such an individual is often termed the 'benevolent dictator' (Linus Torvalds being the obvious example).

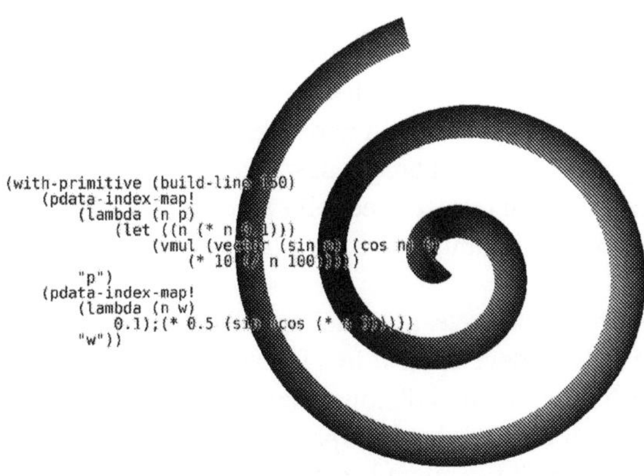

In the case of software containing plenty of ambiguity, too many people can prevent any clear direction. Democratisation or diluting the design process with too many voices is regarded with suspicion by games designers such as Peter Molyneux.[10]

[10]
Molyneux Talks Fable II, Design Gold
http://www.gamasutra.com/php-bin/news_index.php?story=10071

## Applying Free Software Production to Art Making

As goals become more ambiguous, the advantages of open source become more difficult to realise. The free software movement has had tremendous success when the goals are clear and easy to convey, communities can be very large and still work together effectively. When goals become less clear, free software development still works with a clear leading philosophy (usually an individual, or a very small group), but can become more problematic. When decisions become based on personal philosophy rather than technical reasons there is more chance for conflict.

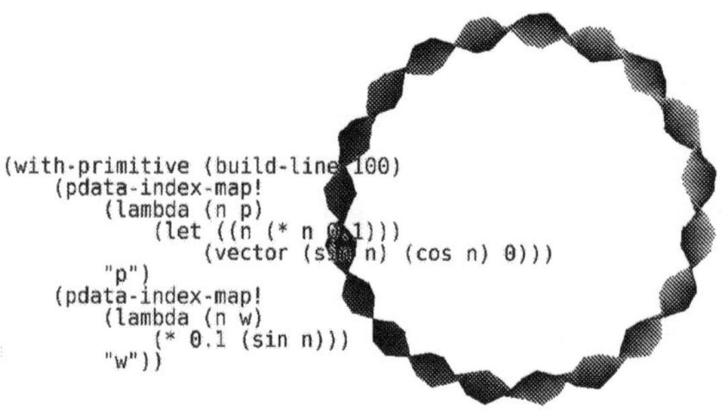


This may explain why there are plenty of quality free software game engines[11], where the goals are easy to communicate, but challenging to implement. While, on the other hand, there is a noticeable lack of free software which exhibits game play which breaks new ground. Many computer games available as 'single release' free software, and are not developed by the free software community.[12]

With software art, the single open release model makes most sense. There is much more need to limit development to a few people with a clear understanding of each other, or an individual maker. This is especially true if the intent can only be clearly expressed by the finished article or, much more commonly, if the intent becomes apparent only via the making of the artwork.

[11]
Examples are Irrlicht http://irrlicht.sourceforge.net/, PyGame http://www.pygame.org, SDL http://www.libsdl.org, Allegro http://www.talula.demon.co.uk/allegro/, Crystal Space http://www.crystalspace3d.org, Ogre http://www.ogre3d.org

[12]
Some examples are ID Software's Doom ftp://ftp.idsoftware.com/idstuff/source/doomsrc.zip, ID Software's Quake http://www.idsoftware.com/business/techdownloads/ and Micropolis http://www.donhopkins.com/home/micropolis/

When making art in the sphere of a community (software, or any art form), the most important thing is to take an active role in the community, helping to disseminate knowledge. Releasing your work as free software is a good way to achieve this, giving other people a chance to learn from what you have done – you will benefit indirectly from their increased knowledge, rather than changes they make to your finished project.

## Ending Thoughts

As the goals and intent of a piece of software increases in complexity and ambiguity, the philosophy of the problem space becomes harder to communicate, meaning that larger groups cause problems. When we start to use software to convey some deeper expressions, or the notion of what is fun, an individual perspective is required and the benefits of open sourcing development, or groups in general are less important.

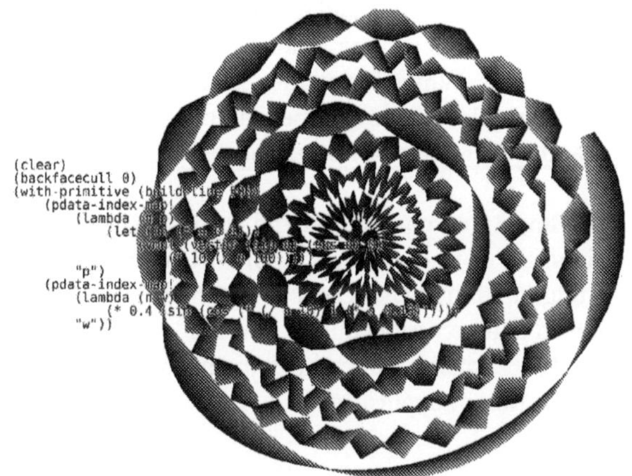


The power of free software is in the vibrancy and strength of it's communities, and allowing new ways of thinking and solving problems to be developed and nurtured. This is an excellent place to be making artwork of any form today, but the realm of free software is politically highly charged, pressure can be put on people, including software artists, to embrace open source methods to the last letter. It needs to be recognised that the development of software for artistic practice has different needs and problems to the more widely understood problem of developing software to achieve goals.

As most software contains many different parts which have different levels of this kind of ambiguity, more exploration of this more fragile, personal side of writing code is needed.

# The Piksel Big Bang

Eleonora Oreggia

## The Festival

Piksel[1] is an international meeting of artists and developers of free software[2] and independent art. It was born from the collaboration of an artist and a programmer, Gisle Froysland and Carlo Prelz, during the development of MoB[3], a real-time video-processing application. The idea became an annual appointment peculiar in shape and content. Its fulcrum is openness, freeness, circulation of knowledge and tools.

[1] http://www.piksel.no/piksel06/about.html

[2] http://www.piksel.no/piksel04/software.html

[3] http://mob.bek.no

The festival, which lasts almost a week and attracts characters from Europe, Japan, Canada, Brazil and elsewhere, features days of workshops, coding nights, and performances. While during the rest of the year communication is generally mediated through the net, in Bergen interaction is analogue and warm and relations are strengthened.

Piksel is a community imagining possibilities and proposing methodologies of development of free software for artistic communication. Discussion happens through mailing lists, access to which is open and the archive of which is indexed and accessible online. It is not a closed elite. Discussion is open, threads are considered public domain. Participation in the festival is through invitation or application.

## Piksel is a Hybrid

This phenomenon bridges between hacker meetings and art festivals. It combines the genuine spirit of exchange, typical of hacker and free software communities, and the critical reflection typical of art practice and creative languages.

This event was created with the intention and the will to collaborate, trusting, on the enthusiastic initial wave, that differences could be integrated, uniting diverse personalities, temperaments and visions under the flag of liberty, circulation of knowledge and information. As if the sense of belonging to a unique community could glue the efforts towards the development of common platforms by chaining different available softwares together. This attempt gave birth to Livido, a framework for sharing video effects between different applications, frei0r, similar but

[4]
Livido,
http://www.piksel.no/pwiki/LiViDO frei0r,
http://www.piksel.org/frei0r Videojack,
http://www.piksel.no/pwiki/VideoJack

[5]
Paul Graham, 'Hackers and Painters', 2003,
http://www.paulgraham.com/hp.html

[6]
see NO FUN!,
http://www.piksel.no/piksel05/expo.htm
DAMAGED GOODS,
http://www.piksel.no/piksel06/exhibition.html
and FUN HOUSE,
http://www.piksel.no/piksel07/exhibition.html

optimized for real-time processing, and Videojack, a utility for piping videos through different applications.[4] Frei0r was the most successful, while Videojack and Livido are still floating in the amniotic limbo of alpha versions.

Yet, the chaotic and anarchist nature of free software which is based on personal inspirations and spontaneous energies, rendered coordination more complicated. The discussion on best structure and development strategy became an infinite process.

Free software is a multiform phenomenon, complex to describe. You can approach it from a political, technical, ethical or economical point of view, and also from a didactic perspective. Within this context, we'll talk about the artisan side, getting your hands dirty, hacking through sleepless nights.

During the creative process both hackers and artists tend to invent techniques to master the environment they are in, with the obsessive tension to realise their purpose, object or manufacture. Breaking conventions, new models are created, unusual and experimental methods and media invented to cover any route and achieve the desired result.

Paul Graham, American hacker, describes the relationship between art and hacking:

> *What hackers and painters have in common is that they're both makers. Along with composers, architects, and writers, what hackers and painters are trying to do is make good things. They're not doing research per se, though if in the course of trying to make good things they discover some new technique, so much the better.*[5]

## Exhibition and Performances

Going back to Piksel, the mingling of art and hacking, a new integral feature of the event is the exhibition, introduced a few years ago. The 2005 show, entitled NO FUN, was dedicated to games. In 2006 the exhibition was named DAMAGED GOODS, and focused on open hardware. The 2007 edition was called FUN HOUSE.[6]

If in NO FUN the critics of the game-as-a-media were pushed to its limits, because of the use of free software and 3D technologies, DAMAGED GOODS opened the doors to hacked hardware and tangible objects, while FUN HOUSE moved further away from screen-based works and has more focus on sound and interaction. For example the work *Waves* by Daniel Palacios Jimenez uses a piece of rope to make a 3D representation of a group of waves floating in the space.[7] The rope, activated by the presence of the spectator, with no need of interface manipulation, starts moving, creating beautiful graphics and brutal, visceral sound. In this iconic work the sound and image are consequences of the same force.

Besides the exhibition, a varied program of audiovisual performances, original and experimental, accompanies the festival's nights. These performances are in general audiovisual interactions based on home-made software, synesthesia and the visualisation capabilities of machines. The visual part is often abstract, sound can be noise...

The technique can be a relevant part of the show, data (information) is often used as raw material, while code becomes actuator and generator of the signal that triggers the aesthetic experience. 'Pattern Cascade' by Dave Griffiths, for example, is a sort of acid-techno machine, a live coding of processes modifying and destroying one another in 256 bytes of memory.[8] These processes and the machine's memory were visualized and projected during the performance.

[7] http://www.waves.stopantplay.com/

[8] http://www.pawfal.org/patterncascade, Performed during Piksel06.

[9] Freej, http://freej.org Effectiv, http://effectv.sourceforge.net Veejay, http://veejay.dyne.org

[10] Denis Rojo

[11] Fukuchi Kentaro

[12] Niels Elburg

[13] Tom Schouten

[14] Yves Degoyon

[15] Artem Baguinski

[16] http://xxxxx.1010.co.uk

[17] http://makeart.goto10.org

**Between Art and Code**

I interviewed Gisle Froysland, main organizer of the event, via IRC. Attempting to propose a probably forefront 'van' writing style, I decided to challenge the rules of canonical journalism by maintaining the text in its original chat form, tuned to the net world. To those readers who will find this paragraph hard or indigestible, I suggest reading between the lines and appreciating the traces of instantaneous simultaneity, and spontaneity, this text is offers.

The following dialogue, here reported almost in its integral form, took place between Italy, Holland and Norway in October 2006, in the temporary chat room #sufloss (irc.freenode.net).

Assuming the role of xname, I opened a channel from Chequepoint, an active anarchist squat in the centre of Amsterdam. Gisle Froysland, connected from BEK, in Bergen, and Silvano Galliani, free software developer, known as kysucix, briefly online from Cimiano, a suburb of Milan, are collectively reflecting on the meaning of art and code, and their mingling.

218:15 -!- Irssi: #sufloss: Total of 1 nicks [1 ops, 0 halfops, 0 voices, 0 normal]
18:15 -!- Channel #sufloss created Thu Oct 26 18:15:45 2006
18:15 -!- Irssi: Join to #sufloss was synced in 0 secs
21:00 -!- gisle [n=gif@191.80-202-240.nextgentel.com] has joined #sufloss
21:01 <gisle> yo!
21:16 <@xname>
21:16 <@xname> hola
21:16 <@xname> sorry
21:16 <@xname> for being late,
21:16 <@xname> i just had an house meeting
21:17 <gisle> that's ok
21:17 <gisle> I'm getting a new kernel
21:18 -!- kysucix [n=kysucix@213-140-22-74.fastres.net] has joined #sufloss
21:18 <@xname> hola kysucix
21:18 <gisle> hola kysucix!
21:18 <kysucix> hola! :D
21:18 <kysucix> :)
21:18 <@xname> kysu
21:19 <@xname> can you save the log
21:19 <@xname> of this chat?
21:19 <@xname> my connection is crappy
21:19 <kysucix> ok
21:20 <gisle> ok, fire away..
21:20 <@xname> so, gisle,
21:21 <@xname> how did the piksel start?
21:21 <@xname> i know its root is actually mob, the software, right?
21:21 <gisle> just remember I'm a very slow typer :)
21:21 <gisle> specially when I have to think…;)
21:21 <kysucix> haha
21:21 <@xname> no problems type as you like
21:21 <gisle> yep, it all started with MoB
21:22 <gisle> back in 2002
21:22 <gisle> after the first prototype we wanted to do a workshop
21:23 <gisle> and also I wanted to invite other developers, not just artists…
21:25 <gisle> back then there was only freej, effectv[and veejay with similar stuff, I think[9]
21:27 <gisle> so, I contacted first Jaromil[10], cause I was following the freej list/project
21:28 <gisle> and he pointed me to Kentaro[11], Niels [12] and others
…
21:28 <gisle> but I also wanted to have pd people involved so i contacted Tom [13] and Yves[14] too...
21:32 <gisle> yep, the first idea was to focus on development and join our efforts
21:32 <gisle> but also to have input from artists
21:32 <@xname> very interesting
21:32 <gisle> yep, the first phase was very enthusiastic
21:32 <@xname> do you know of any other meeting that has this characteristic?
21:33 <gisle> eh, not at the time, no…
21:34 <gisle> we started the piksel list, and there was a_huge_ flurry of ideas going around

21:34 <@xname> like, for example…?
21:34 <gisle> main focus was interoperability
21:35 <gisle> how to combine/expand the different applications
21:35 <gisle> this was the main focus of piksel in 2003
21:35 <gisle> when Livido was born ;)
21:36 <@xname> god bless livido
21:36 <@xname> so you first created the list
21:36 <@xname> and then arranged the festival/meeting ?
21:36 <gisle> yep, we had the list for almost a year before the first workshop
21:37 <gisle> another important guy back then was Artem[15]
21:37 <gisle> very active on the list
21:38 <@xname> so you created a 'community' ?
21:38 <gisle> sure, piksel is also very much a community :)
21:39 <@xname> :)
21:39 <gisle> a very loose one ;)
21:39 <@xname> how did arrange the funding and the practical stuff to start…
21:40 <gisle> we used the normal BEK channels - mainly applied for funding from the Arts Council in Norway
21:41 <gisle> and through PNEK - the production network for electronic arts
21:41 <gisle> PNEK also funded MoB in the beginning
21:42 <gisle> actually the only way to get funding for development…
…
21:43 <gisle> was through PNEK
21:43 < kysucix> ok
21:43 < kysucix> and
21:43 <gisle> now PNEK is reorganizing, and no more money :(
21:44 < kysucix> how do you see piksel evolving through 4 editions ?
21:44 < kysucix> how did it changed? how do you see it now ?
21:44 <@xname> and the community, how did it change…
21:45 <gisle> well, we keep a community 'base' through the original developers
21:45 <gisle> some of which have participated in all editions
21:46 <gisle> but also expand with more people coming and going through the artistic program
21:46 <gisle> the main community channel is still the mailing list
…
21:47 <gisle> we have in a way moved more in the direction of festival
21:48 <gisle> with a larger focus on the artistic program
21:48 <gisle> this is also a result of the development focus not going anywhere :(
21:49 <@xname> so, from the focus on development, with the artist as a user and creator
21:49 <@xname> to the artist as a sort of scientist… or what?
21:50 <gisle> yes, the scientist approach is interesting
21:50 <gisle> specially piksel06 is moving in that direction, with xxxxx[16] collaboration
21:51 <gisle> and more
…
1:52 <@xname> why do you say that the focus on development did not lead anywhere?
21:53 <gisle> well, that's a bit pessimistic maybe, since a lot has been done like Frei0r, Livido, vjack and so on..
21:53 <gisle> but there's not much momentum behind it
21:54 <gisle> and the original collaborative spirit went away
21:54 <gisle> fast
21:54 <@xname> ah! why? what do you mean?
21:55 <gisle> I'm not sure, but I guess developers are even more stubborn and hardheaded than artists are ;)

…

21:55 < kysucix> well, free software development is a really complex phenomenon

21:56 <gisle> yes, that's what we discovered during the 1st piksel

21:56 < kysucix> and yes, to be a free software developer 'in my humble opinion' you *must* be a difficult person ;)

21:57 < kysucix> that gives you the will to go ahead :)

…

21:57 <gisle> also there's things like the pd world vs. the other applications

21:57 <@xname> competition, you mean?

21:57 <@xname> or just parallel worlds?

21:58 <gisle> lots of different approaches - parallel worlds

21:58 <@xname> who knows whether they will ever meet

21:58 <gisle> and no-one have the time/energy to care about the whole system

21:58 < kysucix> competition is a good thing

21:59 <@xname> it depends

…

21:59 <gisle> competition is good if we all share the same goal

…

22:00 <gisle> and use the competition to reach it

22:00 <@xname> so do you think at a certain point the goals where not anymore a common shared field?

22:01 <gisle> yes, it kind of drifted in different directions

22:01 <@xname> which directions?

22:03 <gisle> some want fast results (like me) and some want everything to be discussed in all details

22:03 <gisle> the work done defined directions

22:04 <gisle> like frei0r as a fast result focused on simplicity

22:04 <gisle> kind of proof of concept

22:05 <gisle> and Livido trying to cover all needs, but ends as different forks

22:05 <gisle> also videojack seemed to me first as an easy task

22:06 <gisle> but that shows how naive I am ;)

22:07 <@xname> is the piksel art all floss?

22:07 <gisle> yes and no

22:07 <@xname> …

22:08 <gisle> ideologically it's all floss, and that's the condition in the call for participation

22:09 <gisle> but this year we expanded to hardware as well

22:09 <gisle> and wanted to keep a broad interpretation of the term 'open hardware'

22:09 <@xname> like hackable hardware, for example…

22:09 <gisle> jepp, all the crazy stuff you can do with a soldering iron

22:10 <@xname> do you think floss is important in art? why?

22:10 <gisle> yes, I think floss is very important in digital art

22:11 <gisle> free art needs floss

22:11 <gisle> in the digital domain

22:11 <gisle> too many artists have no clue about the premises for doing what they do

22:12 <gisle> they are dictate by M$ and Apple

22:12 <gisle> and the rest of the industry

22:12 <@xname> a liberation that starts from art?

22:13 <@xname> art as an example ?

22:13 <gisle> no a liberation of society _including_ the arts

…

22:17 <gisle> you have to be able to change the code if you care to

22:17 <gisle> also all the so called 'tools' for artists are made for commercial design

22:18 <gisle> and the 'art' looks according to it

22:18 <@xname> so it is better for art to be autonomous …

22:18 <gisle> sure, up until now almost all digital art has been crap

22:19 <gisle> the whole 'multimedia' thing…
22:19 <@xname> is influenced by the market...
22:19 <gisle> absolutely!
22:19 <@xname> what are the main results from the pasts festivals?
22:20 <gisle> main results? I don't know…
22:20 <gisle> it's more a development of consciousness
22:21 <@xname> interesting
22:21 <gisle> I think also we have paved the way for others
22:21 <gisle> which I like very much
22:21 <@xname> to pioneer
22:21 <gisle> we are gaining interest by lots of people around the world
22:22 <gisle> and some of them are doing similar things
22:22 <gisle> which is good!
22:22 <@xname> is there any festival inspired by the piksel?
22:22 <gisle> yes, just been one in lubljana - by Andraz and others..;)
22:22 <@xname> called?
22:22 <gisle> moment, have to check
22:23 <@xname> k
22:23 <gisle> HAIP 06 - http://www.kiberpipa.org/~haip06/
22:23 <@xname> thanks
22:23 <gisle> and makeart[17], xxxxx
22:24 <@xname> is xxxxx inspired by piksel?
22:24 <gisle> yes, xxxxx and crash started after piksel and with many of the same people
22:25 <gisle> plus we are planning more collaborations xxxxx/makeart
22:26 <@xname> why did you decide to introduce the piksel exhibition?
22:28 <gisle> well, I found out it's much easier to make art happen in a short time than code ;)
22:29 <gisle> we needed a stronger focus on the artistic bit, and an exhibition works well as a 'window to the outside world'
22:29 <gisle> we had a problem of nerdiness
22:30 <gisle> not getting through to the local public
22:30 <gisle> it's still there, but the exhibition helps...
…
22:46 <@xname> and what about music,
22:46 <gisle> what about it?
22:46 <@xname> the focus from video processing is more and more including audio
22:46 <@xname> isn't it?
22:47 <gisle> yep
22:47 <gisle> we needed some fresh blood ;)
22:47 <gisle> repeating ourselves too much, so I decided to loosen up a bit
22:48 <gisle> and also invite some artists directly based on quality
22:48 <@xname> sorry i have bad connection
22:49 <@xname> ok
22:49 <@xname> but isn't this a risk in maintaining a certain identity?
22:50 <gisle> it's important to have a high quality artistic program with a non-compromising attitude
22:50 <@xname> :D
22:50 <@xname> wise
22:50 <gisle> I think that's the vibe of piksel
22:50 <@xname> gisle
22:50 <@xname> it is friday night
22:50 <@xname> i want to ask you a last question
22:50 <gisle> k
22:51 <@xname> what is the future of piksel?
22:51 <@xname> or, how do you imagine it?
22:51 <gisle> by the way, friday is tomorrow ;)

…

22:53 <gisle> yes, the future…
22:53 <@xname> yes
22:53 <gisle> not sure, it's a bit early
22:53 <gisle> to think about next year
22:53 <@xname> to imagine?
22:54 <gisle> well, I like the compact form this year with things happening in parallel
22:54 <gisle> but some things got a bit lost

…

22:55 <gisle> yes, we have to think more about how to do things like that
22:56 <gisle> but I like it as a direction
22:56 <@xname> ubiquitas?
22:56 <@xname> multi-presence?
22:56 <@xname> ;p
22:56 <gisle> more theoretic/practical/philosofic/scientific aspects
22:56 <gisle> code and art in closer relations
22:57 <@xname> they might kill each other
22:57 <@xname> eheh
22:57 <gisle> sure, the big piksel bang ;)
22:57 <@xname> ahaha
22:58 <@xname> ok
22:58 <@xname> so the future is a big explosion
22:58 <gisle> we'll see, next week I might have totally different views

Notes

This text is an updated version of the two articles published in Italian in the online magazine DIGIMAG, http://digicult.it/, November and December 2006.

Acknowledgements

Thanks to Digicult, Silvano Galliani, the Piksel Community, Gisle Froysland, GOTO10, BEK, the Free Software movement, and others.

# Free Studios

Fabianne Balvedi

## Introduction

It is not uncommon today to find the image of open and shared systems associated with the defence of freedom in the fight against a proprietary monopoly. Based on this perspective, free software is almost always appropriated as a banner and a strategic weapon in a counter-hegemonic struggle, which places it in opposition to closed models of information systems.

Although this discourse succeeds in attracting the attention of the mainstream media to questions such as the inequalities present in global technological development and the consequences of patent laws, its failing is that it ignores what are perhaps the most important characteristics of the free software phenomenon: its dynamics of production, its rules for the circulation of products and the behavioural changes towards the medium brought about by the philosophy of its usage.[1] It is different from the proprietary model not just in the nature of its materiality, but, first of all, in terms of the social relations into which it is inserted. Therefore, from this point of view, we understand that it is not correct simply to say that free software is better than proprietary software, but that it is of another order, which is fairer and qualitatively better than the proprietary one. According to De Ugarte, the free software movement is the basis of the first ever large-scale structure based on free property in distributed networks.[2]

While the proprietary model is based on competition and holding back information, the free one is mainly motivated by collaboration and generosity. At any of the levels of interaction, multidimensional developer/user relationships are established which constitute an alternative to the unilateral producer/consumer or provider/client relationships. As a result, the ensuing product is also a process. This process can be defined as a cumulative feedback cycle which makes the network think and is based on the sharing of information as the driving force behind technological innovation and the production of cultural goods.

[1] T. Novaes, F. Caminati, and C. e Prado, 'Sinapse XXI: cultura digital e direito à comunicação' ('Synapse XXI: digital culture and the right to communication'), Paulineas, 2005.

[2] D. De Ugarte, El Poder de Las Redes (The Power of Networks), 2005, electronic book available at http://www.deugarte.com/gomi/el_poder_de_las_redes.pdf

It is worth observing that the coexistence of the process and product variables as the result of a continuous flow of occurrences cannot be understood within the traditional Western logic, that of Aristotle, which is based on the binary values of affirmations. According to this logic, the result of a development process would be just a product, and not the process itself. As for fuzzy logic, it supports modes of reasoning which are approximate, rather than exact, with which we are naturally used to working. Many human experiences cannot be classified simply as true or false, yes or no, black or white. This is also how Estúdio Livre works.

The Estúdio Livre (Free Studio) project is a collaborative environment for research, development, experimentation and production in free media based on the perspective that one of the biggest innovations of the digital world is to be found in the structure of division of labour which takes place in an open network and of which free software is the best example. The methodology proposed illustrates the breaking down of barriers between producer and consumer as an example of collective intelligence as well as of changes in aesthetic, economic and social paradigms in contemporary society.

## The Community – Developers: Art and Science

The use of licenses which allow the sharing and re-use of codes is potentially a huge trump card for the sustainability of an interdisciplinary community like Estúdio Livre, which combines art and science. Stimulating this model of production encourages a space in which science can operate more innovatively and art can become more involved in improving its techniques.

One of the big problems with the dehumanisation of technologies is the failure to question the mechanisms of repetition built into the interfaces of industrial software. In most cases, artists see the computer as a closed box which ends up dictating aesthetic paths linked to standard interfaces. Thus the cultural producer is tied to a blind dependency on new products and formats launched by the industry.

In the case of free software, production follows a rhythm of requests and mutual collaboration in which the developers receive immediate feedback from the artists, who thereby gain more advanced knowledge about the development of their tools since they are no longer trapped within the cycle of industrial secrets. This encourages the deepening of knowledge for the shaping of a personal way of using technology, and the potential for customising the production processes grows, bringing with it also a greater interest in science and the methods which make this possible.

As for scientists, in this environment they find an enormous incentive for creativity. Breaking down the distances between scientific technique and the artist, this environment brings the awareness that producing a code or designing an interface or machine can be a technique loaded with communicative intention – as playful as making brush strokes on a canvas or strumming a guitar. A much less technocentric vision of scientific work is stimulated, bringing back the figure of the inventor and adding poetry to the mix.

[3] L. Lessig, Cultura Livre (Free Culture), Trama, 2005.

## The Community – Artists and Cultural Producers: Collaborative Means of Production

Without a doubt, the way free software is produced represents one of the most successful models of organic and participatory management of collective work ever known. The idea of producing collaboratively, using internet-based interfaces for editing code, version control, discussion forums and email lists, stimulated the construction of systems which are today so proficient for certain application niches that they have overtaken proprietary applications (such as in the case of web servers). This happens because there is also open dialogue between the various parties – this is a more direct and intelligent way to solve problems and implement innovations than in a closed approach in which the parties isolate themselves from everything, cloaked in secrecy.

This vision has had a great influence on how artistic production is seen at the beginning of the current century.[3] It became clear that artistic production could reach its audience directly, without intermediaries and without needing to conform to the aesthetic and marketing demands of distributors (in many case retrograde assumptions, which hamper creativity). This brought with it a better, and more organic, understanding of the artistic field of action. On the other hand, it also generated the need to look again at the question of how this authorship is recognised or remunerated since any consumer could potentially be a distributor or even a collaborator in this production.

One of the solutions proposed and encouraged by Estúdio Livre is support for collaborative production through the use of licenses for sharing. Just as the free software developer shares his or her code using licenses such as the GPL, the cultural producer, through licenses such as Creative Commons, gives the public the prior right to redistribute his or her work, with or without charge, and therefore makes them a partner in the creative production.[4] In this way, a relationship is established in which consumption and production are parts of the same cycle, in which

[4] GPL, http://www.gnu.org/copyleft/gpl.html Creative Commons, http://creativecommons.org

[5] M. McLuhan, and Q. Fiore, The Medium is the Message: An Inventory of Effects, Bantam Books, 1967.

[6] http://www.cultura.gov.br/programas_e_acoes/cultura_viva

the greater profit is the knowledge acquired and the establishment of social networks. Sooner or later, these same social networks will become partners in initiatives for mutual sustainability, creating a chain of production flows which breaks down cultural and geopolitical barriers, making possible autonomous niches which are much more self-referential and aware of their directions and capable of reflecting their socio-economic influences and the role of their production.

## The Environment

Estúdio Livre is a collaborative environment which emerged from the combined perception of people with the most varied backgrounds about the need for research into, and deeper knowledge of, the use and development of free media. The media contextualised through this environment corresponds to communications media, that is, it refers to the instrument or the content form used to carry out the communication process. Since software is an instrument for interaction which makes possible communication between a human and a machine, it may also be considered media, reinforcing McLuhan's hypothesis that the medium is the message.[5] The main objective of Estúdio Livre is active research, supporting and encouraging the production and circulation of free cultural goods, in other words works which can be freely distributed, remixed and retransmitted in a legal way and without any kind of restriction on access. Both virtually and in person, Estúdio Livre's activities and participation take place in the most free way possible. Proposals are made and these are added or other activities removed, depending on the profile of the group in each activity. All the tools in the environment are based on the concepts of free software, open knowledge and technological appropriation. The stimulus for interaction comes from workshops, media labs, free archives, user manuals, forums, personal blogs, research groups, discussions taking place via list and other differentiated tools for collaboration. The maintenance costs for the project include a small part which is voluntary on behalf of the collective and another larger part which comes from its partners: the Free Software Project-Paraná (PSL-PR) and the Digital Culture sector of the Brazilian Ministry of Culture (MinC). PSL-PR was the cradle of the project and administers some of the network services, which the MinC maintains the server and a small team dedicated to the maintenance of the environment. The main reason for this partnership is the support provided to the Cultural Hotspots (Pontos de Cultura) which form part of the Ministry's Living Culture Programme (Programa Cultura Viva).[6]

## The Abstract Environment: Administration and Development

At the moment the tools used for virtual interaction are located on the World Wide Web. The main ones are the public discussion list and the collaborative portal which allow real-time editing of hypertexts as well as upload and download of documents with metadata.[7]

The general public work list was the first virtual environment for interaction amongst the community. Up to now it has been hosted on the Riseup.net technical collective's server. Although we currently have emails and discussion lists[8] under the estudiolivre.org domain we chose to maintain our main list under the Riseup.net domain due to this connection being characterised as a 'knot in the network', in other words, a project which uses resources from another and vice versa. There are people in the Estúdio Livre community who also collaborate with Riseup.net projects, for example, translating its web interface which is originally in English into Portuguese.

The Estúdio Livre website was originally hosted on the Utopia server, then by the Federal University of Paraná (UFPR), and is now at the University of São Paulo (USP). It is programmed in free software and can be developed by any person with technical knowledge of PHP, MySQL, Smarty and CSS.[9] It is based on TikiWiki, a content management system (CMS) designed for communities and distributed under the LGPL license.[10] People without programming knowledge can also contribute via bug reports.[11]

The Estúdio Livre code is a Tiki module which consists of a group of new files, patches and SQL scripts, managed by Polvo, a software written in Perl to carry out automatic publication on the web and locally on the developer's machine.[12] This procedure is necessary to maintain the estudiolivre.org code separate from the TikiWiki code.

The group responsible for the development, maintenance and administration of the site, discussion lists, request verification and organisation of the information is made up mainly of more experienced users, programmers, system administrators, musicians, video-makers and producers who have been using free software for some time.

[7] http://lists.riseup.net/www/info/estudiolivre and http://estudiolivre.org

[8] https://listas.estudiolivre.org/

[9] http://dev.estudiolivre.org

[10] TikiWiki, http://br.tikiwiki.org LGPL, http://www.gnu.org/copyleft/lgpl.html

[11] http://bugs.estudiolivre.org

[12] http://estudiolivre.org/Polvo

## The Abstract Environment: desktop

The main aim of estudiolivre.org is to amass a community which researches, documents, experiments, produces and develops free media. For this purpose, different types of interaction options are available to users. They may either simply search for information or add to or correct incomplete content which they come across during their research. They may also make their own productions available through the Free Archive (Acervo Livre) or download productions by other members of the site.[13] Depending on the license used by those files, users may also remix them and upload them again in a new version. This is only legally possible because the content made available on the portal uses permissive licenses, which facilitate the most diverse types of sharing.

Another resource implemented in the Free Archive are the live channels which make possible audio and/or video streaming.[14] Users can listen to and/or watch someone else's transmission or do their own, as long as they have the necessary tools installed on the computer that will generate the stream.

Access to all of these processes is completely free. However, to interact in this virtual environment, it is necessary to register some personal details on the site. By doing this, the user declares that s/he is aware of the conditions of the site's Terms of Use, thereby taking exclusive, irrevocable and irreversible responsibility for the information provided, as well as for any complaints from third parties about the material contributed.[15]

## The Abstract Environment: the concrete environment

In face-to-face interactions, proactive members of the community promote and participate in workshops and events which involve themes covered by the scope of the project.

The first experience with workshops took place at the Fifth World Social Forum in January 2005 through participation in the activities of the Free Knowledge Lab (Laboratório de Conhecimentos Livres) located at the Youth Camp, which Lawrence Lessig dropped in on and later mentioned on his personal blog.[16] Starting that same year, the Free Knowledge Encounters (Encontros de Conhecimentos Livres) took place all over Brazil, through the partnership with the MinC.[17]

[13] Acervo Livre, http://acervo.estudiolivre.org

[14] Canais ao vivo, http://aovivo.estudiolivre.org

[15] Estúdio Livre being exempt from any obligation related to the exhibition and distribution of the works, and guaranteeing that no remuneration will be due for the material which is licensed, exhibited and distributed by it. See Terms of Use, http://estudiolivre.org/politicadeuso

[16] See http://www.lessig.org/blog/archives/002400.shtml and http://www.lessig.org/blog/archives/002411.shtml

[17] http://estudiolivre.org/Encontros+de+Conhecimentos+Livres

[18] http://estudiolivre.org/

In 2006, a partnership with the regional government of Extremadura in Spain made it possible for seven members of the community to travel to Spain to share knowledge with European activists. Workshops took place in Almendralejo and Barcelona, bringing with them a subtle upgrade in the project's evolution.[18] This trip also encouraged the internationalisation of the site, which gained an interface in various languages, of which the translation of the wiki pages is only the beginning. Despite the mainly nomadic characteristics described above, if we analyse Estúdio Livre as a concept, we can find it applied in various parts of Brazil, such as for example Curitiba, Rio de Janeiro, São Paulo and Belo Horizonte – or even inside the home of a member of the community.[19]

EstudioLivreEspanha

[19] Curitiba, http://www.spet.br/ Rio de Janeiro, http://rio.estudiolivre.org/ São Paulo, http://estudiolivre.org/SampaLab Belo Horizonte, http://estilingue.sarava.org

## Final Considerations

Estúdio Livre's activities are concentrated on supporting the increasing closeness of the development and usage cycles of free software media for the production of other types of media and encouraging sharing and collaboration in this production. Above all it is an environment which draws on volunteers from amongst the community and from those who share these interests for the sovereignty of its principles and autonomy of its proposals. On the other hand, it encourages the participation of its more active members in consultancy and the implementation of projects which require this methodology, using the documentation and works on the site as tools. Estúdio Livre also accepts voluntary donations and partnerships with institutions, governments and companies which are using its material or which would like to encourage specific productions within the community (documentation of a specific software, compilation of documentation, customisation or multimedia production), as long as the objectives of this partnership are coherent with those of Estúdio Livre and the donor or partner in question does not stand for anything which goes against the activism carried out by the community which maintains the project.

The aim is to create a scenario for participatory cultural and technological production, which can generate less alienated reflections than purely entertainment driven consumption and a greater awareness of the social role of everyone involved – those who come to see themselves as part of an independent, open and collective process. We call this aim, Estúdio Livre Phase Two, which sets out to produce something capable of causing the impact that the film *City of God* had on the history of

Brazilian cinema, but, following in the footsteps of the film *Elephants Dream* (which was the world's first open source film and met with critical acclaim), with the differential of free software and the process of methodological sharing.

Bibliography

M. Castells, A Sociedade em Rede (The Rise of the Network Society), Paz e Terra, 1999.

J. Dibbell, 'We Pledge Allegiance to the Penguin' in Wired, Issue 12.11, November, 2004.

P. Levy, As tecnologias da inteligência (Collective Intelligence), Editora 34, 1993.

Notes



The original document is available at:
http://estudiolivre.org/paperEL

# F/LOSS and the Computer Culture of the Maldives

Shahee Ilyas

The development of non-proprietary software will enable poorer countries to abide by the intellectual property rights agreements of World Trade Organization (WTO), which some countries are being forced to comply with in order to receive economic assistance from multilateral development organisations such as World Bank, UNDP and Asian Development Bank. This would also facilitate the growth of a local software development community, which could help both the private and public sectors to drastically cut down costs. With economic advantages such as these and more why hasn't the F/LOSS movement caught on in the Maldives?

[1] Ministry of Planning and National Development , 'Maldives Key Indicators 2006', http://www.planning.gov.mv/publications/yrb2006/Key%20Indicators/Key%20Indicators%202006.pdf (accessed December 23, 2006)

## Maldives

Historically, since people started living in the Maldives as early as 2000BC they lived only in very small communities. Each populated area (island) had an average of less than 200 or so people until the late 1980s and even now there are some with even fewer inhabitants. Very few islands grew to over 10 thousand people but the capital city of Malé presently has a population of over 100 thousand. The population of the Maldives reached 298,842 in 2006.[1] In theory people have always had the choice to migrate to larger islands in order to form larger communities but this was discouraged in the society. One of the apparent reasons for this is poverty, which would force people to share their limited resources if they were to form larger groups. The other is due to people having many things to hide from others in society, especially the status of their lives, as many live a different life than that which they pretend. Throughout time rulers have taken this to their advantage and have kept the majority in smaller groups, in poverty and under suppression.

As in many other poor countries: generations of conditioning and repression have made people resist change. Whenever a person or a group of people came up with a free idea with long term benefits for the community, if the rulers did not get considerable benefits out of it he, she or they would be tortured and executed. With a mentality developed within such a governing framework people are automatically inclined to believe that adapting to new ways and technologies is evil.

The Maldives was a British protectorate from 1887 to 1965. It was a Sultanate until 1968, when it became a republic. The Maldives has had three presidents so far: the third and current president, Maumoon Abdul Gayyoom, has been in power since 1978 (now in his 30th year in power).

In 1997 Maldives was put on the recommended list for graduation from a Least Developed Country (LDC) from 2001 onwards. The government of Maldives argued that it was still too economically vulnerable to totally abandon the benefits LDCs are entitled to receive.

**Computers**

Computers were not very popular in the Maldives until the 1990s. One of the reasons being their unaffordability. Until that point rarely were individuals able to afford to import them and almost no businesses or government offices used computers either (except for a few foreign companies such as the country's only telecom company, the British based firm Cable and Wireless).

In the early 1990s few shops started to sell computers and accessories. Initially there was a tax (import duty) of 25 percent from each computer or computer part imported. The price of a personal computer with an average configuration of that time (with an Intel based 486 processor) was over €3.000 (more than a years' complete salary of a managerial staff ). The import tax was later reduced to 5 percent. Soon after, following trends in neighbouring countries a lot of businesses started to invest in computer retail shops. Their biggest customer was the government. And in the early 2000s the prices of computers were down to an affordable level for the middle classes. In 2007 a Windows based computer with a reasonable configuration was available for less than €350 (less than one month's salary for a worker with managerial job). And there are many shops which allow customers to purchase computers on an instalment basis. From the early 2000s computer users have increased exponentially in the

Maldives. Now almost all households of the capital Malé are equipped with a computer. Like most consumer items, from household items such as needles to industrial machines, computers have never been manufactured in the Maldives.

### Software: Piracy and Copyright

The majority of computer users in the Maldives use Microsoft Windows as their only operating system. There are a few Linux or MacOS users. At the time of writing there is no copyright law in Maldives. There are many advantages and disadvantages of this for a country with a developing economy. Many software vendors were able to sell pirated versions of famous commercial software to locals at a range of prices.

Since early 2000 almost every well known Windows based commercial software was available from the many copyshops around the capital city. Currently the average cost of a CD or a DVD containing commercial software is less than €2 each. It is very common to find Adobe CS3 premium package in one DVD for €5! Availability of Linux or Macintosh based software in this manner is much rarer.

This plays a major role in the non-existence of a community which develops custom software for Maldivian needs. Pirated software is available almost for free, the usage was also free (as in freedom) and it is not illegal in the Maldives yet. Many government offices also use pirated commercial software including Microsoft Office and other proprietary applications. The inability to modify commercial software limits use of this software to only the specified uses in most cases.

Due to the availability of proprietary software at such low cost and the lack of laws to protect their rights, there was little incentive for local programmers to develop their own open source or proprietary software customised for local needs. There exists a few examples of locally developed software for point of sales and accounting needs. These software include specific features necessary for calculating (and cheating) local taxes and serving other accounting needs of businesses. These few local software projects are slowly being replaced by non-bespoke proprietary software developed elsewhere.

## Internet

Dhivehiraajege Gulhun Limited (Dhiraagu), incorporated in 1988, was the country's only telecom company until the year 2004 and was responsible for introducing the internet to the Maldives in 1996.[2] Dhiraagu is a partnership between the Maldivian government and the British telecom company Cable and Wireless. During the first few years basic dial-up service was priced at over €15 per hour for speeds of 28kbps-56kbps via ordinary telephone lines. Introduction of the internet made a great change to the lives of people. Until that time, information was highly controlled and any press or newspapers critical of the government was silenced and prevented from reaching the general public. Critics believed that raising the price of the internet was one of the means adopted to control its use. But this did not stop people from downloading, printing and distributing information from the internet; especially those critical of the government. After a slow beginning, the Internet quickly became the medium of choice for activists, especially those living abroad.

IRC rooms, mailing lists, newsgroups and forums used by Maldivians were around years before the internet was introduced to the Maldives. This use was mostly by small groups of Maldivian students studying in more developed countries. As the online community grew a lot of political discussions took place. With material from these communities, some websites and online newspapers were produced in the early 2000s. This eventually became one of the starting places for internet surveillance by the Maldivian Police (NSS).[3] Heavy surveillance and help from foreign internet surveillance specialists was used to track down and imprison contributors. The creators of Sandhaanu (the most well known internet newspaper critical of the government) were sentenced to life imprisonment in July 2002 and released in 2006 due to increase in international pressure calling for their release.[4]

[2] Wikipedia contributors, 'Dhiraagu', Wikipedia, The Free Encyclopedia, http://en.wikipedia.org/w/index.php?title=Dhiraagu&oldid=92336516 (accessed December 23, 2006).

[3] Michael O'Shea and friends, 'Kotari Chat with the NSS', Maldives Culture, http://www.maldivesculture.com/maldives_nss_chat01.html, (accessed December 15, 2006).

[4] Amnesty International,'Maldives: Fear of torture or ill-treatment/ incommunicado detention/prisoners of conscience', http://web.amnesty.org/library/Index/ENGASA290012003?open&of=ENG-MDV (accessed December 23, 2006).

## Thaana

Thaana the script used for writing Maldivian language, Dhivehi, consists of consonants and diacritic vowels. Thaana is a bidirectional script with letters written from right-to-left and numbers from left-to-right. Maldivians are the only people who use this language and it is the only language many Maldivians use. Until the middle of the 20th century, any mass reproduction of Thaana based publications was executed in pen and ink by hand. With the introduction of printing in the Maldives (in mid 20th century) it was printed from a hand-written stencil as opposed to movable type. Hence there were no fonts except the handwritings of specific authors. Layout and typesetting of newspapers and magazines used hand-written text until the mid 1990s.

[5] In 1988 SehgaSoft became the first registered Maldivian software company. Their other products included, Thaana embedded MLS and a Foxpro based database system for maintaining the Telephone directory developed for Dhiraagu. The main founder of SehgaSoft was a senior staff of Dhiraagu.

To make communications more efficient for use with widespread international technologies, there was an attempt to replace Thaana with Latin in the mid 1970s by the previous government. This was abandoned by the current government in the early 1980s. In the late 1980s Thaana typewriters were introduced only a few years before computers were becoming popular. The price difference was small between a computer with Thaana printing capabilities and a typewriter. So, the life of the Thaana typewriter was very short.

There were many attempts to make a Thaana text processing software capable of writing, processing and archiving documents. Most of these attempts were made with only short term commercial benefits in mind. The earliest successful attempt was embedding a Thaana font into Multi-Lingual Scholars (MLS), a text processing software package developed by an American company, which allowed language packages to be installed and configured during set up. MLS only worked under the MS-DOS environment. In the early 1990s Thaana embedded MLS (distributed by SehgaSoft ) became a necessity in most government offices and many private businesses.[5] Using MLS required a specific range of printers and cost more than the price of a computer at that time. MLS works with a hardware dongle to prevent piracy. With Microsoft Windows MLS and similar DOS based Thaana programmes became difficult to use. Some offices still maintain DOS based machines with MLS just for Thaana text processing. After Microsoft Windows was introduced, some Hebrew and Arabic text processing software were hacked and sold by Maldivian programmers to enable writing Thaana. These included Qtext (Ftana) & Accent Express.

**Thaana Fonts**

In around 1995 the first few Thaana fonts were rapidly distributed among computer users. Some of them were created by Dr. Hassan

Hameed. One of the most common fonts was A_Faseyha, released with this intriguing copyright line:

> *Calligraphy: Abdulla Waheed, Office of the President; Managed by Hassan Shujau; Edited by Hassan Hameed; November 1995; All rights reserved. Based on the 1968 Viyafaari Miadhu Aharee Number.*[6]

Thaana fonts developed by SehgaSoft (in collaboration with Architect & Graphic Designer Mohamed Shafeeq of Group-X GDA Maldives) were soon released to the public.

Although there was a copyright notice on these fonts, they were freely distributed among computer users. Over the years more fonts were released and some based on the previous fonts, often retaining the kerning table, or sometimes the previous copyright notices as well. These fonts were also re-mapped to accommodate the different keyboard layouts, reversed for layout designing purposes (which will be explained later) and adapted to Unicode by others.[7] To an observer this behaviour by the Thaana font users seems similar to adhering to an open source license. There were no reports of any complaints from of the creators or copyright holders of these fonts. From a list of over 100 Thaana fonts currently in circulation, only one font (Thaana Unicode Akeh created by the now defunct Maldivian Internet Task Force in the year 2000) comes with a GPL license.

## Thaana Keyboard

Thaana fonts have three main keyboard mappings, two based on phonetics and the other based on old Thaana typewriters. The typewriter font mapping was meant for use by office clerks who were familiar with the Thaana typewriter layout and the phonetic layouts were introduced for people familiar with the English language which was the case for most computer users at that time. The major difference between the phonetic keyboard and the typewriter keyboard is that the typewriter keyboard is derived from a statistical analysis of Thaana texts, with keys strategically placed to enable increased typing speed.

Though there are three standards, most common are the two phonetic keyboards. The differences between them are very small, but significant. With three standards in use, and two equally common, users viewing or editing documents needed to be familiar with at least two keyboard

[6] Luc Devroye, School of Computer Science, McGill University, http://cg.scs.carleton.ca/~luc/thaana.html (accessed November 17, 2006).

[7] Unicode is a computing standard allowing text to be consistently represented and edited using most of the world's language writing systems.

mappings and needed to have both variations of fonts. Mostly the documents are very messy on screen, but appear fine when printed.

[8] CorelDRAW is a multi-page vector graphic editor very commonly used by Maldivian graphic designers.

## Thaana Recorder

Thaana Recorder is a macro written for Windows Recorder. It adds a 'right arrow key' after each letter typed to make the cursor go to the right hence giving the feel of moving right-to-left while typing. Since it was a macro script for Windows Recorder the source code was open, and there was no copyright notice for it. Along with Thaana fonts this 2-kilobyte macro was distributed from person to person and office to office in floppy disks. It was one of the most common scripts on every Maldavian's computer. It was one of the very first most common and useful open source scripts in circulation, intentionally or unintentionally.

People using this macro/script had many limitations. The text does not flow to new lines and hence it is impossible to do any kind of automatic word wrapping. If there was a need to insert a large portion of text to the middle of an article or to increase or decrease the font size or change the font, almost all the lines of the document required extensive editing. But it was a simple alternative to the high priced 'commercial' Thaana editing software. Many government offices also used this hack to write short letters. The macro was also used by people who made small advertisements or leaflets in Thaana using design applications such as CorelDRAW.[8]

## Reverse Thaana Fonts

A clever way to write right-to-left script was to make a mirror image of a font and using the mirror (scale width to minus 100 percent) function of a graphic editing application to display it correctly. This method was very commonly used from the late 1990s onwards, especially among graphic designers using page layout applications such as Aldus/Adobe Pagemaker. Reversed Thaana fonts gave the flexibility needed to do word wrapping and justify aligning of Thaana text similar to other languages. So this method is still very popular among layout artists. These fonts were also freely distributed from person to person. The main limitation is that it would only work on layout designing software with the mirror function.

Due to these limitations, application of Thaana in computers for anything except text processing was rare or not done at all. Databases, spreadsheets and various other uses were almost never seen. The point of

[9] Allan Wood, 'Test for Unicode support in Web browsers', Allan Wood's Unicode Resources, http://www.alanwood.net/unicode/thaana.html (accessed December 23, 2006).

[10] Haveeru Daily is the longest serving daily newspaper of the Maldives. It is a government aligned newspaper owned by Mohamed Zahir Hussain, a close friend of the current president who also has been serving ministerial positions in the government since 1978.

sales, travel packages and other small tools people used were all in English. In other words a person needed to have a basic understanding of English before being able to use a computer. Some prominent computer programmers in Malé even had the idea of completely changing the Thaana script instead of trying to develop software to accommodate Thaana.

## Unicode Thaana

During 1999, the Thaana range was introduced with version 3.0 of the Unicode Standard.[9] Due to the lack of co-ordination between the Maldivian authorities and the Unicode Consortium only 64 spaces were allotted to Thaana. Although now it is believed more will be necessary to write cursive Thaana. Similar to scripts such as Arabic, some letters can take more forms than just one. In 2001 Windows XP was introduced with Unicode Thaana support. The default Thaana font included in Windows XP is the most unpleasant Thaana font ever produced. Though most of the users were quick to migrate to (mostly pirated versions of) Windows XP, people adapting to use the new standard were rare. Many retained the non-Unicode fonts they had and remained loyal to the methods they were familiar with.

## Thaana on the Internet

Before Thaana was included into Unicode and due to a lack of standard set of rules for writing Thaana on computers, it was extremely difficult to put Thaana on the web. One of the first popular websites that used Thaana was the website of *Haveeru Daily,* http://haveeru.com.mv) during 1997, they used black and white bitmap images of text.[10] A few more websites followed this model, the website of the president's office of Maldives (http://presidencymaldives.gov.mv) also resorted to using bitmap images to display Thaana until 2005. A lot of government websites still use this technique for displaying Thaana text. This technique has a lot of limitations such as slow loading times, not being able to search, copy or paste.

The website of *Haveeru Daily* is among the most visited website and it switched to using dynamic fonts in early 2000. Until now *Haveeru Daily* uses non-unicode Thaana fonts which the users have to download and install to view the website. Using a non-unicode based font makes it harder to integrate their articles into text processing or layout software. This is also one step backward towards creating a semantic Thaana web.

Since the year 2006 there have been a few popular Thaana websites such as the Joomla powered website of *Minivan Daily* (the first daily paper critical of the government, registered in mid 2005, http://www.minivandaily.com) and the locally programmed website of *Jazeera Daily* (http://www.jazeera.com.mv/), which implements Thaana Unicode properly. An open source javascript snippet (JavaScript Unicode Keyboard Handler) developed by a local web developer Jaawish Hameed is being widely used on newly developed websites for mapping keyboard input to Thaana Unicode.[11]

[11] Joomla! is an open source content management system used for developing simple websites to complex web applications.

[12] TRIPS (Trade Related Aspects of Intellectual Property Rights) is a treaty administered by the World Trade Organisation (WTO) which sets down minimum standards for forms of intellectual property (IP) regulation.

## Conclusion

Generations of poverty and long experience of living in a suppressed and non-sharing culture with a huge gap between the poor and the rich has made the emerging middle class more capitalistic and business minded. Those able to find/create/hack even a small software sold it and made quick money out of it even if the product was not completely functional.

Easy and cheap availability of pirated software stopped people from looking for, or creating, commercial or open source alternatives. Since all of the initial generation of computer users were English literate, consumers and developers assumed a basic level of English education to be present for the rest of the users as well. This discouraged people from developing Thaana based software for which there is a great need.

The need for building a F/LOSS movement is stronger now than before. Drafting of copyrights and anti-piracy laws (to abide with TRIPS to get trading international assistance which is essential for the Maldives after its graduation from LDC status) makes the need even more.[12] Open source software is rare now because it is not yet completely necessary and remains without a binding legal framework, proprietary software functions like open source within this society. But this may have to change after the country's economic graduation.

With an increasing number of people using computers, the need for more standards compliant Thaana based applications is now manifold. Though adopting a standard way to use Thaana was difficult and slow, signs of development are now increasing with the advent of Thaana Unicode. Specially on the internet. It is time for a local organisation with support from experts to advocate and widely implement these standards. With the world moving towards the direction of using web based technologies, the development of an open source web based Thaana office suite or an operating system is something to look forward to. This could allow any user with an old machine running Linux with an internet connection (or a local web server running the application) to use Thaana freely via the web browser.

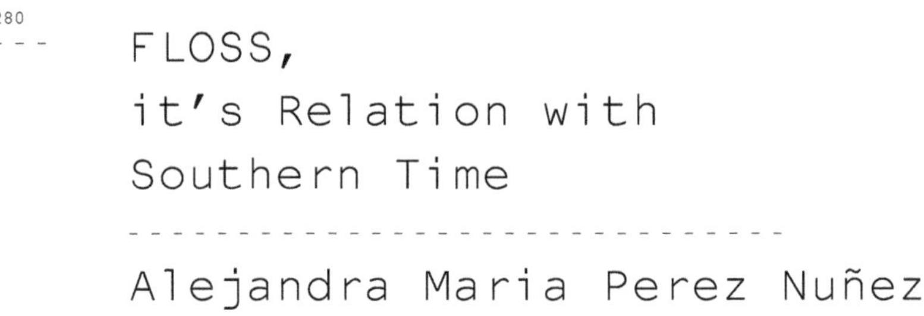

# FLOSS, it's Relation with Southern Time

Alejandra Maria Perez Nuñez

In this report I would like to document a period of meetings held between Barcelona, Bruxelles and Rotterdam between 2003 and 2007. In Rotterdam I interviewed software artist and writer from Berlin Florian Cramer. In Bruxelles, Femke Snelting and Peter Westerman from Constant speaking of their project Open Source Publishing, a suite for graphic design based on FLOSS code. In Barcelona, Yves Degoyon developer of groups; mapOmatix, /etc/groups and the library for video processing in Pure Data Pidip, speaking of Free Libre Open Source software, networks of collaboration. I also include a review about Platoniq and Bricolaje sexual from Barcelona.

The Interview with Florian Cramer was held in Piet Zwart Institute in Rotterdam, the school where he leads a programme based on FLOSS and a critical view of media and digital art. Cramer refers to the economical implications of free software and what are for him the keys to think about innovation in digital art. If we want to reflect upon innovation in software usage we have to think about monocultures in the domain of knowledge production. Yves Degoyon discusses the nature of networks and the processes that materialise networked collaboration. Femke Snelting and Peter Westerman discuss extensively the need for interfaces that might combine the excitement of Linux and of making things open, and look at problems with the existing means of desktop publishing.

I will highlight some elements related to the creation of FLOSS under a southern point of view, in particular the proposal of a group of developers and practitioners in relation to their use of time.

There are differences in the use of time in the south, there are important tensions in relation to methods that will be autonomous and free. There is as well a need to develop coherent practices that will use time outside of Empire. [1] Through work outside the economical time of

[1] 'The empire never ended', Philip K. Dick, The Man in the High Castle, 1972.

unlimited profit we become acquainted with trabajo gratis and useless usage of time. In terms of innovation the south offers examples of experiences related to community mapping, open knowledge banks and a struggle for open intellectual property rights. I will speak about the south as Barcelona but also as Bruxelles, southern with respect to Holland. Rotterdam, south in relation to Amsterdam and Berlin, southern in relation to the rest of Germany and Northern Europe. It is not so much about geographical location as about frames of mind and daily use of time that determines what is conceived as south.[2]

## Barcelona: Time to Stay Together

MapOmatix, coded by Barcelona based developer Yves Degoyon, is an application based on SVG (Scalar Vector Graphics) that allows one to develop maps on the web.[3] It is a geowiki, an open publishing system that allows localization using geographical coordinates. It is, at the same time, a critique of the use of proprietary systems such as GPS and RFID: objective localization systems related to identification and tracking. MapOmatix attempts to overcome the limitations of identification (and egotification) of technologies of tracking through the incorporation of participative variables and experiences of learning together to make cartography and maps. Groups working on psychogeography are also inscribed in the politics of vague time (tiempo vago), time spent without orientation towards consumption. MapOmatix is also an experience of work with open/libre standards and an opportunity for self-mediation. The current situation of MapOmatix is not promising as far as SVG development is concerned.[4] As an open format for high resolution graphics on the web it is somewhat stranded in the middle of the software politics by the existing Flash monoculture.[5] A new implementation of visualizations for collectives, groups and networks is /etc/groups – A Graphical Browser And Search Engine For Networks.[6]

*IRC chat interview with Yves Degoyon developer of /etc/ groups:*

<chevil> There is no software without people and why they do it and in which context

<chevil> There's no software without people and why they are making it <chevil> that might sound easy to say but it's about a historical context, for instance why free software was born in 1990 only?

<chevil> when software exists since the 60's?

<chevil> the history of apple doing their small things in their garage did influence this?

<chevil> I think a model of world domination appeared in the 1990's through software and that provoked that reaction, around 1990

<chevil> mainly born in the heart of the dominators of course

[2] In the sense that Henry Lefebevre formulates the difference in rhythm of Mediterranean cities in Henri Lefebevre, Rhythmanalysis: Space, Time and Everyday Life, 1967.

[3] http://mapomatix.sourceforge.net/

[4] Adobe will discontinue SVG viewer support in 2009.

[5] http://www.adobe.com. 2008.

[6] http://etc-groups.sourceforge.net

<chevil> like a fear of itself
<chevil> now collectives spread, trying to fit their historical practices to the global 'no' to world domination
<chevil> that had a common motto but goals are not clear
<pueblo> You point out a very ideological birth of free software, but inside free software there are various interests <pueblo> Are there people developing without ideology?
<chevil> ok, it might sound abusive to ask an ideological engagement to all, when we are just all playing?
<chevil> I don't think nobody's playing here, as it could be said of 'breaking rules' net-art
<chevil> (thinking of adrian ward and alex mclean and others here)
<chevil> free software as it is, is not pointless
<chevil> it produces empowerment at its best and gets into alternative to corporate business at its worst
<chevil> but always has a goal, not hidden and quite clear
<pueblo> can you explain what is that you point out in the work of adrian ward and alex mclean here?
<chevil> they were just twisting software, not thinking of practical 'applications' <chevil> and I would like to keep doing free software this way
<chevil> but that's not the reality of what we 'produce'
<chevil> at the end, you 'produce' and have bug reports from 'users' on the sourceforge forums
<chevil> so you have users aimed to a goal, and you cannot deceive them <chevil> and you're a free software dealer
<chevil> but you're not even sure you can approve any use of your software <chevil> I've been proposed some work by a surveillance company in Switzerland, so I'm very cautious about what users may want
<pueblo> you have been developing etc groups lately and mapomatix before <pueblo> etc groups is a tool to map and enhance relations
<pueblo> in this period of time, networks are under surveillance
<pueblo> how do you see this problem? Who would be the users of your relational maps?
<chevil> of course, It's not made for surveillance, it's just a formalization of existing networks
<chevil> it's just another way of publishing well-known information
<chevil> and the idea of 'bureau d'études' from the start was to make public such supposedly hidden informations and connections
<chevil> 'secrets de polichinelle'
<chevil> there are just tools to make an easy access to a not-so-hidden information
<chevil> and, anyway nothing would be published without the agreements of its actors
<chevil> you should consider the best protection for any activism is to be well-known and declared, if not, there wouldn't have been such a scandal after the sabotage of the rainbow warrior
<chevil> and it would have been kept 'secret' or 'undercovered' as they would like it to be
<pueblo> well the problem is that to know who goes with whom and who is there has a value, but anyway what is for you the main goal of this network visualizations?
<chevil> these are visualisations right, but also a materializations, maybe not to feel alone is the most important thing
<chevil> If indymedia just cares about having syndication is that it is a power just to communicate different experiences throughout different countries but sharing the same sensibility
<chevil> and if a network exists, if we ever believe it could be useful, that's to share some common experiences, for all the world all looks

now like one (??)

<chevil> I precisely believe in global networks much more than in local networks
<chevil> WAN versus LAN
<pueblo> why is that so?
<pueblo> what is it that you believe?
<chevil> Because it's much more about what is significant in your experience than only collective's conflicts, a subject we should maybe skip
<chevil> anyway, as far as free software is concerned in this, it works to develop with people you have never met in person
<chevil> just because they have the aim, the spirit to do so
<chevil> and you don't need to make a collective with them
<pueblo> In the /etc visualisation for the ESF there were clear aims to help networks of ppl from different countries to be able to visualize their connectedness and participation
<pueblo> correct me if I'm wrong
<pueblo> can you explain more what you mean when speaking of visualizing the rhythm of organisations?
<chevil> I'm not sure that the collectives were ever informed of this
<chevil> all its possibilities, we need to get back on the ground of communication all the time
<chevil> and in every company, 30 percent of the budget is communication
<chevil> but in free software, nobody will do that job
<pueblo> maybe in giss.tv
<chevil> or you get into a company model, which I'd rather avoid <chevil> yes, in giss.tv some might do it
<chevil> giss.tv was aimed to open streaming media to everyone and that's a nice project
<chevil> when it opened possibilities to radios from oaxaca and chile and mexico (segunda campania)
<chevil> it has absolutely little interest to be used in academical institutes in Europe
<chevil> but still we develop things without knowing how they will be used
<chevil> and there there is a very interesting phenomenon
<chevil> I personally, added a clause to the classical GPL license saying : 'not for military or repressive use'
<chevil> and some people from the free software (or were supposed to be) said : this clause is illegal
<chevil> cause it restricts the use of your software
<pueblo> is the same critics that some make to creative commons, what is your position regarding CC?
<chevil> I never gave an ear to that because that's really a attempt to try to look nice and cool, when the goal is the restrictions of rights
<chevil> we should think of the example of the plunderphonics and John Oswald
<chevil> and when Negativeland had a trial with U2
<chevil> people supposedly under CC would do the same trials if they were successful and mocked, you know
<chevil> it's like a declaration of good intents the CC
<chevil> not more
<pueblo> In the current state of development of etc/groups there is a timeline right?
<chevil> nope
<pueblo> you will not do it?
<chevil> in the next versions might be useful
<pueblo> I thought the historical aspect was very important
<chevil> If people think is useful...
<chevil> now, it's more a visualization of the active state of networks
<chevil> and it's hard to collect more information than that
<pueblo> but it's important to know when people got together and when they

broke up
<chevil> yes of course
<pueblo> what is more important for you from etc/groups?
<chevil> the aspect of the 'declaration of good intents' is very important there
<chevil> it's most of the time defeated by practice
<chevil> like when some free software developers can start working for corporate companies
<chevil> although they keep a 'free' version of their software
<chevil> I believe free software can only develop with some public support (universities, art schools, ...)
<chevil> If not, it will not remain free for long
<chevil> I see /etc/groups as a way to communicate
<pueblo> What are the aspects of an active network?
<chevil> well, it should be people really connected in a way, that are still in communication
<chevil> and able to participate in common initiatives
<chevil> but again it's just a tool and you cannot know when it will be used right
<pueblo> On the internet there is an important potential of collaboration, do you think this visualizations of declaring good intentions may become a tool to collaborate?
<chevil> it's something that should be the embryo of wider initiatives
<chevil> but all of this seems idealistic and romantic
<chevil> Right doesn't mean there's one and only way to use it, but in something you might think it's useful
<chevil> people are networking too narrowly with their relatives unfortunately
<chevil> and few connections are opening like a WAN (wide area network)
<chevil> maybe /etc/groups tries to enforce this
<chevil> to see wider networks
<chevil> and common interests
<chevil> well (it will become a tool for collaboration) once it will be filled with the right data, it's still very young
<chevil> the web 2.0 as we can call it just got more and more into ego surfing
<chevil> with networks of friends and relatives <chevil> /etc/groups is the opposite
<pueblo> why is the wider area so relevant for a network?
<chevil> wider area means you concentrate on important things
<chevil> and not waste your time in the blabla of all the blogs
<chevil> you formulate something to the distant and take some distance
<pueblo> you take distance from what?
<pueblo> your ego?
<chevil> let's say from your daily little stories
<chevil> and draw something much bigger <chevil> I never understood why people make these personal blogs
<chevil> after all, they need to read the tabloids <chevil> and tell their little stories?
<chevil> as if they were of the few?
<pueblo> well but in a way people want to mediate themselves, somehow it's better than tv mass control or do you think is the same domination?
<chevil> in the tone and the style, it's the same imitation
<chevil> just to put you as the actor
<chevil> of the same show
<chevil> mediating oneself can be seducing and useful and was one one of the idea of giss.tv
<chevil> But I'm speaking of this personal way of publishing one's stories
<chevil> the diary attitude
<chevil> which might do good to oneself but is mainly without interest for everyone

<pueblo> In many countries the internet is not high on bandwidth and internet is not really a known medium for people, do you think this will change?

<pueblo> don't you see Internet tv as an alternative to tv?

<chevil> well when china will stop censoring contents that will be a step

<chevil> bandwidth is not the only concern

<chevil> and I would not recommend to everyone to be connected

<chevil> It's really not a solution to every issue

<chevil> Internet tv mainly reproduce tv, it's mainly a global VCR

<chevil> where I can see Brazilian tv shows

<pueblo> can you name some innovative examples?

<chevil> well I was seeing giss as 'giss is not tv' it should have been called gint actually

<chevil> and was made for spontaneous transmission

<chevil> of a meditation in Hawaii or another strange thing

<chevil> without presentation and 'tv format'

<chevil> also the streams from Palestine didn't have any subtitles or explanations

<chevil> and it's still open to this kind of experience/ live experiments

<chevil> even though people use it in the traditional way

<pueblo> so what you promote is a sort of 'sense of being there' more than another productive effect?, even if it may be informative

<chevil> yes being there and feeling there are other people out there too

<pueblo> right

<chevil> But precisely not taking the analysis that the tv makes

<chevil> through the grid of economy and history

<pueblo> precisely avoiding it?

<chevil> yes

<chevil> as you should see there is actually just one big tv

<chevil> in several languages

<chevil> getting the same information from the same sources

<pueblo> but how do you avoid into falling into small little everyday stories from groups if you're outside the grids of history?

<chevil> there is not one history, people can reach their own

<chevil> that is more than little histories

<chevil> like the Linux user group of Palestine

<chevil> they have a History not histories

<chevil> but that's not the official one

<pueblo> do they bring together Linux to the Palestinian struggle?

<chevil> well it should be part of the liberation and also to boycott western goods

<chevil> but now all is darkened by violence

<chevil> and it's difficult to build anything in that context

<pueblo> what in your view would be the ideal conditions to make a free software project grow in a community

<chevil> it should be stated that everybody would receive the same support and importance

<chevil> and everybody should keep an 'open mind'

<chevil> that's the most difficult to achieve with people with a scientific background

<chevil> when everybody stays in its domain of competence and doesn't listen to other sensibilities

<chevil> (and that's usually what happens)

<chevil> there is no cross-feeding (of the 5000? (joke))

<chevil> I actually see productive examples of communities in Spain

<chevil>l ike giss.tv is not only programmers..

<chevil> so let's hope this model can succeed

## Rotterdam: Time to Learn

[7] http://puredata.org

FLOSS can be more specific in its installation, development and configuration than the majority of proprietary software. It is not really necessary to be an advanced developer to be able to program an application with FLOSS. This can be observed in the domain of digital arts as for instance in music and Digital Signal Processing. With software as Pure Data, artists are building instruments which don't exist in the market and making applications completely advanced and different.[7] With this graphical programming environment is possible to control robots and systems of sensors. With software like this, even if it is possible to use it as a regular sound editor, its possibilities may go far beyond the domain of the common audio applications that can be currently found on the market. With FLOSS it is also possible to link software in chains, with low level UNIX scripts as 'glue'. It is possible to use software starting from building blocks. Florian Cramer makes the analogy between Lego and Playmobil, since they were very popular games in Germany in the '70s. While in Playmobil all the situations arrive complete and ready to be used, in Lego, many situations and configurations can be built. Building blocks are given to assemble ships and planes. With Playmobil you make everything 'out of the box', something ready to be used. Whereas in Lego or at least in classical Lego the pirate ship is possible but is more difficult to build. But, is also possible to take the building blocks and make something completely different. With Lego it is more difficult because you don't have something ready to use (shrink-wrapped), yet it means that you need to have certain abilities to be able to build the suggested models whilst at the same time there is more flexibility which can serve for unexpected configurations. FLOSS is like Lego, which means that it is more difficult and thus necessary to invest more time. It is necessary to obtain a higher level of ability to be able to use it in a productive way and also you don't have that instant gratification of something that is ready to be used. It is precisely because of these aspects that FLOSS has a special relevance in the domain of digital media and especially in experimental art practices. The model behind Lego has a higher potential and is more flexible, it gives more freedom in relation to the software industry. It gives more freedom to develop everything that you may have in mind and not just what the industry has in mind.

Even if you need to invest more time, perhaps it is this lapse of time that makes learning more effective, full of relations and more enduring. Peter Westenberg from Constant Bruxelles refers to this kind of learning on a user group project of open Source Video Editing and work on the FLOSS video editor Cinelerra.[8] A group of users have set-up a wiki where they document their progress with the tools and tasks used to run an open source video editing project.[9]

[8] http://cinelerra.org

[9] http://osvideo.constantvzw.org/

[10] PeterWestenberg in interview in Bruxelles, November 2007

*It goes from building up a computer that will be running Cinelerra making clear all the prices online and where to find the appropriate hardware. It also includes a pool of links on the web. It all goes in between giving tips and hints based on your own experience but also and for me this is the most interesting part, how to be able to reflect on things that may be very annoying. It allows you to go into a bit of a reflective mode and make more sense and be more sensitive on what you're doing. In a sense is nice to have this continuous reporting going on because it brings you back to reality and you become aware on why you are doing it. It is a simple process but for me is very effective.*[10]

What is the reason for a user to be engaged on her own learning? How is learning affected, influenced, improved by a higher level of observation? Free software proposes a different kind of time compared to closed proprietary applications. In free software time is slower, at least until the learner becomes an expert. Another question, what kind of learning is proposed by closed proprietary applications? To learn procedures without understanding why you are following them sets a fragile condition where you might be adapting your cognition to hidden designs. You might as well be adapting to dependencies that will become artefacts for the way you learn, like the need for menu's, clickable icons, automated menus etc. Time runs fast with proprietary software but, what happens when you want to be independent from added factors in your learning? Some people say that Linux and FLOSS are difficult, but in reality people spend years learning how to use windows and Photoshop.

## FLOSS and computer industry

In relation to the use of software, the main determinant is the computer industry. Movements and tendencies in design and innovation are linked together with the politics of computer software industries.

*It's totally clear that most free software development today is market driven and basically, why is it so? Because despite this 'Lego flexibility' there are some commercial applications with just a lot of economical interest in them. For example most of the internet infrastructure actually works on free software, the whole Domain Name System runs on free software, most mail servers, FTP servers, web servers are run on free software, there are also proprietary ones but in comparison you would see about two thirds of internet server infrastructures are based on free software. Also in embedded devices, for example, if you have TV set-up boxes they often run Linux inside, even if you don't see it from the outside, its just a generic digital video recorder or something like this but it's a Linux box. If you have internet routers, DSL modems often they're Linux devices so there is a real commercial interest in them and for the companies that make them, It often makes sense to invest in free software development because they have a commercial interest in that. So, let's say, a company is developing a router and they're selling the box, but through Linux they get this software for nothing, maybe they need to apply some tricks because of the Linux licensing model, they need to publish these tricks and give them back to the public and this is how the whole system works. A company like IBM has a focus specifically on Linux and Free software and the free software development, it's a completely commercial company with a very large economic interest up to billions of dollars of revenue in cash flow. The point for them is that in the 1990s they restructured themselves from a product company to a service company so what happens is that a company goes to IBM and says for our company we want to have a mail server, we want to have a webserver, we want to have a calendar server and so on and IBM just installs it and you get IBM machines that run these services and you pay quite a fee, you pay 10000 dollars a year and this infrastructure is running, for a costumer of IBM it makes absolutely no difference whether those machines run LINUX or whether they run IBM or other proprietary UNIX. IBM discovered, we make more profit if we put free software onto our computers because we sell integrated services. This also works for the server division of Hewlet Packard for example but it doesn't work in other fields of the software industry and mainly in PC desktop computing, because in PC desktop computing you really have the model of software as of a shrink-wrapped product, as something that you buy in a box. If you buy Microsoft Office if you buy something like 'In design' or any Adobe product, Photoshop, whatever, it's really a box that you buy and install.*

*This is not the business model for most let's say, nonconsumer software, most server software is not sold that way, but through server's contracts. This is why for those companies the server software, doesn't make really a difference whether the software is free or not and using free software saves them money and makes them more competitive.*

[11] from interview with Florian Cramer

[12] http://www.sindominio.net/ bricolaje/brico/tallersnext.html

[13] http://bancocomun.org/

*An economic model behind free software? – it is very capitalistic, because companies like Red Hat or IBM, they make billions with Free software but then if you look on the other hand how many developers really are there employed and get payed and what do they get payed in comparison with what they would get payed in a company like Microsoft or Oracle or let's say BIOS then of course there is also the dark side of Free Software, is that there is a lot of exploitation going on. You have free developers who in many or most cases make unpaid development and that gets commercially exploited on a large scale.*[11]

**Barcelona: Time to Recycle**

Taller de Bricolaje sexual is a project run by Orit Kruglanski and Carla Peirano. Their practice of running DIY sex toy workshops has been mainly developed in Barcelona and they are related to other local instances of work and free/libre economies such as Universitat Pirata, Yo Mango and the now closed cultural community squat center Miles de Viviendas.[12] In relation to the Open free/libre movement, Bricolaje sexual focuses on the use of time so it can be liberated for the manufacture of sexual toys. This liberation refers to time spent to reverse engineer certain sexual toy's technology to be implemented with recycled materials. The liberation operates in making open technical knowledge related to electronics and in experimenting inside other forms of economies like recycling. In contrast with the transnational porn industry, DIY Sex toys use recycled electronics like motors and natural silicons. Sex toys made in these workshop are free from transnational porn industry and it is one example of progress in the evolution towards the recuperation of autonomous time (free for play and pleasure!). The work of Bricolaje is embedded in a larger domain of hardware libre, that has a number of examples in Barcelona and Spain (like arduino.cc from Cuartielles et al, Bruno Vianna (UP, survivalelectronics.org) and the hangar.org electronics workshop)

Another example is Platoniq (Susana Noguero, Olivier Schulbaum and Ignacio Garcia) who perform a practice using libre software and media under Creative Commons licences. They currently work on BCC, (Banco Común de Conocimientos), archives and databases of practices and common knowledge.[13] Together with databases they make gatherings, set up temporary recording studios and create databases about procedures and experiences, they make visible another approach to Free software. We may think of it not only in its technical dimension but in terms of knowledge, a layer of code that overlaps the technical dimension. In the Burn station it is possible to record and play media under Creative Commons licence using free software in a live Linux installation. The group behind Platoniq is a group of audiovisual artists, archive designers and programmers. They work on the perspective of the collector and social organizer. Their new project 'BCC' implies a meeting of people and a creation of systems for knowledge production. Their work involves a reflection about the economy of media and free information as well as a restructuring of time in favour of dedication to collecting and organising experience.

The case of Platoniq is also interesting because in the FLOSS movement the boundaries between developers and users are dynamic and mobile.

> *The Burn Station is a combination of FLOSS applications, which is very characteristic to this type of software and of open code in general since it is software that is very open to hacking and removes the strict boundaries between users and developers, it is open to unusual configurations that can be customized and tailor made and adjusted to the needs of each user.*[14]
>
> *Many times the user becomes a developer to solve its need of design for her own specific machine, a machine that is composed of many different parts and dimensions that surpass the technical realm.*[15]

**Bruxelles: Time to be Autonomous**

An example of the quest for autonomy in labour is the work of Open Source Publishing, an initiative by Constant in Bruxelles.[16] The idea of this group is to make graphic design independent from the monopolies of Macromedia and Adobe. They have developed a repackaging of connected applications: a chain of applications using 'glue' scripts programmed in python. Applications as Inkscape, Scribus and Gimp are associated with each other to obtain all the steps in the production chain of graphical media; posters, brochures, publications and books. The aim is that all steps from desktop to the printer should be solved using FLOSS in order to make a

[14] from interview with Florian Cramer, Rotterdam July, 2005

[15] 'Alongside the proto-machinic tool and technological machines there are also concepts of social machines. For example, the city is a mega-machine; it functions like a machine. Linguistic theoreticians such as Chomsky have introduced the concept of the "abstract machine" inhabiting linguistic or syntagmatic machines. Many biologists today refer to 'machines' in relation to the living cell, to bodily organs, to individuation and even to the social body; here, too, the concept of the machine becoming established. In the domain of idealities - another universe of reference altogether - we are witnessing the broadening of the concept of the machine - that of the musical machine for example, and idea now being developed by a number of contemporary musicians. Logic machine, cosmic machine; some theoreticians are even referring to the earth's ecosystem as a living being, or a machine in my own broad sense of the term. And looking back twenty years or so we might also evoke the "desiring

machines" which take up the theory of psychoanalytical part-objects – the "objet a" as desiring machine – but in the form of elements which are not reducible to objects adjacent to the human body. It is, rather, a question of objects of desire, machines of desire, objects-subjects of desire and vectors of partial subjectification, which open up far beyond the body and familial relations, on to social and cosmic ensembles and all types of universes of reference.' Felix Guattari. On Machines, 1994.

[16] http://ospublish.constantvzw.org/?cat=19

competitive alternative to suites like Indesign or Adobe. This project is far from realisation and has become, for some artists and designers, an area of experimentation and independence from aesthetics and dependencies imposed by transnational software companies. To find out ways to be autonomous from the means of production imposed by transnational software companies and at the same time, of complying with efficiency standards is in itself an alternative use of time in the context of learning.

Femke Snelting is an artist and graphic designer interested in using only FLOSS to realise her practice. In the case of graphic design this is very complicated. Just as SVG, for high resolution work on the web, is not being supported by Adobe anymore, the tools for web design and graphic design are monopolized by the fusion of Adobe and Macromedia. The proposal of Open Source Publishing is not to program an application from zero but to chain the processes of already existing tools. Through python scripts it is possible to connect Scribus, Inkscape and Gimp to design a document and take it to the printer.

*Understanding that design is an interesting and strange discipline that is somewhere between hyper commercialized and totally fixated on efficiency and flow and at the same time it's about representation, it's about language and communication, so it is both very interesting and very uninteresting. For designers to switch to other kinds of software that are not totally fluent, efficient and reliable is difficult, just because of the practical restraints of having to work with deadlines and getting things to a printer and not being able to take risks there. That's one part and the other part is that most of designers, as a result of the Adobe monopoly, because basically there is only one software company that makes professional design software which is Adobe for any package you can think of. Designers have become completely numb and unaware of their relation with software and experience it as completely transparent. There is no sense of what it does, it's like water, air, something that is completely transparent or experience it as completely transparent. That makes it both difficult and extra interesting to try and think about what happens when you step out that neutral habitat into something else.*

*We started to work with a few designers from Brussels and slowly we started to see that at the one hand it was interesting to think seriously about moving our design practice to work to open source not only for the software but also for the way you think of what happens after something is printed and think realistically of what would it mean for an agency or freelance design and also because we were getting jobs, this was interesting, people recognized this as something interesting but there is not much people having that kind of experience to really make things on a professional design level with free software.*

*Over time we decided to start a project much more as a design agency half playing with that idea to try to think about the kind of work processes we were doing and how our economy was working,what is efficiency for us, what is production, how do we deal with time, who takes the risk when something goes wrong? How can you think about software in the kind of history of design tools? But at the same time to make things, to take on commissions and to produce books, magazines and stuff. This is actually what we are doing now which is I think, is a very interesting and exotic stage at the same time is of course scary because that means that also that kind of commercial 'slick' side of design comes closer, because there is always some desire for that either in the ones making or in the ones asking.*

*Open Source publishing as well as the user group of Cinelerra propose a new way of using software that may compete the holistic vision that is imposed by I-life, I-world, I-universe by the everything goes together policy of using software from one specific company 'One of the most exciting learning experiences has been to learn how to work with the command line and I'm not the only one and I see people around me that are making a shift of mind because of understanding or speaking to their computer in a different way but at the same time for making visually complex images it's totally not an option is not possible to do it with the command line it's interesting to think about the relation between a visual world and a scripted world, I'm not saying that they are separate from each other, there is some need for a graphical interface and the problem is that if all energy goes now into a mock interface which is not even so unsuccessful blend of windows and mac trying to be the best of both worlds that's where Gnome and Ubuntu development is in and there is this idea that Graphical user interface is what makes Linux for Human Beings so it means, it's the lowest denominator of use or of imagining graphical interface, meaning that all the*

[17] Interview to Femke Snelting in Bruxelles, November 2007

*energy is put into making it user friendly lower barrier and the result is very disappointing. Not really connected to the kind of excitement of Linux, that of being able to open something up or look at things in a different way. Is not transported to how it is visually developed I find it hard and I really miss that kind of richness of environment but that has not much to do with the shrink-wrapped because I'm totally happy to get rid of that. One of the things I find very interesting to see is how different programs have different histories of doing interfaces and understanding the narrative of the program through its interface. Linux distributions start to shrink-wrap themselves because they don't think interfaces are interesting, There is a split between the idea of 'interfaces are for dummies' and 'good Linux users use the command line'. Interfaces are absolutely vital to creative work, it's just that is maybe not the interface that we know right now. I hope not...*[17]

## Conclusion

In this report I have tried to articulate a number of conversations to show the existence of particular understandings of the relations between time and autonomy. In my view these relations are dynamized by the characteristics of FLOSS and by the communities around it. I have described a few southern examples of Free Libre Open culture that go beyond software. These examples mainly integrate technical aspects with domains that relate to cultural inventiveness and to the autonomy arising from the search for alternative ways of learning, creating and participating. They propose a reinvention of domains that otherwise remains fixated upon a model of time dedicated to production.

Acknowledgments

Thanks to Yves Degoyon, Femke Snelting, Peter Westenberg, Carla Peirano, Orit Kruglanski, Susana Noguero and Florian Cramer for our conversations.

# Open Source Art Again

Rob Myers

*Art is a game between all people of all periods.*
- Marcel Duchamp [1]

The concept of Open Source continues to inspire artists. But it is an intentionally vague concept that is often more confusing than enlightening. Unpacking this concept involves examination of the practices that are associated with it, and the ethical questions that it obscures. This reveals strategies that are of relevance to contemporary artistic practice and can place artists at the heart of current issues of free speech and the laws and technologies of censorship.

## Open Source

The concept of open source comes from computer software development. open source software is software that everyone can recreate and modify. This requires public access to the software's source code. The source code for a piece of software is equivalent to the score or preparatory work for a piece of music, drama or art, and it is similarly required to recreate or modify the finished work.

Closed Source software, as sold by corporations such as Microsoft, does not make its source code publicly available and trying to recreate or modify it is prohibited by law.

Open source was given its current definition in 1998[2] by hackers Bruce Perens[3] and Eric Raymond. For Raymond, the virtue of open source is its efficiency.[4] Open source, he argues, can create better products faster than the Closed Source method of writing software. Many of the most successful software programs in use today, particularly on the internet, have been produced in such a way.[5]

[1] Nicolas Bourriaud. Relational Aesthetics, Paris: Le Press du Reel, 2002.

[2] See http://opensource.org/history

[3] Chris DiBona, Sam Ockman, and Mark Stone, editors. Open Sources: Voices from the Open Source Revolution, Sebastopol: O'Reilly & Associates, Inc., 1999.

[4] Eric S. Raymond. The Cathedral and the Bazaar, Sebastopol: O'Reilly & Associates, Inc., 1999.

[5] For example the Apache web server, the Firefox web browser, the MySQL database and the GNU/Linux operating system. Of more interest to visual artists may be the Gimp image editor, Inkscape illustration program and Scribus DTP package.

The success of open source for software development in an age in which computers are the defining technology and guiding metaphor of society has inspired individuals and groups to try to apply its ideas to other areas of activity such as encyclopaedias, cartography, political activism, philosophy, theory, and art.[6] Yochai Benkler describes this general application of open source as 'commons based peer production': work made collaboratively and shared publicly by a community of equals. This has often proved more problematic than might be expected.[7] The idea of open source as a more efficient means of production doesn't explain why we should want to make philosophy or art more efficient, or what the form or advantage of that efficiency would be.

To take the example of the Open Congress event held at Tate Modern in 2005, artists struggled to find an open source ideology to apply to their art, activists struggled to find an open source ideology to apply to their organisations, and critical theorists invoked Deleuze and Spinoza to try to fill in the gaps.[8] There was a genuine interest in the potential of open source, but frequent confusion over what that might actually mean outside of software development.

The problem is that the name open source was deliberately chosen for its meaninglessness and ideological vacuity.[9] This was intended to make the results of a successful new ideology more palatable to large corporations by disguising its ethical content. That ideology is Free Software.

[6] J. David Bolter, Turing's Man: Western Culture in the Computer Age, Chapel Hill: University Of North Carolina Press, 1984.

[7] Yochai Benkler. The Wealth of Networks : How Social Production Transforms Markets and Freedom. New Haven: Yale University Press, 2006.

[8] See http://www.tate.org.uk/onlineevents/archive/open_congress/

[9] Although there is some evidence that a previous use of the phrase 'Open Source' dates back to at least the late 1980s.

[10] Richard M. Stallman, Free Software, Free Society: Selected Essays of Richard M. Stallman, Boston: Free Software Foundation, 2002.

## Free Software

American computer programmer Richard Stallman articulated the modern concept of free software in 1984 in an environment of increasing restrictions on the use and production of software.[10] free software is not a radical new development, it is a programme of reform intended restore the more freewheeling ethics software development that began to disappear when software became copyrightable in the USA in the late 1970s.

Software is used to achieve many different ends within pluralistic society. Its use is as widespread and diverse as the written word was following the invention of the printing press. Free software can therefore be understood historically and ethically as the defence of pluralistic freedom against a genuine threat. It is an ethical issue, a matter of freedom. This is very different from being a new method of organisation or a more efficient means of production.

Stallman defines free software as a set of Four Freedoms; the freedom to use, study, modify and share software. These freedoms are indivisible.[11] If you have all four freedoms then you are free to use software. If you have only two or three then you are not. There are other definitions of free software but they tend to add redundant or contradictory terms and are best avoided.[12]

[11] Stallman, ibid.

[12] Such as the Debian Free Software Guidelines, see: http://www.debian.org/social_contract

[13] See http://www.gnu.org/licenses/quick-guide-gplv3.html

Once software users' freedoms are restored and protected, in the future by legal reform but until then by measures such as the GNU General Public Licence, this has the effect of encouraging collaborative and public software development.[13] Licences like the GPL are a good example of measures that have been imitated outside of the context of software development. Collaborative, public software development protected by such licences is more efficient and can achieve higher

quality than closed source 'proprietary' software development. It is these effects of the pursuit of freedom that open source focuses on at the expense of obscuring the very causes that produce them.

It is important to remember that these gains, and the existence of commons-based peer production, are effects or products of freedom and the protection of people's rights. Without the guiding principles of the ethics of free software the necessity and direction of open source projects cannot be accounted for. Open source cannot account for itself or suggest which tasks are necessary or important. It may become tempting to compromise some of the Four Freedoms to increase the efficiency or quality that are open source's promises, or in the name of political or economic goals.

This kind of confusion has led to projects such as Wikipedia trying to create an open space for anyone to use as they wish. This leads to Social Darwinism, not freedom, as the contents of that space are determined by a battle of wills. Wikipedia has had to reproduce many of the organisational structures and mechanisms of established free software projects in order to tackle these problems. But people still regard its earlier phase as a model for emulation, when it should probably serve as more of a warning.

Within free software projects, if contributions are deemed to be of acceptable quality, they are added to the project's source code by its appointed gatekeepers. If not, they are rejected and advice given. This methodology is a structured and exclusive one, but it is meritocratic. Any contribution of sufficient quality can be accepted, and if someone makes enough such contributions they themselves may gain the trust required to become a gatekeeper. This hierarchy and the decisions process is public and usually transparent, and if any individuals do not agree with the governance of the project they are free to take a copy of the source code of the project and start their own 'fork' of it.

Free software projects have produced commons based peer production only because of their practical pursuit of freedom. As with the term open source, the concept of commons based peer production easily confuses and misleads. Failing to account for the causes and effects of the pursuit of freedom can render commons based peer production inexplicable and in need of economic or political induction.

This can lead to limits on the very freedom that actually produces the commons in order to protect investment (for neoliberal or robust individualist complainants) or class interests (for paleo-socialist complainants). It is important to not compromise the pluralism produced by the pursuit of freedom in order to answer non-pluralistic concerns. To do so becomes self-defeating because compromising the freedom of others denies the value of them to oneself.

There are strategies from free software that cannot work for art. Software can be replaced with a different, functionally equivalent, piece of software that does the same thing without loss. It is fungible. Art is not fungible. A Picasso is not a substitute for a Matisse artistically. This is not fetishism, it is a product of the fact that an artwork's construction is what it does, you cannot change an artwork without changing its effect. The free software strategy of creating replacements for unfree work therefore cannot work for art. This means that there can be no replacement for Modernist art that will remain covered by copyright and that these limitations must be dealt with through other means.

It is clear that open source obscures the very concept of freedom that leads to the beneficial effects identified by Raymond. 'Commons-based peer production' is no more useful. It is a market-rational economic description of what for many economists seems to be the irrationality of the epiphenomena of free software. Again, like open source, it discards the ethical concepts that lead to its own production.

For all these reasons it is therefore the condition of Freedom rather than the condition of open source that art should aspire to.

## Artistic Freedom

[14] Waldemar Januszczak. 'The Sistine Chapel has a Secret'. The Times, 2005.

Freedom is the principle from which the organisational and economic benefits of open source flow. In applying the ideas of free software, to art we should look first not to the effects of pursuing freedom for software users but to what freedom means for art. To map the concepts of free software into artistic practice the best starting point is to identify the concept or concepts of artistic freedom and to identify the threats against it and opportunities for it.

Freedom applies to individual human beings, not to objects. Artists have always learnt from, imitated, and built on the work of their peers and of previous generations of artists. The history of art consists, in no small part, of the study of genres, schools, iconography, and studios involving many different individuals over many generations. Society has always provided both an audience and inspiration for art in a reciprocal relationship. Successive generations of artists, and artists and society, have collaborated to make the canon of art.

Prior to the extension of copyright to cover art as well as literature, art was implicitly free. The physical artefacts of art were expensive to own and difficult or impossible to transport. But the content of art was free to use by other artists and for critics and commentators to critique. This representational freedom of artists, part of which is the freedom to depict and build or comment on existing culture, to continue the conversation of culture, is in no small part artistic freedom.

Generations of artists could riff on the theme of the crucifixion, and anyone could carve a statue of Venus. The production of Homeric verse was a multi-generational collaboration, and Shakespeare was a notorious plagiarist (or appropriator). Michaelangelo could appropriate Christian and pagan imagery to paint a ceiling:

> *the chapels funny shape [...] has the basic outline of a treasure chest in a pirate movie which was copied from an obscure Christian cartographer called Cosmas, whose chief claim to distinction is that he refused to accept that the earth was round. Cosmas insisted the earth was rectangular, and shaped, as it turned out, exactly like the Sistine Chapel.*[14]

Historically there are examples of artworks, such as Raphael's *Judgement Of Paris* (1515), that we only know from unauthorised copies. Had reproduction of those works been prevented, they would be lost. The same student of Raphael that made these copies won a lawsuit that Albrecht Durer brought against him in 1506 for copying Durer's etchings.[15] This pre-dates the start of the modern concept of copyright by a hundred years.

Marcel Duchamp addressed material and organisational limitations on the creation of art in one of his interviews:

> *When Rubens, or someone else, needed blue, he had to ask his guild for so many grams, and they discussed the question, to find out if he could have fifty or sixty grams, or more.*[16]

It is important to address material and organisational limitations, to create opportunities and support for the creation of art.

Art has always suffered from censorship. Religious, political and cultural restrictions on what can be shown by art have been joined more recently by economic and technological limitations. Calls for religious, political and cultural censorship continue to be a threat to artistic freedom. Opposing them should be a core part of the defence of artistic freedom.

One of the weaknesses of simply imitating the strategies of free software is that software does not suffer from such calls, and so it has no strategies for coping with them. Given this, supporting legal reform and opposing more restrictive laws is vital. But supporting open critique is another way of tackling such calls, and free software does supply means of doing this.

Censorship through restrictive actions have been joined by restrictive laws and now technological restrictions. The chilling effects of these on art are difficult to precisely quantify as they concern work not made and work not seen. But examples may illustrate some of these effects.

Yves Klein patented the recipe for his International Klein Blue pigment in 1960.[17] This would in theory have prevented anyone reproducing the precise colour for twenty years, limiting any artists who wished to comment on Klein's work or to take his ideas further.

Jeff Koons has lost several lawsuits from copyright holders for work that he has used as the basis of artworks, starting with the photographer of a postcard he based the sculpture *String Of Puppies* on [18], although he has more recently succeeded in a lawsuit brought by the copyright holders of photographs that he used as source material for the painting *Niagara*.[19]

[15] Daniel McClean and Karsten Schubert, Dear Images: art, copyright and culture, London: ICA and Ridinghouse, 2002.

[16] Pierre Cabanne, editor. Dialogues With Marcel Duchamp, Cambridge:Da Capo Press, Inc, 1987.

[17] Allegedly French patent 63471.

[18] See Rogers v. Koons, 960 F.2d 301 (2d Cir. 1992)

[19] Blanch v. Koons, No. 03 Civ. 8026 (LLS), S.D.N.Y., Nov. 1 2005

Andy Warhol lost a lawsuit from Patricia Caulfield, the copyright holder of the flower photograph that Warhol used as the source for his 1964 'Flowers' series.[20] The Warhol Foundation allow use of Warhol's images for the creation of art and non-commercial use, although academics do still pay reproduction fees which seems to go against Warhol's own appropriationist spirit.

Warhol and Koons could afford such costs, although the time spent defending lawsuits is time that could better be spent making art. Less established artists can rarely afford the money or the time that legally defending their right to make art demands without assistance.

Tom Forsythe's photographs of a Barbie doll in a blender led to a lawsuit from the corporate owners of the Barbie trademark. Tom fought the lawsuit with help from free speech charity The American Civil Liberties Union. His eventual victory inspired a project to celebrate it.[21]

Painter Joy Garnett used an image that she found on the internet as inspiration for a painting *Molotov*, 2004. After exhibiting it she found herself the subject both of legal threats from lawyers acting for the photographer's agency and of a campaign of support on the internet involving making derivative images of Garnett's own derivative of the image.[22]

Artists can binitiate restrictions around their work as well as suffering from them. Photography of Anish Kapoor's *Cloud Gate*, 2005, was forbidden by the owners of the plaza in Chicago that it was installed in.[23] Photography of Christo and Jean Claude's *Gates* in New York's Central Park was forbidden by the artists themselves[24], although this led to an organised campaign of photography and online parodies in protest.[25]

Even sketching in museums can be affected. When security guards tell children to stop drawing, whether this is a correct application of museum policy or a side effect of a general environment of strong copyright, the effects of copyright have gone too far.[26]

As Joywar and the reaction to *The Gates* show, when media or corporate interests, or even other artists, seek to limit artists and the public from creating their own visual representations civil disobedience is often the result. This is as it should be. Bad law cannot be the limit of society's forms.

[20] McClean, ibid.

[21] See http://www.barbieinablender.org/

[22] See http://www.firstpulseprojects.net/joywar.html

[23] See http://newurbanist.blogspot.com/2005/01/copyrighting-of-public-sp.html

[24] See http://blog.stayfreemagazine.org/2005/02/more_on_christo.html

[25] See http://flickr.com/groups/79972013@N00/pool/

[26] See http://www.boingboing.net/2005/01/08/stop_sketching_littl.html

[27]
Karl Popper. The Open Society And Its Enemies, Oxford: Routledge, 2002.

[28]
Isaiah Berlin, Liberty, Oxford: Oxford University Press, 2002.

[29]
Robert Atkins and Svetlana Mintcheva, editors. Censoring Culture: Contemporary Threats to Free Expression, New York New Press, new York, USA,2006.

Artistic freedom is part of the more general category of freedom of speech within an Open Society.[27] Freedom of speech often becomes 'freedom of expression' in artistic discussion, although 'freedom of representation' might be a more useful concept as art more often causes problems because of what it depicts than how the artist was feeling when creating the depiction.

Support for freedom of speech involves both opposing censorship and providing support for those who would otherwise struggle to have their voice heard. These are the negative and positive freedoms of speech to use Isaiah Berlin's terms.[28] They apply equally to art as to the written or spoken word.

One aspect of art's value to society is that art is free to find new ways of looking at the world. In order to do this, artists must be free to depict whatever it is necessary to do so, however it is necessary to do so. They might be prevented from doing so by new laws, for example by laws against depicting trademarked or copyrighted images or objects. Or they might be prevented from doing so by technology, for example by anti-copying measures on electronic media.

Calling such measures 'censorship' is not historically accurate, and expanding the category of censorship beyond government silencing of opposition is contentious. But there is no word that better fits the prevention of art's creation of new forms by reactionary institutional elements through new legal and technological measures.[29]

A major threat to artistic freedom, then, is censorship in its current legal and technological forms. This is a limit on how art can be created and received, a restriction of freedom. To restore this freedom will require legal reform in the long term, but in the short term artists can look to free software for strategies.

'Free Art' would mean that artists and society are free to produce and deal with art. Free software is concerned with the freedom of computer users to use software. Use in this context means utilisation, not exploitation, use value not exchange value. And it means freedom as a general principle, not something contingent or alienable. Freedom of use does not cover trying to use software to remove the freedom of others to use software any more than freedom of contract covers slavery. Use of software covers production of software as well, since software is used to make software.

Artistic freedom covers the ability of artists, audience, academics and critics to experience, comment on (verbally or in new art), study and produce art [30]. Limiting this freedom is censorship in its expanded sense. Opposing censorship in its expanded sense is the defence of artistic freedom.

Many artists have internalised the Romantic myth of creative genius and see their work as apart from society and needing protection from it through strong copyright and other measures. They have forgotten their own process of learning, their own influences, the criticism and journalism that supports their reputations, and that their audience's attention is part of the value of their art. Artists are tenants of culture, to quote Nicolas Bourriaud quoting Michel de Certeau.[31]

Artists learn from other artists and depict the broader visual environment that is produced by society. Artists are supported by and will learn from critics, academics and theorists. To charge for them to provide this support or to otherwise restrict it is unfair. A backlash against academic image reproduction fees has recently resulted from this situation.[32]

Restrictions on artistic freedom stifle art and reduce its value to society. Appropriation artists and artists who depict contemporary events and the contemporary visual environment will be the first to feel these restrictions. Such art is an 'interrogation of meaning' and will generate precisely the kind of challenges to established or desired meanings that censorship is designed to preclude.[33] These restrictions are being imposed from both within and without the artworld. Art must therefore be part of a broader Free Culture to both defend itself and to avoid causing harm to others.

'Open Content' is a simple mapping of the name open source onto cultural works through the terminology of the recording industry. 'Content' is what entertainment industry middlemen call production-line music and films. Reviewers of disposable pop music use it as an insult.[34] A better term for creative work is 'culture', and as we have established, a more meaningful word than open is 'free'.

'Free Culture' explains both the principle, freedom, and the subject of that principle, cultural as expressed through works and performances. Its advantages are the same as those of free software over open source. The current understanding of free culture was popularised by lawyer and

[30] Following Stallman, freedom always seems to come in fours.

[31] Bourriaud, ibid.

[32] Robert Simon. Editorial. The British Art Journal Vol. IV no. 3, 2007.

[33] Paul D. Miller aka Dj Spooky that Subliminal Kid. Rhythm Science. MIT Press, Cambridge, Massachusetts, USA, 2004.

[34] Charlie Brooker. Supposing ... sandi thom is the musical antichrist. The Guardian, 2006.

academic Lawrence Lessig's book of the same name.[35] Lessig founded the organisation Creative Commons to address some of the issues he identified.[36] Their imitation of free software's licensing tactic has led to a strong association between alternative licensing and the concept of free culture.

[35] Lawrence Lessig. Free Culture: How Big Media Uses Technology and the Law to Lock Down Culture and Control Creativity. The Penguin Press, New York, New York, USA, 2004.

[36] See http://www.creativecommons.org/

[37] Lessig, ibid.

**Licensing**

To protect the freedom of others to draw from and comment on your work is to protect your own freedom to do the same with their work. And with your own work, should you become alienated from it for whatever reason. Licences are a strong way of protecting this. Art as a whole has a social contract but the precise details vary between kinds of art. Appropriation art is the canary in the coal mine of artistic freedom. Once appropriation is restricted, criticism and subsequently the freedom to depict the visual environment as a whole will be restricted.

Alternative licensing uses the tools of copyright licensing to add freedoms rather than impose restrictions. Once an alternative licence is applied to a copyrightable work, such as a piece of art, anyone who copies it or creates new work based on it is free to do so as long as they follow the licence. Ordinarily they would have no such freedom in law, outside of the bounds of Fair Use (or Fair Dealing).

Fair use is mostly an American concept. Other legal systems have more limited exceptions to copyright, and would not allow artistic use of copyrighted imagery under the same terms. Alternative licences are useful for protecting fair use style freedoms in such jurisdictions. Even within American law, Fair use is a legal defence not a right, and must be defended in court if challenged. Against media corporations this will be a very uneven battle, and Lawrence Lessig has described fair use as little more in practice than'the right to hire a lawyer'.[37] So alternative licensing is useful for protecting fair use even within American law.

There are a number of different alternative licences available and several different kinds of licence. Some disallow commercial use. Since the work can be copied for free, and since the person licensing the work may want to use the results in turn, this isn't as useful as it might seem. Some disallow modifying the work, but the work can still be modified under fair use. Some simply allow the work to be copied and used with very few restrictions, but then the freedoms that make that possible can be removed in turn, shutting the audience and the original artist out.

The most successful licences, used by non-art projects such as GNU and Wikipedia allow work to be copied and new work to be based on it as long as people have the same freedoms over any copies or new work.[38] This reversing of copyright to protect rather than remove people's freedoms was named 'copyleft' by Stallman.

The range of work covered by copyleft licences produces a 'commons' of work that people can draw from and contribute to freely. The historical metaphor of the commons comes from land owned and managed by a community rather than a landowner. The often cited 'tragedy of the commons', designed to prove that private ownership is better than common ownership, ignores this fact. It is important to remember that this cultural commons is a product of copyleft, which is a product of the ethical position of freedom. It is not an end in itself. Talk of the commons without talk of freedom can introduce broken metaphors from agricultural commons, or measures to protect the commons that would compromise the freedoms of individuals that give rise to the commons.

By relying on ever-strengthening copyright law, copyleft might appear to support the very thing it is designed to oppose. But this is not the case. If copyright law disappeared, copyleft would lose its force. Licensing is very popular with the 'Web 2.0' internet bubble, where it is seen as a source of free labour for web sites and networks. Web 2.0 is an expression of the information knowledge work culture that Harold Liu identifies as opposed to the literary and artistic culture of history.[39] Objections to licensing from within discourse about both Web 2.0 and knowledge work can be answered with the the argument that is a form of intensification or ironisation of copyright law, a judo throw that uses its opponent's own weight against it.[40]

Licensing is not sufficient for artistic freedom, it is a measure against one specific threat to artistic freedom, the over-extension of copyright. Copyleft licences are also not an end in themselves and must change over time to best protect freedom against any new threats that emerge. New restrictions on freedom such as Digital Rights Management technology did not exist when the first copyleft licences were being drawn up, and modern copyleft licences do indeed tackle them. It is the content of the threat to freedom, expressed in any form be it legal or technological or other, that the form of copyleft licences must change to match in order to protect the content of freedom.

[38] See http://www.gnu.org/ and http://wikipedia.org/

[39] Harold Liu. The Laws of Cool: Knowledge Work and the Culture of Information. University Of Chicago Press, Chicago, Illinois, US, 2004.

[40] Christine Harold, OurSpace: Resisting the Corporate Control of Culture, Minneapolis: University Of Minnesota Press, 2007.

Copyleft was designed to protect the freedom to use computer software. But it can protect freedom of speech and artistic freedom as well. Due to the history of computer programming, programs are created and copyrighted as textual instructions to the computer. Copyleft is a means of removing the restrictions on freedom that copyright imposes not just on software but on any fixed form of expression. Since no small part of contemporary censorship is copyright-related, copyleft can be a useful means of addressing censorship where it is applied.

Copyleft cannot protect freedom where it does not apply. If artists wish to work from art or media that are copyrighted but not licensed, they must fall back upon fair use. If artists wish to depict objects or environments that are trademarks, there are not even licences for that at the moment. Broader reform and ongoing protection against restrictive laws is therefore necessary, copyleft is not in itself a sufficient protection.

This also shows why art should share licences with other media rather than designing specific licences. Doing so gives artists access to those parts of the media that adopt copyleft in return. And it also makes artists work available to critics, academics and other artists who wish to work with it. This can help drive awareness of the artists' work, increasing their reputation and thereby the opportunities and remuneration available to them.

Copyleft for software enforces the social contract of freewheeling hacker software development, but this may be different from the social contract of fine art. The art-specific Free Art Licence is based on copyleft.[41] So is the more general (and more popular) Creative Commons BY-SA licence.[42] The only licence that attempts to enforce the social contract of a particular creative community is the Sampling licence from Creative Commons and Negativland.[43] The Sampling License reflects the standards of the sampling and mash-up musical community, but it has some peculiarities, it is not considered 'free' by any common definition, and has since been deprecated by Creative Commons.

The social contract that the Sampling licence embodies is that of Extended fair use.[44] This allows transformative use and sampling but not wholesale copying. This is similar to the social contracts of appropriation art and of criticism. Copyleft goes further than this, allowing copying and incorporation of the work untransformed.

[41] See http://artlibre.org/licence/lalgb.html

[42] See http://creativecommons.org/licenses/by-sa/3.0/

[43] See http://creativecommons.org/about/sampling

[44] Negativland. 'Two relationships to a cultural public domain', California: Seeland Media-Media, 2005. Included with the CD No Business.

For music, Negativland's focus, such wholesale copying is the hallmark of the peer-to-peer filesharing culture that has emerged following the release of Napster in 1999 and is now a freedom that is taken for granted by most music fans. So, copyleft better fits the audience's expectations here.

To suggest that artists should apply copyleft to their work in order to take a position on artistic freedom in society might appear to replay twentieth century (and earlier) arguments about political commitment.[45] 'It is always with the best intentions that the worst work is done.', to quote Oscar Wilde, and the effects of political volunteerism by artists ranges from the negligible (Surrealism) to the negative (Socialist Realism). But, for artists to protect artistic freedom is not volunteerism, rather, it is key to maintaining the possibility of new forms in art. It is a practical response to the genuine threat of censorship in old and new forms.

[45] Andrew Arato and Eike Gephardt, editors. Essential Frankfurt School Reader, London: Continuum, 1997.

**Collaboration**

Collaboration and appropriation are ways of individuals building on the work of others. Collaboration can be local or distributed, parallel or serial. Collaborators working together at the same geographical location are local collaborators, those working over the internet or meeting only occasionally and otherwise working apart are distributed. Collaboration by a group of people on work at the same time is parallel collaboration, collaboration on a series of revisions of that work over time is serial collaboration, which is also a way of describing appropriation.

The Surrealist drawing game 'exquisite corpse' is local serial collaboration, collaborative projects like GNU and Wikipedia are distributed parallel collaboration. Appropriation and critique are distributed serial collaboration.

Participation is what people generally mean when they say that a project or community is 'open'. People from outside the core of the project can join in and contribute to it. People can join the community without onerous membership tests.

Participation does not necessarily mean collaboration, and participation does not in itself guarantee freedom. It is possible for a group of collaborators to be closed to new members or external collaboration. Any pair or group of artists who collaborate privately do not have a participatory practice. It is possible for a project to be participatory without being collaborative. Social networking sites such as Facebook allow people to participate without necessarily collaborating on projects.[46]

[46] See http://www.facebook.com/

[47] Negativland, ibid

[48] See http://www.washingtonpost.com/wp-dyn/content/article/2007/07/11/AR2007071101996.html

[49] See http://wikipedia.org/

[50] See http://h2g2.com/

[51] See http://www.edge.org/3rd_culture/lanier06/lanier06_index.html

Successful projects have strong social contracts. The existing social contract for art bears more similarities to Negativland's concept of extended fair use than to copyleft.[47] Copyleft is not a match for this but it is a superset of this, and (fine) art objects cannot be replaced by electronic copies of the original.

Collaboration thrives when collaborators know that they will remain free to use the products of their collaboration. Wikipedia and GNU protect this social contract through their licences. The best way of signalling to potential collaborators that their freedom will be protected is to use such a licence. It isn't necessary to be planning to collaborate in order for such licences to be useful. Finished work released into the world with such a licence makes the work of appropriation and critique easier.

It is possible to organise collaboration without respecting the freedom of collaborators. Corporate 'user generated content' initiatives that take copyright from contributors in return for the possibility of a prize remove the freedom of contributors to use their own work. Lawrence Lessig calls this 'sharecropping'.[48]

Projects that deny participants commercial use of their own work have the same effect. And people who come to projects complaining that if only the licence was changed they'd be able to use it in a way that excludes its creators are wannabe 'free riders' by their own, economic, point of view and so should be ignored.

Wikipedia is a project to collaboratively create an encyclopaedia usable by anyone via the Internet. The site is licensed under a copyleft licence, meaning that anyone can add to or use it as long as they don't prevent anyone else from using it.[49] There was another project to create an online encyclopaedia that pre-dated Wikipedia, the h2g2 project, but that was not a freely usable project and as a result ultimately failed both commercially and in terms of popularity.[50]

Voluntary collaboration is not anti-individualistic, despite the charge levelled at Wikipedia by Jaron Lanier that it amounts to a collectivist 'digital maoism'.[51] Individuals can pursue their own ends within a supportive structure and thereby both add value to and receive value from that structure as a whole. But the value of both individual contributions and the structure as a whole can be lost if all contributions are accepted without evaluation or if the project succumbs to structurelessness.[52] The online collaborative literary project 'A Million Penguins' is a classic example of the incoherence that can result from this.[53]

The community arts project Remix Reading ran workshops and accepted contributions through its web site and assembled exhibitions in local arts venues curated from the results.[54] Various student shows run by chapters of freeculture.org[55] followed the Remix Reading model using the image sharing site Flickr to accept contributions and then curating shows both in the real world and in the virtual reality environment Second Life.[56]

These are mostly collaborative exhibitions of free work (and some non-free work under other Creative Commons licences, see the web site Freedom Defined for a good list of free licences), rather than works created collaboratively, although some appropriation and remix art was included.[57] This is a good model for supporting and promoting the production of freely licensed artworks.

When considering collaborative production of work one of the most successful examples from the world of software development is the Linux kernel. Anyone can submit work to be included in the project, anyone can discuss work that is submitted, but submissions are only included in the central repository for the project after evaluation by the project's leaders. Anyone can view that repository, but the project's leadership controls the release of official versions. This ensures both that value can be accepted and included from outside the project, and that substandard work and reworking of the project cannot get into the project or become associated with it.

It is easy to see how this model maps onto collaborative art shows mentioned above but finding evaluation criteria for collaborative production of individual artworks or series of artworks is a difficult challenge. The collaborative image making web site Kollabor8 avoids this problem by allowing each image to be forked from any previous version of an image and the results to be chosen by the audience.[58]

There are more examples of artistic collaboration than might be imagined. Any artistic duo is involved in a collaborative practice. Licensing protects both the freedom of other members of society to appropriate and critique work produced by such artists and the artists themselves to do so should their association end.

[52] See http://flag.blackened.net/revolt/hist_texts/structurelessness.html

[53] See http://www.amillionpenguins.com/

[54] See http://www.remixreading.org/

[55] See http://freeartshows.org/shows/past

[56] See http://flickr.com/photos/sharingisdaring2006/ and http://www.freeartshows.org/shows/past

[57] See http://freedomdefined.org/

[58] See http://www.kollabor8.org/

[59] Raymond, ibid.

[60] Marcel Mauss, The Gift - The Form and Reason for Exchange in Archaic Societies, Oxford: Routledge, 2001.

[61] See http://salrandolph.com/text/8/some-experiments-in-art-as-gift

Individual artists producing what they regard as finished works can support the ability of artists and critics to learn from, comment on, and build on their work with copyleft licensing. This helps anyone whose work might promote the artist. It also encourages and enables collaborations and uses of the work that could not be predicted to the artist and may be of unique value to art and to society.

## Economies

Eric Raymond describes the culture of open source as a 'Gift Economy'.[59] Again, this is a product of Freedom and cannot be substituted for or sustained without it. The concept of gift economies comes from Marcel Mauss' work in anthropology in the first half of the twentieth century[60]. In a gift economy, gifts are given with strong social expectations that gifts will be given in return. It is this social contract that people exposed to the idea of gift economies often forget, regarding gifts as (economically irrational) random acts of kindness where in fact they are more like the enforced sharing of alternative licences (law being a way of enforcing society's norms between strangers).

The free sharing of ideas and iconography in art is a kind of immaterial gift economy. Making a physical gift economy of art can be an interesting commentary on the materialism of the art world even in the era of relational art, and is a good investment in terms of one's reputation.

*Free Documenta* and various other solo projects organised by Sal Randolph, are a good example of creating a physical gift economy.[61] These include organising a global day of events with artists giving away prints of artworks or producing hundreds of blue paintings. Although they may appear to be random acts of kindness they do make a demand of their audience, to reflect the economic and social relations of the artworld. Against the backdrop of the global art market, that is no small demand.

Randolph and her collaborators are giving away works and reproductions of works that have cost money to produce. The freedom to share reproductions of work electronically via the internet reduces the value of copies of easily digitised and reproduced work to almost zero. The music and film industries have panicked in response to this, and have reacted with lawsuits and intrusive propaganda to people who advertise their work for free through sharing it. There is no evidence that they are reacting to a genuine threat or that their actions are affecting peoples' willingness to share.

The gift of near-zero-cost reproductions of recordings of work is not lost revenue, it is promotion. Artists no less than musicians do not make most of their work from selling reproductions of their work and where they do make money from reproductions. They make their money by playing live (residency and show fees, public art fees), private gigs (commissions ) and merchandise (prints and editions of physical artworks, deluxe or personalised recordings or photographs of performances).

Perhaps in order to address such concerns, Creative Commons do provide a pseudo-copyleft licence that only allows non-commercial (NC) use, which might appear to protect artists against economic exploitation. But it allows peer-to-peer sharing of work, which content industry claims is the major source of their loss of revenue, and individuals can print or paint their own copies of work shared in this way.

NC prevents the artist of the original work from using any downstream reworkings of their piece commercially without negotiations that may be unsuccessful. Copyleft in itself is a stronger disincentive to people who wish to simply exploit work without giving anything in return, and NC allows verbatim copying anyway. It discourages critique and thereby promotion. And it prevents artists from recovering the costs incurred in creating derivative works.[62] NC is seductive but ultimately self-defeating.

To quote book publisher Tim O'Reilly, 'Obscurity is a far greater threat to authors and creative artists than piracy.'[63] The Internet is an excellent tool for fighting obscurity and creating opportunities to build reputation, and reputation is key to making a living as an artist. Artists do not generally make a living from selling reproductions of their work, and if they do they can compete on the basis of the quality and authenticity of those reproductions (forged signatures tend to be fairly worthless).

Reputation as capital leads naturally to the idea of a 'reputation economy'. But there is no neat split between a reputation economy and the cash economy that an artist's reputation impacts on. And it is a mistake to try to protect the cash value of an artist's work while they are building a reputation that will increase the value of that work until such time as it can be sold to a traditional middleman.

The Internet has proved a boon for artists, providing means of networking, selling work, and discussing and learning about art globally.

[62] Negativland, 'Negativlands Tenets of Free Appropriation' http://negativland.com/riaa/tenets.html, (undated, 1998?)

[63] Tim Oreilly, 'Piracy is progressive taxation, and other thoughts on the evolution of online distribution', 2002, http://www.openp2p.com/pub/a/p2p/2002/12/11/piracy.html

From community sites like Furtherfield and Rhizome to commercial sites like Saatchi's YourGallery and listings sites like ArtInfo the internet has provided new opportunities.[64]

Unlike recorded music, electronic images of artworks are not a substitute for most artworks, rather they promote the original. An artist and blogger like Joy Garnett, whose paintings draw on media imagery under the American fair use doctrine, can place high-resolution images of her paintings online without fearing that they will be taken by any potential collector as a substitute for buying the original.[65]

[64] See http://www.furtherfield.org/ http://www.rhizome.org/ http://www.saatchi-gallery.co.uk/yourgallery/ and http://www.artinfo.com/

[65] See http://www.firstpulseprojects.com/joy-work.html

Performance, installation and sculpture are unlikely to be affected by electronic copying of images either. Work that is created as electronic images, as video or as software might appear to be more at risk, but as Matthew Barney's 'Cremaster Cycle' shows, it is perfectly possible to sell limited editions of infinitely reproducible art. Attempts led by the music and motion picture industries to restrict how the internet can be used, as government and lobby groups, and attempts to block 'undesirable' content on the internet are censorship in its expanded sense (and in its traditional sense where governments are involved). They provide no benefit to artists and will harm both artists and society's ability to benefit from the new possibilities that the internet affords.

Artists can play an important part in showing that there are substantial uses for the internet that do not involve what its opponents call 'piracy' and can gain economically from the internet whether financially or in terms of reputation.

## Conclusion

Artists are not being distracted by external demands of political commitment when they take on issues of cultural freedom. They are exemplars. Free art and a free culture, is of vital importance for a free society. This freedom may result in commons based peer production, gift economies, reputation economies, increased efficiency and higher quality. But it is important not to confuse the incidental effects of an ideology with its principles. It is these principles that artists should pursue:

It is important to avoid repeating the mistakes of open source when doing so:

– Start from *Free Software Free Society* and *Free Culture*, not *The Cathedral And The Bazaar.*

– Don’t try to organise your organisation in an 'Open Source' way. That methodology is for content, not structure.

– Don’t try to emulate early Wikipedia’s world-writeability. Emulate the meritocratic Linux Kernel development model that Wikipedia is slowly coming to resemble instead.

– Don’t be afraid of matters of principle. Renaming 'Free Software' as 'Open Source' has cost the people who have done so the biggest software market in the US, as the military are much more comfortable with 'freedom' than they are with 'openness'.

There are many ways in which artists can apply the lessons of Free Software to art:

– Artists should become familiar with the concept of artistic freedom, the contemporary status of censorship, and how to protect the former against the latter.

– Artists should campaign to oppose the extension of copyright or trademark law and the reduction of fair use. Where there are opportunities to lobby for extended fair use (such as the 'Gowers Report' in the UK in 2007) artists should make sure their voices are heard.

– Artists should use copyleft licensing to ensure the free circulation of ideas. If the sale of reproductions of work is a concern, investigate services that sell reproductions and experiment with releasing fewer works under a copyleft licence rather than more works under restrictive licences.

– Artists who are interested to do so can investigate the use of collaborative project management.

– Artists who are interested to do so should produce work to show the value of fair use and the public domain.

– Artists who are interested to do so should challenge copyright maximalists and censors by using mass media imagery and transgressive imagery.

– Artists should use Free Software and free (or 'open') file formats for accessibility, and help drive improvement of them.

Applying these concepts to art is neither Digital Maoism nor economic irrationality but an ethical and social stance against the censorious restrictions that threaten to harm art's continued freedom.

= = = = = = = = = = =

## Note on design and fonts

= = = = = = = = = = =

Graphic Design done by
OSP - Open Source Publishing,
at Constant, 292 and Studio Savoie, Brussels.
http://ospublish.constantvzw.org/

Layout: Harrisson and Yi Jang

FLOSS+Art book is typeset with
Libertinage fonts and Not-Courier Sans.

Libertinage Font Set is composed of 27 fonts developed
specifically for this book by Harrisson and Ludivine Loiseau.

"Libertinage A to Z" are fonts where one letter of the latin
alphabet has been derived from the Linux Libertine Font
(http://linuxlibertine.sourceforge.net/).
"Libertinage Full" integrates all the modified glyphs in a
single font.

Libertinage set is released under the OFL License
and is available at:
http://openfontlibrary.org/media/files/OSP/322

Not-Courier sans font is released under GPL2 License
and is available at
http://openfontlibrary.org/media/files/OSP/289

This book has been designed with open source software:
Open Office (text processing),
Scribus (layout and typesetting),
Gimp (bitmap images),
Inkscape (vector manipulation)
and Fontforge (font editor).

Dropped initials were done with Figlet.

= = = = = = = = = = =

About GOTO10

= = = = = = = = = = =

GOTO10 is a collective of international artists and programmers, dedicated to Free/Libre/Open Source Software (FLOSS) and digital arts. GOTO10 aims to support and grow digital art projects and tools for artistic creation, located on the blurry line between software programming and art.

GOTO10 lives on servers, IRC channels, lists and streams. We don't have any static physical meeting place. We organize events throughout Europe, independently and in collaboration with like-minded organizations. Our aim is to live within this network of machines, people and places, to develop and teach new and existing tools, to produce, experiment and play.

All of GOTO10's projects are based on 100% Free/Libre Open Source Software.

http://goto10.org

= = = = = = = = = = =

ACKNOWLEDGMENTS

- - - - - - - - - - - - - - - - - - - - - - - - - - - - - - - - - - -

We would like to thank the following
for their contribution to this book:

- - - - - - - - - - - - - - - - - - - - - - - - - - - - - - - - - - -

The authors:
Fabianne Balvedi, Florian Cramer, Sher Doruff, Nancy Mauro-Flude,
Olga Goriunova, Dave Griffiths, Ross Rudesch Harley, Martin Howse,
Shahee Ilyas, Ricardo Lafuente, Ivan Monroy Lopez, Thor Magnusson,
Alex McLean, Rob Myers, Alejandra Maria Perez Nuñez, Eleonora Oreggia,
oRx-qX, Julien Ottavi, Michael van Schaik, Femke Snelting, Pedro Soler,
Hans-Christoph Steiner, Prodromos Tsiavos, Simon Yuill

- - - - - - - - - - - - - - - - - - - - - - - - - - - - - - - - - - -

The editors:
Aymeric Mansoux and Marloes de Valk

- - - - - - - - - - - - - - - - - - - - - - - - - - - - - - - - - - -

The Print on Demand consultancy team at OpenMute:
Anthony Iles, Simon Worthington, Pauline van Mourik Broekman and
Benedict Seymour.

= = = = = = = = = = =

This publication is made possible with support from:
- the Digital Research Unit at the University of Huddersfield
- Piet Zwart Institute, the Willem de Kooning Academy
- Constant vzw
- OpenMute
- GOTO10

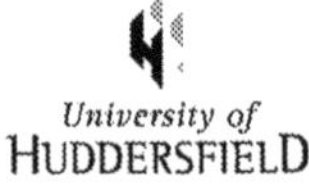


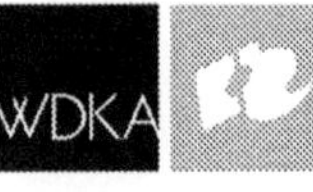


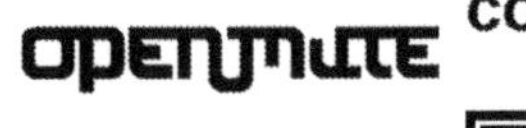


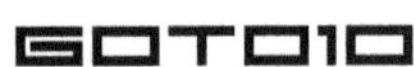

www.ingramcontent.com/pod-product-compliance
Ingram Content Group UK Ltd.
Pitfield, Milton Keynes, MK11 3LW, UK
UKHW041858190726
13854UKWH00002B/969

9 781906 496180